The Soviet-Afghan War

The Soviet-Afghan War
How a Superpower Fought and Lost

The Russian General Staff

Translated and edited by
Lester W. Grau and Michael A. Gress

Foreword by Theodore C. Mataxis

 University Press of Kansas

The Russian General Staff authors' collective is headed by Colonel Professor Valentin Runov, candidate of history. Members of the authors' collective include P. D. Alexseyev, Yu. G. Avdeev, Yu. P. Babich, A. M. Fufaev, B. P. Gruzdev, V. S. Kozlov, V. I. Litvinnenko, N. S. Nakonechnyy, V. K. Puzel', S. S. Sharov, S. F. Tsybenko, V. M. Varushinin, P. F. Vazhenko, V. F. Yashin, and V. V. Zakharov.

Published by the University Press of Kansas (Lawrence, Kansas 66049), which was organized by the Kansas Board of Regents and is operated and funded by Emporia State University, Fort Hays State University, Kansas State University, Pittsburg State University, the University of Kansas, and Wichita State University.

Library of Congress Cataloging-in-Publication Data

The Soviet-Afghan War : how a superpower fought and lost: the Russian General Staff / translated and edited by Lester W. Grau and Michael A. Gress ; foreword by Theodore C. Mataxis.
    p. cm. — (Modern war studies)
    Translated from Russian.
    Includes index.
    ISBN 0-7006-1185-1 (cloth : alk. paper) — ISBN 0-7006-1186-X (paper : alk. paper)
    1. Afghanistan—History—Soviet occupation, 1979–1989. 2. Soviet
Union—Military policy. 3. Soviet Union—History, Military. I. Grau,
Lester W. II. Gress, Michael A. III. Series.
DS371.2.S665 2002
958.104'5—dc21
                    2001006560

British Library Cataloguing in Publication Data is available.

Printed in the United States of America

10 9 8 7

The paper used in this publication meets the minimum requirements of the American National Standard for Permanence of Paper for Printed Library Materials Z39.48-1984.

Contents

Illustrations

FIGURES

PHOTOS

Foreword

Editors' note: General Mataxis is one of the premier authorities in the United States on guerrilla war. During his illustrious career, he fought as an infantry-man in World War II, Korea, and Vietnam. He was continually involved with the observation and study of guerrilla forces. At the end of World War II, when his battalion was deactivated in Berlin, he was put in charge of a prisoner of war camp for German generals and general staff officers. He supervised historians who recorded the German accounts of their operations in the Soviet Union, including the collection of German accounts of German efforts against the Soviet and Yugoslavian partisans. While en route to the Indian Defense Staff College in 1950, he stopped at Singapore where the British instructed him in their ongoing counter-guerrilla efforts in Malay. At the Indian Staff College, he studied the guerrilla aspects of the British-Afghan wars in detail. He graduated from the Staff College in 1951 and then served for a year as an observer in the guerrilla-plagued Kashmir. On his way to the Korean War, he took personal leave to visit French Indochina to observe France's war with the Viet Minh guerrillas.

General Mataxis put his studies of guerrilla warfare to practical use in Viet-nam. From 1964 to 1966, he served as the senior adviser to the South Vietnamese II ARVN Corps. He helped conduct the Vietnamese defense against the lesser known, but more dangerous, Tet Offensive of 1965. When U.S. regular units entered South Vietnam, he took over the 1st Brigade of the 101st Airborne Divi-sion and swept through key provinces in the II Corps Region, fighting Viet Cong guerrillas and regular North Vietnamese forces. In 1968 to 1970, he was assigned as an adviser to the Military Advisory Group in Tehran, Iran, where he advised the Iranians on their covert plans to assist Kurdish guerrillas in eastern Iraq. He returned to South Vietnam in 1970 where he served as deputy comman-der and acting commander of the 23rd Infantry Division. The counter-guerrilla war was winding down and American forces were taking increasing casualties from mines and booby traps. General Mataxis was reassigned to Cambodia with one day's notice. He became the Chief of the Joint Military Equipment Team in Phnom Penh with the mission to build a Cambodian military force of 200,000. However, the American ambassador to Cambodia was more hindrance than help in this effort, and the door was left open to the Khmer Rouge. General Mataxis retired in April 1972 after 32 years of uniformed service.

After retirement from the military, General Mataxis continued his study of guerrilla warfare. He served the Singapore Minister of Defense from 1972 to 1975 as a consultant. During this time, he was able to study the files on the Japanese attack on Singapore and the Malayan Emergency. From 1980 to 1990, he advised and assisted Mujahideen freedom fighters in his capacity as Field Director of the Committee for a Free Afghanistan. He was also active in helping raise support for the anticommunist resistance to the Khmer Rouge in Cambodia. General Mataxis has written extensively about guerrilla warfare and is currently on the faculty of the American Military University where he teaches courses on guerrilla warfare.

As we enter the next millennium, our society is trying to adapt to the impact of an unprecedented and turbulent technological and social revolution. The impact of this revolution is similar to that of the Industrial Revolution on the agricultural society of eighteenth-century Europe and America. The Information Age, with its rapidly expanding technology, has already positioned its guideposts marking our future. Westerners, particularly Americans, love technology. Computers, VCRs, cellular phones, and CD players are commonplace in our homes. Our armed forces reflect this love of technology. We equip our forces with sophisticated equipment and, during times of tight budgets, expect technology to replace expensive manpower. Our view of future conflict is skewed by computer games, popular entertainment, defense contractor pronouncements, and an abiding belief in the omniscience of science. It is prudent for the armed services to incorporate or nullify new technologies as they appear, yet every future war will not be a high-tech war. The military must also prepare for manpower-intensive low-tech wars that may also threaten national interests.

A country or faction within a country can effectively fight a technologically superior state or coalition using guerrilla war. Guerrilla warfare is a test of national will and endurance in which technological advantages are often degraded or negated. In order for a guerrilla war to succeed, a portion of the local populace must support or acquiesce to the presence of indigenous guerrillas in their midst. There must be a willingness to accept considerable casualties–combatant and noncombatant. Guerrillas must have a safe haven and a source of supplies. What guerrillas do not need is military victory. Guerrillas need to survive and endure over the years or decades of the conflict. The guerrillas remained when the French left Algeria and Indochina, the United States left South Vietnam, and the Soviets left Afghanistan. The side with the greater moral commitment, be it patriotic, religious, or ideological, eventually won because of higher morale, greater obstinacy, stronger national will, and the determination to survive.

Guerrilla war does not fit into the popular image of high-tech future war, but it may well be the future war that a high-tech country finds itself fighting. The Soviet Army, a modern, mechanized high-tech force, fought a guerrilla war for over nine years in Afghanistan. Despite their best efforts, the application of overwhelming air power, and the expenditure of national treasure and young lives, the Soviets withdrew from Afghanistan, leaving the field to the defiant Mujahideen guerrilla.

A wise army prepares for future war by examining the lessons of the past. This does not mean that armies should prepare to fight as the last war was fought. Rather, they should draw lessons from the past that will guide the future. The Russian General Staff officers who wrote this book have recorded their experience so that their military can learn from it. Fortunately, their observations are now available to a wider audience. Too many military books only deal with the strategy or tactics of a particular war and ignore the vital issues of force structure, branch missions, combat support, and combat service support. This book examines these issues, as well as dealing with tactics and strategy. It provides a comprehensive look at how a modern, high-tech force attempted to fight a guerrilla war on rugged terrain in the middle of someone else's civil war.

This book is the third in a trilogy by Les Grau covering the Soviet-Afghan War. The first two, *The Bear Went Over the Mountain: Soviet Combat Tactics in Afghanistan* and *The Other Side of the Mountain: Mujahideen Tactics in the Soviet-Afghan War,* the second with coauthor Ali Jalali, covered Soviet and Mujahideen tactics on the battlefield. In this third volume, Les Grau and Michael Gress give the Russian General Staff perspective on the war. They have done a good job in translating, editing, and providing commentary on the text. They have erased much of the awkwardness normally associated with a translation. Their commentary aids the reader without distracting from the main work. This book provides valuable insights for the military professional contemplating the complex issue of fighting or supporting a guerrilla war.

The first two books give an excellent overview of the Soviet involvement in the war and their changing tactics, which they adopted when the Mujahideen resistance failed to collapse (as had the Hungarian and Czechoslovakian resistance after the Soviet invasions of 1956 and 1962). The Soviet invasion shattered the growing detente between the Soviet Union and the West and caused the United Nations to call for "all foreign troops to leave Afghanistan." In the United States, the Soviet invasion was seen as a threat to access of Persian Gulf oil and became a major issue in the presidential election.

With the election of President Reagan, who campaigned on "Peace Through Strength," the United States launched a buildup of conventional and strategic forces and challenged Soviet expansionism. The Reagan administration challenged the Brezhnev Doctrine of "once a communist state, always a communist state," stating that "we do not accept the current expanse of the Soviet Empire as a permanent and irreversible feature of the historic landscape." Shortly afterward, the "Reagan Doctrine" offered support to guerrillas struggling against communist regimes.

The Committee for a Free Afghanistan (CFA) was one of the first Public Volunteer Organizations (PVO) organized following the Soviet invasion of Afghanistan. The administration encouraged the PVOs to back the Reagan Doctrine by assisting anti-communist guerrillas. I was field director of the CFA, and I visited Peshawar, Pakistan, seven times (for one to three months at a time) during the war. Peshawar was headquarters to the seven major Mujahideen factions and was the optimum site to coordinate our activities with these factions and the three million Afghan refugees living in squalid camps along the Pakistan/Afghanistan border. When I first visited Peshawar, I studied the map and was struck by a sense of déjà vu from my experiences in Vietnam. This time, however, I was sitting with the guerrillas in the "Eagle's Beak," which juts into Afghanistan menacing Kabul. Before, I was in Saigon threatened by enemy divisions stationed in the Cambodian "Parrot's Beak."

The Russians divide the war into four phases and outline them in their introduction. The Mujahideen have a different perspective, but also divide the war into four phases. Their first phase was the initial nationwide resistance to the invading Soviets and the Afghan communists that led to the proclamation of *jihad* [holy war]. Their second phase was a reorganization phase in which the Mujahideen structured their headquarters, organized for the receipt and distribution of arms and material, and began training their forces for the prolonged war to drive the invaders out. Their third phase was surviving the Soviet technological onslaught. The Soviets had introduced remote electronic acoustic and seismic sensors that could detect Mujahideen moving some 20 kilometers from Soviet and Afghan communist positions. The combination of sensors and artillery fire was devastating. Soviet radio-activated minefields, night vision devices, and subsonic bullets also decimated Mujahideen ranks. Helicopter gun ships, the "Frogfoot" close air support aircraft, and well-trained Spetsnaz forces were increasingly effective, and Mujahideen morale plummeted as casualties soared. 1985 was the year of decision. Gorbachev ordered his commanders to win the war during that year, and the Soviets launched an all-out effort. The battered Mujahideen held on and began receiving the "Stinger" shoulder-launched air defense missile. "Stinger" changed the dynamics of the battlefield. Soviet jets and helicopter gun ships were forced to fly much higher and lost most of their effectiveness. This signaled the start of phase four for both sides. Gorbachev realized that he had to expand the war significantly or withdraw. He prepared to withdraw. The Mujahideen increased their combat and began organizing and training conventional infantry battalions to fight the Afghan communists after the Soviet withdrawal.

There are several issues in this book that jump out at the reader. First is the extraordinary efforts the Soviets had to resort to in order to protect their fragile lines of communication. Second is that the Soviet Army came prepared to fight the war they trained for–high-tempo, high-speed, mechanized warfare on the Northern European plain or Manchurian plateau. They had to re-arm, re-structure, and develop new tactics and new training while fighting the war. Third, the Soviets attempted to win the war with their high-technology—and were totally frustrated. Despite overwhelming Soviet combat power, the Mujahideen learned to dodge Soviet attacks, work around Soviet technology, and fight another day. In the end, the Mujahideen national will was stronger than that of the Soviet leadership, and the Soviet Army withdrew.

High technology has its place, but too often scarce defense dollars are spent on technology fixes that never accomplish what they promise. NATO's recent operations against Serbia provide an excellent example of the danger of depending solely on technology's promise. For months, NATO air forces pummeled an enemy armed with inferior technology but one with the national will to resist and endure the demands of its stronger and more technologically advanced opponent. NATO failed to prepare for the "worst case scenario" and initially field a ground force in case the aerial bombardments failed to cow the enemy. Serbia's military had excellent camouflage skills and withdrew from Kosovo in good order. Their withdrawal was due to Russian diplomacy and attacks on the civilian infrastructure, not aerial damage to their military. Militaries with inferior technology, but smart leaders, will avoid conflicts where technology will provide an edge. They will opt for urban combat, combat in rough terrain or jungle, or guerrilla warfare. These forms of combat all require quantities of trained infantrymen–an increasingly rare commodity in the U.S. armed forces.

This book provides a rare insiders' look at the Soviet war machine in Afghanistan. The lessons derived apply universally to other armies. The military professional will be well served by studying this appraisal by other professionals.

Theodore C. Mataxis
Brigadier General (Retired)

Editors' Preface

The Russian/Soviet General Staff has a reputation for thoroughness, extensive record keeping, and a highly professional analysis of war experience to garner lessons learned from war and conflict. In fact, the most thorough analyses of Union cavalry employment in the U.S. Civil War were conducted under Russian General Staff guidance in 1875 and 1913.[1] Similar detailed studies were undertaken for the Russo-Japanese War, World War I, the 1920 Soviet-Polish War, and the Russian Civil War. When Hitler invaded the Soviet Union in June 1941, the Red Army was in desperate straits and chronically short of experienced officers. Yet the Soviet General Staff dedicated several of its best and brightest officers to recording the events and experiences of that fighting. Their primary purpose was not so much to record history as to conduct operations research to capture the lessons from their early mistakes and successes so that the Red Army could improve its performance throughout the war. These lessons were collected by selected officers at army and *front,* then compiled and published as classified documents for use by division, army, and *front* commanders throughout the war. The process worked, and Soviet performance improved steadily throughout the war. By the end of the war, the General Staff had produced a 60-volume classified study of war experience.[2]

Western analysts assumed that the General Staff was continuing this valuable tradition during their fighting in Afghanistan. Although the conflict was smaller than the major wars in Europe or China for which the Soviet Army was preparing, it was the largest Soviet expeditionary force launched outside Soviet borders since the Hungarian uprising in 1956 or the Czechoslovakian invasion of 1968. In 1995, I, editor Les Grau, learned that a General Staff study of the Soviet-Afghan War existed. I began inquiries among Russian military friends and acquaintances and learned that the study was awaiting publication. However, the Russian Armed Forces lacked funds, and very little was getting published by the military press. The General Staff authors, wanting to get this information to the serving officers, then offered the manuscript for commercial publication in Russia. However, Russia was too involved with trying to make its way into the marketplace and the world economy. Russia was also fighting another brutal guerrilla war in Chechnya, and the war-weary public was tired of anything dealing with the Soviet-Afghan War or other military developments. Russian publishers ignored the manuscript. I was approached by a Russian acquaintance and finally acquired the manuscript and publishing rights.

The first thing we discovered is that the process used to develop the material in the manuscript is different than that of the World War II war experience volumes. There was no organized General Staff program to collect, access, and analyze the Afghanistan combat experience. Rather, various Soviet staff colleges and branch schools collected information from their student officers who had served in Afghanistan. Other important material was preserved in individual journals and diaries. The 40th Army, the primary Soviet formation in Afghanistan, had also collected a great deal of material on the war but had destroyed most of it prior to, or shortly after, its withdrawal from that war-torn land. Since the war, the Soviet Union and then Russia were involved in a series of small, brutal conflicts in Northern Ossetia, Azerbaijan, Georgia, Turkmenistan, Tadjikistan, and Chechnya. Colonel Runov, a rising General Staff officer, realized that the experience gained in Afghanistan would be very useful in these similar conflicts and formed an authors' collective to create a retrospective analysis of the Soviet-Afghan War. He assembled a group of officers within the General Staff and outlying staff colleges. The authors were officers from the different branches, most of whom had served in Afghanistan. They had access to a variety of material through their various branches and personal contacts. They prepared this manuscript to help the struggling Russian Army meet the challenges of future guerrilla war.

The book has an introductory chapter. Following chapters deal with the organization and training of the Soviet forces and the forces of the Democratic Republic of Afghanistan; the organization and training of their enemy—the Mujahideen; and the conduct of major operations in Afghanistan. There are chapters for combined arms (mechanized infantry); combat arms (airborne, air assault, artillery, armor, and army aviation); combat support (reconnaissance, engineers, combat security, and chemical); and combat service support (supply, maintenance, transportation, finance, post exchange, housing, and medical). The final chapter draws conclusions on the entire war. Many of the same vignettes that were used in *The Bear Went Over the Mountain* are also found in Chapter 5 (combined arms) of this book.[3] This is because the primary data for both came from the archives of the Frunze Combined Arms Academy in Moscow. However, this book extends well beyond the scope of combined-arms infantry combat to provide an in-depth look at how the various branches fought, interacted, and served during the long Soviet-Afghan War.

Why did the General Staff fail to document and analyze the Soviet-Afghan War in the same fashion as they had done with previous wars? The most likely explanation is that there was an ideological blind spot in the Marxist-Leninist tenets. Marxism-Leninism defined several categories of just wars—most dealing with revolutions against capitalist states or wars fought by socialist states against capitalist states. There was no provision for a popular uprising against a social-ist state.[4] Therefore, since the Mujahideen uprising did not fit within the Marx-ist-Leninist definition of a just war, the General Staff was constrained in dealing completely with it—and so tried to ignore it. Colonel Runov, now an officer of the Russian Army, was no longer constrained by Marxist-Leninist dogma and chose to fill the void with a retrospective study.

There are some disturbing revelations in this book. First, the real Soviet casualties from the war are still a secret, but almost double the official figures released by the Gorbachev regime in a great show of glasnost (openness). The official figures are 13,833 40th Army dead, but the actual figures are in the vicin-ity of 26,000. Second, the Soviet military had thoroughly penetrated the Demo-cratic Republic of Afghanistan (DRA) long before the invasion. Soviet advisers permeated the ministries of government and the units of the military. Soviet mil-itary advisers were found down in each battalion of the DRA Armed Forces. A battalion of Soviet Special Forces (Spetsnaz) provided security for the DRA president. This battalion of Soviet Central Asian commandos dressed in Afghan Army uniforms and helped secure the official residence. A Soviet squadron of Central Asian pilots wore Afghan Air Force uniforms and flew aircraft with Afghan tail markings throughout the country. These units were in place up to a year prior to the invasion. Third, despite the Soviet Union's penetration and lengthy experience in Afghanistan, their intelligence was poor and hampered by the need to explain events within the Marxist-Leninist framework. Consequently, the Soviets never fully understood the Mujahideen opposition nor why many of their policies failed to work in Afghanistan.

Several facts place the Afghan War in proper perspective and permit its proper assessment in the context of Soviet military, political, and social develop-ment. First, although violent and destructive, the war was limited and protracted. Its tempo and decisiveness did not match that of the series of short Arab-Israeli wars that scarred the Cold War years. It lacked the well-defined, large-scale mil-itary operations of the Korean War and the well-defined political arrangements that terminated that war. It also differed significantly from the oft-compared U.S. war in Vietnam. In Vietnam, American military strength rose to over 500,000 troops, and the Americans resorted to many divisional and multi-divisional oper-ations. By comparison, in Afghanistan, a region five times the size of Vietnam, Soviet strength varied from 90,000 to 120,000 troops. The Soviet's four divisions, five separate brigades, three separate regiments, and smaller support units of the 40th Army strained to provide security for the 29 provincial centers and the few industrial and economic installations and were hard-pressed to extend this security to the thousands of villages, hundred of miles of communications routes, and key terrain features that punctuated and spanned that vast region.

Second, faced with this imposing security challenge, and burdened with a military doctrine, strategy, and operational and tactical techniques suited to a European or Chinese theater of war, the Soviet Army was hard-pressed to devise military methodologies suited to deal with the Afghan guerrillas. The Soviets formulated new concepts for waging war in nonlinear fashion, suited to operating on battlefields dominated by more lethal high-precision weapons. This new non-linear battlefield required the abandonment of traditional operational and tactical formations, a redefinition of traditional echelonment concepts, and a wholesale reorganization of formations and units to emphasize combat flexibility and, hence, survivability. During the early and mid-1980s, the Soviet military altered its concept of the theater-strategic offensive, developed new concepts for shallower echelonment at all levels, developed the concept of the air echelon, experimented with new force structures such as the corps, brigade, and combined arms battalion, tested new, more-flexible logistical support concepts (for materiel support), and adopted such innovative tactical techniques as the use of the *bronegruppa* (armored group).[5] Afghanistan not only provided a test ground for many of these lower-level concepts, but it also demanded the employment of imaginative new techniques in its own right. Hence, the combined-arms brigade, the materiel support battalion, and the *bronegruppa* emerged on the Afghan field of battle, Spetsnaz units sharpened their skills, and air assault techniques were widely employed.

Third, the inability of the Soviet military to win the war decisively condemned it to suffer a slow bloodletting, in a process that exposed the very weaknesses of the military, as well as the Soviet political structure and society. The employment of a draft army with full periodic rotation of troops back to the Soviet Union permitted the travails and frustrations of war and the self doubts of the common soldier to be shared by the entire Soviet population. The problems so apparent in the wartime army soon became a microcosm for the latent problems afflicting Soviet society in general. The messages of doubt were military, political, ethnic, and social. In the end they were corrosive and destructive.[6]

AFGHANISTAN'S SOCIAL STRUCTURE

Afghanistan is a multi-ethnic southwest Asian state with a long tradition of resistance to central authority and foreign interference. The Pashtun, Tajik, Uzbek, Turkmen, Hazara, Balochi, and other ethnic groups that constitute Afghanistan are 99 percent adherents of Islam, with 85 percent followers of the Sunni sect. The rest are Shia. The prewar population was over 17 million with a literacy rate of approximately 10 percent. The country was primarily rural with some 85 percent of the prewar populace living in rural mountain and desert communities.

The rugged terrain frustrated the development of a comprehensive transportation system and a modern economy. There is no railroad, and truck and automobile traffic are restricted primarily to a highway ring connecting the various cities and Afghanistan's neighbors.

Afghanistan has long been a loose collection of tribes and nationalities with which the central government has had varying success influencing and controlling. Historically, the people have been known for their remarkable Islamic and ethnic tolerance. Still, tribal rivalries, tribal intractability, and blood feuds, coupled with the ambitions of local chieftains, have frequently fomented war between various regions and with the central authority. Afghanistan is at a geographic crossroads that has witnessed the passage of many warring peoples. Each of these has left its mark and involved the people of Afghanistan in conflict. The people of Afghanistan have usually mobilized based on their kinship identity. It is a country composed of fairly autonomous "village states" spread across the entire country.[7] Afghans identify themselves by *Qawm*—the basic subnational identity based on kinship, residence, and sometimes occupation. This instinctive social cohesiveness includes tribal clans, ethnic subgroups, religious sects, locality-based groups, and groups united by interests. The *Qawm,* not Afghanistan, is the basic unit of community and, outside the family, the most important focus of individual liberty. Leaders of the various *Qawm* perpetuate blood feuds and settle them as well. Afghanistan's ancient roots and strong bonds of kinship may retard progress, but they also provide a means to cope when central power has collapsed. Historically, the collapse of the central government of Afghanistan or the defeat of its army has never resulted in the defeat of the nation by an invader. The population, with its decentralized political, economic, and military power, has always taken up resistance against the invader. This occurred during the Anglo-Afghan Wars of 1839–1842 and 1878–1880 and again during the Soviet-Afghan War.

Unlike the Communist guerrilla movements in China and Vietnam, the Mujahideen guerrillas were not trying to force a new ideology and government on their land. Rather, they were fighting to defend their families, their *Qawm,* and their religion against a hostile, atheistic ideology, an alien value system, an oppressive central government, and a foreign invader. Individual groups, initially unconnected to national or international political organizations, spontaneously defended their community values and traditional way of life.

THE GREAT GAME[8]

Russia expanded her empire into Central Asia beginning in 1734, and her interest in Afghanistan was apparent by the late 1830s. The term "the great game" describes the Russian and British struggle for influence along the northern frontier of British India and in the entire region between Russia and India.

Afghanistan was central to this contested area between two expanding empires. Russia described her motives in the region as a desire to abolish the slave trade and to establish order and control along her southern border. The British viewed the Russian expansion into the lands of the Caucasus, Georgia, Khirgiz, Turkmens, Khiva, and Bukhara as a threat to her borders. The British believed the Russian motives were to weaken British power and to gain access to a warmwater southern port. Britain described her own actions in the great game as defensive measures to protect the frontiers of British India.

The great game spilled over into Afghanistan when British forces invaded during the First Anglo-Afghan War of 1839–1842. The British justified their actions as a counter to Russian influence. After hard fighting, the British withdrew. By 1869, the Russian empire reached Afghanistan's northern border–the Amu Darya (Oxus) river. In 1878, the arrival of a special Russian delegation in Kabul led to another British invasion and the Second Anglo-Afghan War. After more hard fighting, the British again withdrew. In the Anglo-Russian Treaty of 1907, the Russians agreed that Afghanistan lay outside its sphere of interest and agreed to confer with Britain on all matters relating to Russian-Afghan relations. In return, Britain agreed not to occupy or annex any part of Afghanistan nor interfere in Afghanistan's internal affairs. This treaty held until 1919, when Afghan troops crossed into British India, seized a village, and tried to incite a popular revolt in the region. The British responded with a third invasion–and the Third Anglo-Afghan War. The political settlement resulted in Afghanistan's full independence from British influence.

THE SOVIET UNION'S TURN

From 1919 until 1978, Afghanistan's foreign policy balanced the demands of her immediate neighbors and those of external powers such as the United States, Germany, and Great Britain. Normal relations with the Soviet Union led to increased Soviet investment and presence in the country. In April 1978, a small leftist band of Soviet-trained Afghan officers seized control of the government and declared the establishment of the Democratic Republic of Afghanistan (DRA), the newest client state of the Soviet Union. President Nur M. Taraki, the putsch-installed Marxist leader, announced a sweeping program of land redistribution, changed status for women, and the destruction of the old social structure of Afghanistan. The program ran counter to the national social structure and mores, and, consequently, the new government had little popular support. Armed resistance grew and civil war broke out. Religious leaders issued statements proclaiming *jihad* against the communist regime and bands of Mujahideen (holy warriors) formed to defend the faith. Desertions swept the army of the DRA, so that, by the end of 1979, the actual strength of the army was less than half its authorized 90,000 men. In March 1979, the city of Herat rebelled and most of the

Afghan 17th Infantry Division mutinied and joined the revolt. The DRA Air Force bombed the city and the 17th Division. The DRA then retook the city. Thousands died in the fighting—including some Soviet citizens.

The DRA was a nominally socialist state governed by a communist party. The state controlled the cities, and tribal elders and clan chiefs controlled the countryside. The communist party itself was split into two hostile factions that spent more effort fighting each other than in trying to establish socialism in Afghanistan. In September 1979, Taraki's Prime Minister, Hafizullah Amin, seized power and murdered Taraki. Amin's rule was no better and the Soviet leadership watched with alarm as this new communist state spun out of control. Leonid Brezhnev, the Soviet Union's aged and infirm General Secretary, determined that direct military intervention was the only way to rescue his client state from complete chaos.

The obvious models for intervention were Hungary in 1956 and Czechoslovakia in 1968. These models served the Soviet General Staff as planning guides. General Pavlovskiy, the Chief of Soviet Ground Forces, who commanded the Soviet invasion of Czechoslovakia in 1968, led a group of 50 Soviet officers on a lengthy planning reconnaissance throughout Afghanistan during August through October 1979. However, the general staff planners failed to note that Afghanistan was involved in a civil war and that a *coup de main* would only seize control of the central government, not the countryside. Although the units of the 40th Army were briefed at the last minute, the Soviet 1979 Christmas Eve invasion was masterfully planned and well executed. The Soviets seized the government, killed the president, and installed their own man in his place. Apparently, the Soviet plan was to stabilize the situation, strengthen the army, and then withdraw the bulk of Soviet forces within three years. The Soviet General Staff intended to leave all fighting to the armed forces of the DRA. However, Afghanistan was in full rebellion, the demoralized DRA army was unable to cope, and the probability of a defeat following a Soviet withdrawal haunted the Soviet Politburo. Invasion and overthrow of the government proved the easy part. Now the Soviet 40th Army found itself drawn into fighting hundreds of guerrilla groups throughout the country. The 40th Army's instincts were to fight the war that they had trained for, using large-scale, high-tempo operations. But the war was actually fought at the low end of the tactical spectrum where platoon leaders tried to find and fight small, indigenous forces that would stand and fight only when the terrain and circumstances were to their advantage.

The military leadership kept recommending withdrawal, but there was little help for the embattled 40th Army from its political masters. General Secretary Brezhnev became incapacitated in 1980 but did not die until November 1982. No one was really in charge in the Soviet Union and all decisions were made by the collective leadership in committee. Brezhnev was succeeded by the ailing Yuri Andropov, who lived less than two more years. He was succeeded by the faltering Konstantin Chernenko in February 1984. General Secretary Chernenko died in March 1985. Finally Mikhail Gorbachev came to power. He did not immediately address the war in Afghanistan and 1985 proved the bloodiest year of the war. It is a matter of debate whether Gorbachev initially sought military victory or whether the orders for the increased tempo came from other quarters. Finally, however, it was apparent that the Soviets could not win the war without severe international and internal repercussions. In early 1986, Gorbachev announced a program to "Afghanize" the conflict and began to negotiate a withdrawal in earnest. The 40th Army began to withdraw in 1988 and completed its withdrawal on 15 February 1989. The Soviet intervention reportedly killed 1.3 million people and forced 5.5 million Afghans (a third of the prewar population) to leave the country as refugees. Another 2 million Afghans were forced to migrate within the country.

Initially the Mujahideen were local residents who took up arms and came together into large, unwieldy forces that seized district capitals and looted arms rooms. The DRA countered these efforts where it could. The Mujahideen then coalesced into smaller groups centered around the rural village. Their commanders were usually influential villagers who were already community leaders. Few had any professional military experience other than conscript service. The rebellion against the DRA was widespread but uncoordinated.

The Soviet invasion changed the nature of the Mujahideen resistance. Pakistan and Iran nervously considered the increased presence of the Soviet military on their borders and began providing training and material support to the Mujahideen. The United States, Peoples Republic of China, Britain, France, Italy, Saudi Arabia, Egypt, and the United Arab Emirates began funneling aid to the Mujahideen through Pakistan. Various Afghan political factions headquartered in Pakistan began representing the various Mujahideen groups and serving as focal points for aid. Pakistan required that the various ethnic and tribal Mujahideen groups join one of these major factions in order to receive aid. Eventually there were seven major factions—three moderate and four Islamic fundamentalist. The Pakistani authorities favored the most fundamentalist groups and distributed aid accordingly. This aid distribution gave Afghan religious leaders unprecedented power in the conduct of the war and undermined the traditional authority of the tribal and village leaders.

The Mujahideen were unpaid volunteers with family obligations. This meant that they were part-time warriors and that the spoils of war played a major role in military actions. Mujahideen sold captured weapons and equipment in the bazaars to support their families. As the war progressed, mobile Mujahideen groups of young, unmarried, better-trained warriors emerged. Sometimes these Mujahideen were paid. They ranged over a much larger area of responsibility and were more responsive to the desires of the factions.

The strategic struggle for Afghanistan was a fight to strangle the other side's logistics. The Mujahideen targeted the Soviet lines of communication (LOC)— the critical roads over which the Soviet supplies traveled. The Soviets attacked the Mujahideen logistics in two phases. From 1980 to 1985, the Soviets sought to eliminate Mujahideen support in the rural countryside. They destroyed crops and irrigation systems, bombed granaries and rural villages, mined pastures and fields, machine-gunned herds of livestock, and launched sweeps through rural areas to conscript young men and destroy infrastructure. This turned Afghanistan into a nation of refugees and forced the Mujahideen to transport food along with weapons, ammunition, and other materials of war. The Mujahideen responded by establishing logistics bases inside Afghanistan. After 1985, the Soviets concentrated their fight against these bases.

This book is a professional examination of this long war. Unlike many military histories, it does not dwell exclusively on the combat. Rather, it presents a unique look at the role and missions of all the branches involved. It will probably be the only General Staff examination of that war since contemporary Russia is involved in a series of guerrilla conflicts. Russia's military barely has time to draw breath from the conclusion of one such contest before it is involved in another. In the long term, the value of this General Staff retrospective is that it provides a critical examination of how a modern mechanized force with over-whelming technological superiority became embroiled in someone else's civil war on rugged terrain. It shows how the war was fought to a military draw and a political defeat. It is a testament to the inherent strengths and weaknesses of a guerrilla movement and the minimal operational impact that technology has on that type of war. It shows how quantities of quality light infantry are essential to successfully fight this type of war, but, more importantly, it provides a unique look at the role of the other combat, combat support, and combat service support branches in conducting this type of war. It shows how the branch efforts were integrated and how the Soviet penchant for large-scale sweeping operations obstructed tactical combat and the goal of gaining an advantage over their enemy. Finally, it shows some of the disillusionment with the Soviet system that the soldiers brought home with them. Their loss of faith spread to the general Soviet society and proved a key element in the eventual collapse of the Soviet empire.

Editors' comments are enclosed in brackets, put in footnotes, or added to the end of each section in italics. The maps are copies of original Soviet hand-drawn maps from after-action reports and planning sketches. We translated the Soviet maps, but left the original Soviet map symbols. For those not familiar with Soviet map symbols, a Key to Map Symbols is provided. A glossary is also included. The Russians use the word formation to indicate divisions and brigades, units to indicate regiments, and separate battalions and sub-units to indicate battalions, companies, and platoons. We have followed that convention. Times are given in military time using the 24-hour clock.

Lester W. Grau
Michael A. Gress

Acknowledgments

Many people contributed to this book. First and foremost, Colonel Valentin Runov and his authors' collective wrote the book. Colonel Viktor Murakhovski brought the manuscript to our attention and arranged for its transfer and the assignment of publishing rights. Colonel Tod Milton and Lieutenant Colonel Henry Nowak, then army attachés in Moscow, provided needed interface throughout the transfer. Colonel (Retired) David M. Glantz provided guidance, direction, and peer review. General (Retired) William Odom provided suggestions and peer review. Robert Love, Graham Turbiville, Jake Kipp, Tim Thomas, Bill Mendel, Lieutenant Colonel Karl Prinslow, Lieutenant Colonel Bill Flynt, Linda Pride, and Alice Mink of the Foreign Military Studies Office provided help and encouragement. Ali Ahmad Jalali and John Sray provided a critical read of our final effort. Brigadier General (Retired) Theodore C. Mataxis wrote the Foreword. Michael Briggs, Susan Schott, Jessica Pigza, and Dorothea Anderson helped guide the book through publication. And our long-suffering wives and children endured our exile behind the computer screen with grace and good humor. We thank you all.

We dedicate this book to soldiers everywhere, who pay for the politicians' mistakes.

General Staff Introduction[1]

The Limited Contingent of Armed Forces of the Soviet Union entered the territory of Afghanistan in the last days of December 1979 "with the mission of rendering international aid to the friendly Afghan people and establishing advantageous conditions to prevent possible actions by the governments of neighboring countries against Afghanistan." Thus, with these extremely vague goals and limited military planning time, the Soviet peoples were cast into a bloody war that would last for nine years, one month, and eighteen days. The war took the lives or health of 55,000 Soviet citizens and did not result in the desired victory for the government.

At the same time, the unsatisfactory political and military-strategic results of the war should, in no way, reflect adversely on the quality of the Limited Contingent of Soviet Forces,[2] especially in the area of operational art and tactics. During the course of the war, Soviet operational art and tactics developed under the particular conditions of Afghanistan—the physical geography, the local economy, the peoples, the history, and the internal and foreign affairs of the last decade.[3]

Afghanistan is a Middle Eastern state located in the southwest region of Central Asia. Its territory covers 655,000 square kilometers [252,830 square miles], or an area roughly equal to France, Belgium, the Netherlands, and Denmark combined. Its 5,421-kilometer [3,366-mile] border shared 2,348 kilometers [1,458 miles] with the Soviet Union, 820 kilometers [509 miles] with Iran, 2,180 kilometers [1,354 miles] with Pakistan, and 73 kilometers [45 miles] with China. Part of the Soviet-Afghan border was defined by the river channels of the Amu Darya[4] and Panj rivers. The Iran-Afghan border runs through plains, hilly country, and desert. Most of the Pakistan-Afghan border and the China-Afghan border run through mountain massifs. Afghanistan is land-locked, and the shortest distance between its southern border and the Indian Ocean is approximately 500 kilometers [311 miles].

1

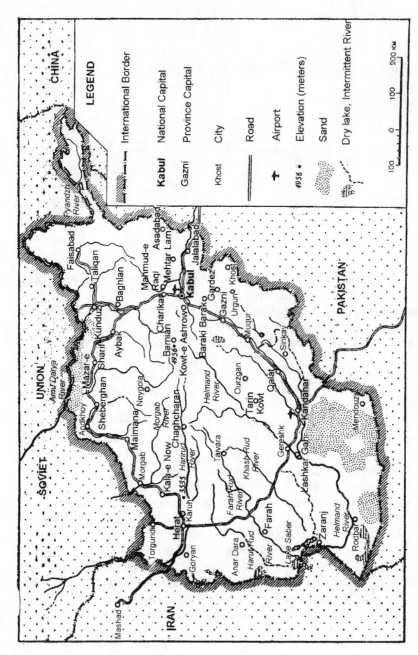

Map 1. Map of Afghanistan

Looking at the geophysical features of Afghanistan, it is a subtropical mountain-desert country located on the eastern edge of the Iranian plateau. It is a vast dry desert that extends from the numerous plateaus of the Near and Middle East (Map 1). About 85 percent of the territory is covered with mountains. They run through the middle of the country and sharply divide the country into two border regions—a northern and a southern. Between these lay interior plateaus and vast deserts.

The Paropamisus and Hindu Kush mountain chains define northern Afghanistan. These chains extend some 1,200 kilometers [745 miles] from the then-Soviet border to Iran along the Paropamisus plateau. The width of this mountain massif stretches from 300 to 500 kilometers [186 to 311 miles]. Mountain ranges crest from 2,000 to 7,750 meters [6,562 to 24,428 feet]. Conventional combat is not possible in this region.

The nearly impassable Suleiman mountain range stretches some 700 kilometers [435 miles] along Afghanistan's eastern border with Pakistan. This mountain range is 250 to 400 kilometers [155 to 248 miles] in width and the mountain peaks extend from 2,000 to 3,500 meters [6,562 to 11,484 feet] in height. These mountains run parallel to each other at several places, creating separate narrow dry canyons. Primary ground traffic with Pakistan and India move along these canyons. Small military units can operate in these canyons.

The Gazni-Kandahar plateau, about 20 percent of Afghanistan, lies between the Hindu Kush and the Suleiman mountain ranges.

In the north, the Paropamisus mountains [Safid Kuh] join the Bactrian plain that extends to the Karakum desert. The Bactrian plain is a sand-covered belt dotted with many oases and cut up by a dense grid of irrigation canals.

The western plain follows the Afghan-Iranian border from the Harirud river to the Farahrud river. This plain is 500 to 1,200 meters [1,641 to 3,937 feet] above sea level.

The zones of sandy desert are the Khash, Deshti-Margo, and Registan, which extend from the west to east some 540 kilometers [335 miles] and north to south some 580 kilometers [360 miles]. This area allows limited deployment of forces.

The country has a poorly developed highway network. There are only some 19,000 kilometers [11,800 miles] of road, or some three kilometers of road per 100 square kilometers [4.8 miles per 100 square miles]. The primary road network is a rough circle connecting Kabul, Puli Khumri, Mazar-e Sharif, Andkhoy, Herat, Kandahar, and Kabul again. It has an asphalt, concrete, or crushed rock surface. However, no more than 25 percent of Afghanistan's roads are paved and the rest are dirt. The carrying capacity of the paved road network is 6,000 to 8,000 vehicles every twenty-four hours while the carrying capacity of the dirt road network is two to three times less. The majority of the road network is difficult to travel due to the varying width of the road (three to ten meters) [10 to 33 feet]; the large number of bridges, tunnels, and high-mountain sections; and the virtually impassable condition of the roads during winter.

The river network is spread very irregularly across Afghanistan. There are many rivers in the mountains, but the few rivers on the plains are widely separated. Most of the mountain rivers originate high in the mountains and have a current of three to five meters per second [10 to 16 feet per second]. The depth of these rivers varies by season and day. They carry the most water during the March to April spring flood and during the July to August snow melt.

The Amu Darya is the mightiest river in the northern part of the country. It has a width of 120 to 1,500 meters [131 to 1,641 yards], a depth of two to ten meters [6.5 to 33 feet], and a current of two meters per second [6.5 feet per second]. Another northern river, the Harirud, forms 96 kilometers [60 miles] of the border with Iran.

The Helmand river is the mightiest river in the southwest of the country. It stretches 1,150 kilometers [714 miles], has a width of 90 to 350 meters [98 to 383 yards], and a depth of one to two meters [three to six-and-a-half feet]. The speed of the current is one to two meters per second [three to six-and-a-half feet per second].

The Kabul river flows in the eastern part of the country and is joined by the large Kunar river. In the area around Jalalabad, the Kabul river spreads to a width of 200 meters [219 yards] and has a depth of five to seven meters [16 to 23 feet].

All the rivers of Afghanistan, with the exception of the Amu Darya, can be forded during part of the year, but during high water, they are serious obstacles.

Ground cover in Afghanistan, although not abundant, is sufficiently varied. Less than 5 percent of the land is forested. At elevations of 1,500 to 1,800 meters, drought-resistant plants such as loco weed and camel thorn thrive. Sagebrush, Russian thistle, and saxaul grow in the desert. In the eastern border regions with Pakistan, there is a moderate area of Himalayan-type forest. Here, an evergreen oak grows up to elevations of 2,500 meters. Pine, fir, and cedar grow up to elevations of 3,300 meters. Elfin woods and alpine meadows are located higher up.

The climate of the country is subtropical to sharply continental, due to the dryness coupled with the fluctuating daily and seasonal air temperature. July is the hottest month in most of the country, when the average monthly temperature ranges from 30° to 52° Celsius [86° to 122° Fahrenheit]. The maximum summer temperature of exposed surfaces reaches 70° Celsius [158° Fahrenheit]. January is the coldest month, except in the mountains, where February is the coldest month. Then, the average monthly temperature ranges from -2° to -14° Celsius [28° to 7° Fahrenheit]. Snow cover in the valleys and plains is 10 to 15 centimeters [4 to 6 inches] and up to two meters (six and a half feet) in the mountains. Blizzards can last for several days.

Strong winds prevail in the mountain valleys, particularly within the mountainous section of the Termez-Kabul road, where winds reach 50 meters per second [112 miles per hour]. Heavy wind squalls often sweep mountain tops and mountain passes.

The conduct of classic military operations and combat, using the existing regulations and manuals of the Soviet Armed Forces, was practically impossible in light of the extremely difficult physical and geographic conditions.

The economic infrastructure and limited extent of development of the theater also prevented the conduct of large-scale, intensive military actions in the country. Industrialization of the country was just beginning, with some 200 to 300 plants and factories that produced less than was necessary for the normal functioning of the country. The annual production of electric energy fluctuated between .8 and 1.1 billion kilowatt hours, while gas production fluctuated between 2.5 and 3 billion cubic meters [88 to 106 billion cubic feet]. Annual coal production was between .15 and 2 million tons. Steel production was from .9 to 1.1 billion tons, and cement production was from .1 to .2 million tons.

There was no military industry in the country. During the war, the government built military maintenance and repair facilities, including an automobile repair plant and repair shops for armored vehicles, wheeled vehicles, artillery, and small arms.[5] However, the output from these facilities was decidedly inadequate and unable to support the combat readiness requirements for armaments and military equipment.

Over 85 percent of the population of Afghanistan was involved in agriculture. This included farming and animal herding by nomads and semi-nomads. Farming took place along river valleys and by oases. There, they raised wheat, corn, barley, rice, lentils, peas, beans, cotton, sugar beets, and other crops. Edible crops are grown across the Bactrian plain, while cotton is grown in the north of the country. Sheep raising is the most developed and widely spread form of livestock production. The number of animals is strictly limited by the available forage and the very limited number of veterinarians. Horses and large-horned cattle are raised in the northern region of the country. Camels are raised in the south on the plains and flat lands. During a good harvest year in peacetime, Afghanistan's agriculture was only capable of providing the minimum necessary food and resources for the local economy. In wartime, however, Afghanistan was unable to provide the necessary materials to support armed forces. Generally speaking, Afghanistan's economy, which was geared primarily for export, was not able to support military actions by a large contingent of forces committed into Afghanistan for operations and combat.

Afghanistan's population is about 17 million people. The average population density is some 25 people per square kilometer [65 people per square mile]. The population density increases around the cities of Kabul and Herat, where it is 300 and 150 people per square kilometer, respectively [777 and 387 people per square mile, respectively]. On the other hand, in the southern deserts and the central and northeast mountain areas, there are practically no people at all.[6]

Afghanistan has over 20 nationalities belonging to various language groups. The Pushtun are the largest group, consisting of approximately nine million people. The Tadjiks have over four million people, the Uzbeks about one and a half million people, the Hazara about 1,400,000 people, and the Turkmens about 1,100,000 people.[7] About 85 percent of the population are peasants. No more than 600,000 people work in industry. Spiritual leaders constitute a large group of the social strata. The majority of the population is settled; however, some three million people are nomads. The educational level of the country is very low, with some 80 percent illiterate. The overwhelming part of the population are Muslim, with 90 percent of these Sunni and 10 percent Shia.

The history of Afghanistan is one of resistance to various conquerors, armed bands, and coups d'etat. It is interesting that Alexander the Great, while conducting his conquest toward the east, took five years to break the resistance of the Pushtun tribes.[8] Ten centuries later, Arab conquerors met the desperate resistance of the Afghan tribes. Six times they launched an offensive against Kabul and the area of the central plateau. Each time, they were forced to withdraw, having suffered heavy casualties.

Ahmad Shah Durrani founded the first, central, independent government on the territory of contemporary Afghanistan in 1747. Ahmad Shah expanded his government and the boundaries of his realm into the Durrani Empire by conquering the Punjab, Kashmir, Sind, Sirhind, Baluchistan, Khurasan, Balkh, and several other regions bordering on the southern bank of the Amu Darya. The khans of the Abdali tribe took the ruling positions in the newly formed government. The subordinate Afghan tribes retained their family/tribal structure. All internal questions of tribal life were settled at a *jirgah*—a council of tribal members. The majority of the tribes were exempt from paying taxes because they furnished soldiers to the Shah. These military levies led to the increased militarization of the tribes. The khans of the tribes used this militarization in their attempts to break away from the central power. This was the primary reason for all the rebellions and mutinies that marked the history of Afghanistan from the end of the eighteenth century to the start of the nineteenth century. As a result, the heirs of Ahmad Shah spent most of their gains, and in 1818, the Durrani Empire split up into four kingdoms: Herat, Kandahar, Kabul, and Peshawar.

In the 1830s, the Kabul Kingdom began expansion, but this was interrupted by the English invasion of 1838. The First Anglo-Afghan War, 1838 to 1842, began when an English corps entered southeast Afghanistan and, by 1839, occupied Kandahar, Gazni, and Kabul. However, the Afghans resented the foreign conquerors and began guerrilla warfare against the British. This led to a massive rebellion in Kabul in November 1841 that resulted in the destruction of the occupation army and the death of Shah Shuja, the British-supported figure head. The remaining English forces withdrew at the end of 1842.

Dost Mohammad was the leader of the unified forces of the Afghan government in their common armed conflict and victory over the aggressor. In 1855, he annexed Kandahar into the Kingdom of Kabul, and in 1863 he annexed Herat. His

successor, Emir Sher Ali, who ruled from 1863 to 1879, continued the centraliza-
tion of power by annexing Badakshah—the northern region of Afghanistan up to
the southern bank of the Amu Darya. Sher Ali strengthened the central power of
the government and significantly increased the strength of the army, which
showed a determined resistance to the second British invasion of 1878 to 1880.

As before, a British occupation corps (over 36,000 strong) invaded
Afghanistan and seized Kandahar in January 1879. The British did this to force
Emir Yaqub Khan to sign the Gandamak agreement. Under the terms of the
agreement, Afghanistan subordinated itself to the British government and ceded
the regions of Kurram, Pishin, and Sibi to the British.[9] These conditions were
unacceptable to the government in Kabul [the king] and the people of
Afghanistan. The treaty elicited a powerful popular insurrection against the
British that began in September of 1879. On 27 July 1880, Afghan forces anni-
hilated a British Brigade at Maiwand, near the city of Kandahar. Simultaneously,
the British garrison in Kabul was caught in the grip of a siege by some 100,000
Afghan rebels.[10] England was forced to abandon her plans for the conquest of
Afghanistan and withdraw her forces from the country. However, London man-
aged to exploit a change of government and signed an agreement with the new
Emir, Abdur Rahman, on 12 November 1893. This agreement left Britain in control of Afghanistan's foreign affairs. More importantly, the agreement set
Afghanistan's eastern boundary—a boundary that exists today.[11]

Toward the close of the nineteenth century and in the early part of the twen-
tieth century, Afghanistan established a relatively centralized government with a
standing regular army and defined economic and political relations with neighboring countries, including Russia. Afghanistan remained neutral during World
War I (1914 to 1918), despite the efforts of the German and Austrian missions,
sent to Kabul in 1915 and 1916, to bring Afghanistan into the war on their side.

In February 1919, Emir Amanullah Khan decided to take advantage of the
results of the Great October Socialist Revolution and the civil war in Russia. He
declared Afghanistan's independence on 28 February. This served as the cause
for the Third Anglo-Afghan War (3 May to 3 July 1919) in which the 340,000-
man British Army met the 40,000 Afghan Army.[12] At first, the British forces pre-
vailed in the Battle for the Khyber Pass. On a different axis, through Waziristan,
advancing Afghan forces were checked at the Thal fortress on 27 May. Simultaneously, the Pushtun tribes along the border rose in revolt. This uprising reinforced the independence movement in India. These uprisings forced London to
seek a truce, which they signed in Rawalpindi on 8 August 1919. Preliminary
peace talks continued, and the final peace treaty between Great Britain and
Afghanistan was signed in November 1921.

The victory of the Afghan people in this war and the Red Army's destruction
of British interventionists in the Caspian Sea region led to a significant [interna-
tional] step as the fledgling Russian Soviet Republic recognized the sovereignty
of Afghanistan on 27 March 1919. On 28 February 1921, the Soviet-Afghan

Treaty of Friendship was signed in Kabul. This was the first treaty that Afghanistan had signed with a great power as an equal. On 24 June 1931, Afghanistan and the USSR concluded an agreement on neutrality and mutual nonaggression. The term of the treaty was for ten years and was renewable. It was renewed four times, the last time being in December 1975.

The progressive reform of Afghanistan continued from 1919 through 1928. In 1923, the government proclaimed the state's first constitution. This constitution was not supported by the tribal leaders, clergy, and peasants. This led to an uprising against the government at the end of 1928 and a military coup in October 1929. General Mohammad Nadir Shah, the former Minister of War, was crowned king and established a new ruling dynasty.[13] His new constitution of 1931 reinforced and supported the participation of the tribal aristocracy in government.

On 7 September 1939, after the beginning of the Second World War (1939 to 1945), the Afghan government announced its neutrality and maintained this stance throughout the war. At the same time, the economic situation in the country became progressively worse. This led to the growth of an antigovernment mood, especially among the young and the embryonic national bourgeoisie, which in turn led to the founding of various opposition parties and groups. This led to a series of regime plots, government negotiations, and the resulting plunge into the abyss of civil war.[14]

In the mid 1960s, the progressive [communist] part of the officer corps of the Armed Forces of Afghanistan clandestinely formed the Army Revolutionary Organization with the goal of overthrowing the monarchy. In July 1973, the army launched a coup d'etat that overthrew the monarchy and established a republic. Mohammad Daoud headed the new government, but he was unable to bring stability to the country. This led to conspiracies by former high-placed officials, generals, and officers. Their attempts failed and the organizers were executed. The country and army were buried in an avalanche of persecution and repression.[15]

In January 1965, the illegal Peoples Democratic Party of Afghanistan (PDPA) was founded. It was headed by Nur Mohammad Taraki, and one of the members of the central committee was Babrak Karmal. From the very first day, there were serious differences between these two leaders that led to Karmal's expulsion from the central committee. His place was taken by Hafizullah Amin. As a result, the party was split into two factions, both of which fought independently for their goals. However, Daoud's opposition politics against both factions of the PDPA and also the repression of PDPA members quickly led the factions to bury their differences and reunite to fight the regime. On 27 April 1978, the PDPA seized control of the country. The prime minister and head of state was N. M. Taraki; his vice president was B. Karmal.

The reforms that Taraki undertook were not supported by members of the government, the army, or the people.[16] Waves of unrest rocked the new administration and brought new leaders to the surface; one of the more active was

Hafizullah Amin. On 14 October 1979, there was a coup d'etat and a usurpation of power. N. M. Taraki was brutally murdered by Amin's supporters. A new wave of repression poured over the army and country. However, this did not guarantee the viability of the new regime, which was secretly opposed within the government and openly opposed by armed opposition groups. Moreover, this armed opposition began to grow in strength and spread throughout the country.

Originally, the Islamic fundamentalist movement provided the foundation for the armed opposition. The Islamic fundamentalist movement arose in the mid-1960s and promoted the rebirth of Islam, based on its original principles and cleansed of its later developments.[17] In 1968, supporters of the fundamentalists joined together in the Union of Muslim Youth. This union's mission was to combat any member of the country's ruling clique who pandered to the modernization of Islam or the penetration of the country with communist ideas. The union established their program and became a permanent resistance in irreconcilable opposition to all the successive regimes that ruled Afghanistan for short or long periods of time.

In June of 1975, the fundamentalists attempted to overthrow the regime of M. Daoud. They started the insurgent movement in the Panjshir valley, some 100 kilometers north of Kabul, and in a number of other provinces of the country. However, the government forces easily smashed the insurgency, and a sizable portion of the insurgents left the country and settled in Pakistan, where they had complete freedom of action. In May 1978, the insurgents founded their first base in Pakistan to train armed bands for combat in Afghanistan. Afterwards, similar centers were founded in Iran and also in Saudi Arabia and Egypt. The primary source of manpower for these armed bands was the many Afghan refugees who, by the fall of 1979, numbered several hundred thousand.[18]

Ethnic minorities also provided strong armed resistance groups that wanted to seize some power and control from the majority Pashtun. Through the efforts of the fundamentalist and ethnic groups, armed insurrection flared in Nuristan in October 1978 and then in Herat in March 1979. In April and May of 1979, the rebellion spread to Baglan, Oruzgan, Farah, Badghis, Ghowr, Logar, and so on throughout the provinces of Afghanistan. "Free Nuristan" was proclaimed in the spring of 1979, and by August "Independent Islamic Hazarajat" with its 3,000-strong "Union of Islamic Warriors" sprang into being. The armed insurrection against the central power and various nationalities began, and, as a result, many regions of the country came under the complete control of the Mujahideen. The Mujahideen established "Islamic Committees" backed by their armed might to rule these areas. Reinforced resistance groups went on the offensive and advanced on the cities of Herat, Kandahar, Jalalabad, and Khost. In the summer and fall, powerful unrest shook the cities of Ghazni, Gardez, Asmar, and others. In June through August, the Mujahideen repeatedly made attempts to seize Kabul, its environs, and the capital airport.[19] Civil war raged throughout the country in 1978 and 1979. Neither of the opposing sides could attain a quick victory over the other without significant help from the outside. Under these circumstances, the ruling circles in Kabul looked to the Soviet Union for help.

Soviet-Afghan military cooperation has a long history. As far back as 1919, the Soviet government gave Afghanistan gratuitous aid in the form of a million gold rubles, small arms, ammunition, and a few aircraft to support the Afghan resistance to the British conquerors.[20] In 1924, the USSR again gave military aid to Afghanistan. They gave them small arms and aircraft and conducted training in Tashkent for cadre officers from the Afghan Army. Soviet-Afghan military cooperation began on a regular basis in 1956, when both countries signed another agreement. The Soviet Minister of Defense was now responsible for training national military cadres. In 1972, up to 100 Soviet consultants and technical specialists were sent on detached duty to Afghanistan to train the Afghan armed forces. In May 1978, the governments signed another international agreement, sending up to 400 Soviet military advisers to Afghanistan.[21]

The DRA and Moscow signed a Treaty of Friendship, Good Neighborliness, and Cooperation in Moscow in December 1978. The treaty allowed the government of Afghanistan to request that the government of the Soviet Union send forces into Afghanistan and provided the legal basis for such an action. The government of N. M. Taraki repeatedly requested the introduction of Soviet forces in Afghanistan in the spring and summer of 1979. He requested Soviet troops to provide his security and to increase the effectiveness of the fight against the Mujahideen. On 14 April the Afghan government requested that the USSR send 15 to 20 helicopters with their crews to Afghanistan, and on 16 June the Soviet government responded and sent a detachment of tanks, BMPs, and crews to guard the government of Afghanistan in Kabul and to secure the Bagram and Shindand airfields.

In response to this request, an airborne battalion, commanded by Lieutenant Colonel A. Lomakin, arrived at the Bagram airfield on 7 July. They arrived without their combat gear disguised as technical specialists. They were the personal bodyguard for Taraki. The paratroopers were directly subordinated to the senior Soviet military adviser and did not interfere in Afghan politics.[22]

After a month, the DRA requests were no longer for individual crews and subunits, but were for regiments and larger units. On 19 July, the Afghan government requested that two motorized rifle divisions be sent to Afghanistan. The following day, they requested an airborne division in addition to the earlier requests. They repeated these requests and variants to these requests over the following months right up to December 1979. However, the Soviet government was in no hurry to grant these requests.

In the first days of December, the Soviet Minister of Defense, Marshal of the Soviet Union D. F. Ustinov, informed a very small group of necessary personnel in the Ministry of Defense of the possibility that the political leadership of the country might decide to send Soviet Forces into Afghanistan. On the 10th of

December, the General Staff of the Armed Forces of the Soviet Union received orders to prepare to conduct a parachute landing with an airborne division and to increase the combat readiness of two motorized rifle divisions. This was the beginning of the establishment of the group of forces that would become the 40th Army. General-Lieutenant Yu. V. Tukharinov was designated to command it.[23] The Kremlin made the final decision to commit Soviet forces to Afghanistan on 12 December 1979.

On 13 October, an operational group was formed in the Ministry of Defense. It was headed by the first deputy to the chief of the General Staff, General of the Army S, F. Akhromeyev.[24] Its function was to coordinate the activities of the representatives of all the Soviet departments, forces of the 40th Army, and Soviet apparat should major forces be committed to Afghanistan. The operations group left immediately for Afghanistan.

On 13 December, Colonel-General Yu. P. Maksimov, the Commander of the Turkestan Military District, approved the plan for the introduction of the Limited Contingent of Soviet Forces (LCOSF) into Afghanistan and sent it to the Commander of the 40th Army, General-Lieutenant Yu. V. Tukharinov. At the same time, officers from the general staff and Turkestan Military District formed a skeleton command and staff element for the embryonic 40th Army. Members of the Military Council included the Chief of Political Affairs, General-Major A. V. Toskaev; Chief of Staff, General-Major L. N. Lobanov; and Chief of Intelligence, General-Major A. A. Korchagin. Not wasting any time, they began intensive preparations for the impending intervention. The preparations were practically open as the force depended on the mobilization of assigned reservists. On the training areas, there was an uninterrupted movement of assigned combat subunits, while in the area around Termez, troops prepared to cross the Amu Darya river.

A general directive for total mobilization and an increase in readiness was not issued. The forces were brought up to readiness by separate orders after the receipt of appropriate oral orders from the Minister of Defense of the USSR. In all, about 100 large units, units, and institutions were brought up to full TO&E manning. Over 50,000 officers, sergeants, and soldiers were mobilized from the reserve. Divisions and regiments were filled out first, and then the combat service support and repair units and other support units of the 40th Army were filled out. Some of these support units were already moving with the intervention force before they were completely filled. This was the largest mobilization in the Turkestan and Central Asian Military Districts since the Great Patriotic War.[25] The Minister of Defense set the time to cross the international border at 1500 hours Moscow time (1630 hours Kabul time) on 25 December.

Everything was ready at the appointed time. The day before, the First Deputy to the Minister of Defense, Marshal of the Soviet Union S. D. Sokolov, arrived from Moscow and moved into the command post of the 40th Army.

Colonel-General Yu. P. Maksimov, the commander of the Turkestan Military District, was also there. The crossing of the Amu Darya river began in the evening twilight. A BMP-mounted motorized rifle battalion (MRB), serving as the advanced guard for its parent motorized rifle regiment (MRR), began to cross the pontoon bridge. The motorized rifle division[26] (MRD) to which the MRR belonged had built the bridge practically on the move. The battalion moved deeper into Afghanistan. Behind it, the main body of the division followed all night long.

At 1900 hours on 26 December, the division was issued new, unexpected orders—change the direction of march and move to Kabul to arrive by 1700 hours on the following day.[27] At that time, the main body of the 103rd Guards Airborne Division had landed at Kabul airfield and an airborne regiment had landed at Bagram airfield. The airborne division was commanded by Colonel I. F. Ryabchenko. The Soviet forces and advisers already in country reinforced the security of important administrative centers, airfields, and radio and television stations. At 1930 hours, the 103rd Guards Airborne Division, commanded by Colonel Ryabchenko, seized all the key political and military installations in Kabul and the surrounding area. This denied entry of Amin supporters to the capital. On the night of 27 December, a Soviet Motorized Rifle Division[28] crossed into western Afghanistan. By 28 December, its regiments had taken control of the city of Herat.

By mid-January 1980, the main body of the 40th Army was located in Afghanistan. The 40th Army consisted of two motorized rifle divisions, an airborne division, an air assault brigade, and two separate motorized rifle regiments. Within the first six months of 1980, the 40th Army was reinforced with another motorized rifle division and two separate regiments.[29] At that time, the overall number of Soviet forces reached 81,800 personnel, of which 61,800 were in combat units of the ground forces and air force. After that, the size of the LCOSF continually grew. Thus, the war required a lot of men and materiel, not only to initially enter the war in Afghanistan, but also to support the essential changes that came with the revision of the theory and practice of preparing the commanders, staffs, and forces for this kind of war.

In light of the defining military-political missions and ongoing combat, the conduct of the Soviet-Afghan War can be divided into four phases.

PHASE ONE (DECEMBER 1979 TO FEBRUARY 1980)

This phase began with the entry of Soviet forces into Afghanistan, their stationing in garrisons, and their final organization for securing bases and various installations. During this phase, the enemy deployed comparatively powerful forces against the Soviet forces. The Soviet forces did not avoid direct conflict with them. The Soviet forces, fighting alongside DRA forces, took the most difficult missions for themselves. The Afghan forces were poorly trained to conduct independent actions and played a secondary role in the fulfillment of operational and tactical missions.

PHASE TWO (MARCH 1980 TO APRIL 1985)

Active combat characterizes this phase. Soviet forces undertook combat on a wide scale, mainly employing only Soviet forces, but also conducting joint actions with regiments and divisions of the DRA. By the start of this phase, the enemy, having suffered heavy losses, was switching to guerrilla tactics and moving into the mountains. Principally, these tactics consisted of avoiding combat with superior Soviet forces; conducting surprise action against small groups; and refusing to fight conventional, positional warfare while conducting widespread maneuver using autonomous groups and detachments. If the Mujahideen were unable to avoid combat, they reverted to close combat where it was difficult, if not impossible, to use air strikes and artillery fire against their dug-in firing positions. Under these circumstances, the Soviet forces attempted to conduct "combat operations" with a clear superiority in forces and means.

PHASE THREE (APRIL 1985 TO JANUARY 1987)

During this phase, the Soviets conducted a two-step conversion from primary active combat to supporting Afghan forces with aviation, artillery, and engineer subunits. Soviet motorized rifle, airborne, and tank subunits mainly became the reserve to raise the morale and warrior spirit of the Afghan forces. Soviet Spetsnaz[30] forces continued to operate to stop the supply of weapons and ammunition from across the border. During this phase, Soviet authorities withdrew six Soviet regiments into the Soviet Union.[31]

During the third phase of the war, the brunt of the fighting was transferred to the Afghan forces. Soviet forces withdrew from large-scale operations and primarily conducted small-sized ambushes based on intelligence reports. However, from time to time, Soviet forces conducted large-scale operations. Basic missions during this period were LOC security, security of key military and civil installations, and convoy escort.

PHASE FOUR (JANUARY 1987 TO FEBRUARY 1989)

This phase was marked by Soviet forces' participation in the Afghan government's program of national reconciliation. During this time, the Soviet forces conducted virtually no offensive actions and went into combat only when attacked by the Mujahideen or when supporting combat by Afghan forces. During this phase, the Soviet forces prepared for their total withdrawal.

The military-political missions assigned to the Soviet forces over the various phases of the war in Afghanistan were also among the important factors that impacted on the formation and development of this part of the military art. Other factors include the special conditions of the country during the 40th Army's stay, the 40th Army organization, the weapons and tactics of the enemy, and the combat capabilities of our own divisions, regiments, and subunits.

Editors' comments: The explanation of Afghan history is couched in Marxist-Leninist terms and reflects the thinking that drew Soviet forces into the Afghan civil war and kept them there. Thus, the Afghans had a "Marxist-Leninist revolution" (actually a coup d'etat) that had to be defended against "Chinese and Western intervention." The United States had lost its influence and listening posts in Iran with the downfall of the Shah. The Soviet leadership was convinced that the United States was trying to move into Afghanistan to make up for this loss. When Amin made some tentative moves for economic assistance from the United States, the Soviet leadership felt threatened and acted. Soviet Spetsnaz killed Amin and installed Babrak Karmal in power. This was a coup de main disguised as an invited intervention. The Soviet need to cast history in "scientific" Marxist-Leninist terms detracted from their ability to understand Afghanistan and to make rational foreign-relations decisions concerning their neighboring state.

The Soviet state had a long, close relationship with Afghanistan beginning shortly after the Bolshevik revolution. Soviet diplomats, economic advisers, military advisers, scholars, and engineers were continually resident in or visiting Afghanistan. Afghan students attended Soviet universities, military academies, and training courses. The Soviet Union had an unparalleled opportunity to study Afghanistan. What is amazing is how the need to see everything through Marxist-Leninist filters and the Soviet compartmentalization of information blurred the General Staff perception of the realities of Afghanistan. This perception continues to the present day.

Despite the Marxist-Leninist ideological slant and the over-arching political issues associated with the war, this General Staff study is remarkably free from discussion of the political issues that surrounded the war. International politics are given a light treatment, and the book concludes with a summary that includes the betrayal of the soldiers by their own political masters. For all of that, the book is a military study that is uncommonly clean of the political factor for a book written by officers heavily schooled in the Marxist-Leninist tradition.

1

Phases and Course of the Conflict[1]

Despite the fact that the operational decision to send the LCOSF into Afghanistan was made thirteen days before it crossed the border, individual units began to penetrate the border and move into Afghanistan at the beginning of December 1979. However, they were not told why they were taking such actions.

On the 13th of October, the Ministry of Defense formed an operational group headed by the first deputy to the chief of the General Staff, General of the Army S. F. Akhromeyev.[2] The group's function was to coordinate the actions of the representatives of all the Soviet departments, forces of the 40th Army, and Soviet *apparat* should major forces be committed to Afghanistan. The operations group left immediately for Afghanistan. They made themselves familiar with the situation and signed the invasion plan.

The concept of the operation was to commit the LCOSF into Afghanistan along two ground approaches and an air corridor. The LCOSF would quickly seize all the important population centers and support the planned *coup de main* to seize the government (Map 2).

On 13 December, Colonel-General Yu. P. Maksimov, the Commander of the Turkestan Military District, approved the plan for the introduction of the Limited Contingent of Soviet Forces (LCOSF) into Afghanistan and gave it to the Commander of the 40th Army, General-Lieutenant Yu. V. Tukharinov in his (Maximov's) office. At the same time, a skeleton command and staff element for the embryonic 40th Army was formed with officers from the general staff and Turkestan Military District. Members of the Military Council included the Chief of Political Affairs, General-Major A. V. Toskaev; Chief of Staff, General-Major L. N. Lobanov; and Chief of Intelligence, General-Major A. A. Korchagin. Not wasting any time, they began intensive preparations for the impending intervention. The preparations were practically open. It depended on the implementation of the mobilization of assigned personnel. On the training areas, there was an

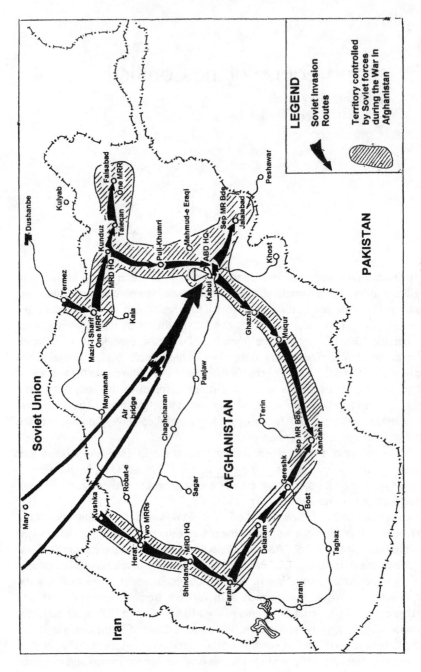

Map 2. Invasion and occupation of Afghanistan

uninterrupted movement of assigned combat subunits, while in the area around Termez, troops prepared to cross the Amu Darya river.

The general directive for total mobilization and an order for the increase in national readiness was not issued. The forces were brought up to readiness by separate orders after the receipt of the appropriate oral direction by the Minister of Defense of the USSR. In all, about 100 large units, units, and institutions were filled out to full TO&E manning. Over 50,000 officers, sergeants, and soldiers were mobilized from the reserve. Divisions and regiments were filled out first, and then the combat service support and repair units and other support units of the 40th Army were filled out. Some of these support units were already moving with the intervention force before they were complete. This was the largest mobilization in the Turkestan and Central Asian Military Districts since the Great Patriotic War.[3] The Minister of Defense gave the time to cross the international border at 1500 hours Moscow time (1630 hours Kabul time) on the 25th of December.

Everything was ready at the appointed time. The day before, the First Deputy to the Minister of Defense, Marshal of the Soviet Union S. D. Sokolov, arrived from Moscow and moved into the command post of the 40th Army. Colonel-General Yu. P. Maksimov, the commander of the Turkestan Military District, was also there. The crossing of the Amu Darya river began in the evening twilight. A BMP-mounted motorized rifle battalion (MRB), serving as the advanced guard for its parent motorized rifle regiment (MRR), began to cross the pontoon bridge. The 108th Motorized Rifle Division[4] (MRD), to which the MRR belonged, was commanded by Colonel V. I. Mironov. The battalion crossed the river and moved deeper into Afghanistan. Behind it, the main body of the division followed all night long. Having completed the march, the division concentrated in the area of Baghlan, Kunduz, Puli-Khumri, and Deshi on the evening of 27 December. At that time, the division was issued new, unexpected orders—to change their direction of march and enter Kabul on the following day by 1700 hours.

At that time, the main body of the 103rd Guards Airborne Division had landed at Kabul airfield and an airborne regiment had landed at Bagram airfield. The airborne division was commanded by Colonel I. F. Rabchenko. The Soviet forces and advisers already in country reinforced their security at important administrative centers, airfields, and radio and television stations. At 1930 hours, the 103rd Guards Airborne Division, commanded by Colonel Rabchenko, seized all the key political and military installations in Kabul and the surrounding area. This denied entry of Amin supporters to the capital.[5] On the night of 27 December, a Soviet Motorized Rifle Division[6] crossed into western Afghanistan. By 28 December, its regiments had taken control of the cities of Herat and Shindand. The division's zone of responsibility extended to the city of Kandahar.

By mid January 1980, the main body of the 40th Army was located in Afghanistan. The 40th Army consisted of two motorized rifle divisions, an airborne division, an air assault brigade, and two separate motorized rifle regiments.[7]

In all, there were some 52,000 personnel. This was considered sufficient to guarantee the viability of Afghanistan. It was thought that Soviet forces would not have to fight during the invasion and subsequent stationing of Soviet forces. It was felt that the mere presence of Soviet forces would serve to "sober up" the Mujahideen. Soviet military assistance would primarily be moral support to the DRA.

The entry of Soviet forces into Afghanistan was the signal to overthrow the government. On 27 December, a small group of conspirators deposed and executed Amin.[8] Babrak Karmal became the republic's Prime Minister and the general secretary of the PDPA [and head of the Revolutionary Council—the head of state]. The first act of the new government was to release 15,000 prisoners from jail. Political prisoners, draft dodgers, and deserters were set free. However, these measures did little to normalize the situation in the country. The majority of the population viewed the arrival of foreign troops without enthusiasm. The opposition immediately took advantage of this feeling, because they saw Babrak Karmal as not only a political enemy but also Moscow's protégé. There were two results from this outcome. First, the opposition movement spread practically over the entire territory of Afghanistan. Second, after a period of relative calm, the opposition began armed aggression, particularly against the Soviet forces.

In light of the defining military-political missions and ongoing combat, the conduct of the Soviet-Afghan War can be divided into four phases.

The First Phase (December 1979–February 1980) began with the entry of Soviet forces into Afghanistan, their stationing in garrisons, and their final organization for securing bases and various installations. They also conducted combat to support the completion of their mission.

Already at the time of the initial intervention and garrisoning of Soviet forces, it was necessary to seek combat with the enemy. Lieutenant Colonel Nikolai Ivanovich Mamykin was a direct participant in those events. He remembers how, during the first phase of settling into Afghanistan, Soviet forces were kept in garrison and were not used for combat. However, the Soviets were fired at by the resistance. Even though they were not participating in combat missions, they were suffering casualties and had to return fire. The Afghan soldiers determined that the Soviet armed forces were responsible for the trial that their revolution was now undergoing. Babrak Karmal expressed this mood from the beginning to the leadership of the operations group of the Ministry of Defense and requested that Soviet forces enter into active combat insomuch as he did not trust his own army. This request produced the desired effect. The commander of the Soviet forces was ordered to begin combat together with Afghan units. They determined that the primary mission to destroy the opposition must be accomplished by the Afghan army, but that the Soviet forces were capable of assisting any given mission.

The winter of 1979–1980 was hard for the Soviet combatants. The hope was that the principal mission of armed combat with the opposition would be accomplished by the Afghan army, but this did not occur. Measures to raise the combat potential of the government forces were weak and ineffective. Therefore, Soviet forces bore the brunt of the combat with the detachments of the armed enemy opposition. The Mujahideen formations that fought the Soviet forces were comparatively strong forces and they did not back off from direct contact. This allowed the Soviet forces to destroy strong antirevolutionary groupings near Faizabad, Taleqan, Takhar, Baghlan, Jalalabad, and other cities.

The leadership of the Afghan opposition, having clashed with a mighty military power, quickly realized that if they maintained their large, fairly conventional forces, they would be destroyed. They abandoned their large-scale tactics and divided their formations into guerrilla groups and detachments of 20 to 100 men that began to conduct guerrilla warfare. The Soviet forces now were faced with the question of how to employ its forces and resources against small, exceedingly mobile groups of Mujahideen using maneuver tactics. Attempts by the senior leadership to deploy large, combined-arms formations to conduct a classic offensive and pursuit against Mujahideen detachments did not work.

This raises a number of issues about the inadequate preparation of Soviet forces. The massive experience that Soviet forces gained in their fight with the Basmachi movement[9] was simply forgotten. The more recent experience of Fascist Germany during the Second World War and the experience of other armies that conducted counter-guerrilla actions in local wars were practically ignored.[10] Therefore, the Soviet forces in Afghanistan had to use trial and error to formulate a new military art to combat their unaccustomed foe. This decreased the effectiveness of their combat actions and resulted in unwarranted casualties. Nikolai Ivanovich Antonov, who was the Deputy to the Operations section of a division, remembers an operation in February 1980 in which the enemy skillfully took advantage of Soviet miscalculations. A battalion neglected to post flank security when it left garrison for a march through the mountains and suffered significant casualties. The enemy allowed the Soviet reconnaissance group and the lead company of the battalion to pass through the ambush kill zone. The enemy opened up on the middle company in the column from both sides. From the intensive fire, observers were able to determine that the enemy force was 60 to 80 men. However, the enemy action was so unexpected that the commanders at all levels were confused and dumbfounded and not a single commander gave an order to return fire. When the order to return fire was finally given, the enemy abandoned his positions and left the area unimpeded and unhurt.

During the first phase of the war, the majority of Soviet forces and equipment was dedicated to securing regime installations and the lines of communication (LOC). Up to 35 percent of the force was committed to this mission. There were additional security missions that involved security and defense of airfields, military installations, and Soviet-Afghan economic cooperative projects. Convoy escort demanded still more security forces.[11] All of these missions had specific requirements. The Soviet forces did not have the experience or knowledge to carry out these missions successfully, and the hierarchy had not foreseen the need to train officers to fulfill these tasks.[12] There were no answers in the regulations and manuals, so these missions had to be conducted by trial and error.

The major difficulties in deciding how to deal with the various operational and tactical missions were further complicated by the living conditions of the Soviet forces. At the start of 1980, there were no cantonments or garrisons prepared for the LCOSF in Afghanistan. The command was able to place a small part of the units and subunits in more or less acceptable military garrisons. The bulk of the force remained in the field in tent cities. In order to prevent enemy surprise attacks, the commanders established security posts and mine fields on the main avenues of approach.

The command became quite efficient in moving forces from one region to another. During these shifts, some forces did not always pick up their mine fields prior to the move, and it happened that Soviet soldiers were blown up by Soviet mines when they moved into the recently evacuated area.

The second phase of the Soviet intervention in Afghanistan lasted from March 1980 to April 1985. It was characterized by the conduct of combat on a wide scale, mainly by Soviet forces, and sometimes in cooperation with Afghan divisions and regiments. The 40th Army was reinforced with the 201st Motorized Rifle Division and two separate motorized rifle regiments. The overall size of the Soviet force reached 81,800, of which 61,800 were in combat units of the ground and air forces.[13] The force included about 600 tanks, 1500 BMPs, 2900 BTRs, 500 aircraft and helicopter, and 500 artillery pieces of various calibers.

The opposition, having suffered significant military casualties in the first phase of the war, moved their main forces into the mountain region, which is difficult to enter and where it is practically impossible to use modern combat equipment. Further, they managed to blend into the local population. The Mujahideen were able to employ various tactical techniques. Thus, when they would encounter a superior Soviet force, they, as a rule, would withdraw from battle. At the same time, the Mujahideen would never miss an opportunity to launch a surprise strike, usually with a small force. As a rule, during this phase, the armed opposition forces abandoned positional warfare and widely employed maneuver. The Mujahideen could only be forced to accept battle under compelling circumstances. These circumstances included defense of a base or base region or when the Mujahideen were encircled and had no other options. In this case, the blocked Mujahideen detachments moved into close combat, where it was practically impossible for the Soviets to use their aviation and which sharply restricted their possibility of using artillery, especially from indirect firing positions.

This situation forced the Soviet forces to find new forms and methods to destroy the enemy. They determined that the only way to achieve decisive results was to liquidate the Mujahideen's regional bases. Special attention was focused on this mission. However, to fulfill this mission required a significant amount of forces and equipment. Taking into account that the bulk of the forces were occupied with other missions, it was difficult to pursue this mission with the forces of just one formation.[14] Very often it was necessary to unite forces from several divisions and to form a single operational command (the 40th Army staff). Such a form of military actions were called combat operations or, in the broader realm, simply operations.

In the contemporary military-scientific interpretation of the term "operation," an operation is the sum total of coordination and cooperation efforts by aim, place and time of the engagement, battle, and strike, carried out in a Theater of Military Actions (TVD) or on a strategic or operational direction with a single concept and plan for the decision of strategic and operational missions. The experience of the Great Patriotic War demonstrated that the minimum amount of forces required for an operation were 70,000 to 100,000 personnel.[15] In Afghanistan, the understanding of the term operation included several different possibilities and forms in the action of forces. The required size of operational formations and the issue of who would direct the combat actions saw operations devolve down to armies, divisions, and even regiments. As a rule, the conduct of army operations called for a force of one or two motorized rifle, as well as airborne, artillery, and engineer units and subunits—a total of 10,000 to 15,000 personnel. These operations were planned by the army staff and directed by the army commander. Division and regimental operations were conducted by the forces of the division and regiment and directed by their commanders. Combat was conducted over most of the territory of Afghanistan. The incidence of combat was especially intense along the main highway network and in the east along the Afghan-Pakistan border.

By 1982, the operational maneuver base element for a raid operation had become a reinforced battalion. The wide variety of possible battalion maneuvers included flanking and enveloping attacks as well as air assaults by air assault forces landing from helicopters. The conduct of these raids proved that commanders and forces were accumulating experience and increasing combat mastery. But they did not always result in the desired outcome. Major S. N. Petrov remembers one such incident.[16] Intelligence sources indicated that a group of 40 well-armed Mujahideen were in the town of Sherkhankel (Map 3). This town was in the area of responsibility of one of the Soviet regiments.

"The 3rd Parachute Battalion, as the alert subunit, was ordered to move to Sherkhankel and destroy the enemy at 0200 hours, 20 March 1982. An artillery battalion and four Mi-24 helicopters were in direct support.

"The battalion commander decided to move at night with an approach march. A combat reconnaissance patrol would move some 300 meters in front of the main body. The march route was down a wide, straight road, along the left side of which stretched an adobe wall. On the right side of the road was a cement-lined canal that was five meters wide and 2.5 meters deep.

"Suddenly, through a firing port cut through the adobe wall, the enemy

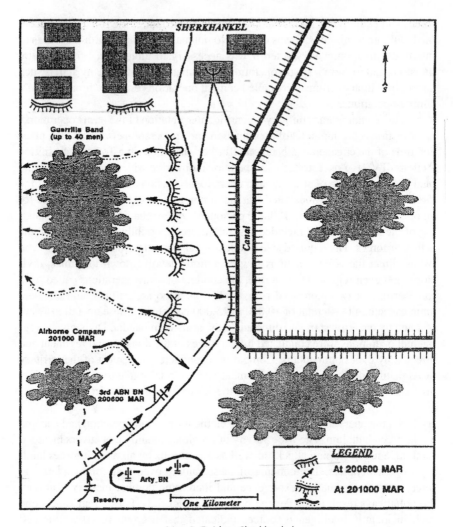

Map 3. Raid on Sherkhankel

opened fire with a grenade launcher at the reconnaissance platoon. Practically simultaneously, a machine gun opened fire on the reconnaissance patrol. The machine gun was in the houses, some 150 meters away. The paratroopers, attempting to take up firing positions, fell under the enemy's fire. The battalion commander called for artillery and air support. The assigned mission was blown, however, and the battalion commander belatedly decided to use maneuver to encircle the Mujahideen. The Mujahideen struck a short, powerful blow and then hid, using the system of *karez*.[7] The battalion had eight KIA and six WIA. Two of the dead were officers. The battalion abandoned further action and returned to base.

"My memory often returns to this tragic moment. I seek an answer to the tormenting question—was there a way to avoid this tragic outcome? Of course, with hindsight, you have 20/20 vision. This aside, I have determined the following miscalculations, which had an adverse effect on the ability of the alert subunit to carry out its assigned mission. First off, the battalion commander did not consider that combat in Afghanistan did not always start where you planned it. It might begin suddenly at any location which is to the enemy's advantage at any time of the day or night. This incident showed how an adobe wall running parallel and close to a road always presented a serious danger for Soviet forces. They provided the enemy secrecy and surprise. This factor was not studied. Second, the battalion column only had security to the front and was moving on a single axis. This made maneuver very difficult. If there is a possibility to move on two roads, with flank security, this may force the enemy to abandon his ambush. Third, in this incident, there was no reconnaissance and the soldiers were not in full readiness to use their weapons."

At this time, the inadequacies of heavy military equipment, which had limited application in mountainous terrain, became apparent. Tanks, BMPs, and self-propelled artillery were road bound and lacked the operational expanse for their employment.[18] Contemporary high-precision jet aircraft were unable to support ground forces effectively with air strikes. Using helicopter gunships, the Soviets were able, for the first time, to establish more effective methods of combating the Mujahideen in the mountains. This use of the helicopters was severely limited later by the introduction of the man-portable Stinger air defense missile. This appreciably decreased the results of operations and combat which frequently did not achieve their projected goals.

It became more obvious to the Soviet command that they would not be able to completely destroy the Mujahideen in a short period of time using the forces of the LCOSF. The main reason for this military failure, as defined by the survival of the Afghan Mujahideen and their definite expansion of the scale of guerrilla warfare, was not military, but political. The Parcham party, headed by Babrak Karmal, had come to power but did not live up to expectations. The new government rehabilitated people convicted by Amin's government and set out on a course of reinforcement and intrigue. Their premature and not-fully-thought-out reforms led to the growth of dissatisfaction in the villages. The Afghan Army, despite its increase in personnel and its saturation with Soviet weapons and military equipment, remained almost completely incapable due to the political instability in the state. Therefore, the Soviet forces were further pulled into the civil war.

The Soviet government and the Soviet High Command did not study Afghanistan's national-historic factors before committing Soviet forces into that country. If they had, they would have found a history of many centuries of resisting various conquerors. The Afghan considers any foreigner carrying weapons in the country as an alien occupier who must be combated. The Soviet High Command made a serious initial error. At first, the majority of the Soviet personnel in the units that entered Afghanistan were Soviet Central Asians. The High Command felt that Soviet soldiers from these nationalities would be better accepted by their ethnically linked peoples of Afghanistan. However, the presence of Soviet Central Asians had the opposite effect. The Pushtun tribes, which were an active element in the antigovernment movement, were historically enemies with the Central Asian peoples to their north.[19] The appearance of Uzbeks, Tadjiks, and Turkmens served as the final irritant, which the counter-revolutionary agitators and propagandists exploited. The strength of the armed opposition grew. Thus, in 1981 to 1983, the number of armed combatants who were members of Afghan Mujahideen groups was estimated at some 45,000 personnel. By 1985, this number grew to 150,000. They controlled all the main agricultural areas of the country. The combined Soviet-Afghan armed forces operating in Afghanistan were about 400,000, of which some 100,000 were Soviet.[20] The Soviet-Afghan forces controlled the cities and the main road network linking the cities.

The Mujahideen's armed resistance continually grew in scale and intensity. Most often their strong formations of semi-regular forces conducted maneuver offensives and defensive battles. In the second half of 1984, the Mujahideen attempted to form "Islamic regiments" based on separate bands of Mujahideen. These "regiments" consisted of three to five battalions and had a total of 500 to 900 personnel. Occasionally, these regiments were united in "fronts"—consisting of several thousand personnel.[21] In addition to small arms, the fronts were armed with mountain artillery, mortars, and surface-to-surface rockets. The Mujahideen established regional bases in the almost-inaccessible mountains. They fortified these bases and protected them with interlocking, multiple-tiered defensive fires.

The bulk of Mujahideen were members of regional groups and detachments. The local tribal leaders and regional authorities were their "field commanders," whose goal was to organize the tactics and conduct armed conflict in the areas bordering on the regions where they lived. As a rule, these formations lacked an established force structure and organization. When in danger, these Mujahideen would melt into the local population where it was practically impossible to identify them. The composition of these detachments and groups were not homogeneous by social-ethnic stratus. Similar formations were frequently composed of members of the same national-ethnic group. In the majority of cases, the commanders of these local guerrillas had no direct contact with the Afghan counter-revolutionary groups located outside Afghanistan [an overstatement]. Their main advantage was the active support of the local populace.

The semi-regular formations were usually found in their bases and in the Afghan refugee camps in Pakistan and Iran. They had good military training and were adequately armed. These formations were not restricted to combat in only one region, but were highly mobile. These detachments and groups received concrete missions. After they carried them out, as a rule, they returned to their bases where they were refitted, rearmed, and rested. By the calculations of Western analysts, these semi-regular forces did not constitute more than 5 to 8 percent of the entire resistance. There were many unsavory elements in the ranks of these groups and their actions had a particularly violent character when dealing with the local populace. There were incidents of forced impressment, robbery, murder, and so on [again, an overstatement]. These acts built a wall of clear alienation between the opposition and the Afghan people. The semi-regular formations were based on class structure, political goals, and the platforms of the emigrant opposition organizations. These organizations were split by internal quarrels and ideological fights and these splits were their chief weakness that prevented coordination. Often, armed conflict broke out between the organizations. Terrorist groups were part of the armed formations that functioned in the cities. They established a diverse network of very clandestine cells. Side by side with the commitment of terrorist acts of sabotage and diversion, the underground leadership inspired mass disorder by penetrating the DRA party apparatus, army, and special services with the goal of undermining the government from the inside.

In this phase, one of the main missions in the fight with the armed opposition was to deprive the Mujahideen of their source of reinforcements by persuading the refugees to return home to Afghanistan. But the resolution to this problem directly depended on the refugees' belief in the selected political course of the government. In reality, as the result of egregious government errors, the number of refugees not only did not decrease, but grew to about 5,000,000 people during the second phase of the war. All military attempts to prevent the arrival of fresh Mujahideen in Afghanistan were unsuccessful.

Realizing that the main methods of fighting the armed opposition could not be military actions by regular forces, but determined social-economic, political, and organizational-propagandistic methods by the government, the Soviet forces in Afghanistan modified their tactics. They abandoned the conduct of large-scale field operations against separate detachments and groups of Mujahideen and concentrated their main efforts on retaining strategically important regions and the lines of communication. Secure LOCs were necessary for providing the local inhabitants with necessary food and goods.

However, in practice, these political steps did not always yield the desired results, mainly because of the weak hold that the government had in the countryside. The result of the many Soviet and DRA operations was to establish government power, the so-called nucleus in the hamlets and villages. These nuclei included a representative of the PDPA, the KHAD, the Ministry of the Interior, several other departments, and representatives from the directing workers patriotic organization, and representatives of the clergy supporting the DRA. Up to a platoon of soldiers were provided to safeguard the detachment. The problem with these detachments was that there were too few of them and that they wielded no real power. The detachment leaders were unable to conduct political work with the populace since they did not have the authority. The influence of these detachments was limited, as a rule, to the village in which they were located.

Upon completion of the operation, the forces left the occupied region and returned to their base camp or transferred to a new contested area. The unharmed Mujahideen would return to the region, reestablish their bases, and drive out or destroy the DRA detachment. This happened repeatedly. For example, during the second phase of the war, the Soviets and DRA conducted six operations in the Pandjshir valley. However, the government control of the region never improved. In the end, the LCOSF conduct of active combat was affected by the amount of available personnel. About 40 percent of the force was used to guard installations and provide security for the population.[22] First of all, it was necessary to build and improve a large number of military garrisons. This required a massive amount of building materials and equipment, most of which came from the USSR. The amount of cargo grew to a flood. In order to comply with the missions to support the construction and provide the necessary reserves for the LCOSF, they deployed a large number of guard battalions. Thus, on 1 December 1981, eight separate guard battalions joined the 40th Army. They were stationed in Bagram, Jalalabad, Kandahar, Sorubi, Shindand, Kabul, Ghazni, and Konduz. However, this force, as time would demonstrate, was insufficient. In March 1984, an additional two guard battalions were formed and stationed in Kabul and Konduz. Consequently, despite the stationing of a separate support battalion in Kabul and an army material support brigade in Puli-Khumri during the first phase of the war, by the end of the second phase of the war, these forces were insufficient to carry out these assigned security missions. The facts speak eloquently about the living conditions in the garrisons where the LCOSF were stationed. Practically every garrison had the facilities not only for sleeping, but also had large shower and bath complexes, libraries, clubs, and so on. The security systems for the garrisons were improved. Mine fields were laid on the approaches to the garrisons, guard posts were located at entry points, and garrisons were built around critical installations.

During the third phase of the war, April 1985 to April 1986, the 40th Army grew to its peak strength. It included four divisions, five separate brigades, four separate regiments, and six separate battalions.[23] There were some 29,000 major pieces of equipment in the 40th Army, 6,000 of which were tanks, BTRs, and BMPs. Four aviation and three helicopter regiments were assigned to the commander of the 40th Army to provide air support. There were 108,800 personnel in the LCOSF, of which 73,000 were in combat units. This was the most combat effective grouping during the entire period of the LCOSF's sojourn in Afghanistan. However, at that time the approach to the employment of the 40th Army changed.

In conjunction with the change of leadership in the USSR, the first open discussion of the Afghan War aired. It was depicted as a harmful phenomena imposed on the country and the people by a small group of old politicians. In conjunction with this discussion, there was a tendency to continually withdraw Soviet forces from active combat, to lessen the frequency and scale of operations and combat, and to shrink the boundaries of guarded regions. Frequent operations conducted by DRA forces were supported with Soviet aviation, artillery, and engineers. The Soviet High Command undertook large-scale operations only in extraordinary situations. An example of this is the operation conducted in 1986 to destroy a well-equipped Mujahideen base in Khost district [Zhawar 2].

During this phase of the war, the Afghan government began work to establish armed self-defense detachments. They met with local tribal leaders and elders. Where the government was able to reach agreement with the leaders and elders, antigovernment activity lessened and the inhabitants, constantly beset by the civil war, gladly returned to peaceful pursuits. The DRA government had its greatest political success in establishing peace with the Pushtun tribes located on the Pakistan border. These talks with local leaders and religious authorities had positive results in various regions of the country—especially in the north.

Along with these steps, the primary task of strengthening the DRA armed forces continued. They adapted measures to strengthen military discipline, began a decisive battle against desertion, and proclaimed complete freedom of religion. TO&E slots for mullahs were created in military organizations and steps were taken to implement their incorporation.

The reaction of the opposition to the lessening of the combat activities of the Soviet forces was not commensurate. On the one hand, the opposition used the pause to expand their sphere of influence in the country, primarily along a peaceful ideological course. On the other hand, they feared that the majority of the peasants would abandon the war and quickly return to a peaceful life. The Mujahideen leaders needed to continue to support tensions in the country and to fan the flames of civil war. The fundamentalist groups located in the provinces of Logar, Kandahar, and Paktia continued their combat. Therefore, in May 1986, General-Major V. P. Dubynin, directed by the leadership of the 40th Army, conducted a series of combined operations in these provinces using Soviet and DRA forces. In the same year, the Soviets conducted a combined operation near Khost to destroy a regional opposition base.[24] They planned this operation using DRA ground forces supported by Soviet air power. The commander of this operation was Deputy DRA Minister of Defense General-Major Naby Azim. In the course of this operation, it became clear that the DRA force would not be able to carry out the mission and this would further impact on the morale and authority of the DRA. Therefore, Soviet forces participated in this operation, covering the DRA flanks and rear and providing fire support. The DRA acted independently during the destruction of a small group of the opposition.

A main event of the third phase of the war was the withdrawal of six regiments of the 40th Army from Afghanistan. The withdrawal occurred in the second half of 1986 and involved two motorized rifle, one tank, and three air defense regiments. As a result of this withdrawal, the 40th Army shrank by 15,000 personnel, 53 tanks, and 200 BMPs and BTRs.[25]

At the start of the fourth phase of the war, the Central Committee of the PDPA conducted an emergency session in December 1986. The plenum decided to adopt a course of national reconciliation. By this time, it was clear to reasonable people that there was no military solution to the Afghan problem. Adopting this course of national reconciliation made it impossible to bring about the end of the war using military means. However, putting the politics of reconciliation into practice would become possible only after laying out the necessary groundwork that involved an entire complex of preliminary measures provided through Soviet initiatives. The main and decisive step was the agreement between the governments of the DRA and Soviet Union on the start of the withdrawal of Soviet forces from Afghanistan. This was dependent on an agreement on the cessation of military aid to the Mujahideen from Pakistan and other countries. The Soviet Union, realizing that new political thinking refused a military solution to complicated political questions, went to Geneva where the governments of Afghanistan and Pakistan entered negotiations assisted by the USSR and the United States. The negotiations resulted in the Geneva Agreement for the Resolution of the Political Situation around Afghanistan.

Beginning in January 1987, the Soviet forces, for all practical purposes, ceased offensive combat and fought only when attacked by the Mujahideen. There was one exception in 1987 when the Soviet and DRA forces conducted the mightiest operation of the Afghan War. Operation Magistral was conducted in Paktia province to supply necessary goods to the beleaguered city of Khost over the road from Gardez. The strength of over five divisions was massed to destroy the powerful Mujahideen force and open the blocked road. In the ensuing action, the Soviet forces seized control of the vital sections of the road and then trained and prepared for the withdrawal from Afghanistan.[26]

In 1988, the Nadjibullah government feverishly began to convert national reconciliation into political reality. The PDPA's primary mission was to strengthen and consolidate the party rank and file. The DRA foreign policy attempted to develop relations with all countries, avoiding alliances with any one bloc. The DRA military continued to adopt those measures necessary to become an independent force capable of protecting the country. However, none of these measures were realized by the end of the war.

The opposition rejected the government's call for national reconciliation. The opposition leaders declared that *jihad* would continue as long as a single Soviet soldier remained in Afghanistan. The oposition increased agitation and propaganda among the population, intensified their combat actions, and conducted a series of terrorist acts.

Relations with Shiite Iran and the armed detachments of its adherents and fanatics in Afghanistan was a complicated and difficult-to-resolve issue in the politics of reconciliation and cease fire. Iran was not one of the four signatories to the Geneva agreement and refused to sign as one of the five interested countries. Iran was not subject to pressure by international authorities and did not agree to quit supplying military assistance to the opposition. Further, Iran did not agree to liquidate Mujahideen training centers located on its territory. Despite these conditions, on 7 April 1988, the Soviet Union decided to withdraw the entire Limited Contingent of Soviet Forces from Afghanistan. The withdrawal would be conducted in two stages. The first stage would be conducted from 15 May to 16 August 1988, during which the size of the force would be halved. Then, following a three-month break, necessary for resolving organizational missions, the second stage, covering a three-month period, would follow from 15 November 1988 to 15 February 1989.

The withdrawal of the force in two stages was planned and conducted as a large-scale army operation involving a large quantity of forces and resources. Fortunately, the withdrawal was conducted successfully. The armed formations of the opposition, prepared for widescale combat with the DRA forces, did not contest the withdrawal of the formations and units of the 40th Army. On 15 February 1989, the last unit left the territory of Afghanistan. Thus these forces returned to their people, having been sent to another country on the whims of a few Kremlin politicians. Their history is written in the blood of thousands of people on the soil of Afghanistan.

Editors' comments: During the second phase of the war, the Soviet leadership determined that the strength of the Mujahideen was greatly enhanced by the popular support they enjoyed among the local populace. The local populace fed and housed the Mujahideen, which greatly eased the Mujahideen logistics effort. Subsequently, the Soviets decided to break the link between the people and Mujahideen by driving the population from the countryside. Soviet aircraft bombed and strafed the countryside while helicopter gunships shot up herds of sheep, goats, and camels. Soviet artillery pummeled the countryside. The countryside was blanketed with scatterable mines, particularly on paths, pastures, and farm land. Some seven million Afghans became refugees—traveling to Pakistan, Iran, or the cities of Afghanistan. This depopulation of the countryside made the Mujahideen logistics much more difficult. Now, in addition to his ammunition, his food had to be carried in from Pakistan or Iran.

To compound the Mujahideen logistics problem, the nature of the guerrilla war changed over time. During Phase One and into Phase Two, many Mujahideen armaments were simple—World War I bolt-action rifles and earlier vintage weaponry plus a few World War II machine guns. Over time, the Mujahideen acquired AK-47 Kalashnikov automatic assault rifles, RPG-7 anti-tank grenade launchers, light mortars, and land mines. Their new armaments made the Soviets reluctant to get closer than 300 meters to the Mujahideen (300 meters being the maximum effective range of the AK-47 and the RPG-7 against a moving target). This reluctance to come within close combat range led to the Mujahideen acquiring heavier crew-served weapons—heavy machine guns, recoilless rifles, surface-to-surface rockets—which had a longer range. However, transporting these weapons, and their heavy ammunition, created severe problems for the Mujahideen logistics effort.

1985 was the year of decision and the bloodiest year of combat. Initially, the decision was made to seek military victory. Who made that decision is still a matter of debate. General Secretary Gorbachev was new in the job. His Ministry of Defense and General Staff may have decided to win the war militarily while political leadership was diverted to power consolidation in the Kremlin. Alternatively, Gorbachev may have given orders to win the war to attempt to beat the Mujahideen while secretly preparing to engineer a withdrawal without his military's knowledge. The Mujahideen were badly hurt by the efforts of 1985 but did not break. In October 1985, Gorbachev persuaded the Politburo to "Afghanize" the war and withdraw. This decision was announced in early 1986.

Les Grau has developed the Order of Battle for the 40th Army in 1980– 1981, 1988, and following the first part of the withdrawal on 15 October 1988. The order of battle chronicles the growth of the 40th Army and continued difficulty in putting together sufficient combat power to fight the Mujahideen due to the need to protect and secure cities, garrisons, and the lines of communication. This order of battle is included as Appendix 1.

Modern armies think in terms of tactics supporting operations and operations building campaigns. This theoretical framework failed in the Soviet Army in Afghanistan, as large-scale operations proved ineffective and were practically a hindrance. Still, the Soviets continued to mount operations. The Soviet Army was probably the world's most operationally competent army in terms of theory, planning, and execution. Historic Soviet victories were operational and Soviet war-fighting was operationally oriented (compared to Western armies that had more of a tactical orientation). Afghanistan, however, was a tactical war and Soviet tactics were initially inadequate for fighting guerrillas. Despite the relative ineffectiveness of Soviet operations, they are a good way to keep track of the military course of the war. A brief synopsis of the major operations of the war follows:[27]

1979

15–21 March. Anti-Communist demonstrators seize Herat. The Afghan 15th Division, ordered to restore the situation, joins the opposition. Between 28 and 200 Soviet civilians and advisers butchered in Herat. Herat is bombed by Afghan and Soviet aircrews, leaving an estimated 5,000 Afghan dead.

April. Soviet-piloted Mi-24 HIND helicopters support a DRA offensive in the Kunar valley that kills an estimated 1,000 when the village of Kerala is razed.

17 May. Afghan mechanized brigade from the 7th Division defects to the resistance.

July. Battalion of Soviet paratroopers lands in Bagram airbase to protect Soviet helicopter force.

August. 5th Brigade of the 9th Afghan Division mutinies and joins resistance in the Kunar valley.

August–October. General Pavlovskiy, Chief of Ground Forces (and Soviet commander of the invasion of Czechoslovakia), leads a group of 50 Soviet officers on a planning reconnaissance throughout Afghanistan.

14 September. Prime Minister Amin's faction kills President Taraki in a gun battle. Amin becomes president.

October. Insurrection in the DRA 7th Division.

24 December. Soviet airborne division begins air landing in Kabul.

27 December. Soviet divisions cross border and begin advance south along the eastern and western highways. Soviet airborne and Spetsnaz forces overthrow government and kill the president.

28 December. Barbak Karmal declared new president of the Democratic Republic of Afghanistan.

1980

1 January. Kandahar revolts and Soviet citizens and troops are hacked to pieces.

21 February. Kabul protests the Soviet occupation and hundreds are killed and thousands are arrested (and later executed). Anti-Soviet riot in Shindand put down by Soviet forces.

February. Soviet sweep of Kunar valley.

March. The Soviet push into Paktia results in the loss of a Soviet battalion. Soviet sweep of Kunar valley.

April. Soviet offensive in Pandshir valley.

May. Soviet sweep of Ghazni. Soviet sweep of Kunar valley.

June. Soviet sweep of Ghazni.

September. Soviet sweep of Kunar valley. Pandshir I.

October. Pandshir II.

November. Soviet sweep of Kunar valley. Soviet sweep of Wardak province. Lowgar valley offensive until mid-December.

1981

February–May. Fighting in Kandahar.

April. Pandshir III.

June–July. Nangahar offensive.

4 July. 108th MRD offensive in Sarobi valley. Heavy fighting in Herat.

August. Pandshir IV.

5 September. 5th MRD offensive in Farah province.

October. 5th MRD sweeps around Herat. Unsuccessful DRA operation at Marmoul Gorge, Balkh province. Soviet offensive in Kandahar.

December. Combined sweeps with DRA and 66th MRB in Nangahar. Fighting in Herat.

1982

January. Fighting in Herat.

February. City fighting in Kandahar.

May. Pandshir V, largest operation yet launched in retaliation for attack on Bagram air base. 108th MRD governing headquarters for composite force drawn from three divisions (108th MRD, 201st MRD, and 103rd ABD).

July. Sweep against Paghman hills near Kabul.

August–September. Pandshir VI.

November. Laghman valley offensive.

1983

January. Lowgar valley offensive. Soviets negotiate cease-fire in Pandshir valley.

April. Sweeps around Herat.

June. Ghazni offensive.

August. Paktia province offensive.

November. Shomali offensive.

1984

April. Gora tepa offensive. End of cease-fire in Pandshir valley. Pandshir VII, largest offensive yet, launched under control of 108th MRD. Operation also includes push up Andarab valley and Alishang valley. Soviets garrison lower valley and fighting continues throughout summer.

June. Lowgar valley offensive. Herat and Kandahar offensives.

July–August. Lowgar and Shomali valley offensive.

August–October. Relief of Ali Khel garrison in Paktia by 70th MRB and 345th ABR.

September. Pandshir VIII.

October. Fighting in Herat.

November. Paktia operation.

December. Kunar valley offensive with 66th MRB, 345th ABR. Lasts until February.

1985

April. Maidan valley offensive.

May–June. Kunar offensive and relief of Barikot garrison.

June. Pandshir IX launched in retaliation for fall of Pechgur.

July. Heavy fighting in Herat and Kandahar.

August–September. Paktia offensive. Largest offensive since Pandshir VII. Relieved Khost, but failed to take Zhawar.

1986

March. Offensive around Andkhoy.

April. Paktia offensive takes Zhawar.

May. President Karmal replaced by Najibullah. Offensive in the Arghandab near Kandahar.

June. Khejob valley offensive.

August. Lowgar valley offensive.

October. Six Soviet regiments withdrawn.

November. 66th MRB offensive in Naizan valley.

1987

January–February. Temporary cease-fire for national reconciliation.

May–June. Arghandab offensive. Paktia offensive near Jadji.

14 July. Loss of Kalafghan garrison in Takhar province.

November–January. Operation Magistral to relieve Khost.

1988

March. Offensive to relieve Urgun in Paktia province.

April. Kandahar to Ghazni offensive.

14 April. Geneva Accords signed (talks in process since 1982).

April. Soviet withdrawal from Barikot, upper Kunar valley and Ali Khell, Chowni and Chamkani in Paktia, Qalat in Zabul.

May. 66th MRB withdrawal from Jalalabad.

15 October. Half of Soviet force withdrawn.

1989

15 February. Last Soviet combat units withdrawn.

2

Organization, Armament, and Training of the Limited Contingent of Soviet Forces and Government of Afghanistan Armed Forces[1]

Combat in Afghanistan provided an in-depth check of the viability of the organization of Soviet formations, units, and subunits; the quality of Soviet weapons and equipment; and the level of training of the Soviet forces and their leaders. Combat demonstrated that not all of these were up to the demands of counterguerrilla warfare fought on rugged terrain.

ORGANIZATION AND EQUIPMENT OF SOVIET FORCES

The Soviet forces were organized into formations and separate subunits. Bearing in mind that the war was primarily a tactical war, the bulk of the combat fell on the shoulders of the subunits—especially the motorized rifle battalions and companies.

The motorized rifle battalion (MRB) consisted of three motorized rifle companies (MRC), a mortar battery, five separate platoons (antitank, grenade launcher, air defense, signal, and support), and a battalion aid station.

The MRC averaged 80 to 100 personnel. It had a command element and three motorized rifle platoons (MRP). The MRP had a command element and three motorized rifle squads (MRS). The MRP was mounted on three BMP or BTR armored personnel carriers.

The first year of combat in Afghanistan showed that the battalion's firepower was inadequate for conducting independent actions. Therefore, the battalion was appreciably reinforced with firepower for independent combat missions. These reinforcements could include up to a company of tanks, one or two artillery batteries, a platoon of ZSU 23-4 self-propelled antiaircraft automatic cannons used to fire at ground targets, a sapper platoon, and one to two chemical squads. In addition, for especially critical missions, the battalion might be supported by an artillery battalion, two or three sections of fighter bombers, two or three sections of helicopter gunships, and two or three sections of armed transport helicopter gunships (Mi-8tv).

During the course of the Afghan War, motorized rifle subunits were equipped with the tracked BMP-1 or BMP-2 infantry fighting vehicle or the wheeled BTR-60PB, BTR-70, or BTR-80 armored personnel carrier. These vehicles provided increased fire power, mobility, maneuverability, and protection from enemy weapons.

BTRs basically met the demands of the war. At the same time, combat uncovered some serious shortcomings in the construction of the BTR. The BTR-60PB was first issued to Soviet forces at the end of the 1960s. During the course of the war, these were replaced by the newer BTR-70. Superficially, the armaments and components of the BTR-70 were analogous to the BTR-60PB. Both machines were designed to transport personnel on the battlefield and to provide fire support to those personnel once they dismounted. They each have four axles and eight wheel drive, which provides great cross-country capability and the ability to overcome a variety of obstacles. There are some improvements in the BTR-70 to include a 25 to 30 percent increase in side armor. The overall dimensions of the BTR-70 were slightly decreased. Steps to allow access through the vehicle sides were added between the second and third wheels. This decreased the time required to dismount the vehicle by some 14 to 20 percent. Exiting the BTR-70, as opposed to the BTR-60PB, is not from atop the vehicle, but from the sides with the hatch doors facing outwards. This allows uninterrupted observation of the battlefield and the ability to fire over the hatches and from the gun ports that are built into the sides and roof of the vehicle. The BTR-70 has more powerful engines—two 115 horsepower engines that increase the average speed of the vehicle by some 15 to 20 percent.

An important addition to the BTR-70 was the addition of an automatic fire-fighting system. The possibility of a fire is further reduced by a reinforced compartment that isolates the fuel tank from the rest of the vehicle. These improvements made the BTR-70 more effective on the battlefield.[2] However, some minor problems remained when these vehicles were used on rugged mountain-desert terrain.

Subsequently, the armed forces began receiving the BTR-80 in 1985. There were several new features in its design. The outward appearance of the BTR-80 differed little from its precursors but it incorporated several major improvements. Its length was increased by 115mm, its width was increased by 100mm, and its height was increased by 115mm. The overall increase in dimensions allowed the factory to install a single powerful diesel engine in place of the twin engines. The diesel engine was better suited to mountainous terrain and running in the rarified atmosphere in the high mountain passes. Therefore, the BTR-80 was more mobile and maneuverable. The new BTR was also better armored. In addition to the increased armor, the BTR-80 was equipped with reactive armor that protected the upper portion of the vehicle from shaped-charged rockets. The design bureau had studied the experience of unfortunate BTRs blown up by mines. If a BTR-60PB or BTR-70 hit a mine, not only was the BTR destroyed, but the crew was killed. If the new BTR hit a mine, the blast only destroyed the transfer case and wheels while the driver and occupants survived unscathed.

Combat showed that the new BTR was not free of shortcomings. It was still vulnerable to heavy machine-gun fire and antitank shaped-charge projectiles. Therefore the soldiers undertook additional field expedient measures to protect the vehicle and crew. Soldiers built stand-off chicken-wire screens on automobile spring frames to protect the vehicle sides. They built additional screens from rubberized sheeting that they hung between the wheels. They protected the BTR turret by mounting the spare tire on it. To protect the crew, they strapped on water cans and oil cans as well as boxes of sand and sandbags. However, the adoption of all these field expedient measures greatly increased the weight of the vehicle.

In the final analysis, the BTRs, particularly the BTR-80, were combat effective in the high mountains despite dust storms and high temperatures.

There were two models of BMPs in Afghanistan—the BMP-1 and the BMP-2. The BMP-1 was first issued to Soviet forces in the mid-1960s. It performed very well in the first phase of the Afghan War. It carried a 73mm smoothbore cannon, a coaxial 7.62mm machine gun, and an antitank guided missile mount. When these were combined with the weapons carried by the on-board motorized rifle squad, the BMP-1 could carry out a variety of fire missions while stopped or moving. The armor on the BMP-1 protected its occupants from small arms fire.

At the same time, the BMP-1 was not without its serious deficiencies. It had a large number of vulnerable spots, all of which were well known by the enemy. Combat disclosed shortcomings in the armaments of the BMP-1. The 73mm cannon's range was too short and the initial velocity of its round was too slow. Its accuracy was subject to various outside influences including side winds and temperature variables. Further, the maximum elevation of the gun was limited, which restricted its ability to conduct effective fire in the mountains.

Unit personnel worked to correct the deficiencies. They reinforced the floor under the steering and transmission housings. They replaced the hard, fixed driver's seat with a seat equipped with shock absorbers. They added additional outside armor to the vehicle sides and turret. However, despite all their efforts, they were unable to resolve the problems. Therefore, the BMP-1 was gradually replaced by the BMP-2 during the course of the war.

The BMP-2 was introduced into the armed forces in 1985. Externally, it was similar to its predecessor. However, its armaments' upgrade significantly improved its combat potential. The BMP-2 mounted a new 30mm automatic cannon in place of the 73mm cannon. The 30mm cannon had a two-belt feed, a two-plane stabilizer, and a greatly increased maximum gun elevation. The 73mm cannon had no gun stabilizer. The designers improved the turret so that the antitank guided missile could be launched while the gunner remained inside the vehicle. The interior of the BMP-2 was redesigned to better accommodate the crew. Now, both the commander and gunner could aim and fire the 30mm automatic cannon and its coaxial machine gun. These changes allowed the BMP-2 to be used effectively on flat land as well as in the mountains.

Motorized rifle forces often employed air defense subunits armed with the ZSU 23-4 "Shilka." This four-barreled system is highly accurate, rapid firing, uses powerful ammunition, has a maximum angle of fire that is practically vertical, and is highly reliable. The ZSU 23-4 proved effective against an enemy deployed in the mountains out to a range of 2,500 meters.

The personnel of the motorized rifle subunits fighting in Afghanistan were armed with a variety of small arms and crew-served weapons. These included the 7.62mm AKM and AKMS assault rifles; the 5.45mm AK-74, AKS-74, and AK-74U assault rifles; the 7.62mm RPK light machine gun; and the 5.45mm RPK-74 and 7.62mm PK medium machine guns. Snipers were armed with the 7.62mm SVD sniper rifle. Besides these, motorized rifle subunits, in some instances, were armed with the 12.7mm NSV, DShK, and 14.5mm KPVT heavy machine guns. Officers, warrant officers, drivers, and other designated personnel carried the 9mm PM pistol.

The 7.62mm AKM Kalashnikov, which the Soviet soldiers were armed with during the first phase of the war, proved to be a reliable automatic weapon in all instances. It proved highly accurate, comparatively lightweight, hardy, and simple to operate. At the same time, it had a few drawbacks. Among them primarily was the hard recoil that, during burst firing, threw the firer's aim far off target. Therefore, in the middle of the 1980s, the Soviet troops in Afghanistan exchanged the 7.62mm for the 5.45mm AK-74 assault rifle. Considering that both models were designed by Soviet weapons designer M. Kalashnikov and are very similar to each other, the new assault rifle was more reliable in combat and easier to use. Its smaller-caliber bullet has a high muzzle velocity and less flight stability, which support flatter trajectory, good penetration, and lethality. The mild recoil when firing the small caliber cartridge allows accurate firing and tight shot groups, especially during automatic firing. Additionally, the reduced weight of the cartridge increased the number of rounds that could be carried. The DRA soldiers were enthusiastic about this weapon.[3] The enemy also highly valued the combat capabilities of the new assault rifles and strove to capture them as trophy weapons in combat.

The short-barreled AKS-74U was designated primarily for assault troops. It has a folding stock and shortened barrel. The short barrel significantly reduced the combat capabilities of the weapon. It reduced the maximum range by two times and the firing pattern spread out significantly. Even with these drawbacks, the AKS-74U assault rifle remained an effective firearm and was irreplaceable in close combat.

A small part of the motorized riflemen were armed with the 7.62mm SVD Dragunov sniper rifle. The Dragunov was first issued to Soviet forces in 1963. It

Model	RPK	RPK-74	PKM	KPVT	DSHK	NSV Utes
Caliber mm	7.62	5.45	7.62	14.5	12.7	12.7
Weight with box of ammunition, Kg	5.6	5.46	7.5	161.5	155	46.8
Number of rounds in ammunition box	40	45	100	40	50	50
Muzzle velocity meters per second	765	960	825	1000	850	845
rounds per minute; semiautomatic	40	50	--	--	--	--
rounds per minute; short bursts	150	160	250	80	80	100
Maximum effective range, meters	1000	1000	1500	2000	3500	2000
Maximum range	1500	1350	3800	4500	5000	6000

Figure 1. Basic data on machine guns

has an optical scope and can fire accurately out to 1,300 meters. The SVD provided serious trouble to Mujahideen snipers hidden in the mountains.

Officers, warrant officers, and some sergeants and soldiers were armed with the 9mm Makarov pistol for self defense.

Crew served weapons used by the Limited Contingent of Soviet Forces in Afghanistan included light, medium, and heavy machine guns and various grenade launchers.

During the first phase of the war, the Soviet forces had both the 7.62mm RPK and 5.45mm RPK-74 light machine guns. Later in the war, all the 7.62mm light machine guns were replaced by the 5.45mm models. The main reason for this change was the replacement of the 7.62mm AKM assault rifle with the 5.45mm AK-74 assault rifle. The leadership wanted to ensure that the squad machine guns and assault rifles could use the same ammunition.

The modernized 7.62mm PKM Kalashnikov medium machine gun was issued to motorized rifle forces. It was a powerful weapon that could destroy point and area targets with high accuracy out to a range of 1,500 meters. However, its comparatively heavy weight did not permit aimed fire when moving with dismounted soldiers. When the weapon was dismounted, it was fired from a fixed bipod or the special tripod designed by the Stepanov design bureau.

In special circumstances, in order to increase the fire power of motorized rifle subunits, the leaders would attach KPVT, DShK, and NSV heavy machine guns to the units to destroy enemy deployed in the open and in trenches to a distance of 2,000 meters. More detailed characteristics of the heavy machine guns are shown in Figure 1.

The AGS-17 automatic grenade launcher was first introduced into combat with Soviet troops in Afghanistan. This 30mm grenade launcher was known as the *Plamya* or flame. It was designed to destroy enemy personnel and weapons in the open. The grenade launcher rapidly fires 30mm grenade rounds. The unitary round consists of a cylindrical metal casing containing the primer, propellant powder charge, and grenade. The propellant charge is relatively small, engineered to propel the grenade at 185 meters per second to a distance of 1,700 meters. The bursting radius of the grenade hurls lethal fragments out to 25 meters. The AGS-17 has two rates of fire—semiautomatic and full automatic. In the semiautomatic mode the AGS-17's rate of fire is up to 50 rounds per minute and is up to 100 rounds per minute in the full automatic mode. The "Flame" uses the firing recoil to drive back the bolt and other moving parts for semiautomatic or full automatic fire. In the event the barrel overheats during firing, it can be quickly exchanged with the spare barrel. The 17.7 kilogram system is comparatively light and mobile. The AGS-17 has a three-man crew that can accompany a column of motorized riflemen, carrying the system across irrigation canals and over adobe walls and up mountains without undue exertion. The AGS-17 can also be mounted on a combat vehicle and equipped with an electric drive. In this configuration, it can be used to conduct direct fire from the vehicle without exposing the crew to return fire from enemy snipers.

Possessing a high rate of fire, tight shot groups, rapid deployment into action, and excellent maneuverability, the AGS-17 provided reliable fire support in Afghanistan. During raids, sweeps, and other offensive combat, the AGS-17 provided support to first echelon subunits from directly behind their combat formations or on line in the gaps between formations or on the flanks of formations. Should a march column encounter enemy resistance, AGS-17 crews would quickly occupy firing positions and provide covering fire for the Forward Security Element and the deploying main body.[4] In the defense, the AGS-17 crews provided barrier fire or concentrated their fires on the advancing enemy to the front or flanks of the subunits.

The RPG-7 and take-down airborne RPG-7D antitank grenade launchers were widely used during the war in Afghanistan along with the improved, tripod-mounted SPG-9M recoilless rifle. They were effective in destroying various light field fortifications such as adobe walls and stone barriers. The fragments from the exploding warhead also made these effective antipersonnel weapons. The RPG-7 and RSG-7D are lightweight and can effectively destroy targets out to 300 meters; they can fire four to six rounds per minute. The heavier, tripod-mounted SPG-9M recoilless rifle can destroy targets out to 800 meters and fire five to six rounds per minute. The tactical and technical characteristics of these weapons are shown in Figure 2.

Hand grenades were also effective weapons in Afghanistan. Offensive hand grenades included the RGD-5, RG-42, and RN models. Defensive hand grenades included the F-1 and RGO models. The shaped-charge RKG-3 antitank grenade was also used. At first, Soviet forces were only equipped with the RGD-5, RG-42, and F-1 hand grenades. These grenades entered the Soviet inventory in the late 1940s and early 1950s. They are effective weapons but all have one signifi-

Characteristics	RPG-7	SPG-9	AGS-17
Weight in kilograms	6.3	47.5	31
Caliber in millimeters	40	73	30
Maximum range	500 meters	1300 meters	1700 meters, 350-400 meters minimum range
Rounds per minute	4-6	5-6	50-100
Maximum effective range	330 meters	800 meters	1200 meters
Muzzle velocity	140 meters/second	435 meters/second	185 meters/second

Figure 2. Tactical and technical characteristics of RPG-7, SPG-9, and AGS-17

Characteristics	RG-42	RGD-5	F-1	RGN, RGO, RKG-3
Bursting radius	25 meters	25 meters	200 meters	25-200 meters
Fuse burning time	3.2-4.2 seconds	3.2-4.2 seconds	3.2-4.2 seconds	point detonating
Weight in grams	420	310	600	310, 530,1070
Average throw	30-40 meters	40-50 meters	35-45 meters	40-50, 40-50, 15-20

Figure 3. Basic characteristics of hand grenades

cant shortcoming. There is a delay of some 3.2 to 4.2 seconds between throwing the grenade and its detonation. In the mountains, this gives the enemy sufficient time to take cover behind a nearby boulder or ledge. Further, this delay presents a danger to the thrower should the grenade begin to roll back down the slope after it is thrown. Therefore, the Soviet Army issued the new RGN and RGO grenades to its forces in Afghanistan. These grenades are equipped with sensors and detonate upon impact with any surface. Soviet forces used the RGK-3 shaped-charge anti-tank hand grenade to destroy particularly well-constructed edifices and to blow up enemy equipment. Basic hand grenade characteristics are found in Figure 3.

For the first time in the history of the Soviet armed forces, Soviet soldiers used a wide variety of armored flak jackets for individual protection during the Afghanistan war. At the start of the war, there were not enough flak jackets for everyone. Therefore, flak jackets were issued to soldiers going into direct combat or to those on combat duty. The first battles proved that flak jackets reduced fatalities by two or three times. This made the procurement of sufficient flak jackets a priority, and, by the end of 1988, all the personnel of the 40th Army had flak jackets.

There were five flak jacket models issued during the war. The first model was the Zh-RI issued in 1980. It weighed four kilograms and was fairly comfortable; however, it failed to provide adequate protection. The 6B3 and YaB4 flak jackets were developed to correct the shortcomings of the Zh-R1. They were issued in 1983 and 1984 and proved more capable of stopping an aimed bullet. However, they both weighed about 10.5 kilograms (23.15 pounds) and were very uncomfortable when worn in the mountains or when it was hot.

In 1985–1986, the Soviets began issuing the Zh-85t and Zh-85k flak jackets. They weighed about 7.5 kilograms (16.5 pounds) and provided chest protection from a bullet fired at the front and spinal protection from fragments impacting in the back. But the area of the body that these flak jackets covered was inadequate. Therefore, these flak jackets were replaced in 1988 with the Zh-86 single-piece flak jacket that covers 1.6 times more body area. The Zh-86 uses titanium alloys, ceramic armor, and specialty steel.[5]

The weapons, equipment, and protective equipment determined the combat effectiveness of the LCOSF in Afghanistan.

Editors' comments: The 40th Army units, weapons, equipment, and training were all designed for large-scale, high-tempo, short-duration conventional war on a European or Chinese battlefield. The 40th Army was not prepared for the rugged terrain, tough guerrilla enemy, and lengthy commitment. Its organization, weapons, and equipment performed less than optimally in Afghanistan. The army needed fewer tanks and more helicopters, fewer air defense systems and more reconnaissance, and more maintenance, supply, transport, and medical units.

The Soviet Army, with its emphasis on high-tempo operations, was particularly ill equipped and ill prepared for tactically intensive guerrilla warfare. The Soviet vision of high-tempo operations reduced tactics to a series of simple, deeply engrained battle drills. The Soviet motorized rifle soldier rode and fought from his BMP or BTR and only dismounted for the final assault—if necessary. While this arrangement may have proven effective against NATO or China, it was not effective against guerrillas in the mountains and desert. The soldier's equipment was designed for use in conjunction with a combat vehicle—not in extended, dismounted patrols and combat on some of the most inhospitable terrain of the planet. Soviet weapons were designed to put out a great volume of suppressive fire that would keep a defending enemy's head down while the combat vehicles rolled over his position. Combat in Afghanistan required longer-range, more-accurate fire that killed, rather than suppressed, an enemy. The Mujahideen seldom fought doggedly for positions that could be overrun by combat vehicles. Soviet weapons were simple, rugged, and generally soldier-proof. However, the characteristics that the designers incorporated were often inappropriate to the war in Afghanistan.

TRAINING OF SOVIET FORCES

Combat in Afghanistan demanded a special approach to the training of personnel, subunits, and units of the 40th Army. This was complicated by the rugged physical geography of the theater; the fact that Soviet Military theory and practice did not deal with counter guerrilla warfare; the frequent rotation of personnel; and the requirement to limit casualties.

When the Soviet forces entered Afghanistan, they not only had no practical skills in the conduct of counter guerrilla warfare, they also did not have a single well-developed theoretical manual, regulation, or tactical guideline for fighting such a war. There certainly was enough worldwide experience in the conduct of counter guerrilla war, such as the Germans fighting the Soviet partisans in World War II or the Americans fighting the Viet Cong in Vietnam; but no one had studied the problem in the Soviet Union. There were no directives on training the force for this type of war; however, the necessity of such training was already evident during the first months after the 40th Army's arrival in Afghanistan.

No less serious a shortcoming than the training of the LCOSF was its poor suitability for conducting combat in mountain-desert terrain. Relying on the training normally conducted by the forces in the Turkestan Military District and utilizing divisions, regiments, and personnel from the Central Asian Republics simply did not work. The supposedly trained forces had to be retrained in tactics for combat in mountains, desert, and green zones from the very start.

It was vital to quickly draft new training guidelines to prepare the force to conduct counter guerrilla warfare in the difficult physical and geographic conditions of Afghanistan. The operations section in the army and the operations sections in the divisions began assembling a digest of documents of generalized combat experience that had to be inculcated in the force. They prepared guidelines for the employment of weapons and combat equipment in the mountains and desert. They published several handbooks on Mujahideen tactics, camouflage techniques, reconnaissance, discovering and disarming various mines and booby traps, and so on. They did everything possible to quickly integrate new methods and techniques of conducting combat into the force in Afghanistan.

A serious difficulty in training was the high turnover of personnel. Personnel served for a limited tour of duty in Afghanistan. Furthermore, the annual casualties incurred by the 40th Army influenced the availability of trained personnel. The combat tour of Soviet soldiers and NCOs was limited by their total service obligation of two years and the necessity to conduct preliminary training in training units located in the Soviet Union. The maximum combat tour for NCOs and soldiers was 18 to 21 months. Officers and warrant officers normally served a two-year combat tour. This was simply not enough time to completely master the combat skills required in this war.[6]

A significant difficulty in training the force was the replacement of casualties, an inevitable occurrence during combat. When they decided to send troops into Afghanistan, the leadership of the Soviet Union and her armed forces had to consider the probability of casualties as well as other issues. However, casualties were greater than forecast. It has been determined that during the ten years of war, the war dead[7] of the 40th Army exceeded 26,000, including 3,000 officers.[8] The numbers are significant. Preliminary data in Figure 4 show these casualties.

Year	Total Casualties	Officer Casualties
1979	up to 150	up to 15
1980	approximately 2800	approximately 320
1981	approximately 2400	approximately 300
1982	approximately 3650	approximately 400
1983	approximately 2800	approximately 350
1984	4400	up to 500
1985	approximately 3500	approximately 380
1986	approximately 2500	up to 300
1987	approximately 2300	up to 280
1988	approximately 1400	approximately 130
1989	up to 100	up to 15
Total	26000	2990

Figure 4. Soviet 40th Army war dead, derived from preliminary data

In order to stem the continual loss of 40th Army personnel from casualties and normal rotation, the Soviet forces had to conduct basic training for some 40,000 to 50,000 personnel every year and then complete their training during the course of their tours of duty in Afghanistan. Initial officer training prior to assignment to Afghanistan was conducted in the USSR. In October 1984, the General Staff directed that an officer training battalion be established in the Turkestan Military District. About 200 reserve officers were activated as training cadre for this battalion. The battalion was brought up to strength with an influx of new lieutenants who were commissioned at military schools in 1983 and 1984 as well as some officers sent on temporary duty (TDY) from other military districts. By the end of 1984, the fluctuating size of this training battalion was stabilized at 500 personnel. From September 1985, the battalion was staffed exclusively with graduates of military schools. They conducted initial officer training for officers of all branches and specialties prior to assignment to Afghanistan.

This training was based on individual skills and organizational experience derived from the conduct of combat in Afghanistan. It included a comprehensive study of enemy tactics and the combat lessons learned by the LCOSF, as well as weapons training and employment of equipment on mountain and desert terrain.

Sergeants and specialists (tank, BMP, and BTR drivers and gunners) had corresponding training in training regiments in the Soviet Union before deploying to Afghanistan. The sergeants and soldiers trained in training regiments located in the Turkestan Military District. Several categories of specialists received their pre-Afghanistan training in other military districts. The Commander in Chief of Ground Forces issued directives determining the quantity of specialists who would be trained to replace the rotating personnel and to establish a reserve pool of trained personnel who would replace casualties. In the meantime, line units in the military district trained other drivers, grenadiers, machine gunners, snipers, and the like. In the spring of 1987, pre-Afghanistan training was increased from three months to five-and-a-half months.

When officers, warrant officers, sergeants, and soldiers arrived in Afghanistan, their training did not stop but continued throughout their tours. The commander's combat and political training plan included all ranks and categories. The training was based on combat in mountain and desert terrain and on lessons learned in previous operations and combat. It particularly concentrated on commander's hard-learned experience in working out the organization for combats, the command and control of TO&E and attached forces, and also the development of initiative, creativity, and the capability for independent resolution of various combat missions. Commander's training was conducted during breaks between combat missions and on the days that were free from alert duty and from post, camp, and station details.

In 1980 and 1981, commander's training was based on the existing commander's training program developed for peacetime training in the Soviet Union. However, it became readily apparent to the Soviet forces in Afghanistan in those first years that this training program was unsuitable. It was designed for preparation of military specialists necessary to fight classic war with a different type of enemy. It was not designed to train to fight the Mujahideen in a counter-guerrilla war. However, the switch from stereotypical tactical ideas to tactics to deal with completely new, extraordinary military circumstances was not rapid.

As far as possible, lessons learned from recent combat were included in the planning and conduct of training of command personnel. The majority of the plans for this training was done by the operations section of the 40th Army and the operations sections of the divisions and major units. At the start of 1982, they initiated a new officers' training program that incorporated previously missing material. Further, the new program was more in tune with the combat situation faced by the units and subunits in the difficult, rapidly changing circumstances. The training focused special attention on practical experience and skills in the organization for combat; the battle command and control of forces and resources of subordinate, attached, and supporting units and subunits; the mastery of the techniques and types of armed combat with the Mujahideen in the difficult mountain-desert terrain; the inculcation of positive military experience; the development of initiative and military cunning and the acceptance of reasonable risk; and the creation of high moral and military qualities among the personnel. This was a more goal-oriented approach to training officers and sergeants for future combat.

Analysis of select daily actions by Soviet forces in Afghanistan suggested special approaches to planning commander's training. First of all, it addressed periodic planning, the composition of training groups, the organization of training, and the selection of the more likely forms and methods of conducting training.

Commander's training for officers in divisions and regiments was planned throughout the training year. Commander's training for battalion officers was included in every training period, while company officers had monthly commander's training. Training groups were constituted. These conducted training for various groups of officers—battalion, company, and platoon commanders. The training groups also combined officers and sergeants in one training collective—usually during the limited training time available prior to combat missions. When the commander conducted his training, not only combined arms officers were present, but also the commanders of attached subunits, aviation forward observers, and artillery fire direction officers, as well as the chiefs of the combat command and control group and representatives of supporting aviation units and subunits. This permitted working out coordination while conducting commander's training preparing for impending combat missions.

There were many peculiarities in organizing training. In peacetime, commander's training was conducted one day a month, except in those months when the regional commanders' assembly was held or when the unit was out in the field for range firing. In Afghanistan, commander's training for officers, warrant officers, and sergeants was a seven-day course, and after 1985 a twelve-day course. During the commander's training, battalion, company, and platoon commanders were given two-day courses on tactics, reconnaissance, fire support, technical support, engineering support, and a hands-on course driving military vehicles. Then, the warrant officers and sergeants took a similar course. Further, officers were trained in communications during radio exercises and command-staff exercises. The capstone of the training was a tactical exercise where the commanders honed their skills while practicing the control of a battle.

Commander's training used realistic times for determining preparation time for the various types of combat. Thus, commanders and staffs had five to ten days to prepare for a scheduled operation and three to five days for an unscheduled operation. Preparation for an ambush or convoy escort mission took two to three days. However, due to the limited amount of time available for these training exercises, they concentrated on working out issues of troop control in battle. The predominant method of instruction was the group exercise and a short tactical exercise without troops. Lectures and seminars were far less common at commander's training. The usual training session consisted of an introductory narrative, an explanation, a demonstration, and then a practical exercise or hands-on training. The practical exercise required a particular site. In this approach to training commanders in a limited amount of time, it is more effective to master the lessons on unfamiliar terrain on which they must conduct a concrete military action.

When troops were not involved in battle, commander's training was conducted at commanders' assemblies as well as scheduled commander's training. This commander's training was conducted monthly. There, the main attention was devoted to general subjects and instilling routine combat experience. Commanders' assemblies were held every six months. At the assemblies, they studied shortcomings in combat experience while determining and working out the procedures to overcome them.

The thematic approach to training, as a rule, was oriented to the nature of impending combat. Commanders at all levels worked with the same tactical problem. The training consisted of determining the missions of subunits in upcoming combat. At this training, the representatives of attached and supporting units and subunits trained alongside the combined arms officers. This permitted easier coordination and troop control.

The 40th Army command placed special emphasis on the conduct of after-action reviews. They were conducted in accordance with the following schedule:

- in divisions and regiments—monthly and when necessary, immediately after the completion of a battle
- in battalions and companies—following every battle, within three days of returning to base camp
- in platoons and other small subunits—immediately after the end of the combat

The after-action review analyzed the tactical situation in detail and delineated the actions of every commander and subunit while carrying out their combat missions.

Training the privates was no less serious a matter. Before assignment to Afghanistan, all privates completed a two-month course in one of the divisions of the Turkestan or Central Asian Military Districts. This training was designed to acclimate the soldiers to the severe climate of mountain-desert terrain. Further, it improved their professional skills and provided moral-psychological steeling to the younger generation. Once they arrived in Afghanistan, all soldiers received one or two months of additional training in their regiment before being sent into combat with their subunits.

Lieutenant Colonel B. Karagodin, who commanded a motorized rifle regiment in Afghanistan, stated that "commanders at all levels always valued their young lads and did not permit unseasoned soldiers to go into combat." When new soldiers arrived in the regiment, they were assigned to a special training subunit under the tutelage of specialists who were experienced in combat in mountain-desert terrain. If it was impossible to train new soldiers in a regiment, they were assigned to subunits that had experienced sergeants and soldiers in them. Such a systematic approach to training supported the replacement of young soldiers and reduced battle casualties.

In this way, during the conduct of combat, the LCOSF established a well-defined system to train commanders and forces that was updated continually. The main thrust of this process was to make all training as close as possible to actual combat. At the same time, the continual loss of rotating cadre and the corresponding loss of developed and tested combat experience, leadership, and techniques had a negative effect on the training process.

Editors' comments: The training of the Soviet forces in Afghanistan was often an extension of the peacetime training regimen. The training program described above is the same system that was used in the military districts of the Soviet Union. The political training, the full-field inspections, and the repetitious drills often degraded, instead of improved, combat readiness. Training in the combat zone is necessary, but routine nonessential training does no good. The airborne, air assault, and Spetsnaz forces had more flexibility in the conduct of their training—to better results.

The revised casualty figures are eye-opening. The actual Soviet dead are almost twice the official figures. When the official figures were released and published in G. G. Krivosheev's Grif sekretnosti snyat *in 1993, scholars were astonished with President Gorbachev's openness (glasnost). This authoritative book listed Soviet dead and wounded for all wars and skirmishes since the founding of the Soviet Union. Only later did scholars, such as David M. Glantz, discover that the dead and wounded from entire operations in the Great Patriotic War (World War II) were excluded from the count. While Gorbachev feigned openness, Krivosheev's book was apparently designed to stop debate and research into casualty figures. It appears that the Soviet casualty count for Afghanistan was significantly undercounted—as was their casualty count for World War II.*

ORGANIZATION AND TRAINING OF THE ARMED FORCES OF THE DRA

During the planning of various operations and combat missions, the 40th Army coordinated closely with the armed forces of the DRA. The armed services of the DRA were the ground forces, the air force, air defense forces, and border guards. In addition, the DRA armed forces included territorial forces, civil defense forces, special forces, maintenance and support forces, and military educational institutions and academies. The average strength of the DRA Armed Forces varied between 120,000 to 150,000 over time.[9]

The DRA army was divided into 4 army corps, 13 infantry divisions, and 22 brigades (3 tank, 1 mechanized, 11 border, 1 artillery, 1 air defense, 2 support, 2 "Commando," and 1 "Guards"). In addition, there were about 40 separate regiments that belonged to various branches and services, with the bulk of them assigned to the territorial forces. These regiments had different purposes and were subordinated to the Ministry of Defense, the corps, or other organizations. Besides these, there were more than 30 separate battalions and squadrons spread throughout the branches, special forces, and in supply and maintenance. They were either centralized under the MOD or subordinated to the corps.

This large number of organizations with varying structures had a negative impact on the overall readiness of their armed forces. Therefore, in the 1980s, the army high command continually undertook measures to raise the combat readiness of their units and subunits. In the middle of the 1980s, part of the separate battalions were combined into regiments. All divisions were converted to a single, standard TO&E structure. Along with this, combat subunits were freed from security duties. This resulted in a greater quantity of forces available to conduct combat and improved the troop control of regiments and divisions.

The Afghan Army was mainly equipped with Soviet-manufactured weapons and equipment. They had about 800 tanks; 130 BMPs; over 1,220 BTRs [BRDMs] and BRMs; over 2,600 artillery tubes, multiple rocket launchers, and mortars; 300 aircraft and helicopters of various types and functions; and some 13,000 trucks. This amount of material was sufficient not only for the conduct of combat but also for army-sized operations.

At the same time, the Afghan High Command experienced a series of problems using the weapons and equipment. In the first place, they had trouble setting up a repair system. This was due to their underdeveloped maintenance infrastructure and their lack of highly qualified specialists. Other problems included their ineffectual training of their young specialists and their understrength tank and vehicle crews. These problems resulted in the incorrect use of weapons and equipment and their premature breakdown.

Afghan Armed Forces officer training was principally conducted at three military institutions. One of them prepared combined arms officers, the second prepared air force and air defense forces officers, and the third prepared officers for technical specialties. Further, there was a higher officers' course in Afghanistan that introduced officers to new methods of armed conflict and the development of military art. There were also some military lycee that were similar to the Soviet Suvorov military secondary schools.[10] A portion of the Afghan officer corps was trained in Soviet military institutions.

The level of training of military specialists in the Afghan military academic institutions during the first years of the war proved inadequate to the demands of the time. Therefore the country's military-political leadership implemented a series of measures in the mid-1980s with the aim of correcting these shortcomings. They increased the courses of instruction. The higher officers' course was expanded from three to six months. The course of instruction at two of the three military academies was expanded from 21 months to 3 years. Only the combined arms academy remained at 21 months. Officers and generals who taught at the military academic institutions were required to pass an attestation board. Reserve officer training was established in four civilian institutes of higher learning in Kabul—at Kabul University, in the political institute, in the medical school, and in the teachers institute. There were over 3,000 students enrolled in this officers' training.

The DRA army used commander's training to perfect the professional preparation of their commanders. This was conducted regularly two days a month.

Commander's training was also conducted at commanders' assemblies held once every training cycle [a training cycle runs one-half year]. Commander's training was also conducted during the course of the weekly training program for combat. The basic thrust concentrated on training the commanders and staffs to organize for combat and control their forces during the course of conducting that combat.

This system of training supported the Afghan Army requirements for a qualified officer cadre. At the same time, this system had many deficiencies. Rank and position depended on friendship, family relations, and which communist party faction the officer belonged to.[11] There was no tightly controlled system that ensured that those officers and specialists who had completed military academic institutes were placed in the jobs requiring that education. Several officers were removed from leadership positions for no good reason and transferred to less important jobs. Others received very responsible posts without prior experience in the given military specialty.

Even worse was the condition of the soldiers and sergeants [the conditions of service for Soviet soldiers and sergeants was also grim]. These were conscripts drafted under the provisions of the DRA law on universal military service for the entire male population. The DRA conscript system consisted of 46 military commissariats of which 12 were located in Kabul, five in regions, and 29 in the provinces.

The military conscript system was not able to carry out its assigned missions fully. They conducted the call up, drew up the rolls of liable registrants, and arranged for deferments. The military commissariats were only able to draft 65 percent of the required personnel for the military contingents.

Besides the conduct of the draft, the military commissariats were also special regional planning offices created by the divisions and regiments. Their spheres of responsibility were the separate rural regions and territories that were controlled by the opposition. They planned and conducted local special operations in Mujahideen territory. Not surprisingly, during these operations, they press-ganged conscripts. Conscripts constituted over 70 percent of the soldiers in the army. The rest were volunteers. As a rule, the volunteers became junior commanders and specialists after basic training. Training regiments and schools trained junior commanders and military specialists, including communicators, border guard sergeants, maintenance and supply specialists, drivers and mechanics, and so on. The rest of the new soldiers were trained in training battalions located in the divisions, in training companies located in the brigades, or in the ground forces training centers. There were 15 ground forces training centers that trained sergeants and military specialists. Basic training lasted one month, whereas sergeant and specialist training lasted three to four months.

The Afghan Army had an annual training plan to provide combat experience to their forces. There were two training programs available for combat regiments and divisions. Selection of one of these programs depended on the condition and type of unit involved. There was a seven-day training program for those regiments that were scheduled to enter combat soon. There was a 20-day training program for those regiments returning from combat for replacement and refitting.

During training, they paid particular attention to managing and coordinating actions with reinforcing elements. They persistently inculcated tactical experience in training in the conduct of air assaults, flanking and raiding detachments, breaching large minefields, overcoming detachments and groups of Mujahideen, putting up a stubborn resistance from prepared fighting positions, and attempting to ward off enemy attempts in a direct clash.

The Afghan Army had many significant training shortcomings. Subunits and units did not always conduct the seven-day training program prior to combat. Regiment, battalion, and company officers were poorly prepared to direct subunits in combat and to use communications properly. Units and subunits were insufficiently trained to maneuver around the flank of enemy strong points, to conduct ambushes, and, particularly, to fight at night. For these reasons, Afghan commanders were, as a rule, unable to conduct large-scale combat independently and constantly turned to the Soviet command for help.

A no less significant shortcoming was the lack of personnel in the divisions and units. On the average, even the combat subunits were 25 to 40 percent below TO&E strength [this is optimistic]. The main reason for this was not only the conscription shortfall, but also the massive desertions. Every month, an average of 1,500 to 2,000 men deserted. As a result, the large units and units had a tendency to shrink. The main reasons for the desertions were the low level of political understanding of the soldiers and their complete lack of understanding of the goals and missions of armed conflict [or perhaps they understood the goals of a foreign occupation quite well].

Under these conditions, the territorial forces were very important. The DRA began to organize them after the Presidium of the Revolutionary Council of Afghanistan passed the law "On the place of territorial forces in the Armed Forces of the DRA" in December 1984. Their goal was to attract senior members of the opposition and opposition armed forces and separate tribes, which conducted their relations independently, to the government side. These territorial units consisted of separate units and subunits that were incorporated into the government corps, divisions, and regiments that were located in their areas. These forces were composed of volunteers, which earlier belonged to the armed opposition, as well as tribal members temporarily drafted into military service. Combatants in the territorial forces were trained in the nearest regular military unit. The term of service was no less than three years.

The territorial units and subunits were located on their own territory. At least 30 percent of the force was located at the kaserne of the territorial unit and carried out military duties. The rest stayed at home waiting the signal to assemble from their commander. The leader of the territorial unit was selected from among candidates proposed by tribal elders and former leaders of the opposition. The unit chief of staff and chiefs of services were regular Afghan officers.

Editors' comments: This study gives short shrift to the DRA Armed Forces that were supposed to take on the bulk of the combat. Although the 40th Army and the DRA were supposed to work closely together, relations between Soviet and Afghan forces were not always good. The DRA units were riddled with Mujahideen sympathizers who readily provided detailed information about upcoming operations and combat to the opposition. Naturally, the Soviets were reluctant to share information and planning with the DRA for fear of compromise. This led to a mutual mistrust and, occasionally, hostility.

Soviet and DRA forces were almost always combined for block and sweep actions and the DRA forces would conduct the sweep. On other actions, where the two forces worked together, the Soviet planners usually put DRA forces forward to draw fire. Soviet advisers served with DRA units down to separate battalion level. Adviser to a DRA unit was considered a hardship assignment by Soviet officers. The living conditions were not optimal, the language and cultural differences made them feel uncomfortable, the presence of covert Mujahideen in the units made them feel insecure, and adviser duty was not considered a stepping stone to promotion.

3

Organization, Armament, and Tactics of the Mujahideen[1]

In Afghanistan, the Soviet forces encountered the combat formations of the government's opposition—the Mujahideen. This was an unusual type of enemy for the Soviets. The Mujahideen directed parties and organizations of varied political and ideological convictions—from the pro-Monarchists to the ultra-leftists.[2] The history of these formations and their development is quite stormy.

At the end of the 1970s, particularly after the April revolution,[3] a large number of Afghan opposition organizations and groups concentrated in the Pakistan border region next to Afghanistan. In June 1981, these coalesced to form the Islamic Unity of Afghan Mujahideen [*Ittehad-i-Islami Mujahideen-i-Afghanistan*] (IUAM). In March of 1982, they split into two parts: the "Group of Seven" (IUAM-7), which was a union of fundamentalist organizations; and the "Group of Three" (IUAM-3), which was a union of traditionalist organizations.[4]

In May 1985, both groups rejoined within the framework of the IUAM to establish an organized opposition that was known as the "Peshawar Seven." It consisted of the Islamic Party (HIH) *(Hezb-e-Islami-Gulbuddin)*; Islamic Society (JIA) *(Jamiat-i-Islami)*; Islamic Revolutionary Movement (IRMA) *(Harakat-e-Inqilab-i-Islami)*; Islamic Union for the Liberation of Afghanistan (IUA) *(Ettihad-i-Islami)*; Islamic Party (HIK) *(Hezb-e-Islami-Khalis)*; National Islamic Front of Afghanistan (NIFA) *(Mahaz-e-Melli Islami)*; and Afghanistan National Liberation Front (ANLF) *(Jebh-e-Nejat-i-Melli Afghanistan)*. Despite the reunion, these opposition parties differed significantly from each other in their political programs and their leaders' goals for the war. The influence of these factions varied by region.

The Islamic Party (HIH)[5] *(Hezb-e-Islami-Gulbuddin)* pursued the goal of establishing an Islamic state in Afghanistan and spreading the message of Islam throughout the world. The majority of its adherents were Tadjiks and Pushtuns who lived in the northeast, east, central, and southwest of Afghanistan. The HIH had less influence in the southeast and northern parts of the country. The highest party organ was the central committee headed by the party leader—Emir Gulbuddin Hikmatyar. Hikmatyar is a Pushtun from the Kharoti tribe. He was born in the Imam Sahib Region of Kunduz Province in 1944. He graduated from the engineering faculty of Kabul Polytechnic Institute.[6] He is a skilled orator, ambitious, cruel, purposeful, with a strong will and an authoritarian leadership style.

The Islamic Society (JIA)[7] *(Jamiat-i-Islami)* had the same goals as the HIH. However, the JIA included not only Tadjiks and [smaller groups of] Pushtuns, but also Turkmen and Uzbeks. The JIA had its biggest influence in the western province of Herat. It leader was professor of theology Burhanuddin Rabbani, who is a Tadjik born in 1941. He graduated from the Kabul Theological Lycee and then from the Theological Faculty of Kabul University. He was characterized as pragmatic and flexible in his dealings with the United States.

The Islamic Party (HIK)[8] *(Hezb-e-Islami-Khalis)* split off from the HIH in 1975.[9] The party contained a group of elderly mullahs and ulamas[10] who had little concern for contemporary political affairs but were politically fundamentalist and had the fanatical desire to return the practice of Islam to its form from the Middle Ages. The party was chauvinistic and Pushtun, adhering to terrorism, sabotage, and the most barbarous methods of war. Its leader was Mawlawi Mohammed Yunis Khalis, a Pushtun from the Khugiani tribe. He was born in 1920 in Wazir Khuchiyani in Nangrahar Province. He is renowned among the Pushtun tribes as a religious authority and poet. From 1963 to 1973, he led a group of mullahs called the "Taliban" who conducted propaganda in the mosques of Kabul.

The Islamic Union for the Liberation of Afghanistan (IUA)[11] *(Etihad-i-Islami)* sprang up in March 1982. It was organized by the agreement of various fundamentalist leaders in order to gain a numerical advantage over the traditionalists within the IUAM framework. Its leader was Abd Al-Rab Abdul-Rassul Sayaf, a professor of theology who was born in 1945 in the Paghman region of Kabul Province. He came from a poor peasant family. He graduated from the Theological Faculty of Kabul University. He attended the Al-Akhzar Moslem University in Egypt in 1970. He then taught in the Theological Faculty of Kabul University. Following the April Revolution of 1979, he emigrated to Pakistan and joined the fundamentalist opposition.[12] He was a supporter of Gulbuddin Hikmatyar.

The Afghanistan National Liberation Front (ANLF)[13] *(Jebh-e-Nejat-i-Melli Afghanistan)* was founded in Pakistan in 1979. Its goal was to establish an Islamic society based on justice, equality, observance of the principles of *sharia* law in the guidance of the country, and support of individual and social freedom in accordance with fundamentals of Islam. The front was open to all Moslem believers regardless of their political and religious views and position in the previous regime. The members of the front included ulamas, intellectuals, government statesmen, and officials of the previous regime. The ANLF had its most influence in the provinces of Kabul, Logar, Kunar, Nangrahar, and Paktia and in the eastern border areas that are inhabited by Pushtun tribes. Separate detachments of the ANLF fought in the north in the provinces of Faryab, Takhar, and

Kunduz. The ANLF leader is Sebqhatullah Mojadeddi, who was born in Kabul in 1925 in a hereditary spiritual Sunni family called the "Hazarats." He graduated from the Al-Azhar University in Cairo, Egypt.

The National Islamic Front of Afghanistan (NIFA)[14] *(Mahaz-e-Melli Islami)* was founded in 1978 in Pakistan by the distinguished and refined religious public figure, Pir Sayed Ahmad Gailani. It was not a contemporary political organization with clear-cut programs, regulations, and structure. First off, it was a conglomerate of followers, Sufi who supported the Moreed (Leader) Gailani— the head of his family.[15] Sufis, for century after century, considered the head of this family to be the lineal descendent of the prophet Mohammad and the spiritual leader. NIFA members were primarily Pushtun who followed the Sunni sect. Gailani was born in 1931 in a hereditary family of "Hazrat"[16] of Arabian descent, a founder of the respected Sufi order of the Qadria sect. The main title that Gailani holds is that of Pir (Saint, Elder), a reflection of his lineal descent, which provides many followers for him in Afghanistan.

The Islamic Revolutionary Movement (IRMA)[17] *(Harakat-e-Inqilab-i-Islami)* was founded in the summer of 1973 in the Pakistani province of Baluchistan. It was a reactionary organization headed by well-known religious figures and ulamas, with its second tier of leadership being ulamas and mullahs who had a great deal of influence on village life. The founder of the movement is Mohammad Nabi Mohammadi, born in 1920 in Logar Province. He studied the fundamentals of Islam with the ulamas of the province. In 1946, he received permission to teach the fundamentals of Islam. He became an ardent nationalist and anticommunist and an enemy of the progressive forces.

IRMA had some 10,000 members and about 25,000 followers.[18] The areas where IRMA was most active were the provinces of Kabul, Logar, Gazni, Paktia, and Zabol. Pushtuns were the dominant group in the organization. IRMA's armed detachments were primarily made up of peasants from the southern region of Afghanistan. IRMA was characterized by being irreconcilable to the national democratic power, cruel to the peaceful populace, and especially so to the supporters of the government who fell into their hands. The warriors of IRMA's armed detachments excelled in religious fanaticism.

The organizational structure of all the opposition parties in the "Peshawar Seven" was primarily the same. Every party had a headquarters, a secretariat, and a necessary number of commissions.

Other than their anti-Soviet feelings and irreconcilable enmity to the government, these organizations and their leadership lacked a common platform. They all viewed the future of Afghanistan differently. One fought for the foundation of an Islamic Republic, another saw itself as the future leader, while a third was disposed to founding a different form of theoretical Islamic government in Afghanistan. Despite the attempts of reactionary Islamic regimes to establish a singular political and military structure on the Mujahideen, they did not succeed.

The many "coalitions" and "unions" were temporary and, mainly, the result of the attempts of special services [CIA and ISI] to somehow unite the counter-revolutionary movement.

The Islamic committees were the link between the parties and the populace. They were composed of leaders, who in the majority of cases received special training in Pakistan or Iran, and also local influential religious agents, former feudal lords, and important land owners. Islamic committees were stationed, as a rule, in fortresses where they were carefully guarded. The composition of the committees differed. The composition depended on the scope of their activities, the size of the population, and the armed formations in the area of operations. In the majority of cases, the governing body was 5 to 30 men.

The Islamic committees of several villages or subdistricts were subordinate to a central committee based on the district. The more influential of these were combined into a union with activities spread over a sizable territory. The union was composed of three to seven Islamic committees.[19] The party leadership coordinated the work of the committees and unions directing their efforts and providing orders and directions, as well as periodically summoning the leaders of these organs to conferences held outside of Afghanistan.

Islamic committees were organized into five sections: leadership, party, military, economic, and financial.[20] The military section planned and personally directed the combat of the detachments and diversionary and terrorist groups.

Islamic committees conducted an active program of subversion among the populace and the personnel of the armed forces of Afghanistan. The main subversive work was the organization and conduct of widespread anti-government and anti-Soviet propaganda. The goal of this propaganda was ideological conditioning of the population and armed forces personnel to draw them into armed combat against the government of Afghanistan and its armed forces. Further, these organs also distributed weapons received from outside the country, conducted the recruitment of men into combat detachments, coordinated their combat actions, established and collected local taxes, and recruited for the counter-revolutionary Islamic organizations.

The Islamic committees paid special attention to the armed forces of Afghanistan. They conducted active ideological work in the divisions and regiments of the Afghan army. Their goal was to demoralize the armed forces, encourage desertion, and recruit these deserters into the opposition. These reactionaries hindered the recruitment of young men into the army, with threats and substantial force. Young draft-age men left their villages and cities for the mountains, where the committees recruited them into their own armed forces.

As a rule, subdistricts and separate districts were under the influence of the Islamic committees of one party. The presence of Islamic committees of more than one party in these locales resulted in civil strife, which was often resolved by armed conflict.[21] For example, during the second and third phase of the war, the leaders of several detachments in Kabul Province approached the Soviet

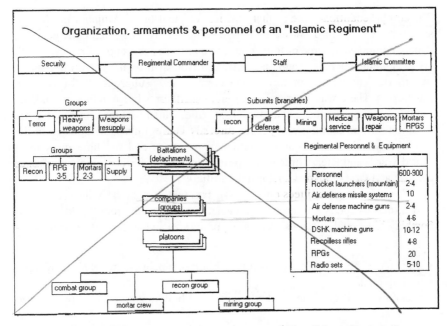

Figure 5. Organization, armaments, and personnel of an "Islamic Regiment"

Command with plans for local combat to liquidate the Mujahideen groups of other parties. They did this to gain personal control over the entire province.

The opposition armed forces did not have a fixed composition. At various times, their overall strength fluctuated between 40,000 to 60,000 men [this is a guess]. The more powerful formations, which constituted up to 85 percent of the opposition forces, were concentrated around Kabul, and also in the central, northeast, southeast, and southern provinces of the country.

There was no definite TO&E structure for the armed formations of the opposition, with the exception of the "Islamic Regiment" (Figure 5). Islamic Regiments were always located in the border regions of Pakistan and Iran and only entered Afghanistan for specific military missions. After they accomplished their missions, they recrossed the border. These regiments were well armed and wore a standard uniform. One of these Islamic Regiments fought in Kunar Province in the second phase of the war. They were equipped with the latest automatic weapons and wore a lightweight black uniform.[22]

The majority of the Afghan Mujahideen leaders determined that guerrilla tactics and the rugged terrain limited the size of guerrilla formations to nothing larger than a group or detachment. Their tactics were the surprise night raid and surprise night attack, which they skillfully applied to inflict appreciable casualties on government forces and Sarandoy subunits to destroy important military, economic, and administrative objectives.

The combat group was the primary tactical element of the Mujahideen. It consisted of 15 to 50 men and included a commander, two or three bodyguards, a deputy commander, three or four scouts, two or three subgroups of riflemen with six to eight men per subgroup, one or two air defense machine gun crews, one or two mortar crews, two or three RPG crews, and a subgroup of four or five minelayers. There was a variety of different small arms in a combat group. During the initial phase of the war, the "Boer" rifle, which was manufactured at the beginning of the century, was very common.[23] During subsequent phases of the war, the Mujahideen employed automatic weapons and machine guns from World War II and later. Combat groups employed the DShK machine gun for air defense and the 60mm mortar for light artillery.

The combat group, as a rule, was garrisoned in a single village and concealed their weapons and ammunition nearby. The combat group could carry out a variety of tactical missions, depending on its size and armament. Primary missions included:

• sabotage of nearby LOCs (blowing up bridges, pipelines, and electric pylons);
• mining roads;
• attacking small garrisons and administrative buildings to destroy or terrorize them, and;
• participating in combat as part of a larger, more powerful formation.

The combat group's light armaments allowed it to maneuver freely and further allowed it to swiftly withdraw from combat or to retreat in the event the combat group encountered a superior force.

The combat detachment was the basic tactical planning element of the Mujahideen. Depending on the situation, the combat detachment might consist of 150 to 200 men (Figure 6). A combat detachment might be garrisoned in one locale or in a fortress or it might be spread throughout several villages with one or two men living per house with the local inhabitants. Besides small arms, the combat detachment might have more effective fire support and air defense systems. They might have 82mm mortars, antitank recoilless rifles, and 14.5mm air defense machine guns.

The combat detachment, depending on its size and armament, could conduct independent combat missions or join with larger, more-powerful formations. Combat detachments often provided convoy escort and security for caravans passing through the territory they controlled. When necessary, detachments could quickly abandon their area of operations (AO). If so, they would leave their heavy weapons behind in prepared hiding places that were well camouflaged.

Small diversionary-terrorist groups of eight to ten men were located in the interior provinces. Their members were usually young, physically fit men who were trained for three to six months at a training center across the border. These groups conducted sabotage and terrorist acts. As a rule, these groups did not participate in the

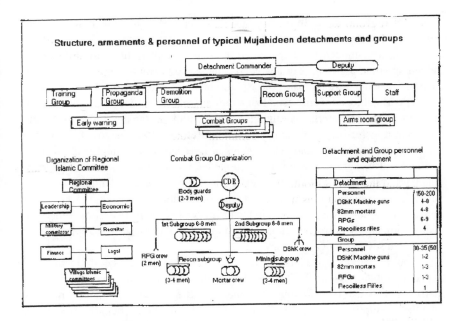

Figure 6. Structure, armaments, and personnel of typical Mujahideen detachments and groups

opening of combat actions. Many combat detachments and combat groups found it necessary to quickly dissolve into the local population, of which the diversionary-terrorist groups were already a part. Between actions, the diversionary-terrorist groups stored their weapons in secret, multiple hideouts that were known to only a limited number of local inhabitants. Often, they would hide their weapons in the women's quarters of a house, where entry by men was strictly prohibited by the Koran. Combat groups and detachments gathered at the predetermined time and place to conduct combat missions. The Mujahideen knew the area well and could quickly move into the mountains on foot. After carrying out their mission, they could store their weapons in their assigned secret hides, and then the Mujahideen, who wore the same clothing as the local populace, could disperse to their villages.

The Mujahideen divided up the entire territory of Afghanistan in accordance with their needs and interests. Depending on the conditions in the zone, it might be further subdivided. From those zones that the Mujahideen controlled, they would occasionally sally forth to conduct an attack, shelling attack, ambush, or other action. In those zones where the Mujahideen mingled with the populace, they would act in secret to carry out their missions. In those zones that were controlled by the government, the Mujahideen would secretly sneak in and remain there only for the duration of their combat action.

In those zones of responsibility where strong Mujahideen groups established their regional bases, they located these bases on difficult terrain close to the region of future combat. In these bases they established a combat and material reserve, a command and control system, an early warning system, an air defense system, a Mujahideen training center, a weapons repair shop, an ammunition reloading point, a garage, a prison, a hospital, and a personnel rest and relaxation center. In such a regional base, there could be up to 500 personnel at one time.

The Mujahideen would establish temporary bases for weapons, ammunition, and other combat material. Along the borders with Pakistan and Iran, they would establish transfer bases on caravan routes in the mountain passes. They would establish supply groups and detachments at intervals where they would distribute and sell weapons. These supply points were controlled by an identity card and pass system and had an observer organization, an early warning system, an air defense system, and a guard system. Sometimes transfer bases were combined with regional supply bases. In the territory of Afghanistan, there were eighteen major supply bases, which included nine regional bases, two supply transfer bases, and seven supply transfer points.

The Mujahideen leadership attached serious significance to ideological work with their personnel. They developed the spirit of Islam, nationalism, and personal responsibility for the outcome of battle in every Mujahideen. They instilled discipline and responsibility with strict methods including the death penalty. The normal life of the Afghan people allowed the Mujahideen to easily withstand burdens and deprivations, participate in guerrilla actions, and show an indifference to death.

In addition to a fanatical faith and the desire to do combat with the "nonbeliever," the Mujahideen required good military training. During the active financial and military support of the Mujahideen by the United States and its partners in NATO, the backers established a network of camps, centers, and points in the territory of Pakistan and Iran to conduct all forms of training. The training included command and staff colleges, commissioning schools, and short courses. The Mujahideen leadership cadre of major armed formations attended courses in higher and mid-level military institutes of Pakistan. In addition, they established over 100 training centers for ringleaders, instructors, air defense gunners, scouts and saboteurs, mortar men, and radio operators. 78 of these centers were in Pakistan, 11 were in Iran, 7 were in Egypt, and 5 or 6 were in China. The instructors and teachers of these centers were Pakistani military officers and reservists, military specialists from the United States, China, Iran, France, Saudi Arabia, Egypt, England, and Japan. There were some 15,000 instructors in these centers. The centers could handle up to 50,000 trainees. Every month, some 2,500 to 3,000 saboteurs and terrorists graduated from these courses.[24]

In addition to direct assistance from government channels, Washington, DC, encouraged so-called "patriotic" and "private" organizations and groups to collect the means for subversive missions and to conduct an active campaign to aid the further spread of American interference in the internal affairs of Afghanistan. Among these organizations were the "Federation of American-Afghan Actions,"

"Southern California Aid to Afghan Refugees," "Society for a Free Afghanistan," the "Non-Official Committee for providing aid with weapons," and so on.

The U.S. special services [CIA] directed and coordinated their activities. Instructions for actions were directed toward the further expansion of the armed conflict by the forces of counter revolution, and to dragging out the decision of this so-called "Afghan question" for an extended period of time. With this established goal, all activities of the American administration were carried out simultaneously to achieve it. The most important of these was the increase of financial aid, which was necessary for purchasing weapons, ammunition, combat equipment, and also to distribute funds to stimulate the Mujahideen to participate in combat.[25] They constantly put pressure on the leaders of the main counter-revolutionary organizations with the goal of prodding them into an actual union to combat the DRA and Soviet forces.

In their turn, the special services of the United States [CIA] and Pakistan [ISI] continually attempted to tighten control over the actions of the armed formations with the goal of creating an effective system of supplying them with everything necessary and increasing the levels of trustworthiness of the data reported to the staffs about the result of combat, sabotage, and terrorist acts. They paid significant attention to giving an improved standard of living to the Afghan refugees, which was the primary source for filling the ranks of the Mujahideen. Besides that, most of their personnel and resources were directed toward perfecting the methods and capabilities of conducting counter-revolutionary combat, propaganda, and agitation among the Mujahideen, emigrants, and also the Afghan people, particularly the young.

All the foregoing measures, as a whole, were rigorously fulfilled. Summing up the results of the end of the second phase and the start of the third phase of combat, the leaders of the Mujahideen stated that the rebel movement successfully tested new methods of conducting combat against the DRA forces. By concentrating their forces and equipment in positions prepared in advance, they were able to conduct intensive fire. Thus, their detachments and groups were able to exert serious pressure on the conduct of Soviet and DRA operations in the southeast areas, particularly during the Soviet/DRA initial stages and as the Soviet/DRA troops were moving into the combat zone. In doing this, they managed to show foreign governments the ability of the opposition forces to stand up against DRA forces when backed with an uninterrupted flow of weapons and ammunition. It was noted that the supply of armed formations in base areas was carried out under the direct control of the leaders of their primary parties and that special commissions of foreign representatives were involved as well. Due to this assistance and stringent control, they succeeded in beginning to structure their formations by branch. The leadership of the counter-revolution felt this had a positive influence on strengthening the rebel movement, improving a greater degree of organization and improving the command and control and supply. They became more like a real military force. The Mujahideen leadership felt that in the future it would be possible to begin creating a so-called Islamic Army.[26]

While conducting combat, the Mujahideen gained experience in quickly refitting their groups and detachments with reinforcing personnel and equipment in the border regions and on the territory of Pakistan. The outcome was that the LCOSF in Afghanistan was confronted by large, well-supplied, and well-organized Mujahideen armed forces that were well-versed in guerrilla tactics in mountain-desert terrain.

The basis of the tactics of the Mujahideen was that of the surprise attack by small detachments and groups to destroy enemy subunits, seize [if only temporarily] separate administrative centers, spread their zone of influence, and replenish the weapons and ammunition of the detachments and groups.

The Mujahideen divided combat actions into offensive (or frontal, by Mujahideen parlance), defensive, guerrilla, and actions to support vital activities of the force.

Offensive and defensive combat has a limited application in guerrilla war and the Mujahideen employed these forms very rarely. They conducted offensive combat to seize important administrative centers, contested territory, and isolated objectives, outposts, garrisons, vital sections of road, and so on. As a rule, the Mujahideen would plan and conduct offensives in the border provinces, where they could quickly receive reinforcements from Pakistan and, in the case of a setback, retreat across the border [it happened, but not as a rule]. While planning, the Mujahideen devoted special attention to surprise, initiative, reconnaissance, early warning, the maneuver of forces and equipment, and independent combat formations during the implementation of the plan. It should be noted, in particular in the Province of Kunar, that the Mujahideen received support in their offensives from artillery located in the territory of Pakistan. During the organization of the offensive, the Mujahideen paid particular attention to the selection of the time, place, and direction of the attack. The Mujahideen ensured that they had numerical superiority over the DRA forces as they maneuvered their forces and equipment into the designated region at the designated time, after which they would secretly move to the line of attack. Simultaneously, the covering force would move to the area on another approach. They would cover the withdrawal of the main body after the attack.

As a rule, the offensive was short-term, especially if it did not turn out well for the Mujahideen. In this case, the Mujahideen would quickly break contact under covering fire and move behind protective mine fields to withdraw along a previously selected route. They did not want to use a large collection of crew-served weapons to support the withdrawal of their groups and detachments since it made them less mobile. They mainly used these weapons to gain an advantage in the mountains but not on the plains, due to risk of capture by Soviet or DRA forces.

The Mujahideen went on the defense in order to hold on to their bases located in various important regions, to cover the withdrawal of their main body during a DRA strike, and to evade open combat. Permanent Mujahideen base garrisons of combat groups and detachments were the first line of defense for Mujahideen bases, defensive lines, and protected zones. They paid particular attention to the defense of mountain passes, canyon mouths, and dominant heights. Villages were important sites for Mujahideen defense.

While organizing a defense, the Mujahideen established a system of observation, fire support, and obstacles. Observation was established starting at the furthest approaches to the defense. Fire support utilized the natural defensive features of the terrain. Firing positions for weapons systems supported continuous, lethal, shifting fire on the approaches to the defense and, in the mountains, any attempts to attack the heights. They habitually put artillery and mortars in caves and rocky shelters in a three-tiered configuration. They positioned mountain air defense mounts and heavy machine guns, such as the DShK, on the commanding heights. The Mujahideen built trenches that resembled vertical mine shafts to protect the air defense weapons. They thoroughly camouflaged these sites. The sniper and DShK machine gun occupied the most important positions in the Mujahideen fire plan in the mountains and populated areas. The DShK position had no overhead cover so it could fire at both ground and air targets. Often these positions were made of concrete and had special slit trenches to protect the personnel. Main positions were connected by slit trenches on all sides and were used to protect personnel from aircraft and helicopter gun ship attack. Recoilless rifles and antitank grenade launchers were positioned in the lowest tier. Mortars and mountain guns often were sited in the second tier. Small arms positions were selected in order to cover mountain passes and trails and various bottlenecks.

In populated areas, the Mujahideen crew-served weapons were placed behind adobe walls that were up to two meters thick and up to three meters high. The Mujahideen knocked passages through the walls. They placed several weapons systems, particularly DShK machine guns, on the roofs and the upper floors of buildings. They built multiple firing positions for machine guns, recoilless rifles, and RPGs. They mined the approaches to the defense and around the firing positions.

In the mountains, the Mujahideen would build their trenches and other defensive works with stone and, in populated areas, with sandbags. They thoroughly camouflaged their firing positions. They would use caves, crevices, and buildings to hide their weapons.

The Mujahideen conducted a stubborn defense in the mountains. During air strikes and artillery strikes, the Mujahideen would move into covered shelters, and, after the air or artillery strike ended, they would reoccupy their fighting positions. The Mujahideen would conduct concentrated fire against an advancing force. Often, they would use a phony withdrawal to draw their enemy into a prepared fire sack. To conceal their actual firing system, they would use the fires of a diversionary group. In the event that the enemy had a significant superiority, the Mujahideen would lay down a short burst of fire on the advancing foe and withdraw along a planned marked path to a new assembly area or defensive position.

The withdrawal of the main body from occupied positions was conducted under covering fire from a rear guard occupying prepared positions. Sometimes the withdrawal from a defensive position would also be covered by an ambush or a minefield. When the Mujahideen conducted a defense, they would choose an area that they knew well which had an escape route from encirclement. Often the Mujahideen would withdraw at night and infiltrate through positions of the advancing force. After withdrawing from an encirclement, the Mujahideen groups and detachments would occupy a new, advantageous position, if possible in the enemy rear area. In this event, they would open fire at the enemy's back in a surprise attack. For this, they would rely on the fire of their snipers and their DShK machine guns.

If the Mujahideen were defending a populated area, they would establish initial positions on the outskirts and open a concentrated fire with all of their weapons on the approaching enemy. After that, they would withdraw into the depths of the village where they would occupy new defensive positions in the houses and behind the thick adobe walls. The Mujahideen wanted to fight the enemy forces and equipment in close combat in the bottlenecks and crooked passages of the villages where it was practically impossible to use armored vehicles, artillery, and air strikes effectively. Combat in built-up areas was particularly harsh and resulted in heavy casualties on both sides.

Guerrilla tactics were the Mujahideen's primary form of armed combat with the DRA. Not only the armed Mujahideen formations, but also a significant portion of the ordinary populace used these tactics throughout the entire territory of the country. The goal of these tactics was to inflict damage on the DRA organs and forces, wear them out, and significantly weaken them. Guerrilla tactics included ambushes, raids, shelling attacks, mining roads, sabotage and terrorist acts, and other actions. The intensity of incidents of guerrilla actions varied with the seasons of the year.

The more active forms of combat, with the exception of mining roads, were conducted in the spring and summer. This can be explained by the fact that the majority of mountain passes used by the caravans are closed in the winter. This created significant difficulties in supplying the Mujahideen. Besides that, the heavy snow cover in the mountains during the fall and winter forced the Mujahideen down into the valleys and spread them out throughout the peaceful population. Further, guerrilla actions decreased during planting and harvest time, and in Afghanistan, there are two to three annual harvests. The majority of Mujahideen took part in agricultural work. Guerrilla actions by the Mujahideen were prepared for after conducting a thorough reconnaissance of the DRA and Soviet forces. The Mujahideen founded a system of observation in every province. The system relied on a wide net of informers among the local inhabitants, military forces, and DRA organs. Islamic committees were instantly informed about the formation of convoys and their departure times and directions of movement. After the receipt of such information, the Mujahideen planners could plan combat or take necessary steps to evacuate detachments and temporarily hide weapons, ammunition, and other supplies.

During the course of the war, the Mujahideen used various forms of combat, chief of which were ambushes, raids, and shelling attacks. Also, they emplaced many mines and conducted a lot of sabotage and terrorist acts. Further, they mounted tactical actions to provide security to their caravans.

The Mujahideen used ambushes to cut off the supply of commercial and civilian cargo, supply themselves with weapons, ammunition, and other supplies, and to physically eliminate DRA soldiers. They used the ambush very often. For example, in the three years of 1985, 1986, and 1987, they conducted over 10,000 ambushes.

The Mujahideen, as a rule, would ambush roads, paths across mountain passes, canyons, and various narrow areas. In the mountains, they sited ambushes on slopes or mountain crests, the entry or exit to a canyon, or a section of road going through a pass. In green zones, the Mujahideen would site their ambushes at likely rest areas for DRA and Soviet forces or along the approach to an expected action. During the ambush, the Mujahideen would fire from the front and from the flank. They would set up their ambushes with several positions so that they could attack their enemy when he was moving in columns and then when he deployed into combat formation. In built-up areas, the Mujahideen would ambush from behind adobe walls and from houses in order to deceive the enemy and draw him into a fire sack in an area where the road is narrow or a cul-de-sac.

Usually, the Mujahideen would set their ambushes at night. However, they also conducted daylight ambushes, usually late in the day when their enemy was tired and less observant. Ambushing late in the day also allowed the Mujahideen to break contact and withdraw under the cover of darkness and lessened his likelihood of being hit by enemy aviation.

Most often, Mujahideen ambushes involved small groups of 10 to 15 men. Their combat formation consisted of look-outs and three or four subgroups (Map 4). The look-outs established observation posts in the mountains or near probable enemy convoy routes. If they were near the road, the look-outs were unarmed and they passed themselves off as peaceful locals, such as shepherds or peasants. There were Mujahideen ambush sites where they used children as look-outs. The base element of the Mujahideen ambush was the firing subgroup, which contained the bulk of the personnel and weapons of the group. It was located in the center of the ambush formation, parallel to and in close proximity to the kill zone. Their positions were thoroughly camouflaged. The width of the deployed firing subgroup was some 150 to 300 meters. Grenade launchers, machine guns,

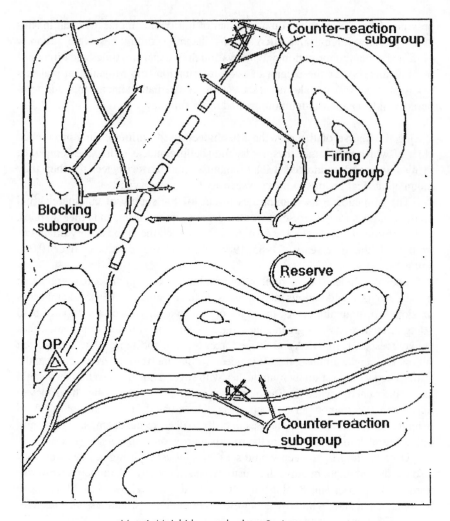

Map 4. Mujahideen ambush on Soviet convoy

and snipers were located on the flanks of the firing subgroup. The Mujahideen would emplace their DShK machine guns on dominant heights where they could fire on ground and air targets.

Besides the firing support group, the Mujahideen would constitute blocking subgroups[27] and a reserve. Blocking subgroups were intended to prevent the enemy withdrawal from the kill zone or prevent enemy movement in another direction. The commander would use the reserve subgroup to reinforce the firing subgroup or to cover the withdrawal of the Mujahideen from the ambush site. Often, the Mujahideen would constitute a "counter-reaction" subgroup.[28] This subgroup would function outside of the ambush area and tie down the enemy reserves. The look-outs and commander would communicate with each other using prearranged audio or radio signals. The Mujahideen had ready access to small American, Japanese, and Western European radio transmitter/receivers.

The purpose of the Mujahideen ambush was to quickly rip apart the convoy, and, therefore, they would allow the combat security element or the bulk of the convoy to pass unmolested and then hit the vehicles remaining behind and the technical support vehicles. Very often, they would strike at the lagging vehicles or small convoys traveling without sufficient protection or air cover. If the Mujahideen ambush had a counter reaction subgroup, this group might open fire on the convoy first, in order to pin down the combat security element in a fire fight. At that point, the vehicles following the combat security element were already without protection as the firing subgroup would open up on the convoy and inflict heavy casualties.

When the convoy would enter into the kill zone, the first shots of the snipers were directed against the drivers and senior commander and command and control vehicles in order to block the road, disrupt the command and control, and spread panic. At the same time, other Mujahideen would open fire on the other vehicles using small arms against trucks and jeeps and RPGs, recoilless rifles, and heavy machine guns against armored vehicles.

If the Mujahideen ambush was effectively repulsed by an organized effort, the Mujahideen would quickly abandon their ambush and hide themselves and not offer any particular resistance. If a convoy had excellent reconnaissance, a good convoy escort, and also air cover, the Mujahideen would not usually risk an ambush.

The Mujahideen conducted raids against security outposts, small enemy garrisons, depots, bases, and government institutions. Most often, they would use a group of 30 to 35 men to conduct a raid. Their combat formation consisted of a forward patrol and four subgroups: suppression, main, engineering, and covering (Map 5).

The forward patrol consisted of two to three men who usually preceded the main body on horseback or foot. They would move to the objective secretly, disguising themselves as the local populace. They would approach the objective and set up observation. Once the forward patrol was convinced that the enemy did not expect an attack, they would give a signal to move up the rest of the force. The suppression subgroup would eliminate sentries and support the movement of the engineering and main subgroups. The engineering subgroup would neutralize mines and support the approach of the main subgroup to the objective, which the main subgroup would then seize or destroy. The covering subgroup would cover the withdrawal route from the enemy, hinder the employment of the enemy reserve, and support the main subgroup as it broke contact and withdrew following mission accomplishment. During the withdrawal, the Mujahideen paid particular attention to misleading their enemy. As part of this, the personnel split

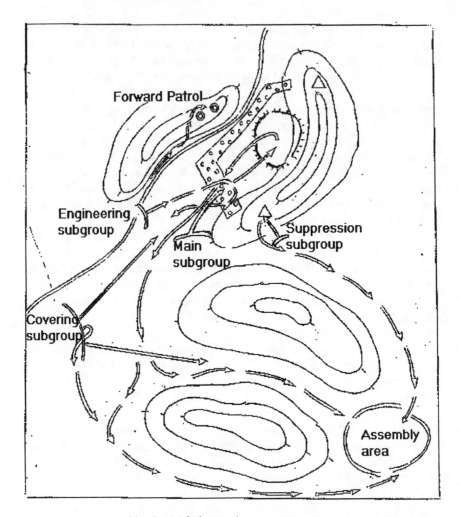

Map 5. Mujahideen raid on a security outpost

into small groups and moved by different routes to their designated assembly area.

During the course of the war in Afghanistan, the intensity of Mujahideen raids constantly grew. Thus, in 1985, the number of Mujahideen raids was about 2,400, in 1986, almost 2,900, and in 1987, 4,200.

Once the Mujahideen began receiving Chinese-manufactured rockets, they expanded their shelling attacks widely. To conduct a shelling attack, the Mujahideen would designate a small group of 3 to 15 men to transport and launch 10 to 15 rockets. The Mujahideen surveyed firing positions that they normally located near villages within range of Soviet artillery posts. This put the villagers in danger of death from return Soviet artillery fire. They mounted the rockets on homemade tripods and aimed them at the target. On the signal from the lookout, they would launch the rockets, after which the group would take cover. Sometimes, when the Mujahideen wanted to launch a large number of rockets, they would use mechanical timers that they could program into an electronic circuit.

As a rule, these shelling attacks were not very effective. The shelling attacks were directed against various targets—to create panic among the peaceful populace and to cause stress in the Soviet and DRA garrisons. In the border region with Pakistan, they would often launch 20 to 800 rockets per day. All in all, during the period April 1985 to January 1987, the Mujahideen conducted over 23,500 shelling attacks on military and government targets.

One of the basic forms of Mujahideen guerrilla tactics was mine warfare. They laid many mines on all the roads to pursue an end—to stop or seriously retard the movement of military columns or government convoys carrying vital material. The Mujahideen devoted particular attention to mining the main roads: Kabul-Kandahar-Herat; Kabul-Hairatan; Kabul-Jalalabad; and Kabul-Gardez-Khost. They used various mines and demolition explosives—principally of foreign manufacture. They placed their mines and *fougasses*[29] ahead of time on the road or in close proximity to the approaching forces and vehicles. The more common sites that the Mujahideen used to place his mines and *fougasses* included the following: sections of road outside built-up areas; sections of mountain road running along a mountain ledge, along a river, in canyons or in other sites where it is impossible or difficult to bypass or repair the passage; entries and exits on major roads; approaches to springs of water and stream and river fords and crossings; damaged sections of road; canyon exits onto roads; and sites that are ideal for a rest halt or extended break.

The Mujahideen laid pattern minefields (with mines laid equally along the entire stretch of a route) as well as small irregular groups of three to five mines. The mines were buried in various patterns: at a single point, in a checkerboard pattern of several points, or grouped along the roads. Mine groups normally were an antitank mine surrounded by three to five antipersonnel mines. All mines were carefully hidden to blend in with the area. Often they would pour water or strew ashes from burnt straw over the loose ground covering a mine in order to help the ground harden. In order to provide a uniform background to the mined area, they would put their mines and *fougasses* in cattle trails and cover the mines with manure.

When the Mujahideen were going to emplace a large quantity of mines, they would use a specially trained group of four to six miners. Often, they would enlist the services of the local inhabitants and even children. Given a little training, the locals could also plant mines. At the places that they had planted mines, they would establish visible posts to warn drivers about particular stretches of road and pedestrian paths. Usually, there was an established fee for this warning.

The Mujahideen leaders paid great attention to sabotage and terrorist actions. These were carried out by specially trained groups and detachments of varying strengths. Usually groups were divided into sections by the type of mission they performed. Thus, for example, the first performed attacks on sentries, the second (technical) would support the conduct of sabotage close to the objective, the third was designated for taking out lines of communication and fighting reinforcements.

Sabotage was usually conducted one or two hours before dark. The more common types of sabotage included damaging military equipment and power lines, knocking out pipelines and radio stations, and blowing up government office buildings, air terminals, hotels, movie theaters, and so on.

Terrorist groups had three to five men in each. After they received their mission to kill this or that government statesman, they busied themselves with studying his pattern of life and its details and then selecting the method of fulfilling their established mission. They practiced shooting at automobiles, shooting out of automobiles, laying mines in government accommodation or houses, using poison, and rigging explosive charges in transport. From 1985 through 1987, there were over 1,800 terrorist acts recorded. Moreover, in 1985 there were some 450 acts, whereas there were 600 in 1987.

The high tempo of combat conducted by the Mujahideen resulted in their receiving the type of material they wanted. For every captured or killed Soviet soldier, the Mujahideen was paid a monetary reward of 250,000 Afghans ($1,250). For a Soviet officer, it was doubled to 500,000 Afghans ($2,500). For every tank or IMR that they destroyed, they received 500,000 Afghans ($2,500).[30] For every aircraft or helicopter they destroyed, the Mujahideen received 1,000,000 Afghans ($5,000).

The Mujahideen mounted tactical actions to provide security to their caravans, which were the only way to transport the faction's weapons and ammunition into Afghanistan from the neighboring countries. Weapons and ammunition caravans were composed of the transportation element and the security and escort element. The weapons and ammunition were usually transported in their original packing cases in the bed of a truck, trailer, automobile, animal-drawn cart, or pack animal. Caravans could be large (10 to 15 trucks or 50 to 100 pack animals) or small (two to three vehicles or three to five pack animals). For convoy escort, the Mujahideen usually used Subaru or Toyota trucks (less often the GAZ-53) and motorcycles. Sometimes they transported weapons on buses and tractors with trailers. During the transfer of weapons into Afghanistan, should the caravan travel on the highway, the weapons would be hidden on the bottom of the truck bed under cargo, sacks of flour, sacks of grain, firewood, and so on.

In order to cross the border, the Mujahideen used over 50 routes, which split into a large number of roads and trails suitable for the movement of mechanical, animal-drawn, or pedestrian traffic. In all, there were 99 caravan routes in Afghanistan, of which 69 were vehicular and 30 were for pack animals.

Experience showed that the Mujahideen used many variants and methods to deliver weapons and ammunition to Afghanistan. As a rule, the conduct of a caravan involved representatives of the Islamic Committees, who determined the distribution of weapons and ammunition. Considering the heightened danger of conducting weapons caravans, the Mujahideen would select the more convenient caravan routes, which would allow them to escape confrontation with armed forces and, when necessary, conceal themselves from air actions. Before the caravan would leave the assembly area, the Mujahideen would do a careful reconnaissance of the entire length of the route, which was as necessary as selecting the guide. The reconnaissance group and the foragers moved on the march route. They, as a rule, provided communications, in accordance with prearranged signals, necessary legal documents for Afghanistan, and letters of recommendation for the leaders of the detachments through whose area of operations the caravan would pass. Besides these, the last was a Mujahideen order to guarantee the safety of the caravan route in the area of responsibility of the local commander. In addition to the reconnaissance and movement of the group, the march commander also had the responsibility for spreading disinformation during the course of the caravan.

Usually a caravan moved in three elements. The advance guard moved first. This was a group of 10 to 15 Mujahideen moving on trucks, motorcycles, horses, or foot. The main body moved behind the advance guard. It could be divided into several groups, moving apart from each other at no set distance and having a proper guard. Behind the main body was the caravan rear guard. It consisted of five to ten armed Mujahideen.

In the event of a confrontation with Soviet or DRA forces, the advance guard would tie down these forces in order to secure the withdrawal of the main body of the caravan. In the case that the escape route of the caravan was blocked, the Mujahideen would try to move the trucks with their weapons out of enemy fire. In extreme circumstances, they would blow up the trucks along with their cargo. The main mission of the convoy escort and protection force was to guarantee the uninterrupted delivery of the cargo to the designated site. In this, they used contiguous detachments from the territories through which the caravan passed.

However, caravans did not always reach their designated sites. Sometimes, the cargo was intercepted by detachments belonging to other factions. In this case, relations between the factions became strained and could result in armed conflict between the factions, which might last for several months.

In some cases, the strong factions would use captured trucks and armored personnel carriers that were manufactured in the Soviet Union. The Mujahideen would use these to carry their cargo. They would dress their people in DRA uniforms and provide them with the necessary documents. Carelessness at the road control posts allowed the Mujahideen unimpeded delivery of arms and ammunition in the western areas. In extraordinary circumstances, the caravan would off-load and hide its arms and ammunition in cemeteries, *karez,* and caves, or distribute them among the inhabitants for safekeeping. The transport had to be driven back or destroyed in place. The pack animal would have to be abandoned or sold to the local inhabitants. The Mujahideen would disperse into the villages or leave the dangerous area. When the danger passed, the caravan might reform completely or partially and continue to move to the designated region.

Thus, the LCOSF had to contend with these developed Mujahideen tactics. The Mujahideen combined the tactics of the offense and defense with a wide variety of guerrilla tactics. Naturally, the Mujahideen used their more successful tactics whenever possible.

Editors' comments: The Mujahideen used tactics that, in many cases, had not changed appreciably for a century. The British developed a set of effective tactics to counter these tactics. These British tactics generally still applied; however, ranges had changed with technology. The Soviets did not consult the British experience and this was a war in which technology played a limited role. Mujahideen tactics were adapted when necessary to deal with new systems such as the close air support aircraft, the helicopter gunship, and the antipersonnel mine—the technology that had some impact on the Mujahideen. For a detailed examination of Mujahideen tactics, see Ali Ahmad Jalali and Lester W. Grau, The Other Side of the Mountain: Mujahideen Tactics in the Soviet-Afghan War *(Quantico: U.S. Marine Corps Study, 1998).*

What is apparent from this chapter is that the Soviets did not have a clear understanding of their opposition and that the Russians still lack this understanding when looking back in retrospect. There is a Soviet desire to impose structure and order on the unstructured and disorderly Mujahideen. There is a Soviet need to quantify the unquantifiable. There is faulty Soviet intelligence involved in the basic task of identifying the major opposing factions. There is an inability to understand the enemy, since the Soviet perception of that enemy is filtered through the prism of Marxism-Leninism—and that prism disallows any popular uprising against a Marxist-Leninist state. Despite all their efforts, the Soviets did not understand who they were fighting.

4

Operational Art[1]

The 40th Army planned and conducted combined-arms operations to carry out large-scale missions. Depending on which country the troops belonged to, the operations were subdivided into independent and combined operations and employed the forces and resources of the entire army or part of the army.

Independent operations were especially widespread during the second phase of the war. In Afghanistan, these were conducted exclusively with the forces of the 40th Army and planned and directed by the army leadership. During the time that the LCOSF was in Afghanistan, they conducted approximately 220 independent operations.

Combined operations were widely employed in the third and fourth phases of the war. They were conducted according to plans developed by the Soviet Command and carried out by Soviet and DRA forces. There were more than 400 combined operations conducted during the entire course of the war in Afghanistan.

The composition of the forces and resources required for the conduct of each operation was determined by its scale, location, the nature of enemy actions, the selected plan to destroy them, and the peculiarities of the terrain. When determining the forces and resources required, planners learned that fighting guerrillas in the mountains requires significantly more forces and resources than operations conducted under ordinary circumstances. Counter-guerrilla operations required the participation of four to five combined-arms divisions plus regiments of various branches of service and special forces. At the same time, during the course of the war, there often were sites requiring smaller-scale partial operations. For these, the army command would select a regiment from one or more combined-arms divisions and reinforce it with supporting regiments and subunits as well as 40th Army special forces. Besides these ground forces, operations used aviation on a wide scale. The amount of aviation employed depended on the region where the enemy was located, the status of enemy air defense, the season, and the time of day.

Operations were conducted to support the following goals: destroy powerful enemy groups in enemy-controlled regions; secure military and government installations; support the passage of supply convoys; and withdraw Soviet forces from Afghanistan.

Operations to destroy powerful enemy groups in enemy-controlled territory were offensive operations; however, in the course of such an operation, separate axes might revert to the defense. The organization and conduct of offensive operations were more complex than other types of operations. At the same time, the expenditure of forces and resources in an offensive did not always achieve the desired results. Nevertheless, the Soviet command denied the 40th Army the adequate resources necessary to undertake such costly operations in order to effectively influence the military-strategic situation in the country, but required the 40th Army to undertake them anyway. An example of such an operation is one conducted in the valley of the Panjshir river and surroundings (Parwan Province) in May 1982. The heightened interest in this region by both of the contending sides was readily apparent. The Panjshir river valley winds for almost 250 kilometers through the mountains of the Hindu Kush. It is one of the main arteries that unites the central provinces of Afghanistan with Pakistan. This region was the center of the strongest opposition party—the Islamic Society *(Jamiat-i-Islami)* (JIA) headed by Rabbani. There are large deposits of emeralds, rubies, and lapis lazuli in the valley. Mining these provided the opposition with funds to purchase arms and ammunition from across the border. Therefore, it was not surprising that the JIA chose the Panjshir river valley and its surrounding mountain massif to position the "Central Guerrilla Bases" that served to train the armed Mujahideen detachments and to provide them with arms, ammunition, food, and other supplies—not only in the valley, but also in the surrounding provinces.

In May 1982, the guerrilla main force of over 5,000 combatants was concentrated in the Panjshir river valley. The Mujahideen defense was designed using the mountainous characteristics of the terrain. Basically, the defense consisted of individual strong points located on dominant heights, in canyons, and in various excellent defensive positions. Strong points were also established in fortresses and the outskirts of villages. Every strong point was defended by a garrison of 10 to 20 men and equipped with several firing points made out of stone. The staffs and Islamic committee centers were spread out, as a rule, in the best guarded points. Each was guarded by a 30-to-50 man detachment armed with small arms and man-portable air defense missiles. Mujahideen artillery firing positions were located near thoroughly camouflaged crevices and caves. The artillery pieces and mortars were kept under cover and only set up in the firing positions during fire missions. This type of defense used significantly fewer forces to control the region and was much harder to find with reconnaissance and to engage with artillery and air strikes.

Preparations for the Panjshir operation began with a thorough reconnaissance of the enemy. The reconnaissance hoped to determine the strength and location of enemy forces and weapons, the location of enemy strong points, and other important military and economic sites. As a result of the reconnaissance, by the start of the operation, they had discovered 95 Mujahideen detachments and groups totaling up to 3,000 men, 16 Islamic committees, up to 100 air defense systems, two reserve training centers, and several supply points. Considering that reconnaissance data, as a rule, never discloses more than one half of the actual situation, the Soviet command concluded that there was a strong enemy force in the valley and decided to destroy it. The planners estimated the composition and location of the main Mujahideen force and determined their own force structure and the necessary missions required to destroy the enemy on this very difficult terrain.

For this operation, the LCOSF designated one regiment each from two motorized rifle divisions [108th and 201st] and the 103rd Airborne Division, the 66th Separate Motorized Rifle Brigade, and subunits from the 860th and 191st Separate Motorized Rifle Regiments and the 345th Separate Parachute Regiment. Further, regiments and subunits of supporting branches, as well as front and army aviation were committed to the operation. Regiments from three different DRA divisions were committed to the operation as were DRA subunits from the "Commando" brigade and a separate infantry regiment, as well as subunits from the DRA KHAD. The forces committed totaled about 12,000 personnel, which was about 2.5 times greater than those of the enemy.

The concept of the operation envisaged two thrusts: the main attack would advance up the Panjshir river valley from Bagram to Evim, while the diversionary attack would advance to the north along the Gorband river valley (Map 6). Soviet and Afghan forces were combined for the conduct of these offensive thrusts by its motorized rifle divisions and regiments. Further, these thrusts were to be combined with aviation strikes and an air assault to destroy the enemy in the river valleys and establish control over this important strategic region of Afghanistan. The scale of this operation stretched over 60 kilometers of front and up to 220 kilometers in depth. Planners determined that the operation would last for 13-to-15 days. Therefore, the average rate of advance had to be 15-to-18 kilometers per day.

The operational formations of the force included a first echelon, a combined-arms reserve, artillery groups, special forces, and rear services elements. The air echelon was an independent element of 20 Soviet and Afghan battalions.

Operational planning was conducted—paying attention to the particulars involved with participation of the divisions and regiments of the Afghan Army, as well as their militia and organs of their state security—by KHAD. The drafting of the operational plan was restricted to a very limited number of officers. Moreover, all of these were from the 40th Army staff.[2]

The 40th Army planners intensified their efforts, and by the end of April, they had worked out the operations plan and had it approved. They had also

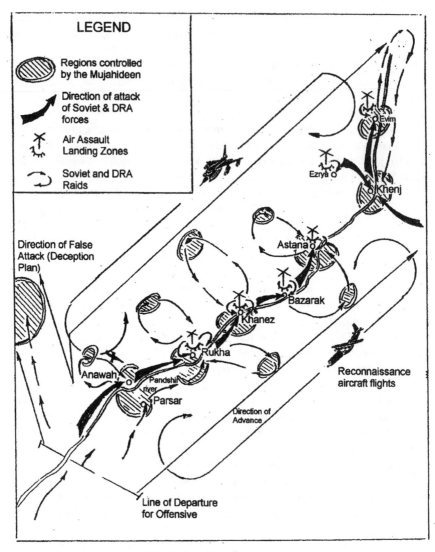

LEGEND

Regions controlled
by the Mujahideen

Direction of attack
of Soviet & DRA
forces

Air Assault
Landing Zones

Soviet and DRA
Raids

Direction of False
Attack (Deception
Plan)

Reconnaissance
aircraft flights

Line of Departure
for Offensive

Direction of
Advance

Evim

Ezrya

Khenj

Astana

Bazarak

Khanez

Rukha

Anawah

Pandshir
river

Parsar

Map 6. Panjshir valley operation

worked out a partial disinformation and camouflage plan employing various branches, special forces, and various services. This deception plan posited an advance along the Gorband river bed to deceive the Mujahideen as to location of the main thrust and the time that the offensive would begin. The 40th Army provided the deception plan to the Afghan high command as the real plan. The enemy quickly learned about the plan.

The main thrust attack was thoroughly planned in great secrecy. The operations section of the 40th Army worked up maps depicting the starting situation as well as their initial combat deployment. They worked out signals for troop control, instructions for equipping the force, and ordered flights to obtain aerial photographs of the future combat region. All of these documents were placed in sealed envelopes that were delivered to the division and regimental commanders at the 40th Army headquarters just five days before the start of the offensive.

From 5 to 10 May, the main duty of the commanders of the divisions and separate regiments was to conduct their own aerial reconnaissance over the region of impending combat. They refined their missions and coordinated their forces and various branches with respect to missions, coordination lines, times, and types of action.

During their coordination, they defined the axes of advance and march routes for the advancing divisions and regiments, established the boundary lines between forces, determined the landing zones for the air assault, determined the sites to construct obstacles and destroy enemy obstacles, determined the link-up line between advancing forces, determined the order of combined actions during the capture of important objectives, and also troop control signals and mutual recognition signals. The commanders coordinated their ground movement with supporting artillery and aviation, paying particular attention to the optimum distribution of targets between artillery and aviation and determining the times to conduct the aviation strikes or to open fire with the artillery. They paid particular attention to thoroughly coordinating the actions of aviation and artillery during their shifts of fire between one target and another. In these instances, they determined the time of the strike, the flight route of the aviation, and the firing trajectory of the artillery. Further, they coordinated the tentative schedule for artillery suppression of enemy air defense systems along the flight route and in the area of aviation employment.

It was particularly difficult for commanders at all levels to coordinate their actions with the Afghan regiments and subunits. In order to preserve the secrecy of the operations plan, coordination was conducted in a very compressed time, as a rule, only on the map and often after receiving the mission just before moving the force to the area of operations. Sometimes, coordination was done while the force was deploying into combat formations. As a result, the effects of this type of coordination were most often extremely limited.

Simultaneously, the commanders and staffs intensely prepared their forces for the impending battle. They conducted a series of staff communications exercises at army, division, regiment, and battalion level. Regiments conducted live-fire exercises. All preparations concluded with the conduct of a full-field layout in garrison.[3] Following this, units had two to three days to correct deficiencies and load gear onto their armored vehicles and the trucks of their transportation battalions.

Preparation of the air assault forces received special attention since the operation planned to use a large quantity of these air assault forces. Helicopter lift capacity was a function of the elevation of the landing zones above sea level. Lift ships could normally carry ten men. On this operation, the landing zones were often 1,500 to 2,000 meters above sea level. Planners divided the landing zones into four categories. Lift ships could carry eight men into the category I LZs (under 1,500 meters in elevation). Lift ships could only carry seven men into the category II LZs (1,500 to 1,800 meters in elevation), while they could carry only four or five men into category III LZs (1,800 to 2,000 meters in elevation). Lift ships could only carry four men into Category IV LZs (over 2,000 meters in elevation). Soviet and Afghan air assault troopers were divided into helicopter lifts and met with the helicopter crews early on. Air assault issues were resolved, such as loading and landing procedures and fire suppression of the enemy located nearby the LZs. Commanders of the air assault units were divided among the lifts. Thus, the regimental or brigade commander would fly in after the first lift had secured the LZs. He would then take command of the air assault while one of his deputies at the airfield organized the dispatch of the helicopters and the launch of subsequent lifts. These measures prevented the accumulation of forces at the air field and supported the organization of the air assault in the assigned region.

Supply activity ran parallel with planning the operation and preparing the force for action. Hundreds of tons of ammunition, food, fuel, and other stocks were laid in, as Bagram air base became a supply distribution point. Fork lifts stacked the cargo in various depots.

The army chief of staff headed an operations group that controlled the forces during the course of the operation. The operations group consisted of the chiefs of branches, sections, and services. Besides the operations group, the division commanders controlled their forward regiments and coordinated their movement with that of their neighboring units. The 40th Army constituted an additional three operational groups from branch and services officers to help control the initial phase of the operation.

Before the start of this important operation, as part of the preparations, reliable guides were selected from among the local inhabitants of the Panjshir valley. Every battalion had a guide.

The Panjshir operation began on the 15th of May 1982 and had four phases. The first phase lasted from 15 to 16 May with the diversionary attack into Gorband Province to deceive the enemy as to the location of the main attack. The deception plan achieved positive results. The enemy commander perceived the diversionary attack as the main attack and hastily began to transfer additional forces from the outlying region, and even from the Panjshir valley, into the Gorband river valley.

The two days of the first phase were sufficient to concentrate and deploy the main groups of Soviet and Afghan forces north of Bagram at the entry to the Panjshir river valley. The 40th Army operations group command post was also deployed there. They were joined by the columns of personnel carriers of the air assault battalions loaded with supplies for 12 to 15 days of combat. The personnel of the air assault subunits remained in their base camps.

On the night of 16 May, 11 reconnaissance companies seized the dominating terrain controlling entry into the Panjshir valley. Their triumph was conducted practically without a fight. Artillery moved forward and occupied firing positions and began computing firing data. On the following night, one of the motorized rifle battalions entered the valley and advanced some 10 kilometers to seize several dominant heights in the valley. In this way, they formed the spring board for the operation's main thrust.

The second phase of the operation (17 to 22 May) started at 0400 hours on the 17th of May. After launching a massive aviation strike along the entire depth of the valley, an artillery preparation began on the enemy strong points that they had discovered. Then, Soviet and Afghan units moved into the offensive on the main attack axis. Motorized rifle subunits moved on foot along both sides of the river under covering fire from their *bronnegruppa*. They occupied one height after another, destroying any enemy that they encountered.

One hour after the start of the offensive, a Soviet motorized rifle battalion and an Afghan infantry battalion air-landed near the towns of Rukha and Bazarak. The mission of these battalions was to seize the dominant heights near the LZs and prevent the withdrawal of the enemy into the depths of the Panjshir valley. A massive air strike on the LZs preceded the air landings. During the air landings, aviation conducted bombing runs and strafing attacks on enemy positions located on nearby heights. Such fire support suppressed the Mujahideen firing accuracy and minimized casualties during the air landing. At the same time, the suppression of enemy air defense systems was not as successful. The Mujahideen shot down two helicopters and damaged several others during the air landing at Rukha.

The Soviet command determined that an inadequate number of air assault forces were able to land during the first lift. Therefore, they repeated the aerial preparation of the LZ with frontal aviation and Mi-24 helicopter gunships. This support allowed the successful landing of successive lifts.

During this first day of phase II, six battalions (three Soviet and three Afghan) air-landed with a total of 1,200 men some 40-to-50 kilometers into the valley and some 80 kilometers from Bagram air base. The air assault subunits, using the factor of surprise, captured LZs and dominant heights, destroyed existing enemy strong points, and organized a perimeter defense.

The successful action of the air assault forces enabled the advancing ground forces to advance on Anova simultaneously along three approaches—along the existing road paralleling the Panjshir river bed and along the mountain canyons affiliated with villages to the north and south. The force advanced in columns. The lead column of the main body was the advance guard, composed of a motorized rifle battalion reinforced with tanks and self-propelled howitzers. These subunits used all their firepower to suppress enemy firing points and support the actions of the Movement Support Detachment [MSD—OOD in Russian], which was following them.

The division MSD, as a rule, had a mine neutralization platoon, a sapper company, an engineer road repair company, and tank and motorized rifle companies. The MSD was organized into a reconnaissance group, a mine neutralization group, an obstacle removal group, a road repair and bridging group, a mine-laying group, and a reserve. The tempo of the MSD moving through an area filled with mines, obstacles, and destroyed sections of road is slow and does not exceed two kilometers an hour. This predetermined the low tempo of advance of the advance guard and columns of the main body. On the first day, they averaged one to two kilometers an hour.

The rugged terrain, the fragmented nature of the Mujahideen defense, and the presence of a large number of manmade obstacles called for the application of new methods by the advancing force. The new method tried included the simultaneous fire destruction of the enemy to the depth of the assigned mission; with the follow-on destruction of the enemy in the valley by ground forces; and the tactical envelopment of the enemy by air assault forces. This combination action prevented enemy maneuver, broke up enemy armed formations, and created the conditions to defeat the enemy in detail.

The frontal advance along the Panjshir river valley was combined with actions by part of the force to bypass and take the dominant terrain with a flanking attack. As a rule, they usually took canyons dismounted, after which the *bronnegruppa* rejoined the subunit. Depending on the terrain and the width of the canyon, the *bronnegruppa* would move along the stream bed of a small stream or along the side of a road, prepared to open fire on an opposite slope or the ridge controlling a height. During a confrontation with the enemy in a canyon, they would hit the enemy with helicopter gunship fire, artillery fire, and mortar fire. After this, they would use a subunit to bypass the ridge on the height to create a fire sack and complete the destruction of the Mujahideen. Simultaneously, they would employ remotely delivered mines on paths and mountain passes leading out of the valley to the north and south. This served to isolate the battle area from the influx of fresh reserves from the neighboring regions around the Panjshir and to prevent the withdrawal of remaining, defeated groups into other provinces.

On the morning of the second day, the 40th Army reinforced the forces in the vicinity of Mata with an air assault landing consisting of one Soviet battalion and one Afghan battalion. They seized an advantageous LZ, captured dominant terrain, prevented the withdrawal of the enemy to the east, and prevented the arrival of enemy reserve from the Andarab river valley. Motorized rifle and air assault subunits, supported by frontal and army aviation, first seized an LZ. Then they destroyed the enemy and occupied the dominant heights, thus severely restricting enemy maneuver.

On 19 May, a Soviet and an Afghan battalion air-landed in the Astana region and a similar force landed in the region of Mata. A day later, four battalions (two

Soviet and two Afghan) landed in the region of Evim to the depth of 100 kilometers in the Panjshir valley. In this fashion, during the course of four days from the start of the offensive, the Soviet command inserted 65 battalions into the enemy rear using helicopters.

Despite the massive use of air assaults and the successful coordination of aviation and ground forces, the enemy continued a stubborn resistance. He reverted to a positional defense, concentrated his main forces on favorable dominant high ground, moved them along parallel valleys, and positioned them on the mouths of tight canyons. The enemy established multi-tiered defenses everywhere and used all crevices, crags, caves, grottos, and heights for firing positions. Between the heights, the enemy established shaping and canalizing positions that they would occupy in the course of battle with flanking groups and detachments. This defense pinned down the advancing ground forces. Soviet and Afghan government forces suffered many casualties in personnel and, especially, equipment.

Every day the 40th Army began combat with a fire preparation conducted by supporting artillery and aviation. The length of the fire preparation depended on the quantity of fire strikes and scheduling. As a rule, the fire preparation lasted for 26 to 30 minutes. Every howitzer battery planned fires on one or two targets. A special feature of the fire preparation was that the fire was conducted simultaneously by all artillery systems. One firing battery was dedicated to each target. In several instances, each multiple rocket launcher vehicle had a single target. Ammunition expenditure depended on the character and terrain of the target area, but each target received from 40 to 120 artillery and mortar rounds.

The artillery preparation of the attack conformed to the principles of concentration of fire, fire on individual targets, and fire to the depth of the subunits' combat mission. During this phase, each maneuver battalion was supported by the fire of one or two artillery battalions. The effectiveness of the artillery fire first of all was achieved by the artillery schedule and then the extent of fire support. Artillery expenditure on an enemy artillery piece or mortar during the period of the artillery preparation numbered 200 to 600 rounds each.

As the Soviet/Afghan forces advanced and shattered the enemy's established defenses, the character of enemy actions gradually changed. The enemy transitioned from a positional defense to a maneuver defense and then back again to a positional defense. Leaving a small force as a rear guard, the Mujahideen moved their main forces into the depths of the canyon where they established a new defense.

Combat showed that, as a rule, frontal attacks by Soviet and Afghan forces did not succeed. During the air strikes by fighter bombers and close air support aircraft and during the artillery strikes, the enemy would successfully withdraw his forces and weapons along communication trenches cut in the slopes to preserve their combat power. As the advancing force went over to the attack, the Mujahideen forces and weapons would return to their prepared positions and put up a stubborn resistance. However, not a single Soviet or Afghan commander decided to change his tactics during the operation. The Soviet/Afghan force slowly displaced the enemy from his occupied positions, but did not inflict significant casualties on the Mujahideen. Only by the end of 21 May were Soviet and Afghan forces able to enter the towns of Mata and Pasi-Sheun-Mardan to link up with the air assault troops. This link up marked the completion of the second phase. The enemy abandoned the main part of the territory he controlled and suffered significant personnel and equipment losses. The average rate of advance of the force was 8 to 10 kilometers per day.

The special characteristics of the second phase of the operation were that the Soviet/Afghan forces used tactical air assaults widely, they actively fought at night, they achieved surprise, and quickly destroyed the enemy while suffering minimal casualties.

Following this battle, the valley was completely free of enemy forces and the enemy air defense system ceased to exist. The Soviet command then began the third phase of the operation, which continued for three days (22 to 24 May). The goal of this phase was to seize the road junction near Evim. Caravans from Pakistan brought weapons, ammunition, and other military cargo to the Mujahideen through this road junction.

To accomplish this mission, the Soviet command launched an air assault near Evim—some 220 kilometers from Bagram. The air assault force consisted of two battalions (a Soviet and an Afghan battalion) of about 600 men.

The aviation preparation of the Evim LZ began two weeks prior to the air assault. Approximately 130 air sorties carried out the preparation. Reconnaissance data pinpointed the enemy firing positions located on the LZ and the air strikes hit them. An air preparation was conducted on the LZ immediately prior to the air landing. The LZ was located close to the dirt-strip airfield at Evim.

The first lift captured two dominant heights within a three to four kilometer radius of the airfield and then moved to clear the boulders and obstacles off the runway. Further landings and resupply were carried out using the captured runway.

After all the air assault forces landed, they widened the battle zone and advanced on some villages. The enemy, in order to escape encirclement and destruction, began to withdraw into the mountains. As darkness fell, his detachments, numbering up to several hundred men, separately attempted to storm the heights occupied by the air assault troopers. However, all these attacks were unsuccessful. By the end of 24 May, Soviet and Afghan subunits had solidly fortified the area they seized and effectively cut the important enemy LOCs.

A particular feature of the air assault was the flight approach that was conducted at a height of 4,600 to 4,700 meters—which is at the upper limits of the Mi-8mt helicopter for altitude, speed, and carrying capacity. Due to the extreme height of the mountain passes and the extended distance of the LZ from the Bagram airfield, Mi-24V helicopter gunships were not able to provide covering fire for the air assault. Therefore, air cover for the air assault was provided by a group of MIG-21BIS and SU-25 aircraft from frontal aviation.

Conducting an air landing in this theater (TVD) in the designated region in a limited period of time required the movement of a significant quantity of material from the depots established at Bagram. During the course of 3 days, 30 helicopters conducted 3 lifts a day to move 180 tons of ammunition and 30 tons of food and other supplies to the Evim LZ. The helicopters moved under the protection of frontal aviation to resupply the forces and maintain it in a high state of combat readiness. The demands of the situation increased the demands on the pilots, who had to fly up to seven combat missions a day with a daily average of nine hours in the cockpit for army aviation crews and a daily average of four hours in the cockpit for frontal aviation crews. These times were significantly above the norm. The fourth phase of the operation (25 to 28 May) involved the withdrawal of the main body of Soviet forces from the combat zone. This was carried out in sequence according to a synchronized plan. Part of the dominant terrain was transferred to Afghan forces. Under the cover of strong points established on high ground and a strong detachment to support the movement, the force began to withdraw.

The last force out of the valley was the rear guard, which was composed of three Soviet and three Afghan battalions. By the end of 28 May, the force was concentrated in the region of the Bagram airfield. Transport aircraft and helicopters began returning to their regular airbases. *Bronnegruppa* moved under the cover of a small force and air cover to complete the march on their own. Thus, the 14-day Panjshir operation was successfully completed. In the course of the operation, they destroyed the staffs of ten zonal Islamic committees, the united staff of the Province of Astana,[4] the main Islamic committee of the Panjshir valley, the committees of Parvan and Kapista Provinces, weapons depots, ammunition depots, food stores, and other supply depots. They captured a large number of secret documents. Among these were the structure of the leadership of the guerrilla movement, lists of party members of the Islamic Society of Afghanistan with photographs and forms, lists of active members underground in Kabul, the plan for combat against the government and Soviet forces in the coming years, as well as lists of officials marked for elimination.

Of definite interest is the application of forces and resources in an operation conducted by Soviet and Afghan forces in the region of Ghazni from 25 June to 3 July 1982. The operation was somewhat smaller than the Panjshir in the quantity of personnel and equipment and the scale of the action. The Soviet side included the 108th Motorized Rifle Division, the 56th Air Assault Brigade, and the 191st Motorized Rifle Regiment, while the DRA force was the 15th Tank Brigade. The operation was conducted over a swath that was 70 kilometers long and 15 to 25 kilometers wide. The AO covered two regions.

In the Ghazni operation, motorized rifle units and subunits masterfully used the terrain and the absence of a continuous enemy perimeter defense to seal in the enemy with a small force advancing from the front and then attacked on the flank and rear to destroy the enemy. During this action, the Soviets widely employed small enveloping and raiding detachments that bravely penetrated into the depth of the enemy defense and decisively acted to aid the advance of the main force.

This operation especially highlighted the effectiveness of subunits, reinforced with flame throwers, attacking at night. Under the cover of night, they crossed the dead space undetected and approached close to the enemy firing positions. The enemy's heavy weapons were kept in caves and recesses. The force attacked and destroyed the weapons with flame throwers.

The Soviet method of artillery support to the advancing force is particularly instructive. Part of this support included establishing a moving artillery barrage in front of the advancing force while the BMPs, tanks, BTRs, ZSUs, and antitank guided missiles (ATGMs) conducted aimed, direct fire. This effectively suppressed the firing accuracy of the Mujahideen and reduced casualties among the advancing force.

A distinguishing feature of the operation was the key mission to encircle and destroy the enemy grouping in the Ghazni region. The encirclement was conducted by *bronnegruppa,* which secretly encircled a village and occupied favorable lines on the flanks of the enemy. Simultaneously, the dismounted motorized rifle subunits conducted a deep encirclement of positions and closed the ring of encirclement from the west. This cut off the Mujahideen withdrawal route into the mountains. Besides this, the Soviets conducted an air assault to seize a separate dominant height. The encircled enemy was destroyed primarily with air strikes and artillery fire, and then the destruction was completed by advancing motorized rifle forces.

This new method of combating the Mujahideen in the Ghazni operation began with a special tactical unit—the Spetsnaz plus some alert subunits. Their high effectiveness was achieved by having intelligence about enemy objectives. The Spetsnaz subunit and alert subunits acted on this intelligence quickly. They conducted artillery fire on the objectives and fired remotely delivered mines on the enemy as armed forces moved on helicopters to the designated region. Having completed the destruction of the enemy, they returned to base on the helicopters.

In this fashion, the Ghazni operation not only used the lessons learned in the Panjshir operation but also applied several new approaches to combat. In this case, these approaches were unexpected by the enemy and led to success.

The goal of these operations was to destroy strong enemy groups through direct armed conflict. The operations were widespread over Afghanistan. As a rule, they were carried out in phases by strong groups of Soviet and Afghan forces in wide swaths and to great depths. The result of these operations was to force the enemy out of his primary base regions and destroy the enemy detachments in detail.

The divisions and units often took to the field in their own AOs. This happened when the enemy groups were spread out over a large stretch of territory in small detachments. The enemy would occupy villages, canyons, and mountains, where they could not be encircled. Then, the Soviets divided the region into zones, each small enough that they could be managed by a division or by a regiment in an independent action. At that time, the 40th Army commander provided aviation support to those who had the most need of it and used aircraft to block the area of operation. The operations conducted in January 1983 are more instructive of this type of operation. These operations were conducted in the provinces of Kabul, Logar and Wardak against some 20 enemy detachments with a total strength of about 2,000 men.

In these operations, the Soviet command assigned the 108th and 201st Motorized Rifle Divisions, regiments of the 103rd Airborne Division, the 56th Air Assault Brigade, and 40th Army regiments. They divided this vast expanse into zones for tactical groups and operational groups. This allowed the force to act simultaneously against all the enemy groups in the various regions, to pin down the enemy maneuver forces, and to defeat the enemy in detail.

A different, yet effective way to destroy enemy forces was to commit divisions and regiments simultaneously in several different directions. These advances were supported by frontal and army aviation and air assault landings. This approach was used in those circumstances where the enemy groups were located in different directions and at different distances. Therefore, the 40th Army command tried to destroy these simultaneously. To prevent the withdrawal of the Mujahideen into his rear areas, the 40th Army used air assaults to cut them off. The air assault forces would seize high ground and reinforce it for a stubborn defense, thus becoming the anvil. Aviation maintained control over the air space of the entire area of operations and was on call to the ground forces commander who could apply individual and massed air strikes where needed, even out to the operation boundaries and on the approaches. The advancing ground forces developed methods of sweeping an area as they would move from one phase line to the next. This type of operation could last for eight to ten days.

A special type of operation was the operation to safeguard convoys. The most powerful of this type of operation was "Magistral," which was conducted from 20 November 1987 to 21 January 1988. For the conduct of this operation, the 40th Army assembled the 108th Motorized Rifle Division, 103rd Airborne Division, 56th Separate Air Assault Brigade, 345th Separate Airborne Regiment, and the 191st Separate Motorized Rifle Regiment. The Afghan government provided the 8th, 11th, 12th, 14th, and 25 Infantry Divisions, the 15th Tank Brigade, and the Commando regiment (Maps 7 and 8).

During the preparation for the operation, every division and regiment received an independent area of responsibility in which they were to conduct

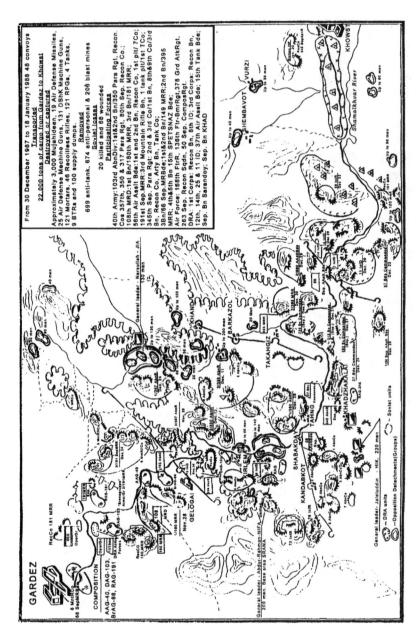

Map 7. Joint combat actions in Operation Magistral

Map 8. Maneuver in Operation Magistral

active combat in order to ensure that the enemy would not break through to the supply convoys. Besides this, aviation was on alert at airfields to conduct air strikes at the order of the combined arms commander.

There were several days from the start of the operation to the movement of the first column as forces seized their areas of responsibility, fortified favorable positions, established fire plans, and organized reconnaissance. In those regions where they discovered the enemy, they destroyed or forced the enemy out with short surprise strikes by ground forces and aviation. As a result of the thorough preparation and precise execution, Operation "Magistral" was a success.

A noteworthy operation for the Soviet forces in Afghanistan was their withdrawal operation from the country. In accordance with the Geneva Agreement signed in April 1988, the withdrawal was conducted in two phases. After transferring part of the combat equipment and weapons to the Afghan Army, the Soviets still had to withdraw 110,000 personnel, 500 tanks, 4,000 BMPs and BTRs, 2,000 artillery pieces and mortars, and some 16,000 trucks. The withdrawal was complicated by the fact that at that time the armed opposition had more than 150,000 men and controlled over 80 percent of the country.

The first stage of the operation lasted from 15 May to 15 August 1988, and the size of the LCOSF was cut in half by force withdrawal (Map 9). The remaining forces, not garrisoning the withdrawal route, moved out of two zones located south of Kabul and Shindand. Following the first phase, there was a three month break, after which the second phase of the withdrawal began. The second phase lasted from 15 November 1988 to 15 February 1989.

Both phases of the operation required a great deal of preparation. Considering the long stretch of the withdrawal route and the severe terrain along the way, both withdrawal routes were divided into 120 to 150 kilometer stretches—each stretch a day's motor march. At the end of every stretch, the march column would concentrate into a prepared bivouac site where they would refuel, carry out routine repairs, feed the personnel, provide needed medical treatment, and allow the personnel to sleep. The prepared bivouac sites were prepared for defense with dug-in positions for tanks and BMPs. There was a prepared fire plan. The site was protected by mine fields. Further, there were coordination plans for convoys and the stationary guard posts that lined the route. Army aviation also supported the march units. Defensive battle planning was conducted between the march columns and army aviation. Detailed artillery fire support was planned to cover the withdrawing units during the withdrawal and for three or four days before each march unit began its withdrawal (Map 10).

During the operation, the demand for aviation support was heavy. Thus, on 5 August 1988, 74 sorties were flown in the Kandahar region. They made 37 bombing and strafing attacks.

Engineering support for the withdrawal was essential. Between 29 June and 9 July, sappers discovered and removed 193 antitank mines, 138 antipersonnel

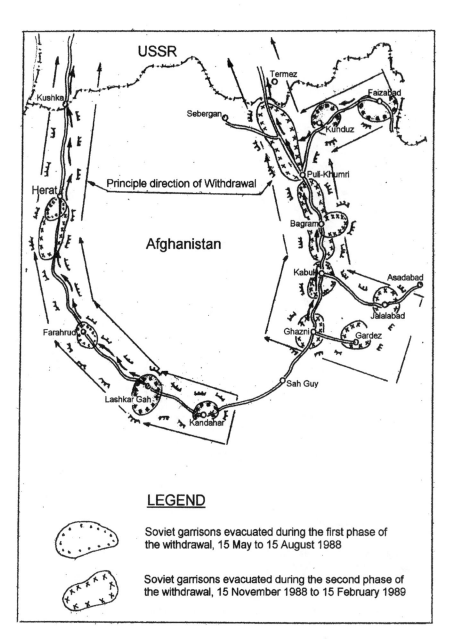

USSR

Kushka

Termez

Faizabad

Sebergan

Kunduz

Herat

Principle direction of Withdrawal

Puli-Khumri

Bagram

Afghanistan

Kabul

Asadabad

Jalalabad

Farahrud

Ghazni

Gardez

Lashkar Gah

Sah Guy

Kandahar

LEGEND

Soviet garrisons evacuated during the first phase of the withdrawal, 15 May to 15 August 1988

Soviet garrisons evacuated during the second phase of the withdrawal, 15 November 1988 to 15 February 1989

Map 9. Withdrawal operation

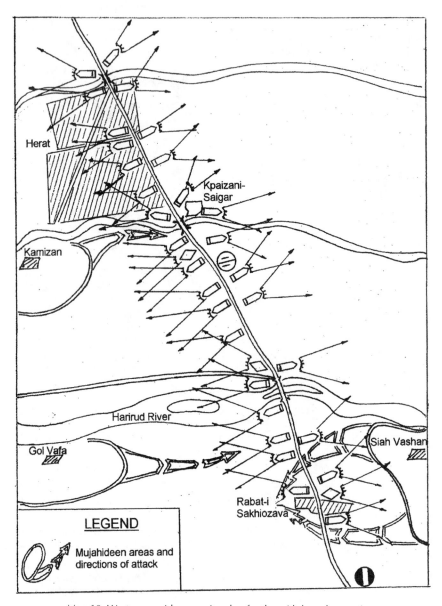

Map 10. Western corridor security plan for the withdrawal operation

mines, and 95 powerful *fougasse* in the Taleqan sector between Kishim and Karashar.[5] All levels of command between separate regiments and the 40th Army constituted movement support detachments to move in front of the convoys and clear the road. It normally took an hour to clear 200 to 300 meters of mined road. The engineers fulfilled their mission successfully.

Soviet forces in Afghanistan not only used the academic examples and methods of the operational art for conducting combat, but they discovered many new methods. It would be a mistake to say that all the operations were successful or that all the results were expected. Most often, operations ended without the destruction of the enemy, and if they forced the enemy out of his occupied positions, he would reassemble and return in force after the operation was over. The practice of massing a large number of regular forces against a small group of irregular forces to fight a guerrilla war on rugged terrain is bankrupt. However, even in these circumstances, when the Soviets were able to effectively coordinate all their forces and achieve surprise, their operations were successful. The war in Afghanistan posed many issues for the Soviet operational art, which await resolution. Unfortunately, no one was even thinking about these issues then—or now.

Editors' comments: The Red Army was victorious in World War II through their mastery of the operational art—based on the skillful employment of large armies, fronts, and groups of fronts. The Soviets were masters of large-scale successive operations with which they kept their enemy off balance and his reserve committed in the wrong sector. The Soviets expected to fight World War III operationally. The Soviet Army incorporated tactical predictability that allowed it operational flexibility. Its structure, weaponry, tactics, and training all supported this operational focus. As a result, the Soviet small unit leaders lacked the tactical expertise necessary to fight a determined guerrilla foe in a purely tactical fight.

When the Soviets invaded Afghanistan, they soon found themselves fighting the Mujahideen. Naturally, the Soviets tried to defeat the Mujahideen with large, sweeping operations. Instead of victory, the operations used a lot of fuel, covered a lot of territory, and accomplished little. Still, the first years of the war were marked by a series of successive operations, more appropriate for the Northern European plain than the rugged mountains of Afghanistan.

Guerrilla warfare is fought at the tactical level. Sometimes, when a large number of guerrillas are forced to defend an area, an operation is appropriate. However, the vast majority of Soviet operations were wasted effort. The best-executed Soviet operations were the invasion, "Magistral," and the withdrawal. The Mujahideen staged few operations, primarily large-scale road blocks and sieges. Mujahideen excelled at traditional guerrilla tactical combat—and Soviet small unit leaders were hard pressed to match them at the squad and platoon level. Squad and platoon level combat is the business of sergeants and new lieutenants. The Soviet sergeants were conscripts who had attended a six-month NCO course.

The lieutenants were fresh out of their commissioning academies. The least-seasoned Soviet leaders were trying to defeat the guerrilla in the guerrilla's back yard. It was an uneven contest that Soviet firepower unsuccessfully tried to offset.

The Soviets only had the one army in Afghanistan, and even when the 40th Army combined with DRA forces, it lacked the amount of forces required for consecutive operations that Soviet warfighting envisioned. Further, after the necessary forces were deployed to guard base camps, airfields, cities, depots, government buildings, lines of communication, and key points, the 40th Army found itself severely constrained in the amount of force that was available to fight. Still, the Soviet experience of war dictated that success came through operations. The 40th Army commanders responded by conducting operations with considerably smaller forces—divisions, brigades, and regiments. Compounding the problem, these smaller forces were composite forces formed for the operation using what forces remained. As a result, under-strength battalions from different regiments and under-strength regiments from different divisions were thrown together. Naturally, these ad hoc detachments and formations did not work together as smoothly as they would under their normal command. Coordination remained a major problem throughout the conduct of Soviet operations. As the troop list on Map 7 demonstrates, even a major operation such as Magistral used composite units.

Operations were within the comfort level of the Soviet commanders in Afghanistan and so they continued them—despite their lack of success. The non-traditional airborne, air assault, and Spetsnaz forces, who were trained to conduct tactical battles independently, were more successful in breaking away from this operational fixation and carrying the fight to the Mujahideen.

5

Combined Arms Tactics

The unique requirements of the Soviet forces mission, the peculiar Mujahideen tactics, and the difficult terrain and climate of Afghanistan required the adoption of different forms and methods of combat. The more typical tactics were the raid, the cordon and search, the ambush, and the convoy escort.

RAIDS[1]

Raids moved subunits along a planned route or direction to a designated finishing point that was located from several dozen kilometers up to 100 kilometers away. In the course of this movement, the subunits would search for Mujahideen detachments and destroy them.[2] A Soviet raiding detachment usually consisted of one or two Soviet battalions mounted on BMPs or BTRs plus reconnaissance, engineer, and artillery subunits. Initially, Soviet authorities required that raids be combined to include Afghan subunits. Raiding detachments were supported by helicopter gunships and transport helicopters as well as aircraft from frontal aviation. A raid would normally last from three to seven days. The Afghan forces provided intelligence on the route and Mujahideen to the raiding detachment commander. Sometimes, guides from the Afghan MVD or KHAD would accompany the raid.

During the first phase of the war, 40th Army reconnaissance only provided the staff with information about the enemy and the area in close proximity to the Soviet base camps. Therefore, the Soviet advisers and the Afghan intelligence organs had to provide the basic data about the Mujahideen locations and activities which the commanders and staffs used for planning raids. The basic data did not reflect the complete intelligence picture or the actual situation. The enemy strength was usually deliberately exaggerated. The DRA [and Soviet advisers] did this in order to convince the Soviets that the DRA forces were inadequate for the task without the participation of Soviet forces. Unfortunately, there were even instances where the intelligence reports were simply lies, and if fire missions were conducted solely on the basis of this data, without cross-checking it, artillery fire and air strikes would fall on the peaceful population. Therefore, all intelligence reports about the enemy had to be checked during the course of the raid by questioning the local inhabitants and interrogating prisoners.

Already by the spring of 1980, the Mujahideen were attacking guard posts, Soviet base camps, military columns, supply convoys, and administrative and industrial centers. The Soviet forces began conducting independent raids as well as raids with the DRA divisions and regiments.

Major A. P. Pivovarenko remembers the first raid conducted by his Soviet subunit in Afghanistan.[3] At the time, he was a reconnaissance platoon leader. "In April to 1980, the situation along a section of the Termez-Kabul highway was very difficult. Mujahideen bands would frequently attack military columns and supply convoys. Therefore, the Soviet command decided that Soviet forces would actively seek combat with the resistance. A motorized rifle battalion that had earlier been securing a section of this road was ordered to conduct a raid from Charikar to Bamian and then to Pandjab. The battalion was reinforced with a tank and reconnaissance company, a self-propelled artillery battery, a platoon of ZSU 23-4s, and a sapper squad.

"This first raid by our battalion began on the night of 20 May (Map 11). At dusk, we set out on our vehicles for the town of Ghorband. At that time shots rang out from the town that, according to agent intelligence, contained a large detachment of Afghan soldiers, who were reported to be preparing to go over to the resistance. In response to the Mujahideen fire, the raiding detachment increased their speed and returned fire as they burst into Ghorband. We killed six Mujahideen, set one BMP and five trucks on fire, and captured two BMPs. Despite the swiftness of our action, the main part of the resistance slipped away from our attack in the direction of the city of Bamian. Our raiding detachment followed rapidly in pursuit. However, as we approached the outskirts of the city, we were ambushed. We lost a BMP and a ZSU-23-4, but no personnel. We launched an attack that evening and finally captured the city. We stayed there for a month. During the course of that time, we conducted two raids near the city, which had no results.

"Only on the 28 of June did our raiding detachment continue to move in the direction of Pandjab. We swept some nearby areas looking for depots with weapons and ammunition, but we did not find any depots or guerrilla bands. After ten days, the battalion had to return to Bamian.

"On 10 July, as the battalion was returning to rejoin its regiment, it was fired on by the Mujahideen from the opposite peak. We lost four men who were killed outright or died enroute to the hospital. This was the price of our first raid."

From this vignette, one can note that the casualties from this raid might have been significantly larger if one remembers that the town was captured from the

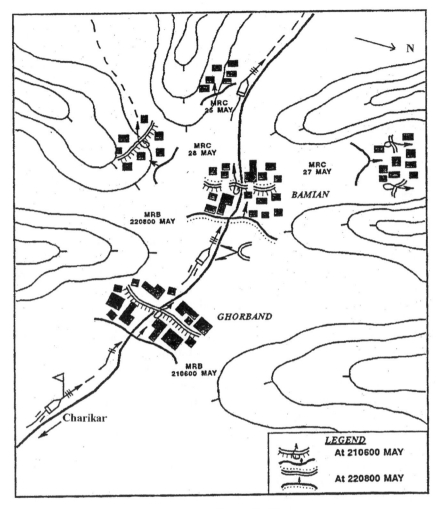

Map 11. Ghorband raid

march without the required reconnaissance. The battalion commander's decision was characteristically unilinear, in that he did not quickly consider the possibility of enemy deception or maneuver. This appears to be a highly visible miscalculation in the commanders' preparation by officers in the beginning of the war in Afghanistan.

Major S. V. Nikitin[4] relates another vignette about an unsuccessful raid by a reconnaissance company from a separate reconnaissance battalion in May 1980. The event occurred in Farah Province. While approaching the foot of the Lor Koh mountains, they discovered truck tracks leading into a mountain canyon. An attempt to enter the canyon on a BMP did not succeed. During the entry into the canyon, the BMP hit a mine. The reconnaissance company then attempted to enter the canyon on foot. They had gone about 200 to 300 meters when one of the reconnaissance groups discovered a large cache of supplies and food on the left side of the road. There was not a single local person anywhere near by. The company continued to move into the canyon where it took a sharp turn to the right. As they entered the turn, a heavy machine gun opened up on the scouts. Three scouts were wounded and sheltered behind a large boulder. Attempts to evacuate the wounded failed since the machine gun fire covered all approaches to the boulder. Only the approach of night allowed the scouts to reach their comrades. By then all three were dead. They recovered the dead and the reconnaissance company left the canyon and blocked the entrance to the canyon.

By the next morning, the Soviets had assembled the separate reconnaissance battalion and a motorized rifle battalion outside the canyon. They launched an attempt to take the canyon by advancing along the roads. However, the subunits were only able to reach the bend in the canyon. They were stopped by the fire from the machine gun which was protected by a stone trench. It should be noted that this attack was attempted without artillery support and the Soviets made no attempt to use maneuver and to cover the advance with fire.

The commander called in an SU-25 close air support aircraft[5] to suppress the machine gun fire. The aircraft accurately bombed the machine gun position and destroyed the machine gun. The reconnaissance battalion, with its commander in the lead, pushed forward in the attack. They successfully carried the canyon bend and advanced another 500 meters into the canyon. At that point, Mujahideen suddenly opened up with automatic weapons, wounding the battalion commander and killing two scouts. Enemy fire pinned the scouts down as they went to ground.

The 40th Army commander[6] arrived on the scene an hour later. He analyzed the situation and determined the mission. He decided to seize the canyon following a ten-minute artillery strike. Plumes of flame shot out as artillery rounds exploded here and there on the mountain slopes. A loud echo floated through the canyon. Then it became quiet. The battalion again began to attack and advanced 75 to 100 meters further when it was met by enemy small arms fire. Two more scouts were wounded. Artillery fire was called in, but they were unable to adjust the fire to suppress the Mujahideen firing positions, so they just fired artillery into the general area. This type of fire in the mountains proved ineffective.

The reconnaissance battalion was unable to seize the canyon and was committed on a different axis. The motorized rifle battalion took over the mission of seizing the canyon and did so in the course of the next two days, thanks to helicopter gunship and aviation support. The enemy left eight dead on the battlefield. Their bodies were hidden in the mountains. As eyewitnesses stated, the personnel of the reconnaissance battalion and the motorized rifle battalion fought heroically. But they lacked combat seasoning; they lacked experience in the tactical lessons of conducting fire and directing subunits in battle. Experience showed that reconnaissance forces and motorized riflemen could successfully conduct combat in the mountains only if they were supported by aviation, helicopter gunships, and artillery. If these fire support systems were provided accurate target data, and if they did not conduct normative area fires, they could achieve excellent results.[7]

Lieutenant Colonel A. L. Makkoveev[8] remembers an incident from his service in Afghanistan. "Throughout the winter of 1979–1980, it was quiet in the region south of Kabul. However, in the spring and early summer, the Mujahideen began actions in the area. Combat with these Mujahideen was complicated by their audacity and decisiveness. After shelling Soviet forces, they would not get involved in a drawn-out fire fight, but would quickly withdraw and hide in the mountains. This situation was intolerable.

"Since reconnaissance had not disclosed the exact location of the enemy detachment, the command decided to conduct a search near the village of Kirgak. They constituted a raiding detachment consisting of the 3rd Mountain Rifle Battalion reinforced with my 7th Motorized Rifle Company mounted on BMPs.

"At 0500 hours on 22 July, the raiding detachment began to move out on the mission. Riding on the BMPs along a small stream, we were able to move four to five kilometers. After this, in view of the increased number of obstacles, the battalion commander ordered my personnel to dismount and move on foot. The BMPs were grouped in an assembly area and guarded by a platoon.

"We were moving dismounted along the crest of mountain #4. The battalion commander, Captain Yu. P. Levintas, ordered my company to sweep through a village located to the right of the height on which we were moving (Map 12). We were to sweep through the village and check for Mujahideen. Then my company was supposed to move out of the village in a column parallel to our present height along a trail and link up with the main detachment. The company formed into a combat line and began to move to the village.

"I positioned my machine gun/grenade launcher platoon[9] on the eastern flank to provide covering fire. In the course of a half hour, my company conducted a search of the village houses and basements. They found no trace of the enemy in the village, and the men of the company concentrated near the bridge to the southwest of the village walls. I took a head count of my men. Everyone was there.

"At that moment, the Mujahideen opened up on us with heavy fire from hill #2. The company went to ground behind the adobe walls and established a defense along the southwest and west outskirts of the village. I decided to send two squads from the 1st MRP to flank height #2 from the right and left. They would move under the company covering fire and then we would destroy the enemy with an attack from the front and rear. At the same time, I also decided to dispatch a patrol squad to the top of hill #1 to seize it. However, just as the squads started to move to carry out their missions, the Mujahideen opened fire on them from heights #1, #2, and #3 and forced them to take cover.

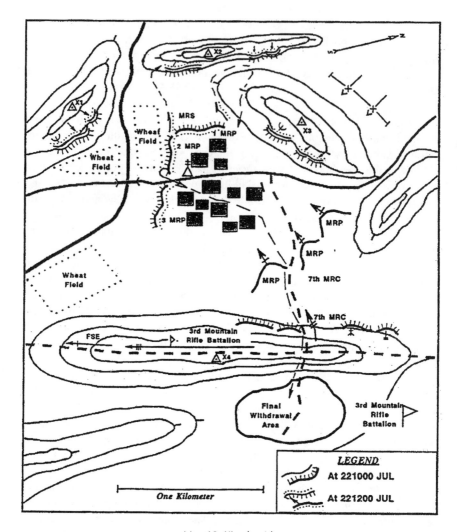

Map 12. Kirgak raid

"After thirty minutes, the battalion commander ordered me to withdraw my company and reassemble on hill #4. During the withdrawal of my company, we were pinned down by Mujahideen fire from hill #3. We were pinned in a fire sac and we were unable effectively to counteract the enemy who held the dominant terrain. They could see every move my force made. I called for help.

"After helicopter gunships destroyed the Mujahideen, the company was able to withdraw at noon and reassemble on height #4. I had dead and wounded. In the course of carrying out my mission, I should have conducted a thorough reconnaissance and seized the dominant terrain where the Mujahideen were able to surprise us and cover the entire area by fire. We learned valuable lessons in fighting the Mujahideen in the mountains."

This example of a first raid showed that the limited time available to prepare the force was primarily spent in formal inspection of weapons, equipment, and personnel gear. Scant detail was devoted to the reconnaissance of the enemy and his tactics. During the raid, the force moved on the roads, which made it easy for the enemy to find them and take countermeasures. This negated the results of the raid and resulted in unnecessarily large losses in personnel, arms, and equipment.

Examples of previous unsuccessful raids were studied when training commanders and forces for combat. Major S. V. Poleshchuk[10] commanded a motorized rifle platoon during a raid. In September–November 1980, Shir Agha led a strong Mujahideen detachment in the villages in the eastern portion of Herat Province. Shir Agha supported the prosperous elements of the villages and terrorized the peaceful populations. He killed DRA Party activists. He attacked DRA guard posts in the east of the province. The DRA Army Commander relayed a request through his Soviet adviser to the Soviet Commander to conduct a combined Soviet-Afghan raid to find and destroy Shir Agha's detachment.

"In the second half of November, we began planning for the raid and preparing the force for it. Two Soviet motorized rifle battalions, a Soviet artillery battalion, an Afghan infantry battalion, and a Soviet tank company made up the raiding force. From ground and aerial reconnaissance, we determined where the Mujahideen detachment was located and its strength—80 men.

"The raid elements began tactical training in blocking villages and destroying the enemy in house-to-house fighting while supported by tanks and artillery. Motorized rifle companies were organized into combat groups and trained for independent actions away from the main body. Tank, BMP, BTR, and artillery tractor drivers prepared their vehicles for winter driving in the mountains. The weapons and combat equipment were cleaned, repaired, and maintained, as was the reconnaissance equipment, including night vision devices. We drew additional clothing and equipment to prevent frostbite. The day before the raid, we were given our orders and we coordinated our actions around the map.

"Early on the morning of 5 December, our raiding detachment completed a 40-kilometer road march and arrived in the area where we expected to find Shir Agha's detachment. We dismounted the force while the artillery battalion occupied firing positions close to the road leading to Herat city (Map 13).

"The dismounted troops formed into a combat line and began moving in a northerly direction. At 1000 hours, the 3rd Motorized Battalion and the Afghan battalion approached the village of Haji Dara while the 1st Motorized Rifle Battalion approached another village located some two kilometers to the northwest. We did not find any Mujahideen in these villages or in neighboring villages. The force conducted a search along the ridge of the Sel Selakoh-i Dawindar mountain range going some 15 kilometers to the east and 10 kilometers to the west of

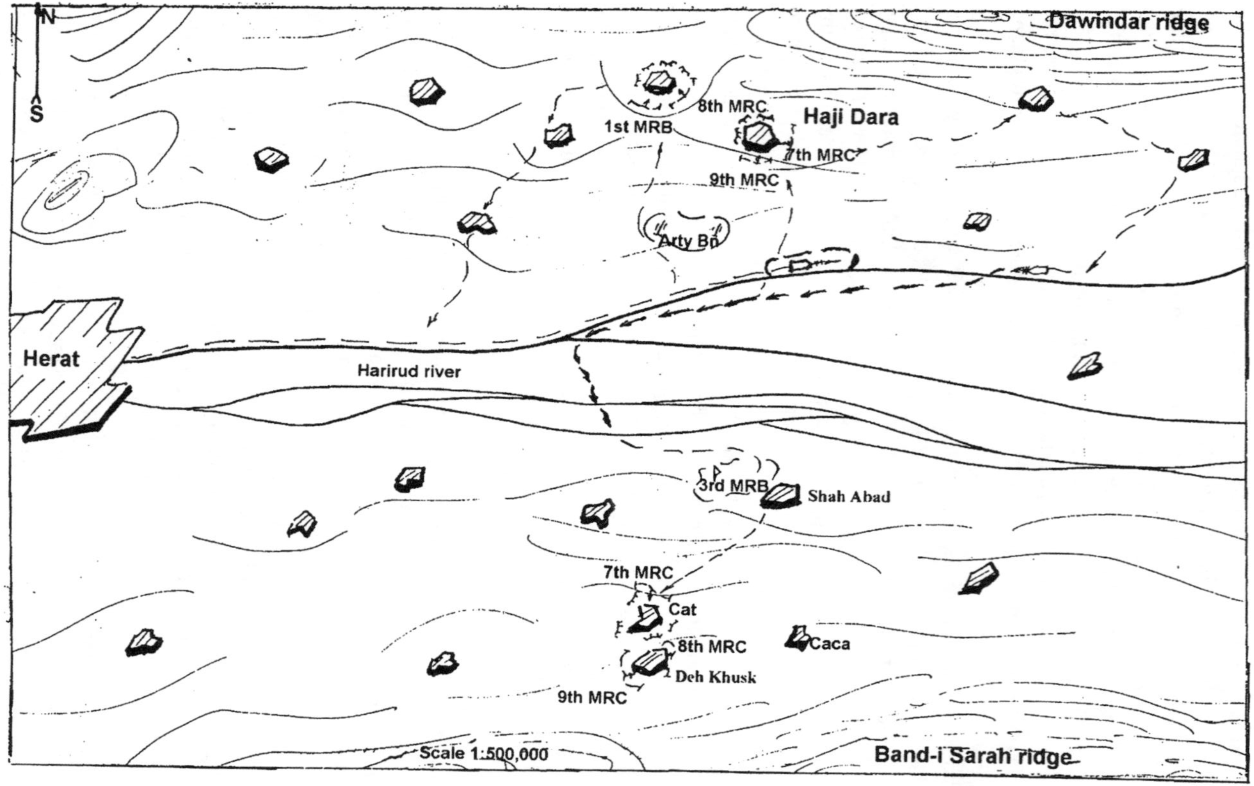

Map 13. Deh Khusk raid

Haji Dara. Then the battalions came down from the mountain to the road. The 1st MRB, the Afghan battalion, and the Soviet tank company returned to their base camps. The 3rd MRB continued the raid moving south to the northwest slope of the Band-i Sarah mountain range. The detachment established a night lager at the village of Shah Abad. The night passed quietly. Early in the morning, Major A. P. Veresotskiy, the battalion commander, briefed his company commanders on the plan for continuing the raid. The dismounted force would secretly move out to the villages of Cat and Deh Khusk. Then, the 7th MRC, reinforced with the mortar battery and an Afghan infantry company, would block and destroy the enemy in Cat village. The remaining force would block and destroy the enemy in Deh Kusk.

"At 0800 on the 5th of December, the detachment continued its mission. After four hours, the forward patrol of the 7th MRC discovered an abandoned Mujahideen ambush site on the approach to Cat. The company was moving in combat groups commanded by Lieutenants A. Chebikin and V. Nakhushev and Warrant Officer L. Samoevskiy. They moved to block the village. They occupied the dominant terrain and sealed all exits from the village. As they were moving to the blocking positions, the Mujahideen discovered the forward patrol. The patrol initiated combat and held the enemy's attention. Therefore, the Mujahideen did not anticipate the sudden appearance of the company at the village. The Afghan company began to sweep the village. Fighting broke out at a house where a small group of men, led by the son of Shir-Agah, were sheltering. But this flare-up was quickly extinguished. We killed 8 Mujahideen and captured 13 more. We captured 40 firearms and a large amount of ammunition. The company lost one KIA and two WIA."

The other companies were unable to accomplish their mission. The 7th MRC was discovered long before the 8th MRC and 9th MRC arrived at the Deh Khusk village. This allowed Shir-Agah and his Mujahideen units to escape into the mountains. Convinced that the enemy had escaped, the detachment returned to base camp.

The raid lasted two days. It was characterized by quick changes in the direction of the force, by deceiving the enemy using the departure of a major portion of the force to base camp, by a high degree of coordination among the personnel, and by confident leadership by the commanders. The preparation of the subunits for the raid was a significant improvement.

The following vignette was widely used throughout Afghanistan for instruction. The first raids demonstrated that raiding detachments that stayed in the valleys and on the roads had little success. The Mujahideen had an excellent system of reconnaissance and information. They not only knew when Soviet forces were moving through their region, but they also knew about the plans of upcoming actions of the Soviet command. As a result, the Mujahideen would select optimum terrain and establish ambushes along the route of the raiding detachment or hide themselves in the mountains, green zones, or villages ahead of time. Soviet subunits that served in raiding detachments learned from the bitter experience of their predecessors to act more carefully, avoid moving in a straight line, and to use a wide variety of deception measures and military cunning.

Captain V. I. Sidyakin commanded a company in 1980 that conducted a raid to seize an enemy objective in a mountain canyon. The terrain was extremely rugged. High mountains with dome-shaped peaks, steep slopes, and canyons retarded movement. Many boulders crowned each height from behind which the enemy could hide poised to fire at any minute.

The company command organized his unit to conduct area reconnaissance and allow it to find enemy strong points, ambushes, and heavy weapons systems. His forward patrol allowed the company to move successfully. He included a maintenance element in order to eliminate mechanical breakdowns quickly during movement. His rear guard patrol followed the column within visual contact and fire support of the main force.

All-around observation was organized along the entire length of the column. Weapons were kept ready for immediate deployment in any sector. As the column approached the mission area, the probability of contact increased. Personnel riding on the armored BMPs became prime targets.[11] The company commander, in order to disperse the motorized rifle men, gave the order to dismount and deploy in combat formation.

V. Sidyakin recalls: "I understood that the enemy which was sheltering in some rugged mountains considered their flanks unassailable. Preceding military experience showed that Soviet subunits did not adapt to the special conditions of mountainous terrain. In the first months of the war, they usually traveled only on the roads, ignoring simple actions such as maneuver, flank attacks, and military cunning. As a result, their combat often achieved limited results as the enemy successfully withdrew into the mountains while the Soviet subunits suffered casualties. After I received my combat mission, I worried about how I could carry out the mission while preserving the lives of my subordinates. In the end, I concluded that, despite the ruggedness of the terrain, it was necessary for part of my force to move along the ridges on the heights to the right of the road. The ridges overlooked paths which seemed to me to be ideal for a Mujahideen withdrawal. I selected a motorized rifle platoon for the mission. I moved the remaining two platoons and reinforcements on the road at a distance from the mountain tops which would preclude destruction of my personnel from a Mujahideen ambush. These platoons moved slowly by bounds from phase line to phase line. I could not allow my platoon on the heights to fall behind the company advancing slowly on the road. If that happened, the value of the platoon would fall to nothing. Therefore, disregarding the tremendous loss of time, we moved very slowly while remaining ready for combat. After the start of a bound forward, the Mujahideen opened fire on the company. My personnel went to ground. I requested supporting artillery fire. After the artillery fire fell, the enemy attempted to withdraw into the mountains. They came under fire from my platoon on the mountain ridge. The Mujahideen did not expect this development and they began to panic. Taking advantage of this surprise, my company quickly attacked to overcome their strong point."

In this vignette, the Mujahideen were forced onto the defense. The situation and terrain allowed the commander to hit the enemy on the flank and rear. That the commander recognized this enabled him to win this tough fight.

However, maneuver during a raid did not always have the desired results. Reasons varied, but most often it was the lack of combat experience of the recently arrived replacement commanders and soldiers, the limited experience of individual officers when commanding subunits in difficult situations, the fast pace of events where senior commanders forced their subordinates to do something in a rush without considering the situation, and the discrepancy between intelligence reports and the actual situation. Several of these factors were apparent during this same raid by neighboring companies moving in another direction.

An entire company was moving along a canyon bottom in combat formation when the Mujahideen opened fire on it. The platoons concentrated their fires against the Mujahideen, and, as their fire suppressed the Mujahideen fire, the company began to move forward. Shortly, however, the company began taking new Mujahideen fire and the motorized riflemen again went to ground. The company commander realized that a frontal attack against a dug-in enemy would not succeed. Therefore, he decided to use two platoons to conduct an envelopment and attack the enemy from the rear. However, this maneuver did not succeed since the Mujahideen grasped the scheme of maneuver and, understanding that only one platoon was to their front, counterattacked. It took a large force to throw back this attack and save the platoon.

A flanking detachment was quite useful in destroying the enemy during the conduct of a raid. Major V. V. Vishnevskiy recalls one instance when he was a motorized rifle company commander in Afghanistan. In March 1981, his company participated in a raid to capture a canyon in Lor Koh mountain in Farah Province. The canyon was T-shaped and was about one and a half kilometers deep. The Mujahideen had weapons and food depots in the canyon. The canyon was well-fortified and prepared for defense. Concrete firing positions were sited in several tiers and various enemy weapons systems were mounted in them. The entrance to the canyon was blocked and mined.

The commander of the reconnaissance company moved in front of the raiding detachment. He decided to penetrate the canyon, bypassing the roadblock and moving up the dried-up stream bed. He did not check out the route, but sent his company to carry out the mission. The company quickly halted after it lost two BMPs to mines. The commander did not withdraw the subunit as he should have, but ordered the company to dismount and to move further into the canyon. The Mujahideen let the scouts come deeper into the canyon and then opened up with deadly fire from both sides of the canyon. The company was caught in a bad situation and was only able to withdraw under the cover of darkness. They brought 12 of their dead out of the canyon that night.

Vishnevskiy considered the bitter lesson of the scouts and decided to act differently. He sent two platoons up the slopes of the canyon at night, and they surprised the enemy guards and seized some enemy firing positions (most of the enemy had gone down into the canyon for food and water). In the morning, the platoons on the height provided covering fire for the third platoon as it advanced along the canyon floor. Success in this battle was determined by the nighttime maneuver of the platoons, for which the enemy was unprepared. On the following day, the main body of the raiding detachment arrived at the canyon, destroyed the enemy, and seized the only water spring in the area. With this, a difficult raid became successful.[12]

A combined Soviet-Afghan raid was more successful. Major K. I. Atangenzdiev commanded a mountain rifle battalion. Around the 10th of December 1981, intelligence reports indicated that an armed group of enemy had gathered in the village of Valikheil in Baghlan Province. Major Atangenzdiev's battalion was ordered to conduct a raid to this region, surround the village, and sweep it. He was reinforced with a reconnaissance company, two ZSU-23-4s, and a sapper squad. Two Mi-24 helicopter gunships were placed in support. Two battalions of the Afghan army would also participate in this raid, which was scheduled for 24 December.

In order to keep the movement a secret and achieve surprise, Major Atangenzdiev decided not to use his armored personnel carriers. He used five local trucks driven by Soviet soldiers. After a two-hour nighttime drive, the raiding detachment was ten kilometers from the objective. They dismounted and moved out. During the movement, the soldiers did not talk or smoke, but remained quiet and undetected. They used night vision devices to augment their observation. As dawn broke on the 24th of December, the village of Valikheil was cut off from the mountains by ambushes laid out by mountain rifle companies and the reconnaissance company.

During the morning, the two Afghan battalions and the 3rd Mountain Rifle Company arrived at the village as previously planned. Their goal was to deceive the Mujahideen in Valikheil village and force them to withdraw to the mountains in the direction the ambushes were waiting. The Afghan battalions began sweeping the village, while the 3rd Mountain Rifle Company held the flanks, not allowing the Mujahideen to escape in a direction not covered by ambushes. At the start of the sweep, the Mujahideen in the village of Valikheil attempted to move up a ravine to reach the mountains, which are some 200 to 300 meters away. However, fire from an ambush cut off this route of escape. Twenty-one Mujahideen were captured, along with weapons and a mine-making shop. This raid was a success due to the skillful combined actions of the Soviet and Afghan subunits, the strict observance of noise and light discipline, and the application of military cunning to achieve surprise.

Actions by alert forces were similar to raids.[13] It is true that alert forces did not go out and search for the enemy. They were directed at already confirmed objectives that were sufficiently important. Alert battalions in divisions and alert regiments in the 40th Army were sent out on missions based on intelligence data some 20 to 25 times a month (240 to 300 times annually). Many of these were successful.

Major V. L. Barnovolokov remembers one such raid. The basis for the raid was the arrest of two Mujahideen RPG-7 instructors in the Anavas canyon. During their interrogation, they described how, after the successful Soviet operation in May–June 1985, the Mujahideen established supply points in small villages, which, as a rule, escaped notice. The captives told how there was a supply of arms and ammunition in one house and medical supplies in another house in the village of Kaayi-Mullovan.

After a quick estimate of the situation and tactical calculations, the commander decided on how to exploit this intelligence with two alert reconnaissance companies. The companies were standing by in full combat readiness. The soldiers of these companies had earlier participated in the destruction of a Mujahideen base in the Anavas canyon and knew the area well. The command determined that the alert force would conduct a 40-kilometer road march with two flanking detachments (a platoon each) to make a surprise approach from the east and west, while the main body would seize Kaayi-Mullovan from the north. Air strikes would prevent the withdrawal of Mujahideen to the south. A special search team would search the village and uncover the ammunition and medical dumps.

At 0700 hours on the 16th of August, the raiding detachment moved out. The detachment consisted of the two reconnaissance companies (without their tank platoons), a self-propelled artillery battery, a sapper platoon, and a flame-thrower squad. The column moved three kilometers behind the movement support detachment. The BMPs and BTRs moved off the road, instead of on the road behind tanks with mine sweeps. As they neared the objective, the flanking detachments (which included sappers and artillery forward observers) increased their speed and, by 0930 hours, had occupied their assigned positions. The helicopter gunships hit the mountain tops, possible observation points, and enemy firing positions. The surprise arrival of the subunits at the village and the helicopter strikes discouraged the Mujahideen. This positively influenced the outcome of the battle, and there were no casualties. The information supplied by the prisoners was accurate. Ammunition stores and medical supplies were in the designated houses.

Combat demonstrated that raids by alert subunits were not always successful. One of the causes of this, as confirmed by Soviet soldiers who fought in Afghanistan, is that the commanders and political workers were oriented on the rapid destruction of Mujahideen and tried to get into a specific region or village for combat as quickly as possible without proper reconnaissance and preparation. During the approach march, they did not always allot sufficient attention to reconnaissance and security. The Mujahideen quickly exploited these blunders and inflicted heavy casualties during Soviet movements.

In conclusion, generally the raid was used widely in the beginning of the second phase of the war in Afghanistan. They were effective more often when Soviet and Afghan subunits had strict, goal-oriented training to conduct raids using reconnaissance, secrecy, and surprise.

Editors' comments: The composition of a Soviet raid was similar to that of the Soviet Forward Detachment in conventional combat. However, the forward detachment was part of a larger offensive force and facilitated the movement of the following force. The raid was a limited action against a specific target and was usually an independent action. Where the forward detachment moved rapidly to move behind the defending enemy and seize key terrain or pin down a reserve, the raiding group moved much slower and searched the objectives for Mujahideen and their weapons and supplies. Map 14 shows how a motorized rifle battalion mounted on BTRs and supported by an artillery battalion, a helicopter gunship squadron, and an air assault company advances north from garrison to attack an enemy village. The raid then moves east, while the helicopter gunships screen its flank, to attack an enemy group. After defeating this group, the raid turns south. Once again, the helicopter gunships screen their flank to prevent Mujahideen escape. An air assault company holds an enemy group in place, while the raiding group and helicopter gunships complete the encirclement and destroy the enemy. The raid group then splits into company columns and moves further south through separate canyons to converge on yet another enemy group before returning to garrison.

The skill required to conduct such a raid took a long time to perfect, and many Soviet units fell short of this ideal. The most common problems with Soviet raids were communications over difficult terrain and the fact that the raids moved on predictable routes and failed to insert a blocking force—so that the raiding group usually only engaged the Mujahideen rear guard. Soviet raids were conducted based on intelligence reports. Many of these intelligence reports were from the DRA. Often the DRA reports were inaccurate or wrong and resulted in Soviet raids that were ineffective or failures.

CORDONS AND SEARCHES[14]

When the Soviet Armed Forces entered Afghanistan, their combat manuals did not consider the cordon and search (block and sweep) as a form of combat. Therefore, Soviet forces considered this a new tactic.

Soviet forces used the cordon and search during the Great Patriotic War and also in the first years of the postwar period when NKVD forces used it in the con-

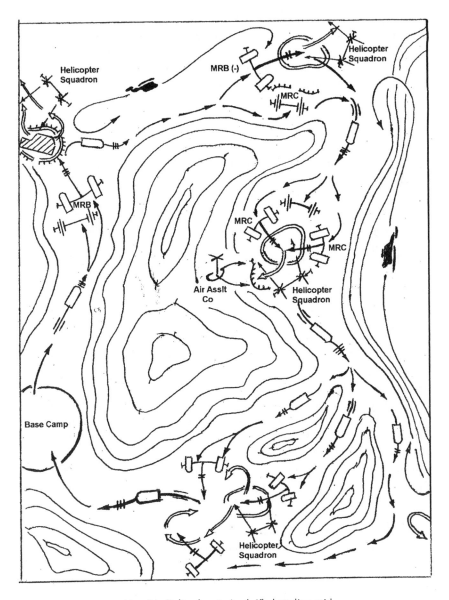

Map 14. Stylized motorized rifle battalion raid

duct of special operations.[15] The NKVD would use the cordon and search in swampy-forested regions. In the sector where the sweep would occur, they would first cut off the routes to block the escape exits of their enemy. During the conduct of special operations in built-up areas, they would check the documents of the inhabitants and inspect the buildings. Armed groups that they discovered were invited to surrender. In the event that the groups refused, they would be eliminated by combined arms combat. In the following years, this tactic virtually disappeared from training and this experience was not used.

In Afghanistan, where there was no front line and the enemy was a guerrilla, the cordon and search proved the basic and more effective tactic against the Mujahideen. Cordons and searches were usually conducted by Soviet and Afghan forces working closely together whenever there was an opportunity to isolate the enemy. Such an action demanded the massing of a significant force. Motorized rifle, reconnaissance, and air assault or paratroop subunits worked with artillery, armor, and sapper subunits.

The cordon and search was conducted in two phases. In the first (cordon) phase, the enemy group was blocked in place, as a rule by Soviet subunits. This was done to prevent enemy withdrawal and to cut him off from outside help from another group. Air assault forces landed on the more remote blocking sites and on those sites that were difficult to reach with combat vehicles. Map 15 shows the employment of helicopters to establish blocking positions against an enemy escape route. [Air assault forces never landed directly on the blocking positions, but at landing zones at which they assembled and then moved to their blocking positions.]

During the second (search) phase, the Afghan army subunits, together with militia and party activists, would destroy or capture the trapped Mujahideen. The Soviet forces would support the Afghan sweep of the isolated site and populated areas. A significant number of forces were required to conduct a successful cordon and search. Thus, a cordon and search in Kama district from 30 March to 1 April 1980 required more than two Soviet motorized rifle battalions, four Afghan infantry battalions, and 100 party activists. In the same year, a cordon and search in Laghman Province used two Soviet motorized rifle battalions and three Afghan infantry battalions.

Conducting a sweep in the mountains, along river flood plains, and along wide canyons required encircling a given region using converging subunits moving from an external circle to its center. Map 16 illustrates that technique. [After the blocking positions are in place, the sweeping group moves through the area between the two rivers.] Also the sweep may be conducted along an axis of advance with the subunits of two sides moving toward each other to a link-up site.

There were several methods of conducting a sweep. In mountain regions, subunits can spread out from a central point in the sweep area moving along valleys in various directions, thus squeezing the enemy into the mountains where they can finally be captured or destroyed.

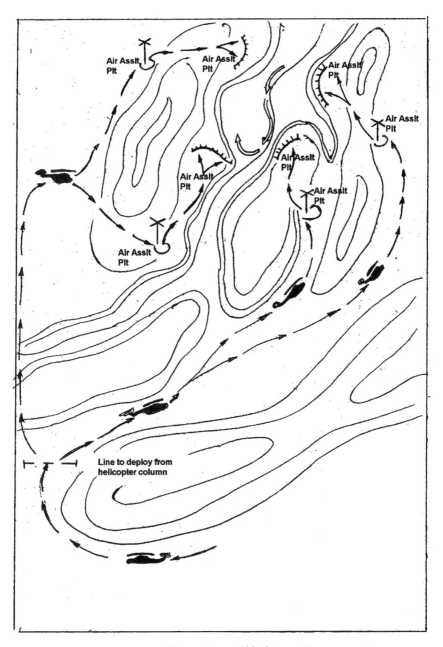

Map 15. Helicopter-inserted blocking positions

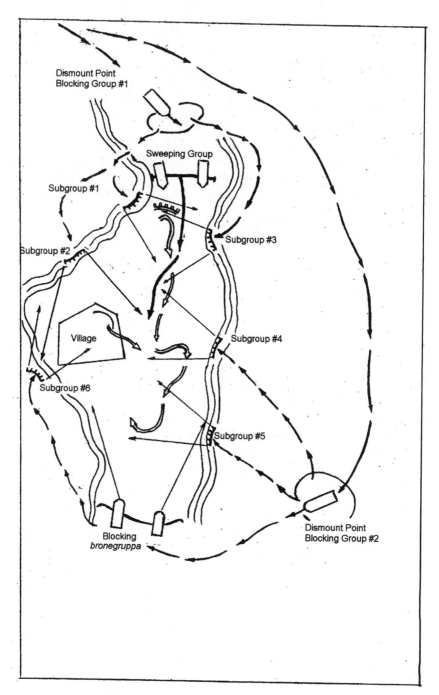

Map 16. Encirclement with converging subunits

During the sweep, motorized rifle forces were usually dismounted. Their armored personnel carriers were used to support them by fire or to kill encircled enemies.

The cordon and search was widely used by Soviet and Afghan forces to fight the enemy located in villages. Thus, at the beginning of November 1981, the advance of winter forced the Mujahideen to leave the mountains and disperse in small villages located one to two days' walk from the Kushka-Herat-Kandahar road. This road was one of the Mujahideen objectives.

The commander of an Afghan regiment received information that a 30-man detachment, armed with automatic weapons, grenade launchers, and explosives and antitank mines had come down from the mountain massif and was located in Nishin village. He passed this information to the Soviet authorities through his Soviet adviser. At 1300 hours on the same day, Captain Yu. V. Ryazanov, the commander of a motorized rifle battalion, received his orders. His motorized rifle battalion, reinforced with an artillery battalion and a tank company and supported with four Mi-24 helicopter gunships, would conduct a 30-kilometer road march and block Nishin village by dawn of the next day. There, they would support an Afghan "Watanparast" battalion so that it could conduct a successful sweep of the village to destroy the Mujahideen.[16]

At 0300 hours, the 3rd MRC commanded by Senior Lieutenant A. A. Kapitonov secretly boarded cargo trucks on loan from the DRA and moved to the village and blocked it from the north and west in order to prevent an enemy breakthrough in the direction of the mountains and the city of Herat (Map 17).

The enemy detected the movement of the battalion main force. The Mujahideen split into two groups and tried to leave the village to the north and west. However, the blocking forces opened fire and forced the Mujahideen to return into the village.

At 0500 hours, the 2d MRC with a tank platoon established a block to the south and east. At the same time, the 1st MRC with two tank platoons occupied an assembly area some two kilometers to the southwest of the village where they remained in readiness to reinforce the blocking subunits. The enemy observed these actions.

The Soviet subunits held their positions blocking the village and waited for the Afghan battalion that would sweep the village. The Mujahideen fired from all sides of the village at the blockers. At the same time, the Mujahideen regrouped, practically unhindered. From their actions, it was clear that there were about ten times more Mujahideen in the village than was originally thought.

At 0600 hours, the enemy went into action. They planned to pin down the northern blocking groups with fire and launch their main attack to the west. The Mujahideen hoped to quickly break through the blocking positions in this attack and then quickly disperse and hide in neighboring villages in order to escape total destruction. In response, the 1st MRC commander, Captain Yu. B. Ryazanov, reinforced the 3rd MRC with two tank platoons and called in artillery fire. The

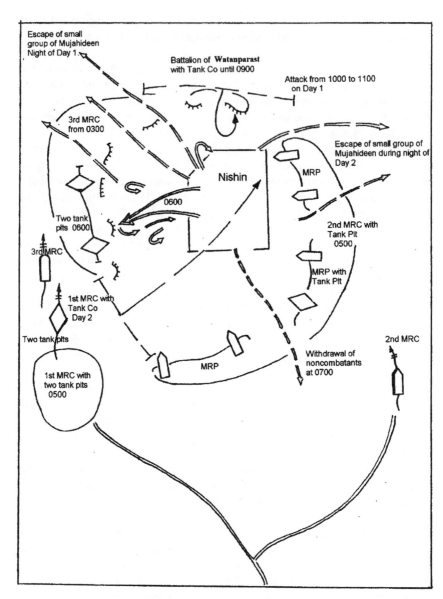

Map 17. Blocking and sweeping Nishin

Mujahideen broke off their attack. The Mujahideen refused the Soviet demands to surrender. The Soviets allowed noncombatants to leave the battle zone after carefully searching them.

At 0900 hours, the "Watanparast" battalion occupied its assembly area some two kilometers to the north of the village. After an hour, this Afghan battalion began its sweep, supported by seven tanks. However, accurate Mujahideen fire forced the DRA troops to go to ground. The DRA force suffered casualties and withdrew to its assembly area. At 1100 hours, the DRA battalion repeated its advance and was driven back again. The ammunition expenditure was tremendous. A new attack, without ammunition resupply, would be pointless. The ammunition resupply finally arrived from the Afghan base camp at dusk. They also provided a hot meal to the personnel since they had brought only enough dry rations for one day.[17]

The "Watanparast" battalion refused to conduct a night attack. The regimental commander ordered the motorized rifle battalion to conduct an attack. At dawn the next morning, the 1st MRC and the tank company attacked, following a 40-minute artillery preparation. By 0700 hours, they had taken the village. However, with the exception of a 15-man rear guard, there were no Mujahideen in the village. Prisoners said that the Mujahideen had exfiltrated through the battalion blocking positions during the night and escaped into the mountains. They had 34 men killed and about 50 wounded. The Soviet and Afghan forces had 13 KIA and 18 WIA and also lost two tanks and one BTR.

Normally, the blocking force was Soviet and the sweeping force was DRA. Occasionally, Soviet forces carried out both missions independently—especially in 1980 and 1981. Major S. V. Poleshchuk remembers that in the middle of spring 1981, the enemy was active in the region of the Kalan-Mirdawoud pass. The enemy detachment that was active in this region was particularly cruel and audacious. They attacked military security posts located in the pass as well as local villages and supply convoys. They assassinated activists who supported communist power. The casualties that the Mujahideen inflicted were appreciable, and the Mujahideen were impossible to apprehend.

On the afternoon of 23 April, the Soviet command learned that Mujahideen would be in the village of Rabati-Payeen the next night. The village was about 70 kilometers from the Soviet base camp. The Soviet command decided to liquidate the enemy. The concept of the operation was that one motorized rifle battalion would move secretly at night and block the enemy withdrawal from the village to the west into the mountains. Another motorized rifle battalion would surround the enemy from the north and east. A third battalion would compress the encirclement and destroy the enemy. In the case of a strong resistance by the Mujahideen, the force would pull back while artillery pulverized them.

As darkness fell, the 3rd MRB, commanded by Major L. P. Zerisonskiy, began its night movement from base camp on its personnel carriers. After two hours, it had advanced 60 kilometers to the Kalan-Mirdawoud pass (Map 18). To go any further on the vehicles might disclose the plan of the operation to the enemy. Therefore, in the interest of achieving surprise and maintaining the secrecy of the approach, the battalion left their personnel carriers with their drivers and gunners while they began to move across the mountains on foot to the village of Rabati-Payeen. The mortar battery carried 82mm mortars. A platoon in every company carried ammunition for the mortars. They also carried the heavy ammunition for the grenade launcher and antitank platoon in this way. They moved about 16 kilometers that night and by dawn were one-and-a-half-to-two kilometers to the west of the village. They positioned ambushes on the eastern slope of the mountain. As a result, they cut off the enemy escape route into the mountains.

The BTRs that the 3rd battalion left parked on the road were placed under the command of the 2d MRB commander, Major V. A. Plotnikov. One-half hour before dawn, his column began to move. At dawn, his force arrived at the village of Rabati-Payeen, deployed into combat formation, and began to envelop the village on three sides.

The enemy sentries gave the alarm only when they heard the noise of the BTRs as they neared the village. The Mujahideen saw that they had only one escape route and began to withdraw into the mountains, where the 3rd MRB was waiting in blocking positions. The 3rd MRB opened up with heavy machine gun, grenade launcher, and mortar fire at a distance of 400 to 600 meters. The enemy was forced to withdraw back into the village where they were surrounded on four sides.

The enemy, taking stock of his situation, adopted some very effective measures for combat in the village. He set up ambushes consisting of a few men positioned in houses, behind adobe walls, and in vineyards. It was very hard to destroy these ambushes with small arms fire. The Mujahideen were protected by thick adobe walls. The antitank platoon and artillery had to destroy this cover. Snipers and grenadiers achieved good results.

The fighting for the village was severe and lasted about five hours. The Soviets killed 40 Mujahideen and captured 14. They killed the Mujahideen leader. This battle finished off this Mujahideen formation and stabilized the situation in the region for a long time.

The more successful cordons and searches of built-up areas to destroy Mujahideen were conducted in accordance with timely, well-developed plans. Conversely, there were many examples where Soviet and Afghan forces rushed to get into position and fell into a Mujahideen ambush waiting on the Soviet or DRA route of advance. Major B. L. Polovinkin remembers one such incident.[18]

Mujahideen mined the road, attacked a convoy, and shelled the nitrogen fertilizer and gas reprocessing factory in his regiment's AO. At 1730 hours on 31 March 1981, company commander Polovinkin was summoned to the division

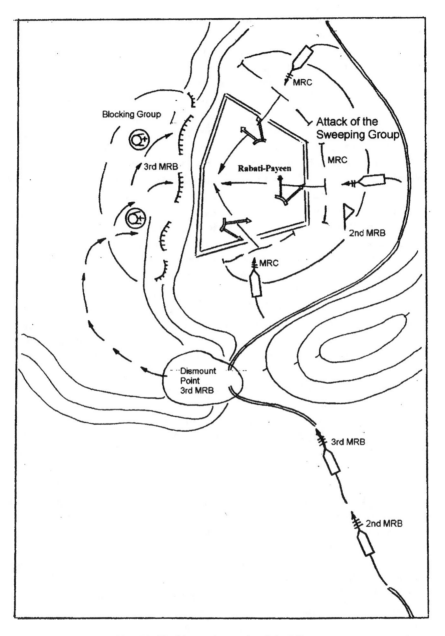

Map 18. Blocking and sweeping Rabati-Payeen

chief of staff and ordered to move to the area of Tagayi-Khodzhasuflai [as spelled] village and destroy the enemy. According to Afghan intelligence, the enemy was a sabotage group armed with two mortars. His reconnaissance company was reinforced with a motorized rifle platoon mounted on BMPs and a commandant's service[19] platoon from the Afghan Army.

His subunit set out at dusk and moved 30 kilometers to the village of Argat. His forward reconnaissance discovered an ambush in the village manned by an unknown number of Mujahideen. Polovinkin made a daring decision. His company slewed the gun turrets of their armored personnel carriers to the right and left and approached the village. His forward patrol vehicles were already in the center of the village when two RPG-7 shots rang out simultaneously. One BMP was knocked out and burning on the road. In order to evacuate the BMP, company commander Polovinkin ordered the company to speed up and move to the village. His BMPs were protected from RPG-7 fire by adobe walls. The soldiers dismounted and occupied the nearby houses and got up on their roofs.

It became quickly obvious that the enemy fire was more intensive from the area of a grape orchard. The company lacked the strength to storm the grape orchard. Four hours after the start of the battle for the village, the 1st MRC, commanded by Senior Lieutenant N. I. Starikov, arrived. The 1st MRC occupied firing positions on the western slope of the ridge. Shortly thereafter, the 2d MRC, commanded by Senior Lieutenant V. N. Korobov, occupied firing positions to the east of the grape orchards while the 3rd MRC occupied firing positions at the entry to the village. By 2330 hours, the village was completely blocked by Soviet subunits. At 0500 hours on 1 April, a DRA force established an interior encirclement of the village.

At dawn, the DRA force began to sweep the village. The enemy put up a stubborn resistance, but finally lost with about 50 KIA and more than 30 captured. The Soviets lost six KIA and five combat vehicles. Afghan losses were slightly higher. The cordon and search of the village had liquidated this group of enemy.

When sweeping built-up areas and regions, the Soviet and Afghan subunits had more success when they were able to secretly occupy their blocking positions. It was not easy to conduct a successful cordon and search in the mountains or where the enemy reconnaissance was thorough. The leaders of the enemy detachments were often immediately informed when the Soviet subunits left their base camps, what their axis of advance was, and when they neared the objective area. As a result, the plans of the Soviet and Afghan forces were often compromised and their actions were often fruitless. Aside from this, the Mujahideen used unusual or unexpected techniques that, as a rule, allowed them to mislead their enemies and achieve surprise.

On 8 December 1980, DRA intelligence agents reported that a 50-man Mujahideen detachment had slipped across the border from Pakistan and crossed the Kunar river at night. Then it stopped to rest in a canyon. The Soviets decided to liquidate them the following night using a reinforced parachute battalion. The concept of the action was to use part of the battalion as a blocking detachment to prevent the Mujahideen withdrawal from the canyon (Map 19). On the following morning, the main body would begin to advance into the canyon. When the enemy discovered the Soviets, they would try to escape into the mountains avoiding combat or, having seized the dominant terrain, conduct a stubborn resistance against the Soviet advance. In either event, the enemy inevitably would be taken under fire by the blocking force.[20]

Late in the evening, a truck convoy moved from base camp with its lights out to the region where the Soviets would conduct their cordon and search. This was some 25 kilometers from the regimental base. Simultaneously another truck convoy moved in the opposite direction in order to mislead the enemy.

A parachute company dismounted from the moving trucks and hiked across the mountains to take up their blocking positions to encircle the Mujahideen from the south. The rest of the force dismounted to the north of the canyon and encircled the Mujahideen from the north. The truck convoy continued three kilometers further north and pulled off into a dry river bed where the trucks were camouflaged and the convoy protected by a designated force. After a difficult ascent to the top of the canyon, the blocking groups occupied firing positions and were concealed by 0400 hours. At 0500 hours, the main body of the battalion, mounted on their armored personnel carriers, began moving into the canyon. At 0600, the Mujahideen sentries discovered the Soviet force. The Mujahideen constituted a rear guard to pin down the armored groups while the rest of the force moved to the mountains. However, the main body of the Mujahideen fell under the fire of the blocking force and was almost completely destroyed. In all, 24 Mujahideen were killed and 4 were captured. One Soviet soldier was wounded.

Despite successes like the above, combat demonstrated that other commanders would repeat the same techniques and procedures over and over again. The results were that the mission was not carried out successfully and the force suffered heavy casualties. Therefore, the commander needed to look for new techniques and procedures with every new mission in order to defeat the enemy.

In the fall of 1981, the command employed military cunning to deceive the enemy and carry out the mission with a limited force. Intelligence reports disclosed that there were two strong enemy groups located in different canyons. The village of Kayum was in one of the canyons and hosted a Mujahideen force of 64 men. The Najmuddin detachment was located in the other canyon and had a force of some 53 men.[21] After detailed study, the command decided to destroy the Kayum detachment. However, in order to deceive the Mujahideen, they spread the word through the representatives of the Ministry of Internal Affairs and the political activists that Soviet subunits and a company of DRA Sarandoy would destroy the Najmuddin detachment the following morning.

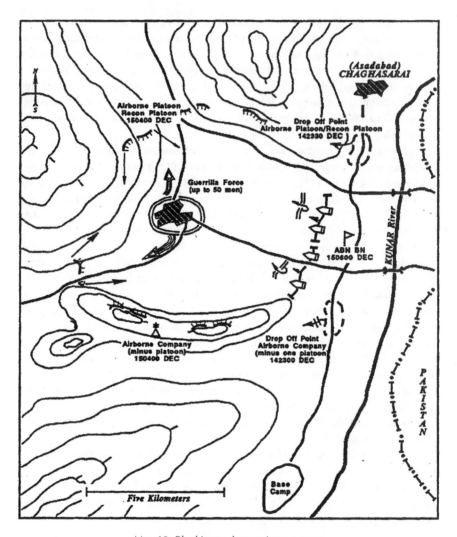

Map 19. Blocking and sweeping a canyon

At 2300 hours, two Soviet motorized rifle companies began to move from their garrison. They completed a 12-kilometer road march and blocked the village where the Kayum detachment was staying. A platoon of Sarandoy and some party activists joined the Soviet force as they positioned outposts on dominant terrain, established interlocking fields of fire, and laid down mines on likely enemy routes of withdrawal.

At 0600 hours, artillery opened fire on an ambush site the Najmuddin detachment had set up. A Soviet deception force made themselves very apparent outside the village where the Najmuddin detachment was deployed. The battalion *bronegruppa* approached the village. Simultaneously, an assault force of two Soviet motorized rifle platoons and a DRA Sarandoy platoon moved up to the Kayum detachment village, dismounted, and began to sweep the village. The Mujahideen were taken by surprise and did not put up an effective resistance. The bulk of the group was captured. A few small groups tried to flee to the mountains where they were cut down by the blocking forces. The Najmuddin group did nothing to help their compatriots in the next valley.

To a great extent, the success of a sweep depended on the actions of the blocking subunits. If the blocking elements managed to get into position without being detected, then the sweep had a good chance of inflicting heavy casualties on the enemy. As the above examples show, blocking positions had the best chance of moving undetected at night or during limited visibility. In a number of cases, airborne forces were used for night movement.

Major A. M. Kovyrshin[22] relates an incident in the region of the town of Ishkamesh, which is located some 60 kilometers southeast of Kunduz. The Mujahideen established a base and training center at Ishkamesh where, according to intelligence reports, they had over 1,000 men, about 70 grenade launchers, 25 DShK machine guns, and about 50 artillery pieces and mortars. Further, the Mujahideen maintained arms, ammunition, and supply depots at Ishkamesh. Mujahideen from this site would go to Kunduz airfield and fire at landing aircraft and they would attack transport convoys on the Kunduz/Pule-Khumri road. This made it difficult to supply and sustain the garrisons and forces located in the province[23] (Map 20).

A Soviet force of two motorized rifle battalions, a separate reconnaissance battalion, a separate helicopter squadron, and two artillery battalions was assembled for the mission. An Afghan infantry division supported the Soviet force. The difficult nature of the terrain and the excellent enemy reconnaissance system did not permit the secret insertion of blocking forces.

Therefore the leader of the operation, Lieutenant Colonel V. M. Akimov, decided to use air assault forces to establish blocking positions and then destroy the Mujahideen with a frontal advance by ground forces.

At 0700 hours on the 20th of January 1984, following airstrikes on Fuloli, Marzek, and Kokabulak regions, the reconnaissance battalion made a heliborne landing there. At the same time, the 2nd MRB made a heliborne landing four kilometers west of Ishkamesh. The heliborne landings were made from Mi-6 cargo helicopters instead of troop transport helicopters. The Mujahideen, used to the cargo role of the Mi-6 helicopters, virtually ignored them as they flew in. The 2nd MRB, commanded by Lieutenant Colonel V. Krokhin, landed and destroyed the enemy in the vicinity of the Kuchi strong point and, by 0830, linked up with the approaching *bronnegruppa* which had driven there under the command of the 6th Motorized Rifle Company commander, Senior Lieutenant R. S. Zarifov. The 2nd MRB mounted its vehicles and conducted a raid on the axis Apikutan-

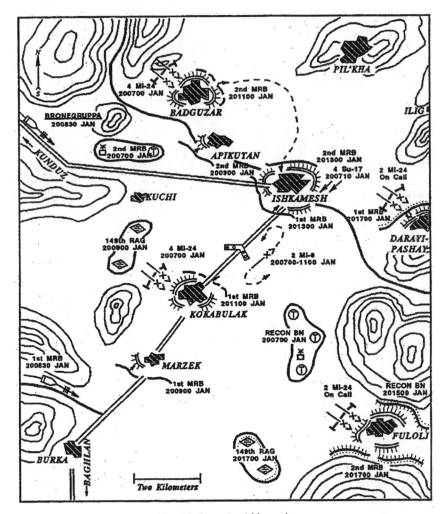

Map 20. Sweeping Ishkamesh

Badguzar with the mission of destroying weapons and ammunition caches. The enemy, while conducting delaying actions, withdrew part of its force into the mountains, while the other part withdrew into the town of Ishkamesh—the main training center of the Mujahideen.

The 1st MRB, commanded by Major A. V. Vlasov, exploiting the success of the reconnaissance battalion, arrived at the villages of Kokabulak and Marzek by 0830. Over the course of the next two-and-one-half hours, they destroyed the enemy in these strong points. By 1300, they approached Ishkamesh from the south. The Mujahideen in Ishkamesh were blocked on two sides.

After a ten-minute artillery barrage, both motorized rifle battalions, supported by a flight of helicopters, launched an attack, and by 1500 hours, they destroyed the enemy in the town. However, part of the Mujahideen broke out of the encirclement and fled toward Darayi-Pashay. The 1st MRB pursued the Mujahideen while the 2nd MRB was ordered to the south of Fuloli to link up with the reconnaissance battalion and join forces to seal off and destroy the enemy in Fuloli.

By 1600 hours, the enemy had concentrated his main forces in the villages of Fuloli and Darayi-Pashay. The Soviet subunits, attempting to preserve the initiative, attempted to seize the villages from the march while mounted on BMPs. They were unsuccessful. Their encirclement attempt was stopped by heavy Mujahideen fire. During the next 24 hours, the motorized rifle battalion and the reconnaissance battalion fought to take the villages and took them only after the Mujahideen used darkness and fog to slip out into the mountains to the southeast. It turned out that there was an inadequate amount of forces available for the area of operation (30 by 10 kilometers). Further, during the planning, the commander had not considered the possibility that the enemy would break out of the encirclement at Ishkamesh and had not taken countermeasures.

An examination of the battle showed that the Mujahideen skillfully avoided the sweeps and that the majority of the groups escaped into the mountains. Mujahideen casualties were about 150 killed and captured. The Soviets captured a large number of weapons and ammunition.

A cordon and search in a green zone was highly challenging. These agricultural areas were particularly difficult, intersected by a dense network of irrigation canals and vineyards. The Mujahideen used the green zones to construct an organized defense, including available houses, adobe forts, thick walls, grape orchard earth works, and even specially constructed firing positions with overhead cover. The green zone presented a serious challenge to advancing forces.

The Mujahideen formations, deployed in green zones with necessary protection, conducted diversionary attacks against Soviet security outposts and convoys, pillaged Afghan truck traffic, and, by such actions, destabilized the surrounding region. Naturally, this was unsatisfactory to the Soviet and Afghan commands. Lieutenant Colonel S. V. Zelenskiy[24] remembers preparing and conducting an operation in the green zone to address this threat. In October 1982, intelligence data disclosed that some ten guerrilla detachments, with a strength up to 300 men, were hidden north of Kandahar city in the green zone that borders the Arghandab river. This fertile green zone stretches for 15 to 20 kilometers along the northern bank of the river and is up to seven kilometers wide. It is an agricultural region of gardens and vineyards bisected by a network of irrigation ditches. It is practically impassable for vehicles.

The brigade received an order to destroy these Mujahideen. The commander's concept was to seal off the north with the *bronnegruppa* of three battalions

(Map 21). Helicopter gunship patrols would fly patrol patterns along the Arghandab river and along the eastern edge of the green zone. Two motorized rifle battalions and an air assault battalion would move on foot to sweep the Mujahideen out of the blockaded area. An artillery battalion would support the action. The force moved to its assembly areas and designated positions at night. By 0500 hours on 6 October, the battalions' *bronnegruppa* had all occupied their designated positions, the dismounted personnel were in assembly areas, the artillery battalion had deployed into firing positions to the southwest of the block-aded area, and the helicopters were on station and flying their standing patrols.

At 0530 hours, the three battalions began their sweep. Enemy groups of five to seven men began long-range small-arms fire on Soviet forces and then with-drew to the northeast. The Mujahideen had experience in similar circumstances and tried to stay as close to the Soviet forces as possible. This prevented the Soviet command from using aviation and artillery and significantly slowed the Soviet rate of advance.

By 1600 hours, the subunits in the sweep had moved some ten kilometers into the green zone. At that time, the 2nd Air Assault Company, moving in the center of the battalion line, made contact with a significant enemy group that was organized and holding its ground. The battalion commander ordered the right-flank 1st Air Assault Company to envelop the enemy force from the right and block the enemy route of withdrawal to the northeast. Then, they were to destroy the enemy in concert with the 2nd Company.

It took the 1st Air Assault Company commander a half hour to form up his platoons and begin the maneuver. Within an hour, he had carried out his mission and his platoons were in blocking positions in the enemy rear across his line of withdrawal. The company commander was located at an observation point at the extreme right flank of his position. He had seven soldiers, including himself, in the command group.

A group of approximately 70 Mujahideen approached the command post. The commander had lost radio communications and could not call in artillery fire. The command group took the enemy under fire and drove them back, but the danger grew. The enemy force attacked three times. During the third assault, the command post was running out of ammunition. Each member of the com-mand group simultaneously threw a grenade and broke contact with the enemy. Enemy losses were twenty killed, while the company had no casualties. Unfor-tunately the Mujahideen managed to break contact with the sweeping force. The operation was called off with the arrival of dusk.

Combat experience in Afghanistan demonstrated the effectiveness of con-ducting a simultaneous cordon and search. However, the command did not restrict itself to only using the block and the sweep together. Often, the block was used to prevent assistance from reaching the enemy from across the borders or for assur-ing the regular flow of traffic on the roads or for supporting other missions.

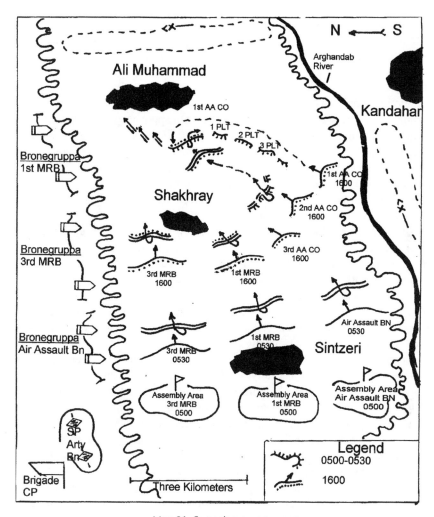

Map 21. Sweeping a green zone

Major A. V. Odinochnikov[25] recalls that in September 1980 the Soviet and Afghan forces conducted a large-scale operation to destroy enemy forces in the area around the city of Herat. The opposition, trying to retain its supremacy in this important administrative and economic region, launched an attempt to provide aid from Iran to the Mujahideen who were encircled in Herat. The motorized rifle battalion, commanded by Major A. P. Cherkashin, was ordered to move to the international border between Iran and Afghanistan and block sections of it from Zyul'fagar to Esdan (a distance of 300 kilometers). His mission was not only to prevent the delivery of aid from Iran to the Mujahideen, but also to prevent the Mujahideen from crossing over the border into Iran. Each motorized rifle company sector stretched about 100 kilometers and each platoon had a separate sector of responsibility of 20 to 35 kilometers.

Movement to the international border was in company and even platoon columns. Since the sectors of responsibility were so wide, they paid special attention to mountain roads and trails that crossed the border. After a short commander's reconnaissance, the Soviets mined these approaches. Mostly, they used antipersonnel mines, except on some separate sections of road where they used antitank mines. They kept the roads and trails under constant observation. These measures also paralyzed the movement of the Mujahideen across the border.

The battalion blocked the sector for about one month. Enemy attempts to provide timely aid to the encircled Mujahideen were skillfully curbed by the actions of Soviet subunits. The Soviets killed and captured several dozen Mujahideen. More than 20 trucks and motorcycles were blown up by mines. After the operation in Herat concluded, the Soviet removed all the bridges and blew them up. Soviet forces blocking the international border were decidedly passive. They used their weapons only as necessary to stop Mujahideen attempts to violate Afghanistan's borders.

Major A. S. Burov[26] recalls when a blockade served to help seize the dominant terrain of Lakarosar mountain and establish a security post on it. This mountain occupied an exclusive tactically advantageous position. The mountain's twin peaks (with heights of 2,530 and 2,470 meters) were about 600 meters apart and overlooked the Shindarak canyon. Intelligence data confirmed that the Mujahideen controlled these heights and lived in nearby villages that are located on both sides of the ridge. From the mountain, the Mujahideen supported the transit of caravans carrying weapons and ammunition. These Mujahideen also periodically conducted shelling attacks on Soviet subunits posted in the valley. The Soviet command decided to destroy the Mujahideen outposts and to establish security posts on the ridge. The mission began at 0530 hours on 2 October 1985 with a 30-minute artillery preparation on the enemy positions. As the artillery preparation ended, the 2nd Air Assault Company conducted an air landing on the 2,470-meter mountain peak. The air assault mission was to destroy the remaining Mujahideen firing positions, block the nearest three villages, and create favorable conditions for the 5th Motorized Rifle Company to establish security posts.

The air assault force blocked the villages and signaled their accomplishment. At 0640 hours, four Mi-8 transport helicopters, covered by four Mi-24 helicopters, air-landed the 5th MRC on the heights. The main force of the company fortified the LZ while the machine gun/grenade launcher platoon and some mine layers moved to the 2,530-meter peak. The group of mine layers descended some 300 meters to lay some mines on the northwest approach when they were met by Mujahideen fire and withdrew to the machine gun/grenade launcher platoon position. Some 30 Mujahideen pursued them. However, the fire from an artillery battery stopped their attack. As a result of this combat, the Soviets captured 18 assault rifles and took three prisoners. The Soviets discovered that when the artillery preparation began, the Mujahideen sheltered in a safe place on the ridge. When they saw the group of mine layers, they decided to capture them. However, they were unsuccessful due to the unexpected seizure of the mountain peak by the machine gun/grenade launcher platoon. The Soviets had one KIA and two WIA. Soviet casualties might have been much heavier if they had not established blocks close to the villages that prevented the villagers from helping the Mujahideen fighting on the ridge.

Sweeps could also be conducted separately, but without a blocking force they were usually less effective.

The enemy could readily maneuver and when necessary could withdraw from battle and hide. The cordon and search, as a form of combat, allowed the Soviets to isolate and destroy the enemy in villages, canyons, and bases. The cordon and search was an effective tactic when fighting armed Mujahideen formations.

Editors' comments: The cordon and search proved an effective tactic but was difficult to implement correctly. If the blocking forces were detected early, or did not arrive simultaneously, the Mujahideen generally escaped, leaving a rear guard and the uninformed to fight the searching element. The use of DRA forces for the search was smart, in that the villagers in the cordoned area were dealing with their own people—and not a foreign invader. However, the DRA had a tendency to loot houses and villages. This brazen theft did nothing to enhance the population's support for its government. Soviet forces also looted, which clearly did nothing to endear them to the local populace.

The most successful block and sweep actions were completed before nightfall. At night, the trapped villagers and Mujahideen found that they could often sneak out of the encirclement undetected, as Soviet encirclements were porous at night.

AMBUSHES[27]

The ambush, as an independent tactical form, was widely used in all types of combat in Afghanistan. They were often used close to the Pakistan and Iranian borders. The essence of the ambush consisted of the secret deployment of the subunit to a site laid out along the route of enemy movement and then opening fire on the surprised Mujahideen to kill or capture them, their weapons, and cargo. Ambushes were conducted by day and night.

The organization and conduct of an ambush in Afghanistan did not differ particularly from the ambush laid out and recommended in the regulations and training manuals. However, there were several peculiarities. The ambushes organized by combined arms subunits in Afghanistan often functioned outside the framework of a simple reconnaissance mission.[28] The Soviets used ambushes to reduce the amount of personnel, weapons, ammunition, food, and other supplies available to the resistance. Ambushes served to inflict appreciable casualties, prevent the arrival of reserves, and block enemy access to the roads, airfields, and other important objectives.

An ambush force normally consisted of a motorized rifle, reconnaissance, or paratrooper platoon or company, reinforced with one to three AGS-17 automatic grenade launchers and two or three sappers or a sapper squad equipped with anti-tank and antipersonnel mines. Occasionally, an entire battalion might be used to conduct an ambush. In this case, the battalion would, as a rule, simultaneously establish two or three ambush sites that would function for four or five days and which were part of a general system of ambushes controlled by the battalion commander.

During the entire time that the ambushes were in position, one or two pair of helicopters were on strip alert at the nearest air base. Further, an alert company stood by with its gear uploaded on its fighting vehicles at the battalion base camp that dispatched the ambushes. The ambush site had enough communications gear to communicate within the ambush and with the next higher commander, as well as the *bronnegruppa,* the supporting artillery, and the helicopter gunships.

Depending on the purpose of the mission, the ambush normally had several groups. The firing group included AGS-17 crews, grenadiers, machine gunners, and snipers who would shoot the enemy in the kill zone. Five to seven brave, phys-ically strong, enlisted men composed the snatch group, which would capture pris-oners, documents, and enemy weapons. The security group, which could be up to a platoon in strength, would cover the flanks and rear of the ambush site and cover the withdrawal of the ambush party as it withdrew to the assembly area and evac-uation site after completing the mission. An observation group provided recon-naissance and early warning from several 2 to 3 man observation posts (Map 22).

The ambush could constitute other groups to carry out specific missions. Thus, a mine-laying group could be formed from attached sappers. Usually the sappers would be protected by some motorized riflemen. Ambush forces equipped with BMPs or BTRs would form a *bronnegruppa* that would deploy to a concealed position no closer, as a rule, than five to seven kilometers from the ambush site. This separation was close enough to allow the *bronnegruppa* to quickly move to the ambush site and support the site with fire. The *bronnegruppa* could also support the ambush force withdrawal at the conclusion of the mission. If the ambush were conducted at night, an illumination group provided battlefield illumination at the ambush site.

The decision to conduct ambushes was made by the senior commander on the basis of intelligence data. There were two variants. The first was to plan an ambush based on the requirements of the monthly reconnaissance plan using already approved ambush sites and times for their conduct. The second was to plan an ambush based on developing operational information. The second vari-ant was more effective.

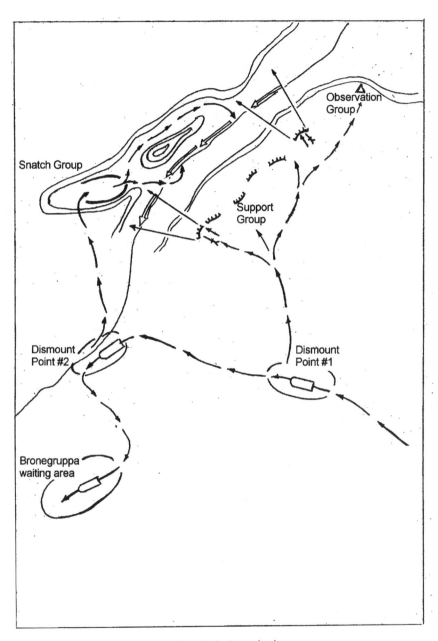

Map 22. Soviet ambush

The senior commander gave the subunits the ambush mission.[29] He provided the necessary information about the enemy. Then he explained the mission of the ambush, the time, location, the dismount point or landing zone, the sequence of actions at mission's end, day and night signals and communication, and the signals to summon aviation support. Besides these, the commander specified the steps to be taken to prepare for the mission, the security and secrecy measures to be observed, and what deception measures to take against the enemy. Since almost all ambushes occurred at night, the commander specified the necessary steps to provide battlefield illumination. When artillery fire was planned in support of the ambush, the commander of the ambush stated what firing batteries would support the ambush and what signals would be used to call for fire and to shift and cease fire.

Outfitting the soldier for ambush was very thoroughly planned. Besides the individual's weapon, he carried one-and-a-half to two units of fire,[30] two to eight hand grenades, a bayonet, binoculars, night sights, illumination flares, and signal flares. He carried enough dry rations for the duration of the ambush and extra water. If it was winter, or he was going into the high mountain area, he received cold weather clothing.

Preparation for conducting an ambush began with the receipt of intelligence data from various sources. From these, if Soviet troops had not been used previously in this area, the planners would determine the reliability of the data, evaluate the terrain, and select the most expedient method of action. They would plan the action, including deception measures, and they would specify the order of withdrawal from the ambush site. With the acquisition of combat experience, they planned the evacuation of dead and wounded, prisoners, and captured weapons. The subunits that were designated for the ambush, as a rule, were well prepared for the mission. The training could run from several hours to several days. The subunit commanders paid a great deal of attention to organizing the ambush and positioning the soldiers on site. As a rule, the training area was normally a long way from the base camp and the selected ambush site; however, they would use terrain similar to the actual ambush site to train on. At this training, they would work out several variants to the planned ambush.[31] They would pay particular attention to coordination and the conduct of uninterrupted, thorough observation.

There was exceptional importance attached to the maintenance of weapons and equipment for combat in the mountains; in extreme heat; under conditions of wide temperature and pressure variables during a single day; in strong winds; in summer sand storms; and in the frost, ice, and heavy snowfalls of winter. Every soldier personally maintained his assigned weapon under the supervision of his commander. Rounds from every lot of ammunition were fired to ensure that the production lot was good. Before going on the missions, all weapons' magazines and ammunition boxes were inspected externally, checking for cleanliness and proper spring tension. All equipment that might rattle was shifted or taped to prevent noise during movement. Batteries for radios and night vision devices were checked. Weapons' silencers were checked. Night vision devices were calibrated. After test firing, all weapons were cleaned, oiled, and wiped down. Grenade fuses were inserted into the grenade bodies.

Ambush parties arrived at the ambush site by various means—on combat vehicles, on trucks, by helicopter, and on foot. As a rule, the movement to the site was at night. The success of the mission often depended on orderliness and attention to detail. An example of this occurred in June 1983 in a motorized rifle battalion in which Major R. S. Zarifov served. The battalion was ordered to conduct an ambush on the southwest outskirts of the village of Navabad. The ambush was supposed to destroy a 200-man Mujahideen detachment in the area.

Navabad is located some 17 kilometers west of Kunduz. The plan was to move during the night of 4 June on armored vehicles to a dismount site and then move on foot to the ambush site. The battalion had only four to five hours to prepare for the mission. At 2200 hours on 3 June, the battalion received the final mission. In order to hide their intentions from the enemy, the battalion was now ordered to move the entire distance on foot at night. This was a distance of about 20 kilometers from the regimental base camp to the ambush site. As a result, the battalion was unable to reach the ambush site in the designated time. Further, the battalion ambush party itself was ambushed at dawn. It took them five hours to extricate themselves and they suffered casualties.[32]

As this example shows, preservation of secrecy and rapid movement are important conditions for the success of a mission. To achieve these, commanders can use various forms of military cunning. Senior Lieutenant V. N. Popov provided one such example when he secretly moved his motorized rifle platoon to the ambush site by using BTRs that were driving their nightly routine road patrol over a fixed route. [His soldiers jumped out of the slow-moving vehicles into a ditch and then assembled to move to the ambush site.][33]

In an April 1987 example, Senior Lieutenant Yu. N. Petrov secretly moved his company on food trucks to a security outpost on the Kabul-Salang highway on the first leg of the journey. The food trucks made a daily run to the outpost, and there was an area in the outpost where the troops could dismount unobserved. On the next leg, the company moved to the ambush site on foot at night. Two days prior, the company's *bronnegruppa* had moved to another outpost as part of a reinforced road security sweep. This split approach by the subunit concealed the presence of an ambush site from the enemy that quickly fell into Petrov's trap.[34]

Considering that the enemy had a high probability of observing the ambush force from its departure from base to its arrival at the mission area, the Soviets used many deceptive and misleading tricks in Afghanistan. The first method included imitating a flanking movement by a *bronnegruppa* to an intermediate objective. The vehicles moved slowly while the ambush party secretly dismounted, and the vehicles moved on to seize the intermediate objective and then waited in readiness to give help to the ambush.

Another method to move troops secretly is to use "twins." The ambush force rides on the top of the armored personnel carriers and the "twins" ride hidden inside.[35] The armored column moves to a dismount point, which is concealed from possible observation, where the ambush party quickly dismounts and the "twins" take their place on the top of the carriers. The armored personnel carriers move on to an intermediate objective where they wait in readiness to support the ambush.

The third method is to move the subunits to a false objective where the ambush personnel dismount and secretly move to the ambush site. The armored personnel carriers move to an intermediate objective and wait for a prearranged signal.

The fourth method had the secret title "Calling it upon yourself." This involved selecting a site to simulate a vehicle breakdown or vehicle disabled by a mine explosion. The crew began to repair the vehicle, while the firing party, originally located inside the armored vehicle, took up positions to kill the enemy. Once the vehicle was "fixed," the convoy moved on, leaving the dismounted ambush party at the selected site.

Ambush parties also moved on helicopters to an LZ located five to twelve kilometers from the ambush site. The helicopters would make two or three false insertions, with the goal of deceiving the enemy as to the site of the actual LZ. Usually, the actual helicopter air landing took place 15 to 20 minutes before dusk. After landing, the subunit would secretly assemble at an assembly point that was located, as a rule, 200 to 400 meters from the LZ. The subunit would move out to the ambush site on foot in the dark.

In all instances where the ambush party moved from the dismount site (LZ) to the ambush site on foot, they moved in one or two subunit columns with the subunit personnel moving parallel to each other within the column (two or three abreast). The column maintained all-round observation, periodically making a short stop to listen and to more carefully observe the surroundings. A forward patrol moved in front of the main body and a rear patrol trailed the column. To provide immediate security and a survey of the terrain, the commander of the forward squad or platoon sent its own patrol forward. As a rule, this patrol consisted of two men armed with weapons fitted with silencers. Being lightly equipped, this patrol could move quickly, freely bypass obstacles, take up opportune firing positions, and, when necessary, initiate quiet combat with the enemy. Over the years, patrolling tactics were refined. During movement, each patrol had its sector of observation. One would look forward and to the right. The second would look forward and to the left. The following was standard operating procedure. If one patrol encountered the enemy, it would initiate fire or hand-to-hand combat while the second patrol would observe. Only in dire necessity would the second patrol fire in support of their comrades. During movement at night or in difficult mountainous terrain with dead space, the patrols moved by bounds using traveling overwatch. At each bound, the covering party would carefully observe the sector and listen. Then they would begin to move to the next designated site some 200 to 300 meters away. During the movement, the soldiers kept their weapons ready to instantly open fire. The following group or platoon would start to move only when the forward group had taken up good positions and were ready to defeat an enemy attack. Thus, bounding from one covering position to another, all the subunits moved through the danger zone. Here, as participants of the events noted, it was very important that every combatant knew his exact responsibilities for observation and opening fire. This was necessary lest the Mujahideen took the subunits unawares. At this moment, the role of the commander was especially important. He must clearly give the order to open fire, and quickly give or refine the mission for observation, illumination, and blinding the enemy.[36]

In the event that the Mujahideen launched a surprise attack during the course of moving to the ambush site, all weapons would return fire to repulse the attack. Senior Lieutenant A. Kravchenko and officers A. Khomenko and V. Kulikov discussed how a special mounting attachment was strapped to the AGS-17 assistant gunner's back so that the gunner could quickly open fire using the prone assistant gunner as a base.

The correct selection of the area and site for the ambush were important factors for its success. Combat experience showed that the ideal location allowed the secret deployment of the subunit to the ambush, supported observation, and incorporated a "fire sack" in the kill zone. Ambushes can be divided into several types depending on the mission, locale, the time it is conducted, and the methods of conduct. Ambushes located along enemy caravan routes were more widespread. The Mujahideen had some 80 such routes they used for transport. Thirty of these routes from Iran and Pakistan were especially active. Arms and ammunition were stockpiled in Iran and Pakistan for transport into Afghanistan. Truck transport carried these armaments to the international border or to the bases in the mountain passes in the border area where the caravans formed up. When it came to selecting the movement route through Afghanistan, the enemy, as a rule, avoided a fixed schedule or routine and frequently changed their methods. The caravan routes that the Mujahideen used offered sections of terrain with good trafficability, maximum secrecy of movement, and invulnerability to air attacks. Usually, the Mujahideen sent scouts forward on the route several days before a weapons caravan crossed the border.

Caravans usually moved during the night, or, if during the day, when the weather was unfavorable to aviation. Lieutenant Colonel S. L. Pivovarov noted that sometimes, if the weapons and ammunition caravan moved during the day, it might "filter" through as a peaceful caravan. This was the case in Helmand Province. On the route selected by the caravan, the usual traffic consisted of trucks carrying contraband or trucks carrying household goods of returning refugees. On these routes, nomads and scouts left markers at designated sites that other Mujahideen and nomads understood. Often, the Mujahideen would drive a herd of cattle along the caravan route in order to find an ambush site and to clear the mines from a section of the route. During the day, the caravan stopped at a preselected, prepared day lager, located, as a rule, in a village, canyon, cave, grove, or other site that was carefully camouflaged. Every caravan selected its own route and determined their final destination. Most often, the caravans moved close to the AOs of active guerrilla bands while moving between intermediate bases and depots. The guerrillas provided movement security by forming a good system of mobile security, reconnaissance, and early warning along the route. The Mujahideen often used the local populace to provide reconnaissance and early warning.

Shortly after encountering their first Soviet ambushes, the Mujahideen began perfecting their tactics of caravan escort. They significantly increased the size of the caravan's mobile security element and developed more precise and tougher meeting-battle drills for fighting their enemy. If the Mujahideen had a sufficient quantity of forces and equipment, they would try to turn the flank of an ambush and destroy the ambushers with an attack on the flank or rear. If they did not have sufficient strength, as a rule, they would fall back to a reserve route under the protection of their covering force. As a result of these Mujahideen countermeasures, platoon-sized ambushes no longer produced appreciable results. Therefore, the Soviets began conducting ambushes with motorized rifle companies and reconnaissance companies reinforced with engineer subunits and supported with artillery fire.

An ambush conducted by a reinforced motorized rifle company to the northeast of Jalalabad at the beginning of October 1986 is instructional and was recorded by Major V. P. Podvorniy.[37] The company covered three possible caravan routes simultaneously. The company reached the ambush site at 2300 hours and occupied positions with overlapping and interlocking fields of fire. Their flanks and gaps were covered with minefields. The enemy did not keep them waiting long. At 0030 hours, the forward security patrol for a Mujahideen caravan moved down route #1 and within an hour was in the kill zone of the second platoon. The Mujahideen caravan stretched 1.5 kilometers behind its forward security patrol. The company commander decided that the bulk of the caravan was located in front of the two platoons and gave the command to open fire. Artillery was called in to strike the caravan rear guard. Part of the caravan was destroyed. The surviving Mujahideen were able to withdraw since the artillery was late in opening fire. The company remained at the ambush site.

At 0500 hours, the caravan again began moving, but this time on route #2. The enemy thought that, as was usual, the Soviet ambush forces were small groups and were unable to cover several routes simultaneously. Further, they knew the ambush tactics of Soviet forces and thought that the ambush group had left the region after opening fire. They were wrong.

When the caravan was in the kill zones of the 3rd and 4th platoons, they were caught in the withering Soviet fire. Part of the caravan was destroyed while the surviving Mujahideen abandoned their cargo and fled into the mountains.

During the spring and summer of 1987, guerrilla forces increased their activity. To support this combat, the Mujahideen leaders increased their deliveries of weapons, ammunition, and other supplies from across the international borders. Owing to earlier experience, the Mujahideen had developed several procedures for conducting caravans. The deliveries would start at the Pakistan border with large caravans of 250 to 300 pack animals delivering to the Mujahideen major supply bases in Afghanistan. From there these large caravans would break into caravans of 15 to 30 pack animals moving across the mountain passes to the base camps of Mujahideen detachments and groups.

By this time, the Mujahideen knew the Soviet subunits tactics well and used this knowledge to good advantage. Thus, if their caravan was traveling during the day and was approaching a likely ambush site, the Mujahideen would block the pass beforehand and hold it for two or three hours until the caravan passed through. The Mujahideen would post two or three armed sentries every 200 to 300 meters on the pass. The caravan would then come through in groups with an hour between groups until they had all crossed this dangerous area. If the caravan were to approach a pass at night, they would send out one or two unarmed patrols at twilight. These patrols were disguised as shepherds and often accompanied by children.

The caravan would start to move after taking due precautions. Five to ten men would move some 200 to 400 meters forward of the caravan as a forward patrol. The caravan moved behind this patrol with drovers moving between every two pack animals. A rear security force of two to three men moved behind the caravan. All the caravan personnel were armed with small arms.

To capture such a caravan took a company reinforced with artillery and supported by helicopter gunships. Aviation reconnaissance provided observation of the area.

The ambush ground force was divided into several groups. Observation posts were stationed on the side from which the caravan would approach. The main force was divided into a firing group, a snatch group, and a support group, which were deployed from 50 to 200 meters from the caravan route. Under favorable conditions, the *bronnegruppa* and supporting artillery were located five to seven kilometers to the rear or the ambush site—or even closer. Helicopter gunships were kept on strip alert at the airfield or on temporary airstrips ready to support the ambush force. All the groups were in radio contact with each other. Such ambushes were, as a rule, effective. An example of such an ambush was one organized at the Yakpay mountain pass in late August 1987 by battalion commander Major B. I. Korotkikh.[38]

The mission to conduct the ambush was issued on 27 August. The ambush site was on the Yakpay mountain pass located some 12 kilometers from the unit's base camp and on one of the enemy's main caravan routes running through this area. The battalion commander was the commander of the 45-man ambush force. The force included 24 air-assault troopers, 12 scouts from a reconnaissance platoon, two RTOs, two sappers, two chemical warfare specialists, the battalion surgeon, and physician's assistant.

Preparation of the ambush party was personally conducted by the battalion commander within a compressed time schedule on terrain that was similar to that of the ambush site. The ambush party was broken down into the various groups and observation posts. Ambush coordination was worked out on the map and on a terrain model. During this advance planning, several ambush sites were selected and several methods for moving the force to the site were considered.

At 2030 hours on 28 August 1987, the ambush party moved out to the ambush site. After six hours, the party finished its ascent into the mountains and went into a concealed day lager some 1.5 kilometers from the pass. Closer toward the evening, the observation posts reported that a caravan was moving in the direction of the village. At dusk, the ambush force moved quickly into the pass, took up positions, and prepared to fight. They waited until 0200 hours on the 30th of August, when the battalion commander decided that the caravan would not move that night. He decided to return to the day lager, pick up the equipment they had left there, and move to a new ambush site located further down into the pass.

During the afternoon, the observation posts reported that 30 armed Mujahideen had moved into the pass and taken up posts. It was clear from this action that the current ambush site would not achieve surprise. Therefore, the battalion commander decided to move the ambush site to a new site and reported this to his unit commander. The unit commander gave permission, and the ambush party began to move at 1800 hours. Conducting a five-kilometer forced march through the mountains, the ambush party arrived at the new site at 2330 hours and prepared for combat in the next 10 to 15 minutes. By that time, a caravan had already started to move up the canyon. The ambush let the forward security patrol go through the kill zone. When the caravan was in the kill zone, the battalion commander gave the order to open fire. The illumination group fired off illumination flares that aided the effectiveness of the firing group. In the course of a few minutes, the caravan was destroyed. There were no Soviet casualties. At 0800 hours, the ambush party linked up with its *bronnegruppa* at the pick-up point.

Conducting an ambush in the desert was particularly difficult, especially in the summer. Desert ambushes were conducted without reliable intelligence about enemy caravan routes that could branch out in any direction and thus become impossible to interdict with small ambushes. Desert ambushes demanded initiative, resourcefulness, and creativity on the part of the commander, who must function independently at the designated ambush site and lead the fight while dependent on the developing situation.

Desert ambushes usually required a small group, most often a platoon. The ambush group would remain on site for five to ten days and "disappear" into the desert, waiting for the enemy trucks at the selected site. The reason for these extended ambushes was the time required to escape the observation of shepherds, who would use smoke to warn the Mujahideen of passing Soviet subunits. These extended ambushes presented an especially difficult problem in supplying the personnel with water and food. Therefore, desert ambushes were usually supplied with up to 1.5 tons of water and firewood for cooking food.[39] Success in the conduct of these ambushes depended to a great deal on the personnel's knowledge of the terrain and their experience in using the terrain to camouflage their positions.

Desert ambushes in the winter were conducted by up to three reconnaissance groups formed from a battalion. These groups would establish operating bases in the desert where they would lager and rest during the day. At twilight, they would leave the lager traveling 30 to 50 kilometers in different directions and carry out their missions. It was very difficult to avoid the shepherds who at the time were driving their herds of sheep in the desert, and the smoke from their fires would surround practically all ambushes.

It was even more difficult to conduct ambushes on enemy-controlled territory. These ambushes required a well-trained platoon, reinforced with AGS-17 automatic grenade launchers and sappers. The company commander would usually lead these ambushes.

One such ambush was commanded by an air-assault company commander, Captain V. A. Stolbinskiy.[40] This ambush was conducted in February 1987 close to the Pakistan border. The difficulty in conducting this ambush was that the ambush party would have to cross three mountain ridges, the approaches to which were under 24-hour observation from enemy observation posts. The "Pipe" outpost was established to break up this enemy observation system. The Soviets conducted three weeks of close observation to find a Mujahideen observation post and to determine the route to the ambush site.

During the course of several days, the ambush force was secretly moved to the "Pipe" outpost under the guise of transferring forces. The commander decided to move to the ambush site on New Year's Eve night (by the Muslim calendar) in the hope that the vigilance of the Mujahideen would be less than usual.

On the night prior to the ambush, the ambush party began moving to the selected site. Some five kilometers from the ambush site, the Deputy Platoon Leader, Senior Sergeant R. A. Usmanov, took command of a 16-man group to cover the withdrawal of the look-outs, snatch group, and covering group. The remaining ten men, led by the company commander, continued to the ambush site, which they reached at 0200 hours. There was no cover near the road, so the company commander decided to shelter in a road culvert over a dry creek bed. Commander Stolbinskiy put five men, including himself, Senior Lieutenant A. Kholod, Sergeant Babaev, Private I. Dzhumaev, and Private A. Sivushkin, in the culvert. The other five men, commanded by squad leader Sergeant V. A. Sakhnov, occupied positions on high ground some 800 meters from the road. They had an AGS-17 and a PK machine gun. They were to observe for and support the snatch group in the culvert. The groups were all in radio contact.

At 0900 hours, Sergeant Sakhnov reported that about 150 Mujahideen gathered in a field some 400 meters from the culvert and were training for battle. Two days passed. No caravan materialized. On the third day, the commander decided to capture one vehicle and withdraw. At noon, some armed bicyclists approached the ambush site. When they were 20 meters from the culvert, the snatch group spilled out on the road and captured the Mujahideen bicyclists. Sergeant Sakhnov reported that a car and some motorcyclists were moving down the road. When the car approached some 70 meters from the culvert, the snatch group ran out onto the road and opened fire. The ambush resulted in five Mujahideen dead, including the leader of a powerful detachment and his adviser, and captured weapons and documents.

The snatch group began to withdraw into the mountains pursued by the Mujahideen from a nearby village mounted on motorcycles and tractors, who tried to cut off their escape route. The company commander called in artillery from the "Pipe" outpost that stopped the Mujahideen pursuit. Fortunately, the platoon returned to the outpost without casualties and with military trophies.

In Afghanistan, ambushes were often sited along probable enemy escape routes from cordon and search operations. Major V. I. Pavlenko remembers one such ambush.[41]

The brigade commander[42] directed the operation and decided to block the village from the north and southeast with two motorized rifle battalions. His air assault battalion and some DRA subunits would conduct the sweep.

A company would move on transport helicopters to establish an ambush preventing enemy withdrawal to the northwest. The company had two hours to prepare for this mission. This time was used to plan the ambush on the map, organize the elements of the ambush, coordinate the actions of the combat groups, and issue the necessary supplies to the soldiers.

That evening, the company boarded the helicopters. The flight took 30 minutes and landed the ambush party some five kilometers from the ambush site. The movement to the ambush site occurred at night, observing secrecy, light discipline, and quiet. Every platoon was split into two groups and moved side-by-side where they could be controlled by hand signs and visual signals. A patrol moved in front of and behind each platoon. A patrol squad moved in front of the company.

When the force arrived at the ambush site, the commander positioned his platoons and squads. He placed forces to block the entrance and exit to the ambush site but left the bulk of his force concentrated in the center of the ambush site. All-around observation was maintained in each platoon and squad while sappers laid mines on the road. At 0400 hours, the company was ready to conduct an ambush.

An hour later, Musa-Kala was blocked in the north and south by Soviet soldiers. Then a thorough sweep of the village began. The Mujahideen joined the fight and, under the covering fire of its rear guard element, tried to evacuate its arms and ammunition stores into the mountains. However, the Mujahideen convoy, loaded with these armaments, drove into the ambush. Five trucks loaded with armaments were destroyed and 46 Mujahideen were killed or captured. The ambush force lost one KIA and five WIA.

Sometimes it was necessary to conduct ambushes inside of the territory controlled by the Soviet forces. Most often this was the result of discovering the presence of Mujahideen forces crossing this territory. To destroy these transiting forces, ambushes were sited along transit routes. The structure of these ambushes were practically the same as that of an ordinary defense.

An example of such an ambush was one conducted by Captain A. A. Tolkachev, a parachute company commander, in Helmand Province in December 1984.[43] The basis for the ambush was an intelligence report that a truck-mounted Mujahideen detachment was functioning in the Soviet AO outside of Kandahar. A 25-man group from Captain Tolkachev's company was selected for the ambush. It was reinforced with five PK machine guns.

The ambush force was moved into position by helicopter. After two false insertions, the group landed some six kilometers from the ambush site. The ambush site was located on a hillside running parallel to the road. On the other side of the road, the force set up some directional mines.[44] The ambush force secretly occupied ambush positions with a frontage of some 250 meters. The site allowed the ambush party to observe the road to a distance of three to five kilometers.

One day, after several hours manning the ambush site, five trucks full of people approached the site. As they drove into the kill zone, a few warning shots were fired over the convoy. The Mujahideen responded to the warning shots with heavy fire, disclosing that they belonged to the Mujahideen and were not simple peasants. The ambush commander gave the signal for the ambush to open fire. In the course of ten minutes, the convoy was destroyed. The Mujahideen lost 44 killed and captured. There were no Soviet casualties.

Thus, combat in Afghanistan demonstrates that the ambush was an effective way of combating the Mujahideen on the routes he traveled. As a rule, subunits conducting ambushes achieved significant results with smaller forces. Ambushes gave the Soviet command the possibility to reestablish control over important sections of terrain used by caravans to transport weapons and ammunition. Success in ambushes depended to a large extent on military cunning, thorough practical preparation of all participants, a well-defined organization, and coordination with supporting elements.

At the same time, combat experience showed that, in a number of cases, ambushes did not accomplish their missions. This occurred when they were often sited in the same location or were conducted using a set pattern of organization and conduct. Further, there were often slip-ups that compromised secrecy and surprise. In these cases, the ambushing force sometimes fell into an enemy ambush and suffered heavy casualties.

Editors' comments: Soviet ambushes were frequently clumsy and ineffective. Ambushes were usually placed after receipt of intelligence data about impending Mujahideen movements. Several days' preparation preceded the ambush. The Soviets seldom routinely saturated a likely area with ambushes in order to deny the area to the Mujahideen and disrupt their resupply efforts. Failure to be more aggressive in employing ambushes meant that the Mujahideen owned the night. The Soviets did not like to be out at night and frequently broke contact when dusk approached. This is a far cry from the Red Army of World War II who were feared for their night tactics.

Soviet ambushes were compact, whereas Mujahideen ambushes were more spread out. A Mujahideen ambush might cover five times the area that a Soviet ambush would with the same amount of men. The result was that the Soviet ambush had a small, but highly lethal, kill zone, whereas the Soviets were often not sure that they were in a Mujahideen ambush or merely drawing harassing fire. Soviet ambushes became larger as the war progressed and company-sized ambushes were not uncommon. It is much harder to set up and maintain a large ambush than a series of smaller ones, but the Soviets preferred the safety of a large ambush party—even if it was not too effective.

In the peacetime Soviet army, ambushes were supposed to be done by recon-naissance forces in order to capture prisoners and documents. Therefore, the 40th Army used a lot of reconnaissance forces for ambush duty. Ambushes are a source of intelligence data, but there are more productive ways to employ recon-naissance forces. In Afghanistan, ambushes were the best way to counter Mujahideen logistics, but the Soviets were never able to seriously impair the Mujahideen resupply effort.

MARCHES AND CONVOY ESCORTS[45]

The large area of Afghanistan, the highly maneuverable combat conducted by the LCOSF, and the continual requirement to supply all sorts of military and eco-nomic goods from the USSR dictated the massive use of truck convoys. These convoys were opportune targets for an attacking enemy. The high vulnerability of truck convoys was a product of the poorly developed road network—a significant part of which wound through the mountain massif. Narrow mountain roads with a large number of serpentine turns and a limited turning radius precluded two-way traffic on some sections of the road. Sometimes the convoys could simply not move without special measures.

The main road network was a circle, running from Kabul to Puli-Khumri, Shibargan, Herat, Kandahar, and back to Kabul. There are seven roads leading off the circle. These roads become narrow passages through high mountain passes as they extend to the international borders with neighboring countries. The most difficult section of the Termez-Kabul road runs through the Hindu Kush mountain massif, across high mountain passes, including the Salang mountain pass, which is four kilometers high. This pass is equipped with a series of galleries and has the highest mountain tunnel in the world. The tunnel itself is 2.5 kilometers long. The length of the entire enclosed structure of tunnel and galleries is over six kilometers long.

The sharp turns and steep up-grades and steep down-grades of the roads seriously hampered the movement of truck convoys. For example, the length of the up-grades and down-grades adds another 80 to 100 kilometers to the Salang pass trip. The majority of the road sections were subject to collapse, landslides, falling rocks, and, in the winter, avalanches and snowdrifts. During the winter, most of the mountain passes were difficult to cross due to sharp up-grades and down-grades and sometimes the ice cover—especially for wheeled vehicles. Mountain streams were a significant obstacle as they were practically impossible to ford during flood time.

If the majority of paved highway roads on the plains can handle 4,000 to 10,000 trucks per day, the high mountain roads can only handle 500 to 1,000 trucks per day. Further, in increased elevation, both men and machines feel the effect of the rarified atmosphere, the sharp drop in temperature, the icy winds, and the thick fog. It has a telling effect on the average speed of a truck convoy. Frequently it is only 15 to 30 kilometers per hour and sometimes falls to five to ten kilometers per hour.

Here, the Mujahideen tactics were based on surprise attacks on the truck convoys using small detachments and groups. The Mujahideen would place mines in the road, try to destroy separate sections of road by digging ditches across the road, shear off pieces of road, artificially narrow the passage way, strew sharp objects on the roadway, and sometimes overturn a large truck on the highway.

The enemy paid particular attention to placing mines and explosive obstacles on the roads. Their methods and techniques of mining varied. Most often, they would mine road sections, road construction, and also bivouac sites and rest stops. Solitary antitank (antivehicular) mines and explosive charges were sited in those places where the destroyed vehicle would stop movement for a long time and aid in the destruction of men and vehicles during ambush. Their ambushes consisted of groups from 10 to 15, up to 100 to 150 men. When selecting an ambush site, the Mujahideen would skillfully use the terrain relief (canyons, nar-row confines, passes, and ledges overlooking roads and galleries). They would arrange their positions, as a rule, at a favorable and concealed location on the slope of a mountain or on the crest of a height, on the entry or exit to a canyon, where the road crosses the mountain pass, and also at the places where the Soviet drivers were likely to rest.

The Mujahideen would deploy some 150 to 300 meters parallel to the road with some 25 to 40 meters between combatants. The Mujahideen's favorite tech-nique was to attack the head and tail of the convoy—simultaneously destroying the gas tankers first. Then the snipers would fire at the command vehicles in order to disrupt battle command and control. As one of the instruction sheets sent into Afghanistan from abroad stated: Q: "When and where is it best to hit a con-voy?" A: "At the most opportune site—at the entrance or exit to a tunnel, at a bridge, at a tight turn, on an up-grade or a down-grade, at a constricted road."

These were the tactics facing the forces that had to guard and escort con-voys. At first, there was no experience to draw on. Acquiring this experience in combat sometimes produced unwarranted casualties.

For example, Mujahideen activities increased in Ghazni Province at the end of 1981. A bitter battle developed along the Ghazni-Kabul road and the Ghazni-Kandahar road. The enemy paid special attention to the conduct of truck convoys transporting military and economic cargo. At the beginning of September, a motorized rifle company, in which Senior Lieutenant V. I. Rovba served as a pla-toon leader, was ordered to escort an 80-vehicle convoy from Ghazni to Kabul and return—a distance of 160 kilometers.[46] Two motorized rifle platoons were detailed for the mission. The company commander would command the mission and could communicate with helicopters over a radio he had from the regimen-tal communications company.

The only preparation that the soldiers had for the mission was drawing their ammunition and cleaning their individual and crew-served weapons. The drivers pulled maintenance on their vehicles by themselves.

The security of the convoy was organized with one BTR at the head of the convoy and two at the tail. The other seven BTRs were spaced throughout the convoy between every 15 or 16 trucks. In the event of a Mujahideen attack, the nearest motorized rifle squad traveling in the convoy on its BTR would pull over to the side of the road from which the enemy was firing and return fire with all of its weapons. Thus, it would provide covering fire for the trucks driving out of the kill zone. Once the convoy was clear, the BTRs would rejoin the convoy and reoccupy their positions in the march column. The main provision, which the company commander ordered, was that under no condition would the enemy be allowed to stop the column. It would be very difficult to get the convoy going again should it be stopped.

The road march to Kabul passed without incident. However, there was a delay in refilling the fuel trucks. This meant that the return trip, which was supposed to begin at 0600 hours, did not start until 1030 hours. The convoy sat on the outskirts of Kabul for four hours waiting for the fuel trucks. While the convoy waited, individual Afghan vehicles passed by. The drivers and passengers could not help but notice the composition and size of the convoy.

When the loaded fuel tankers finally arrived, the convoy set out. After driving for one and a half hours, the convoy entered the minor Kabul river canyon [Khord-Kabul] and traveled through a green zone. Three kilometers ahead of the convoy was an Afghan Army post which guarded a river bridge. The presence of this post had a certain psychological effect and the soldiers relaxed their vigilance as the convoy approached the post. Once the entire convoy was flanked by the green zone, Mujahideen RPG-7 fire opened up on the lead vehicles—the command vehicle and a fuel truck towing a broken-down fuel truck. The fuel truck towing the other fuel truck was hit. Simultaneously, the Mujahideen hit the tail of the convoy and knocked out a trail BTR.

The escort vehicles reacted as they had been briefed and returned fire. The truck column began to drive out of the kill zone while the enemy was rattled by the return fire. The company commander radioed for air support and after 30 minutes, helicopters arrived. They hit the enemy and supported the motorized riflemen in their fight. Soviet losses were one soldier KIA and seven WIA.

Major A. A. Degtev recalls other ambushes in other green zones on the Kabul-Gardez highway. In one of these ambushes at the end of 1983, the convoy lost 16 vehicles and about 10 personnel killed and wounded.

The enemy was especially insidious in attacking supply convoys moving inside cities. The Mujahideen used small groups of 25 to 30 men. They functioned in secret, attacking individual vehicles and convoys alike.

Lieutenant Colonel A. A. Agzamov served in Afghanistan as a platoon leader in a reconnaissance company.[47] At the end of 1981, his company, which was garrisoned in Maimana, was ordered to escort a 120-vehicle convoy from Andkhoy to Maimana. The distance was 110 kilometers. The company was reinforced with a sapper squad, a flamethrower squad, a ZSU-23-4 air defense gun, and some recovery vehicles.

They had two days to prepare for the mission. They paid particular attention to readying the vehicles for the march and to preparing weapons for combat. The deputy commander of a Spetsnaz detachment, N. Beksultanov, was placed in charge of the convoy. After they linked up with the loaded trucks in Andkhoy, the convoy commander specified the composition of the march order, distributed combat power throughout the convoy, coordinated necessary details, and determined the site of the night lager on the march route.

The convoy moved out at 0500 on the appointed day. A forward security patrol (a platoon) moved in front of the convoy. By 0900, the forward patrol reached the village of Daulatabad. They reported back that the village was deserted. This report put the convoy on guard, and the convoy commander ordered increased observation. When the lead vehicles of the convoy began to exit the village, the Mujahideen opened fire with RPG-7s and hit the convoy commander's BMP and a fuel tanker full of gasoline. A fire broke out and the vehicles immediately behind the conflagration were stuck in the narrow streets.

Simultaneously, the enemy opened up with small arms fire. Two more BMPs were knocked out and, as a result, the convoy was split into three sections. The Soviets returned fire, but it was not controlled or directed and, due to loss of control, the return fire was not too effective.

A FAC flying overhead saw what was happening and called in helicopters. The FAC directed their fires as they made gun runs on the village. The trail platoon, under the cover of the helicopter gunships and their BMPs, dismounted and began to sweep the western part of Daulatabad. Faced with this decisive action, the enemy withdrew. However, in the course of this three-hour battle, four soldiers (all drivers) were KIA, six soldiers were WIA, three BMPs were destroyed, and five trucks were burned up.

These early failures could be attributed to the lack of soldiers' moral-psychological preparation and the lack of commanders' skills in organizing battle in this very difficult terrain. There were instances when junior officers lost control in a critical situation, when they were unable to direct fire skillfully with the covering force, or they communicated with helicopters and artillery poorly. The Soviets also did not understand enemy tactics. All these led to unnecessary losses of life and equipment, and not a single convoy was conducted without such losses.

After these early failures, the commanders at all levels began to pay more serious attention to the problem of convoy escort and security. Afghanistan is a mountainous country. General-Lieutenant B. V. Gromov noted that practically everything necessary for life and combat in Afghanistan had to be delivered on trucks. Therefore, over the course of nine years, the Soviets developed a system that allowed them to conduct convoys with a minimum loss of equipment, lives, and cargo. Over the succeeding years, the Soviets began protecting vehicular convoys somewhat differently depending on the level of enemy activity and the terrain. They established permanent security outposts along the route and continued to escort convoys with combat subunits.

Along the main highways, which were guarded by permanent security outposts, the truck convoys moved without a covering force. Security outposts were located to control difficult terrain, namely canyons, mountain passes, serpentine switch backs, in green zones, at the entry and exit to tunnels, and other places at which the Mujahideen could commit acts of sabotage or attack convoys. At every security outpost was an alert force that was on five-minute alert to move to the scene of an attack on a convoy. Also artillery and mortar batteries were ready to open fire. Further, experience of the previous years showed the need to deploy the highway commandant's regiment and subunits of the highway commandant's service on key sections of the highways.[48] The commandant's service would set up mobile patrol points on the highway with their armored vehicles. The highway commandant's service would regulate and direct traffic; dispatch control and security elements during the escort of convoys through tunnels, passes, and other dangerous sections of road; conduct continuous reconnaissance along the roads; render technical aid and fill vehicles with fuel; provide medical assistance to convoy personnel; evacuate sick and wounded; evacuate broken-down and damaged vehicles; and enforce a high state of military discipline.

Dispatcher points were established to control traffic flow on the highways. Dispatcher points consisted of five or six personnel (leader, dispatcher, and riflemen-regulators). They were usually located in troop compounds and in the areas of security outposts. Every dispatcher point had its zone of responsibility. In this zone, they would establish constant control over the moving convoy, provide for its safe movement, and support the efficient transfer of the convoy from one zone of responsibility to the next.

The movement and organization of convoys was controlled by a central dispatch point. The point was composed of officers from the army rear services, the highway commandant's service, the transport service, the operations section, and three shifts of duty dispatchers. Convoy control was carried out by signals, commands, and radio instructions from the dispatcher service at neighboring dispatcher posts and pickets. The convoy commander personally transmitted information. Information about the convoy movements was sent to dispatcher points, security outposts, control posts of the highway-commandant's service battalion, and the command posts of the division and regiment whose AO the convoy was transmitting. Control was handed off as the convoy exited the various zones of responsibility. Information about incidents, shelling attacks, and Mujahideen assaults were immediately transmitted by all communications means.

In order to facilitate the control of moving truck convoys, Colonel E. Mikhalko founded and commanded a group of efficiency experts[49] to design and inculcate a special control system, which was laid out on an automated, electronic map. This map was arranged to allow the expert to see the situation quickly on a selected section of road and to analyze the information to make the necessary decisions and implement them. Thanks to this group, the Soviets always had the necessary highway information to adjust the convoy schedules, remove obstructions and other hindrances, and schedule timely vehicle maintenance and crew rest.

As a rule, convoys formed using vehicles with the same speed, cross-country capability, and freight-carrying tactical-technical characteristics. This allowed the planner to organize by quality and to better schedule maintenance and to facilitate control of the convoy's movement. It was also important to maintain the integrity of the transport subunits. The most sensible truck convoy was one conducted by a transport company. The transport company has its own supply and maintenance capability and an independent organization.

The composition and march order of a truck convoy depended on the situation in which it would carry out the transport, the degree of enemy activity, the condition of the roads and terrain, the degree of technical support available on the roads, and the on-loading and off-loading capabilities at the start point and finish point. Usually, truck convoys had 50 to 80 vehicles. These included command and control vehicles, cargo trucks, and the trail party. Three to five BMPs or BTRs and three to five air-defense machine guns were attached if there was the possibility that the convoy might have to withstand an enemy attack. As a rule, there was one combat vehicle for every 15 to 20 trucks. The trail party included the PAK-200;[50] maintenance trucks carrying spare tires, spare parts, tools, accessories, and lubricants; wheeled recovery vehicles; water and fuel tank trucks; and one or two spare trucks. The convoy commander had the necessary communications to talk to his assigned security elements. Helicopters would escort the convoys over particularly dangerous routes.

Every convoy had a convoy commander. If a subunit constituted a single convoy, the subunit commander was the convoy commander. The convoy commander bore responsibility for maintaining order at the loading area and during the course of the march. He was also responsible for safeguarding the cargo in transit and for organizing close combat to repel a Mujahideen attack.

The convoy commanders paid particular attention to warning personnel about an enemy attack and to the actions to be taken when the warning signal was given. In the event of a Mujahideen attack, the attached security element would immediately accept combat, while the convoy would increase speed and vehicle spacing and move out of the kill zone under the cover of friendly return fire.

If the convoy was pinned down in an attack and could not move, the convoy commander would counter the enemy attack using his earlier-developed battle drills in close coordination with his fire support. He would give instructions to his covering force and quickly inform the regimental command post responsible for the area his convoy was transiting. He would report the attack and the artillery and air support he was currently receiving. After the convoy passed through this dangerous area, it would assemble in a specially designated area.

The convoy escort acted somewhat differently on sections of road where there were no permanent security outposts. It these situations, the convoy escort used specific techniques that it had thoroughly rehearsed earlier.

When a supply convoy had to transit territory controlled by enemy detachments, combat subunits of Soviet and Afghan forces plus artillery and aviation were detailed for security. The combat subunits would block sections of the roadside and escort the trucks along the highway.

Depending on the length of the road march, the terrain, the situation, and the amount of detailed combat subunits available, they would block a section of the roadside or the entire route for one to two days. In the first instance, the subunits doing the blocking for the supply convoy would move to the new section of road to be blocked while the convoy was at a rest stop. They would continue to bound in this fashion, to protect the convoy all the way to the end point.

If the march route was short and there were enough detailed security forces available, the entire road would be blocked and secured simultaneously as part of a comprehensive transportation operation.

A motorized rifle battalion was normally detailed for blocking roadsides. The battalion was assigned a zone of responsibility in which, depending on the terrain and mission, the battalion would create the necessary number of security barriers, outposts, and ambushes. The battalion would construct strong points and prepare a fire plan tied in with engineer obstacles. A motorized rifle company or tank company would usually constitute two to three security barriers and four to six security posts. The security posts were positioned so that they had visual contact with each other and the road. If there were sections of the road that could not be observed from the security outposts, then that section could be secured by an armored block.[51] An armored block consisted of two to three armored vehicles (tanks, BMPs, or BTRs). The commander would daily determine the times to establish and remove the armored block.

The battalion commander maintained a group of three to four armored vehicles at his command post that could rapidly reinforce any section of the battalion zone of responsibility and help repulse a Mujahideen attack. This group was normally reinforced with a mortar crew.

Every evening, the senior headquarters sent a schedule to its subunit commanders who were performing blocking missions. The schedule included every supply convoy that would pass through the subunit sector, the size of the convoy (by cargo vehicles and escort vehicles), and the time of passage. The regiment commander issued the order providing escort vehicles to these transiting convoys. The personnel detailed to blocking duty received this information every day from the regiment. The information the posts received was limited to what they needed to perform their duties.

A movement support detachment cleared the road before the armored blocks were posted on the roadway. A couple of sappers usually checked the deployment site for the armored block. The convoys moved only after all the security elements were in position, and then usually with a combat subunit as an escort.

As a rule, it took two to three days to prepare a combat subunit for escort duty after it received the mission. Preparations included vehicle maintenance; issuing the necessary ammunition, POL, rations, and medical supplies to the companies; assigning personnel to vehicles; and the conduct of training and rehearsals by the company and platoon commanders. The training and rehearsals included assigning observation responsibilities, evacuating broken-down and damaged vehicles, and giving first aid and evacuating the wounded. The commanders gave particular attention to training their snipers, armored vehicle drivers, machine gunners, ATGM crews, flame thrower operators, RTOs, artillery FOs, acting FACs,[52] medics, and sappers.

The convoy usually set out early in the morning and stopped late in the evening. The commander would not allow large gaps between vehicles, since the enemy could use these gaps to mine the road unobserved or to attack solitary vehicles. The perfidy of the Mujahideen knew no bounds. In the later years of the war, the Mujahideen started using "counter-reaction" groups in their ambushes in order to increase convoy casualties on the roads and particularly on urban streets. These "counter-reaction" groups would pin down the Soviet reconnaissance and security forces, and, at the same time, the enemy main force would attack a critical section of the convoy, destroying men and machines.

Lieutenant Colonel D. F. Savchin, who served in Afghanistan as a battalion chief of staff, remembers the Mujahideen use of such tactics in October 1988. His battalion was providing security to an 800-vehicle DRA convoy moving from Puli-Khumri to Kabul. The column stretched out over 50 kilometers in length. As the convoy approached the Salang tunnel, the Mujahideen fired at two BTRs in the middle of the convoy. The BTRs joined battle, and soon all the available security forces were firing at the Mujahideen. Then, the Mujahideen launched their main attack on eight food trucks that were out of view of any security elements. Such tactics helped the Mujahideen destroy 22 trucks before the convoy reached its destination.

In order to prevent similar attacks, combat subunit commanders constituted two reconnaissance elements and two security elements. The first group or a reconnaissance and a security element might battle with the enemy "counter-reaction" groups, conducting reconnaissance and organizing a defense behind adobe walls within a village, while the second group would continue to assist the convoy in its march. Such an arrangement facilitated the quick passage through built-up areas.

Such commanders' initiative and foresight, coupled with their unswerving dedication to working out multiple tactical variants with their subunits, led to their success in the event of an enemy attack. Major A. M. Portnov remembers one such action.[53]

Two air assault platoons, reinforced with a mortar platoon, a flamethrower squad, and two AGS-17 automatic grenade launchers (mounted on BTRs), were detailed to escort a supply convoy the 114 kilometers from Shekravan to Shirkhan. The air assault company commander, A. M. Portnov, was the convoy commander. A DRA Sarandoy company was attached to the escort element. The Sarandoy company personnel were equally distributed throughout the convoy to ride on every cargo truck. The Forward Security Element (FSE), consisting of two BMDs and a BTR, moved a kilometer in front of the convoy.

When the convoy approached Basiz village, the enemy fired on the FSE with grenade launchers and blew up a command-detonated mine. The enemy was trying to destroy the bridge across the canal and the BTR that was on it. Thus, they hoped to stop the convoy. Simultaneously, the enemy knocked out four cargo trucks in the convoy. However, the Mujahideen's initial success did not lead to a great victory.

The security element and an air assault platoon executed a planned battle drill to maneuver behind the enemy and to take him from the rear. The fires from one BMD, an AGS-17 crew, and the mortar platoon were enough to pin down the enemy, who were subsequently surrounded and destroyed.

In another episode, the high level of the soldiers' combat readiness supported a successful mission. Major A. I. Guboglo, who was a platoon leader at the time, recalls the battle.[54]

In the winter of 1982, a convoy, escorted by the 7th MRC, was traveling between Kabul and Ghazni. There were two BTRs at both the head and tail of the convoy. The other BTRs were dispersed between every eight trucks of the convoy. Another platoon served as a reconnaissance patrol and moved ten kilometers in front of the convoy.

As the convoy entered the green zone in the Maliykhel' region and crossed the river bridge, the enemy activated a radio-controlled, command-detonated mine that damaged a towing vehicle. The enemy then opened fire on the convoy from dominant heights. Efforts to clear the road and move to a safe place proved fruitless. Despite the heavy Soviet small arms, BTR, and helicopter gun ship fire, the Mujahideen continued heavy fire on the convoy. The company commander called on the radio for an additional pair of helicopters. Then he ordered the 1st MRP, which had originally acted as the reconnaissance platoon, to attack the enemy and take the height under the covering fire of the machine gun/grenade launcher platoon and the helicopter. The convoy could now resume its march.

This acquired convoy escort combat experience was widely used in the closing phase of the war, especially during the withdrawal of Soviet forces, starting on 15 May 1988 and ending on 15 February 1989. During the withdrawal operation, the Soviets moved more than 100,000 men, a large number of combat vehicles, and a large amount of supplies from 25 garrisons and 179 base camps.

The leaders of the opposition well understood that it would not do to wreck the withdrawal of Soviet forces, a lesson that they had learned and still understood from the Soviet withdrawal of six regiments in 1986. However, the leadership of the Group of Seven insisted on a blood bath. Therefore, the Soviet command paid serious attention to security and convoy escort during the force withdrawal. Hero of the Soviet Union Major S. N. Gushchin's battalion, along with others, supported the withdrawal of forces.

As a rule, a combat mission was issued to a battalion two to three days prior to the convoy. The mission was either to conduct a convoy supporting the withdrawal of forces or to transport civilian cargo back into Afghanistan. During this time, all organization issues were resolved. A day before the start of the operation, the officers of the battalion command post conducted a rehearsal to determine which personnel would participate in the upcoming combat action. The rehearsal included all categories of soldiers—officers, NCOs, and privates. Training and preparations then ensued to ensure that the selected personnel were 100 percent prepared in combat support, maintenance, and supply as well as being morally, psychologically, and physically fit to accomplish the mission.

Depending on the length of the march, the battalion established one or two blocking positions in its zone of responsibility. There was always a blocking position at the convoy finish point. Usually the battalion moved out to position its blocks early in the morning, crossing the departure line at 0500 or 0600 hours. The road march began with a movement support detachment (up to a reinforced MRC). A FSE moved behind it staying within visual and supporting fire range. The battalion main body moved behind the FSE. The battalion rear services followed the main body, and the escorted convoy followed the battalion rear services. A maintenance trail party followed the convoy; a rear security element brought up the rear.

The battalion commander moved at the head of or in the center of his battalion. During the course of the movement, he revised his concept for establishing the blocking position, personally pointed out every possible enemy position along the route, and personally designated firing positions. Sometimes a company commander would take over this duty. As soon as the battalion arrived at the boundary of its zone of responsibility, it would begin establishing the blocking positions. A tank with a mine plow or other engineering equipment would clear the sites of enemy mines before combat vehicles occupied the blocking positions. The machine would dig up the area to clear the space that vehicle tracks would transit. The mine plows would clear firing positions which were one-and-a-half to two times larger than the length and width of the weapons system that would occupy the firing position.

When moving through areas where the Mujahideen might conduct ambushes, the moving tanks and BMPs would shoot at possible Mujahideen firing positions. They would fire at these possible sites while moving at about ten kilometers per hour.

The basic requirement of combat vehicles was to keep in visual contact with your neighbor and stay in a position where you can support your neighbor with fire. In areas of possible enemy contact, it was usual to establish two sites. The battalion CP-OP was sited at the point of probable enemy action, and a firing position was laid out for the mortar battery.

Commanders constituted mobile groups[55] to deal with surprise situations that arose. These groups usually consisted of a tank, the AGS-17 platoon, and one to three mortars. The group commander was usually the company executive officer or an experienced platoon leader. The mortar battery was located where it could coordinate its fires with the supporting artillery battery and provide fire support to the battalion positions. Depending on the situation, the convoy usually arrived in the designated region some one to two hours after the battalion established its blocking positions or on the following day. Such support of convoys was provided by battalions near Kandahar, Charikar, Musa Kala, Farah, Herat, and other critical areas.

In such a fashion, the Soviets acquired rich combat experience in convoy security and escort over nine years of counter-guerrilla war in the rugged, mountain-desert terrain of Afghanistan. At war's end, the Soviets understand the correct role of march security and the positioning of personnel and weapons systems to counter enemy surprise attacks. Further, convoy escort and security in Afghanistan demanded serious modifications to combat equipment and increased the quality of commanders, staffs, and forces training.

Editors' comments: Convoy escort was not a task that motorized rifle forces trained for in the Soviet Union. Rear area security was the responsibility of the KGB and Interior Troops. The 40th Army's LOCs were exposed in Afghanistan, and convoy escort and convoy security became a major task of these combat forces. Convoy security and LOC security tied down a good portion of Soviet combat forces, but it was absolutely essential since the 40th Army was totally dependent on the uninterrupted flow of supplies from the Soviet Union.

The General Staff did not maintain good records on combat experience in Afghanistan, and so the personnel who wrote this chapter utilized the data available in the Frunze Academy. The Bear Went Over the Mountain *is drawn from this same Frunze Academy data. Therefore, some of the material in this volume was previously published in* The Bear Went Over the Mountain. *The editors decided to retain this material. Likewise, where the General Staff decided not to include a supporting map, the editors followed their lead even though these are available in* The Bear Went Over the Mountain. *We apologize to any readers who feel that they are going over the same ground unnecessarily.*

In a scene familiar to hundreds of years of warfare in Afghanistan, a dismounted Soviet motorized rifle company hikes into the mountains. Most of these soldiers have swapped their inadequate issue boots for Chinese-manufactured tennis shoes. (Central Museum of the Armed Forces)

Relegated to firing flares in high-tempo modern mechanized warfare, the ancient 82mm *Podnos* (Tray) mortar became a star performer in the Soviet-Afghan War. (Valentin Runov)

Sappers lead the way. Soviet engineers protected by body armor and using probes and a trained dog gingerly probe for mines in front of the infantry. (Central Museum of the Armed Forces)

Mi-24 "HIND" helicopter gunships in action in the Panjshir valley in June 1985. (Vasiliy Semochkin)

BM-21 "Grad" (Thunderstorm) multiple rocket launcher battery opens fire on suspected Mujahideen positions. (Valentin Runov)

Destroyed Soviet fuel tank trucks on the road near the Salang tunnel. (Central Museum of the Armed Forces)

Aerial photograph of the Panjshir valley. Seven Mujahideen supply trucks are moving by daylight on the road that parallels the Panjshir river. (Central Museum of the Armed Forces)

Not a man from Mars, but a Soviet sapper in a protective suit, which offers complete protection from antipersonnel mines but weighs 28 kilograms (62 pounds). (Anatoliu Avdeev)

The Soviets even used the R-300 "SCUD" missile to fire conventional warheads at remote Mujahideen base camps. When the Soviets withdrew, they left four battalions of SCUD missiles behind to support the Najibulloah regime. (Viktor Murakhovskiy)

Two SU-25 "FROGFOOT" close air support aircraft. Called *Grach* (Raven) by the Soviets, these provided air-ground support. (Vladimir Vinogradov)

T-62D tanks in defensive positions guarding the approach to the Salang tunnel. (Central Museum of the Armed Forces)

Battery of 122mm D-30 howitzers deployed in a circular firing position. Normally, Soviet artillery was positioned in a straight line, but in Afghanistan, they were forced to deploy for combat in any direction. (Central Museum of the Armed Forces)

Artillery fire direction center, where laser range finder helps determine firing data. A visiting Soviet General Major is conspicuous in his saucer cap. (Central Museum of the Armed Forces)

Motorized rifle regiment command post in the field, 1983. (Central Museum of the Armed Forces)

Field repair of a BMD-1 airborne personnel carrier. The turret assembly and gun are being replaced. (Valentin Runov)

In the Afghan desert, water is precious and necessary. Soviet engineers positioned rubber water reservoirs at key points to support their forces. (Petr Skuratov)

It wasn't just a man's war. A female warrant officer who provided medical support to a motorized rifle battalion takes a moment to smell a flower and reflect. (Aleksandr Torgashin)

Back in the USSR. A soldier and his mother meet at Termez as the last of the Soviet forces are withdrawn in February 1989. (Aleksandr Torgashin)

Often soldiers erected monuments to fallen comrades at the place of their deaths. This monument memorializes an officer—"Vitaliy Eliseevich Kretinin, 1 March 1944–12 February 1987." Even these simple markers did not last too long after the Soviet withdrawal. (Central Museum of the Armed Forces)

6

Combat Arms Branch Tactics

Combat in Afghanistan was conducted by the various branches of the ground and air forces. Units and subunits of artillery, armor, airborne, air assault, and army aviation participated in the battles and operations, along with the motorized rifle forces. They developed and perfected various techniques and methods to accomplish combat missions as part of a combined arms group or independently. Many of their techniques and methods set new milestones in developing branch tactics for the special conditions of the war in Afghanistan.

ARTILLERY[1]

The war in Afghanistan demonstrated that the most important condition for achieving victory in combat is to conduct effective fire destruction of the enemy. The main means of conducting that fire destruction was artillery. The LCOSF had TO&E artillery assigned to its divisions and brigades. There was additional artillery assigned to the 40th Army artillery.

The most numerous and probably the most effective artillery systems in Afghanistan were the mortars.[2] They were indispensable for combat in the mountains, for repulsing Mujahideen attacks on security pickets and outposts, and for fighting in built-up areas and green zones.

The Soviet forces used the 82mm *podnos* [tray] mortar and 82mm *vasilyek* [bachelor's button] automatic mortar widely during the war. They were lightweight, aggressive, mobile artillery systems that could effectively support the various combat arms on the plains and, more importantly, in the mountains. The *podnos* could be disassembled and man-packed into the mountains. The *vasilyek* was often mounted in a MTLB[3] to increase its maneuverability and protect it from enemy fire.

For fire missions that required a heftier round, the towed 120mm *Sani*

167

[sleigh] mortar and the towed 240mm M-240 mortar were effective. These mortars were towed into battle behind a truck, BTR, BMP, or tank. They are relatively lightweight and can be manhandled into a new firing position by their crews. Their rounds pack significant explosive power and they have a wide bursting radius. At the same time, since they are towed, they are less maneuverable than self-propelled artillery, and the mortar crews are vulnerable to enemy fire.

The Soviet forces used the 240mm 2S4 self-propelled *Tul'pan* [tulip] mortar for the first time in combat in Afghanistan. This system, which is mounted on a tracked, armored vehicle, can quickly shift positions on the battlefield and destroy the more important enemy targets. It is a particularly accurate weapon when it fires the laser-guided *Smel'chak* [daredevil] round.

In addition to mortars, the Soviets used a variety of howitzers in combat. The towed D-30 122mm howitzer was widely used at security pickets and outposts. The D-30 fires 360° without relaying the piece, ranges over 15 kilometers, and has a wide variety of rounds. The D-30 proved an effective fire support system, primarily when used in fixed positions.

The Soviets widely employed the 122mm 2S1 *Gvozdika* [carnation] self-propelled howitzer and the 152mm 2S3 *Akatsiya* [acacia] self-propelled howitzer for maneuver combat against the enemy. These systems possess great fire power, maneuverability, and crew-protection and were indispensable on the battlefield. The Soviets used the 152mm 2S3 *Akatsiya* widely for firing on fortified positions and for direct and semi-direct firing, as well as assault guns in direct support of motorized rifle forces during the seizure of forward combat bases.

The 152mm 2S5 *Giatsint* [hyacinth] self-propelled cannon was used for especially difficult fire missions. It could fire on enemy targets out to 30 kilometers away. At the same time, the system had a limited sector of fire, and its effectiveness was significantly reduced when used in the mountains against small, highly mobile enemy groups.

The Soviet forces in Afghanistan used various types of antitank systems for fire missions, despite the lack of Mujahideen armored vehicles. The *Konkurs* [competition],[4] *Fagot* [bassoon],[5] and *Metis* [mongrel][6] antitank guided missiles have a high rate of probability of a first-round hit. The Soviets used them to hit enemy firing points located in caves, in stone-constructed field fortifications, and other sites where it was difficult or impossible to use artillery.

As a rule, the Soviets did not use the 100mm MT-12 antitank gun in mobile combat. It was used to protect LOCs and important installations. For example, there is a green zone on the approaches to the Kunduz airfield. The TO&E antitank battalion of the 201st Motorized Rifle Division secured this airfield and shelled the green zone with their 100mm guns. The high rate of fire and accuracy of this artillery system enabled the gunners to rapidly and effectively engage an observed enemy with fragmentation ammunition.

The Soviets also used multiple rocket launchers (MRL) to rain destruction on the enemy during battle. They used the BM-21 *Grad* [hailstorm] and BM-22

System	Maximum range (km)	Rounds per minute	Unit of fire	Weight of the System (kilograms)
82mm mortar "podnos"	4	20	80	40
82mm automatic mortar "vasilyek"	4.27	100	300	600
120mm mortar "Sani"	7.1	10	80	210
240mm mortar M-240	9.7	1	40	3600
240mm self-propelled mortar "tul'pan"	9.7 19.8 w/ rocket-assisted round	1	40	27500
122mm howitzer D-30	15.3	7	80	3200
122mm self-propelled howitzer "Gvozdika"	15.2	5	80	15700
152mm self-propelled howitzer "Acacia"	17.3	4	60	27500
152mm self-propelled cannon "Giasint"	28.5	6	60	9800
BM-21 MRL "Grad"	20	40 round 122mm rocket salvo in 20 seconds	120	13700
BM-22 MRL "Uragan"	50	16 round 220mm rocket salvo in 40 seconds	48	20200

Figure 7. Basic tactical-technical characteristics of tube artillery and MRLs

Uragan [hurricane] MRL which have significant destructive power and a large impact area. They used these systems to kill enemy in the open, deployed on the crests of heights, or on mountain plateaus and in canyons. In some cases, the BM-21 was used to place remotely delivered mines (RDM) in areas it was difficult to reach or to prevent an enemy withdrawal from a cordon and search operation. The wide variety of BM-21 munitions with their various directional systems allows firing out to ranges of 20 to 30 kilometers to create avalanches, fire, and rock slides on enemy territory.

Figure 7 shows the basic tactical-technical characteristics of tube artillery and MRLs.

Mobile reconnaissance posts, sound-ranging systems, radar systems, and fire direction vehicles conducted target reconnaissance and fire direction to support the mission.

The PRP-3 and PRP-4 mobile reconnaissance posts fulfilled a wide variety of difficult missions in the mountains. They not only "triangulated" the enemy, but they also helped adjust artillery fire and illuminated the command post location in the event that it came under attack at night.

It was difficult to use the VPZK and AZK-5 sound ranging systems in Afghanistan. The enemy artillery was small caliber (50mm to 107mm), the enemy positioned his artillery in terrain folds (*karez,* crevices, and the reverse slope of heights) which muffled the sound of his firing, and the enemy was highly mobile. This prevented orientating the sound reconnaissance in the designated region. As a result, the sound ranging systems had limited effectiveness against Mujahideen mortars and rocket launchers firing in the mountains.

These same conditions limited the effectiveness of the SNAR-10 and ARK-1 artillery radar reconnaissance systems in finding the enemy artillery. At the same time, these radar systems were effectively used to adjust Soviet artillery fire, especially at night. The portable ground radar reconnaissance system PSNR-5 was used to detect nearby moving objects. However, it could not be used to adjust fire since it was impossible to determine the point of impact in relation to the target with the PSNR-5.

Combat showed that optical reconnaissance was the best method of artillery reconnaissance in Afghanistan. It produced preferred basic artillery data—the ability to quickly "intersect" the enemy and "produce" polar coordinates (angle of deflection off the gun-target line, range, height). Artillery optical reconnaissance was conducted using optical instruments—the PAB-2A field artillery surveying instrument and the DS-1, DS-2, 1D13, and 1D15 optical range finders. Figure 8 shows the basic tactical-technical characteristics of these artillery reconnaissance systems.

Combat demonstrated that artillery systems functioned effectively while firing at maximum rates and in the complex meteorological conditions of Afghanistan (extreme dustiness and high temperatures [50° Centigrade[7] and higher]). However, there were several precautions that were necessary to ensure firing effectiveness and stability. During preparation for combat, the gun crews needed to thoroughly inspect all the MRL rockets that had been transported off road by ammunition trucks and other transport. This rough transit often separated the warhead and rocket motor. This, in turn, sometimes resulted in the explosion of the round in the MRL launcher during the launch. Intensive operation of artillery systems in the dusty air and high temperatures resulted in the breakdown of mechanisms and assemblies in MRL and cannon. During the firing of the BM-21 *Grad,* the separate adjustment belt of the rocket launcher assembly weakened. Firing the 2S1 and 2S3 howitzers weakened the power ram loading mechanism as well as attached components, assemblies, and instruments on the howitzer hulls and also produced fluid leaks from the weapon's recoil absorbers.

Nature and climatic conditions affect the use of optical-electronic instruments.

System	Range (kilometers)	Accuracy (meters)	Operating sector	How carried	Magnification
1D13 laser range finder	1.45 - 20	1	360 degrees	Man pack	x7
DS-1 stereoscopic range finder	0.4 - 16	15	360 degrees	Man pack	x8
DS-2 optical range finder	0.4 - 20	10	360 degrees	Man pack	x8
PAB-2A artillery surveying instrument	1.0 - 6	-	360 degrees	Man pack	x8
PSNR-5 radar	10 (vehicle) 4 (man)	20	24-120 degrees	Man pack	-
ARK-1 counter-battery radar	15 (artillery) 30 (rocket)	30-90	30 degrees	MTLB CP vehicle	-
SNAR-10 radar	23 (vehicle)	30-50	30 degrees	MTLB	-
AZK-5 sound locator	12 - 16	1% of range	10 - 12 degrees	ZIL131 truck carries 5 pieces	-
PRP-3	8 -10	.1% of range	1 - 1.5 km	BMP-1	x8
PRP-4	10-15	.1% of range	1 - 1.5 km	BMP-2	x8

Figure 8. Artillery reconnaissance system characteristics

The mountain terrain allows the selection of observation points that support long-range direct observation, but low-power observation instruments limit long-range observation. Therefore, more-effective, high-power binoculars (B-10 and B12) were issued for mountain use. At the same time, the high amount of solar radiation limited the effectiveness of laser range finders by overheating the units and ruining their efficiency. Therefore, it proved prudent to equip artillery subunits with both optical and electronic instruments for reconnaissance and observation.

During the course of combat, the artillery of the LCOSF in Afghanistan performed several types of missions: artillery support of large-scale offensives, fire support of motorized rifle or airborne subunits in their zones of responsibility, security and defense of important military and civilian installations, march security and convoy escort, supporting a disengagement from combat, and the withdrawal of forces after mission accomplishment.

To carry out these missions, sometimes artillery would be massed in large artillery groups and other times would be split out by artillery battalion and even by artillery battery. The main difficulty in constituting artillery groups was that 20 to 30 percent of the systems were dedicated to securing installations. Therefore division and regimental artillery groups were constituted with very limited resources, and sometimes the artillery groups were not constituted at all. As a result, motorized rifle regiments often had to fight with only their TO&E artillery support.

The TO&E artillery battalion of the MRR was the basis of the Regimental Artillery Group (RAG) when it was constituted. The TO&E artillery regiment of the MRD was the basis of the Division Artillery Group (DAG) when it was constituted. The bulk of the MRD's artillery regiment was usually attached to the MRRs by artillery battalions and even batteries. However, in most situations, the division commander retained his MRL battalion and one to two batteries of the 152mm self-propelled 2S3 howitzer under his direct command. The motorized rifle battalion artillery (a mortar battery) was normally split among the motorized rifle companies. When an MRC was working in the mountains, they normally had an 82mm *Podnos* mortar platoon and an AT-4 ATGM crew attached from battalion assets.

Neither spreading out artillery nor massing artillery in groups guaranteed quality fire missions. Consequently, the 40th Army convened a commanders' conference involving all command levels to consider the predicament. They decided that in mountain warfare, the basic firing element was the artillery battery and, in some instances, the artillery platoon. Based on this new definition, they planned fire missions against the enemy.[8]

Fire planning against the enemy depended on the situation, the scope of the action, and the type of action.[9] In large-scale offensive operations and in combat during the cordon and search of an area containing a significant number of Mujahideen, there were three phases of fire support—fire preparation of the attack, fire support of the attack, and fire accompaniment of the advancing force into the enemy depth.

Fire preparation of the attack was conducted to inflict maximum casualties on the enemy and to demoralize and limit the effectiveness of enemy personnel, as a rule, to a depth of four to five kilometers. The length of the artillery preparation was determined by the number of required fire missions and the amount of artillery available. Most often, it lasted 18 to 35 minutes. Fire preparation of the attack was planned and conducted within the course of one to three fire strikes. The first fire strike was directed at the first firing line, corresponding to Mujahideen located in firing positions and concealed groups in the villages that would be seized by Soviet subunits (according to the senior commander's plan). The second fire strike would hit targets of the enemy defense located on the second and third firing lines and also on enemy firing positions located on the middle and lower tiers of the mountains. The third fire strike, as a rule, would revisit the targets of the first fire strike.

In some instances, the third fire strike would be a combination of conventional artillery rounds and the creation of a smoke screen on the forward edge of the enemy positions. In addition, the third strike would fire on flanking enemy firing positions located on dominant terrain. However, artillery smoke screens were not widely employed in the mountains of Afghanistan, since it was very hard to lay in a smoke screen without being able to predetermine wind speed, wind direction, and the meteorologic situation in the mountain passages (which caused drafts and other meteorological peculiarities that lessened the effectiveness of smoke rounds).

In 1985, during the independent combat to seize the Mujahideen base at Bayram Shah, Balkh Province, the artillery preparation of the attack was conducted with two fire strikes on the same targets. The first fire strike used delayed-action, high-explosive rounds to destroy the adobe structures that protected the enemy from shrapnel. However, not every 122mm high-explosive round fired at the covered enemy positions was able to penetrate the adobe and destroy the walls, fortress, or other structures. Some of these structures were left relatively intact. After the first strike, there was a tactical pause of 15 to 20 minutes. Then the second fire strike went in on the very same targets—which surprised the Mujahideen since they expected the fire to shift. The second fire strike used a large quantity of high-explosive fragmentation and flechette ammunition, which was extremely destructive on the exposed Mujahideen and their weapons. This kind of artillery preparation proved far more effective and frequently served to completely demoralize the enemy and destroy his defensive positions.

If the situation and terrain allowed, artillery would fire in direct lay during the artillery preparation for the attack. Thus, during the battle for Khanabad City, Kunduz Province, in May of 1986, the Soviets used a battery of 152mm self-propelled 2S3 howitzers in direct lay. They fired at covered positions on the dominant terrain, suppressing several specially designated targets, while the targets were bracketed by other artillery. Direct-lay artillery could continue to fire during the aviation preparation without a risk of hitting friendly aircraft and helicopters with artillery fire.

As a rule, the aviation preparation preceded the last fire strike of the artillery preparation of the attack and was directed at targets located in the enemy base region at a depth of five to seven kilometers from the line of contact.

Artillery support of the attack was conducted, as a rule, using the classifications of fire-fire concentration (SO) and single-line successive fire concentration (PSO). Artillerymen had to combine classifications of fire and apply fire differently than in conventional combat. Thus, during combat near Takhar in Parvan Province, the artillery had the mission of preventing the withdrawal of the enemy from a cordoned canyon into the mountains. The artillery used a three-line standing barrage with 300 to 650 meters between each line of artillery fire. They used three artillery groups that maintained the standing barrage for two hours by firing one round every three minutes. As a result of the establishment of the barrier fires, the enemy tried to escape in other directions. At first, the enemy wandered into a mine field and then into the fires of a blocking group. The enemy was completely destroyed.

Of definite interest is the artillery support of the attack conducted in Baghlan Province in November 1985 during an advance through a zone full of villages. The gunners planned to use the successive fire concentration method on a one-and-a-half kilometer front with a depth of three kilometers. The lines were straight-line map drawings corresponding to the configuration of the blocks of the villages. The gunners determined that the fire on the enemy covered-adobe defensive positions was having little effect. Therefore, they had a 152mm self-propelled 2S3 howitzer battalion conduct direct lay fire on every line of the PSO. These weapons began to destroy the adobe positions on every line of the PSO, after they shifted the artillery fire to firing on the covered firing positions on the consecutive lines. The artillery groups firing on direct lay shifted from one line to another by bounds by battery. Each battery moved 100 to 150 meters forward and reopened fire. As a result of such an integrated fire plan execution, they captured the villages practically without enemy return fire.

Sometimes, during combat in the villages or green zones, artillery support of the attack required the use of an offensive rolling barrage. Intense fire was conducted solely on the designated line. In November 1984, during an advance in Charikar valley (Parvan Province), the Soviet and Afghan forces used moving barrages. The barrage width in dense growth was 200 to 250 meters and 400 to 600 meters in an open area. The average depth of fire destruction of the enemy with a moving barrage was two kilometers. The third piece in each battery fired smoke rounds to mark lines in front of the attacking force and to direct fires. The fire on each line started with an artillery salvo and continued with volley fire until the command or signal was given to shift fire. If enemy resistance continued on one of the lines, then the FO, working with the attacking battalion or company commander, would concentrate fire on the trouble site to suppress the enemy completely.

Overlapping fire strikes were not planned.

In maneuver war, highly mobile enemy groups would quickly try to move out of the way of the "artillery support of the attack" and the "artillery accompaniment of the advancing force" phases of fire support. During these phases, the artillery most often fired on previously determined targets and on those targets discovered through additional reconnaissance to the depth of the planned military mission. The effectiveness of these important artillery phases depends on the possibility of maneuvering the fires and artillery subunits. In an area with few roads that are heavily mined by the enemy, maneuver of the subunits was very hard to accomplish. The solution was to work in accordance with the principle "I fire in support of my neighbor and my neighbor fires in support of me." Fire and subunits would shift wherever it was possible.

In some cases, "fire accompaniment of the force" into rugged terrain was accomplished by batteries, which were held in a special commander's reserve for this role at the beginning of the battle. Then, when their fire power was no longer able to support the destruction of the enemy, helicopter gunships were called in.

In all cases, during the artillery "support of the attack" phase, the control of the artillery was decentralized. As a result, the primary fire support for the advancing subunits was from artillery batteries and artillery platoons that were often attached to motorized rifle battalions and companies. Thus, during a February 1986 advance against an enemy dug in a green zone in Kandahar Province, every motorized rifle company was reinforced with a platoon of 82mm *Podnos* mortars. A mortar platoon of 82mm *Vasilek* automatic mortars stayed under the battalion commander's direct control. Mortar platoons moved 80 to 150 meters behind the advancing dismounted force to destroy the enemy at the command of the supported commander. Further, to provide more volume of fire, each battalion had a platoon of 122mm self-propelled 2S1 howitzers in support. Thanks to such a selection of various fire support systems, the fire missions were successfully accomplished. Witnesses state that during the artillery accompaniment of the force phase, the artillery suppressed 16 enemy firing positions. Two mortar platoons suppressed nine firing positions with an average of 12-to-30 82mm rounds per firing position. The 122mm self-propelled howitzer platoon suppressed the other seven firing positions with an average of 10-to-15 122mm rounds per position.

During the conduct of separate operations and actions, artillery planners must plan artillery support for the moving units and subunits as they leave their base camps, deploy into march column, and conduct the march. Unlike conventional combat, the artillery did not have to prepare to combat long-range artillery, since the enemy had none, but had to contend with destroying Mujahideen weapons systems deployed in ambush against the march columns. This mission was given to the alert forces and the artillery moving in the march column. The alert artillery battery or battalion located in the base camp covered the march unit until it had moved beyond the maximum range of this supporting artillery. Officer FOs were assigned to the motorized rifle battalions and companies so that they could quickly call for and adjust fire for the moving column. When the FO found a new target, he would consult his map, which had all the planned targets drawn on it. He would select the target closest to the Mujahideen and call for fire on that site. He would then adjust the fire from the observed strike of the artillery rounds and shift the fire onto the enemy. If the fire from the alert artillery unit was insufficient to destroy the enemy, the artillery accompanying the march columns would deploy and fire. Accompanying artillery usually fired on direct lay. Such an artillery combination served to successfully combat enemy ambushes.

The 2S1 122mm self-propelled howitzer and the *Nona-S*[10] 2S9 120mm self-propelled howitzer/mortar were best suited to support raiding motorized rifle or air assault forces. They usually deployed by battery or battalion. Prior to the raid, the Soviet planners determined initial targets from aerial, visual, and artillery reconnaissance. They usually fired a three-to-five minute artillery preparation on those targets. Should the Mujahideen open fire on the Soviet forces in the course of the raid, the Soviet gunners would attempt to quickly engage the target before it could escape by registering with one or two ranging rounds and then firing massed artillery fires on the target using normative firing tables for suppression or assured destruction. While pitched battles occurred, the most common activity for raiding Soviet forces was pursuit of a withdrawing enemy. Mujahideen would usually leave a rear guard to slow down the attacker while the main body escaped. The rear guard would try to stay within 200-to-300 meters of the Soviet force to escape Soviet air and artillery. In that case, the Soviet forward observer would spot his first round some 200 meters beyond the enemy and then walk the rounds back onto the enemy.

Rarely would the Soviets use a battery of 2S4 240mm self-propelled mortars for this type of mission. However, with the introduction of the laser-guided *smel'chak* round, this type of artillery system became irreplaceable for destroying well-constructed defensive positions, forts, and stone barriers.

Combat in Afghanistan reaffirmed that when a combined arms commander made the decision to suppress or destroy a target, he must know the technical characteristics and potential of the artillery systems and also have actual experience in directing the fire of his TO&E artillery systems.

A frequent type of artillery support was concentrated fire by a battery or single fire by a single piece.

Often, highly accurate fire support was necessary during the conduct of a pursuit of an enemy, even if it meant the loss of surprise. Very often this occurred where a small friendly blocking position was in close contact with the enemy, which was located 200-to-300 meters beyond the friendly subunit. In such situations, it was necessary to accurately adjust fire onto the enemy by initially firing some 200 meters behind the Mujahideen and then walking the fire forward on top of them. The gunners had to ensure safe fire support during close combat.[11]

When the target could be observed from the firing position, it could be accurately engaged by direct lay out to the maximum range for direct fire. In such a situation, the distance to the target could be determined with the help of a laser rangefinder, or in its absence, by eye with the help of a map. It demanded a high state of professional mastery to determine range in mountains.

With the introduction of the laser-guided round for the 2S4 240mm self-propelled mortar, this system became more effective, and could be used for fire support of forces. Thus, the destruction of a Mujahideen fortress only required one or two rounds. However, the registration on the target still required two-to-three F-864 High Explosive Fragmentation rounds.

A 2S4 240mm self-propelled mortar battery supported an MRR in the Charikar valley in June 1985 to eliminate a Mujahideen detachment belonging to Ahmad Shah Masood. During the attack on the enemy, the center of hard-core resistance was in the fortress (target 35). In the fortress, the Mujahideen concentrated a significant force armed with two DShK machine guns, six or seven RPG-7s, and small arms. Senior Lieutenant A. Beletsky, the mortar battery commander, was ordered to destroy this center of resistance.

The battery commander established an observation post on "Nameless" mountain and used a laser range finder to determine that the distance to the fortress was 2,350 meters. Calculating the firing data, the battery commander first fired a ranging round. After observing the explosion, the commander was able to correct the range and deflection and to fire a *smel'chak* guided round for the next shot. It took 12 minutes to destroy the fortress and demoralize the surviving enemy. It would have required the expenditure of much more ammunition and time to achieve the same results with other artillery systems.

Combat experience showed that the use of smart munitions was expedient not only in the valleys but also in the mountains. They were used with high effectiveness to destroy strong points and individual enemy firing positions located in terrain folds and sheltered in caves.

A special artillery mission was the security and defense of important military and civilian installations. As a rule, the antitank battalions of the motorized rifle divisions were used for these missions. They were armed with the 100mm MT-12 antitank gun and ATGM combat vehicles. Further, artillery battalions of D-30 122mm howitzers were assigned to these missions. The commanders at all levels tried to anticipate enemy attacks with combined artillery and reconnaissance systems.

The Soviets used the "Realiya-U" seismic reconnaissance system[12] extensively to help secure installations. They were used by the alert artillery units and significantly decreased the probability of an enemy surprise attack. In February 1986, Lieutenant T. Kozhbergenov commanded an alert platoon of D-30 122mm howitzers near Taloqan in Takhar Province. Their mission was to prevent an enemy surprise attack as part of a security detachment. Lieutenant Kozhbergenov installed the Realiya-U sensor near a Mujahideen supply trail he could not see from his platoon observation post (Map 23). He then plotted three fire concentrations on the trail.

At 0100 hours, the Realiya-U operator reported that a small caravan of wheeled vehicles, pack animals, and people were approaching. The platoon leader decided to destroy the caravan. As the caravan passed through the most confining terrain, the commander ordered his platoon to open fire simultaneously on all three fire concentrations. The platoon expanded 12 rounds and destroyed two trucks and killed four pack animals and six men. This example demonstrates how seismic sensors and artillery alert units could combine to destroy enemy caravans, particularly at night.

Determining how to provide convoy escort and security with artillery was a complex task. Usually, it was conducted in accordance with one of two variants. In the first variant, artillery was dispersed along the march column in blocking positions, along with blocking tanks and armored personnel carriers. These

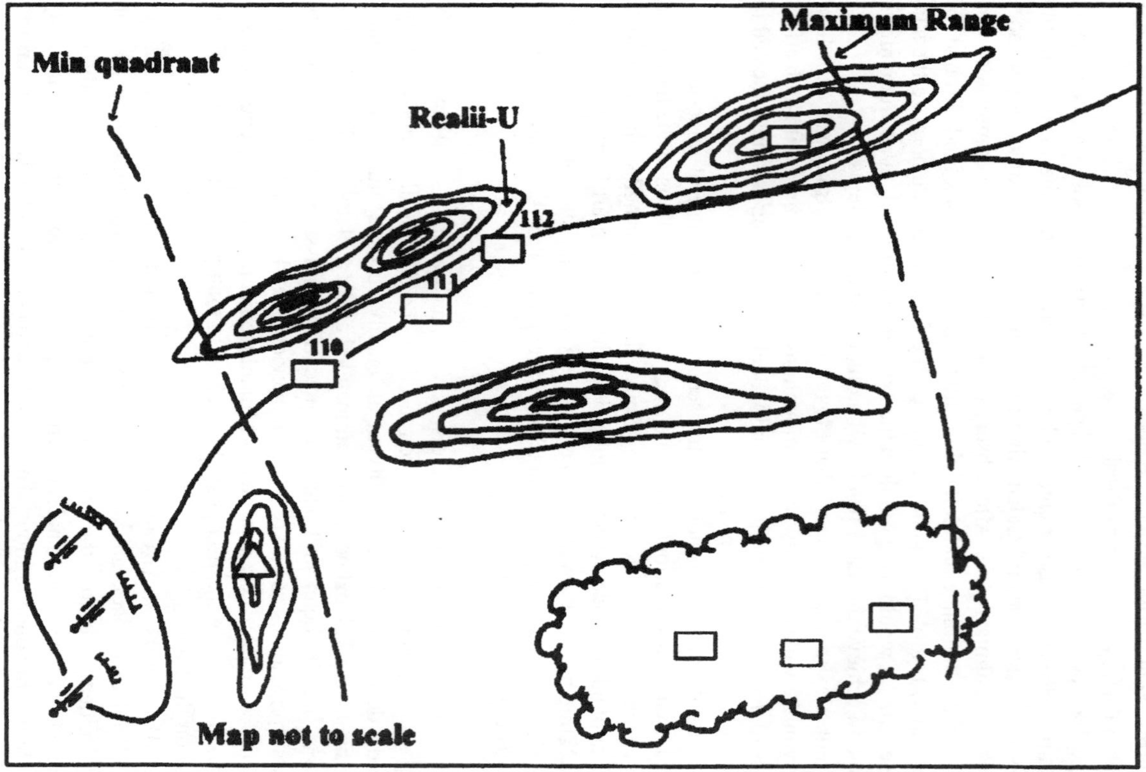

Map 23. Artillery ambush

blocking groups had a great deal of independence and their commanders could decide when to open fire. The blocking positions were sited within direct fire support distance of each other, keeping about 300 to 400 meters between armored vehicle blocks. This deployment created a stationary system of "fire blocs"[13] that secured the passage of the convoy all the way to the finish point (Map 24). If the artillery had to fire on the enemy, it was, as a rule, by direct lay.

The second variant was more complex. The artillery moved with the column in fire support and accompaniment. Artillery moved with the column in three groups. The first group moved at the head of the column. The second group moved in the middle of the column and the third moved at the end. These artillery groups were usually self-propelled howitzer batteries, but sometimes were artillery battalions. Artillery FOs were spaced every 10 to 15 vehicles throughout the column. This spacing ensured continuous fire support, even when gaps developed in the convoy spacing.

As the column started to march, the artillery stationed at the start point provided initial support. As the column reached the maximum effective range of the supporting artillery, the second artillery group deployed into preplanned firing positions located by the road, usually within the artillery fan of the initial supporting artillery. The second artillery group then provided fire support as the third artillery group leapfrogged forward to the middle of the column. As the end of the column passed the second artillery group, the head of the column approached the maximum effective range of the second artillery group. The third artillery group then occupied firing positions, and the second firing group rejoined the column. The Soviet artillery would continue this procedure until the march column closed into an assembly area. This method kept the march column protected by artillery ready to open fire at any minute when called in by the FOs.

Afghanistan demonstrated that organizing support for a convoy demanded close coordination between the combined arms commanders and the artillery commanders, well supported by good communications and experienced FOs.

Support of Soviet subunits as they broke contact and withdrew was a complex task for supporting artillery. Soviet forces, particularly airborne and air assault forces, were at risk when their advance ended and they started to withdraw from the mountains. At the start of the pull back, Mujahideen would occupy the abandoned heights and open accurate fire on the withdrawing subunits, inflicting significant casualties.[14]

Artillery fires became a standard way to allow a Soviet force to break contact and withdraw. Before the Soviet force began to withdraw downhill, Soviet artillery would hit the reverse slope of the mountain crest that the Soviet force was on as well as the flanking slopes of mountains possibly occupied by the enemy and surrounding peaks and trails (Map 25). As the Soviet force began to withdraw, Soviet artillery fire shifted to the crest of the mountain that the Soviet force was on. As the Soviet force withdrew, Soviet artillery fire gradually shifted downhill in a series of lines some 150 to 200 meters apart. The Soviet artillery

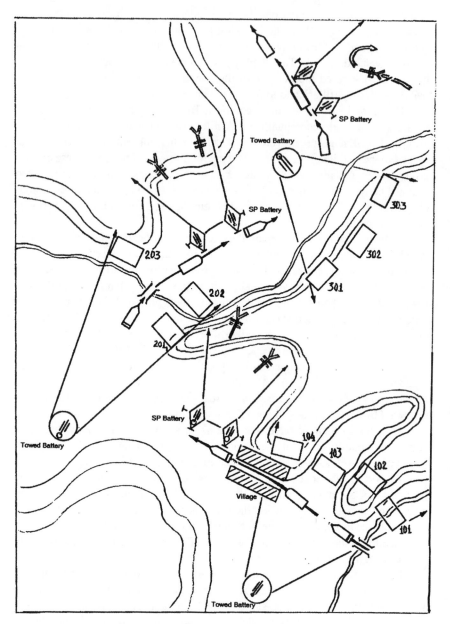

Map 24. Artillery support of a moving force

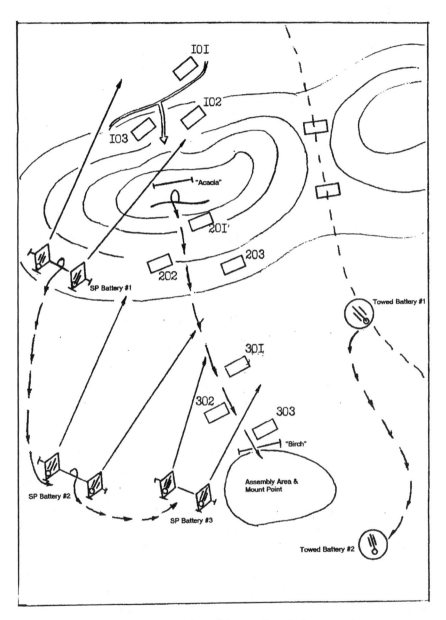

101

102

103

"Acacia"

201

203

202

SP Battery #1

Towed Battery #1

301

302

303

"Birch"

Assembly Area &
Mount Point

SP Battery #2

SP Battery #3

Towed Battery #2

Map 25. Fire support of a withdrawing force in the mountains

continued to hit the mountain and its surroundings until the Soviet maneuver force completed its descent and was some three kilometers from possible Mujahideen small arms fire.

Much of the effectiveness of artillery fire depended on the quality of crew drill and FDC procedures. Afghanistan's terrain demanded particular measures. Artillery reconnaissance played a very important role in Afghanistan. During preparation and combat, artillery reconnaissance was conducted by a special group of scouts and FOs. Each group had an officer FO and one or two scouts and an RTO. These groups established forward and flanking OPs as part of the combat formation or on dominant terrain. The number of OPs, as a rule, corresponded to the number of motorized rifle companies (and separate platoons) and could exceed the number of supporting artillery batteries. The effectiveness of reconnaissance was increased by linking them to artillery, air defense, and motorized rifle subunit OPs in a single system in which every OP had an assigned sector, which was overlapping and was redundant to the others.

Combat demonstrated that optical reconnaissance produced better results in the mountains. Sound and radar reconnaissance had limited application in the mountains, but worked well in valleys, desert, and green zones.

In the mountains, it was difficult for scouts to determine the coordinates of targets. The large DAK[15] and DC[16] range finders mounted on the 1B12 and 1B17 command and control vehicles had limited application in the mountains. The preferred tools in the mountains were the 1D13 lightweight range finder, the PAB-2A[17] aiming circle, and binoculars. Often, the coordinates were determined by eye and large-scale topographic maps, overprinted photo mosaics, and aerial photographs at 1:40,000 scale.

The terrain of Afghanistan often demanded special considerations in electing artillery firing positions and sites to deploy artillery systems. Usually, there was no difficulty in setting up on the plains, but the mountains were another story. There are few flat areas where cannon artillery and MRL can set up. This often meant that cannon artillery and MRL platoons set up right next to each other instead of at the prescribed intervals. In some cases, the firing position might only accommodate a single MRL. The MRL would fire its salvo and then quickly withdraw to reload while the next MRL moved into its place. This kind of rotational firing would continue right up to the completion of the firing mission or the required destruction of the target.

The different features that exist in the mountains led to different firing formations and often required fire not only to the front but also to the rear of friendly forces, using large gunnery shifts. These conditions led to the discovery of new ways to carry out fire missions involving large shifts from the base line of artillery fire.

One of the artillery regiments discovered that in some instances it was expedient to lay the base piece some 1-50 mils[18] left of the base line (major shifts during nonlinear siting of the pieces can be from 0-50 to 1-50 mils). This allowed the turret of the 2S3 152mm howitzer to rotate further to the left with 12 rounds loaded in the ammunition carousel. In this position, without moving the barrel, the crew was able to pull ammunition from the lower ammunition storage racks. As a result, the tempo of the firing was not diminished. This allowed the senior officer in the battery's vehicle to locate some 100 meters to the right of the number one gun to allow maximum traverse of firing (the traverse is 15-00 mils to the right and 8-00 mils to the left[19]). This enabled the battery to conduct firing missions with maximum shifts from the base line and also, no less important, to use the gun sight, when necessary, to adjust the aim.

During combat, the weapons and gun sights of self-propelled howitzer batteries were often laid in by gyrocompass. Combat demonstrated that if the initial angle of orientation was accurately established, then after a few minutes the gunners could use the gyro compass to determine the direction of the axes of the vehicles. During this, it is only necessary to determine the maximum convergence of meridians in the region.

Sometimes, it was necessary to lay the battery's weapons pointing in two opposite directions simultaneously. To establish these parallel fans, the gunners would first lay out one fan in one direction and then the other in the other direction. The accuracy of the lay was worked out in both directions. Usually a rock on the crest of a well-defined landmark was picked as a reference point. During firing, the gunners were able to easily pick that out and make fewer errors. However, during the morning hours, particularly in the fall and winter, fog often masked the mountains. In that case, the senior officer in the battery established an alternate aiming point with his vehicle's view finder.

In mountain combat, batteries were seldom deployed in linear firing positions. Therefore, artillery deployments were often echeloned in the mountains. The base piece was laid on the base line and the senior officer in the battery's vehicle was located 200 meters forward and to the left. In order to preserve the battery angle of fire, the battery was deployed in a circle as much as possible and used the vehicle gun sights to adjust the aim. Besides the primary lay, the battery could fire in five other directions. This resulted in an increased effectiveness in self-defense of the battery firing positions—a very important consideration in Afghanistan.

It was no less complicated connecting the firing positions and the CP/OP in the topography of the mountains. After all, the slightest inaccuracy in the calculations would significantly lessen the effectiveness of fire and complicate the coordination between the artillery, the motorized rifle subunits, and aviation. In the course of combat, there were instances where mistakes in determining coordinates resulted in artillery fire missing the enemy and sometimes hitting friendly forces.

A primary reason for this was that practically no government geodesic survey work had been conducted throughout most of Afghanistan. This complicated the topographic preparation of artillery fire. There is not a single geodesic point along the entire 200-kilometer stretch of road from Herat to Farah. Further, there is a distinct lack of prominent landmarks in that area. If one draws a line on a map, the line will intersect a landmark every 20 to 30 kilometers or more.

Therefore, the primary method of determining coordinates of firing positions was the topographic orientation on the map using the on-vehicle navigational instruments or other instruments to determine location of landmarks. Experience showed that determining coordinates in the mountains using these navigation instruments resulted in an increase of error (up to 10° or 15° laterally) some ten times greater than on the plains. This frequently interfered with utilizing the full potential of the firing systems.

Meteorological support of artillery fire was very difficult in Afghanistan. The primary meteorologic data for firing was provided by the regimental meteorological station, the non-TO&E meteorological posts in artillery battalions, and the meteorological posts of the MRL batteries. There was one artillery ballistic station[20] (ABC-1), an assault meteorological kit[21] (DMK), and a pneumatic cannon[22] (VR-2) available at division to equip these. There were often not enough trained personnel and equipment to support the required missions. The rapid, frequent changes in the meteorological conditions demanded that the conditions be checked twice as often as normal—at least every 30 minutes. During these readings, they would determine the meteorological conditions at the meteorological station and firing positions. Combat showed that in order to get actual meteorological data it was necessary that the meteorological station and the artillery be located at the same elevation and be exposed to the same winds. In the mountains, it was practically impossible to achieve those conditions. As a result, the meteorological errors during preparations for firing at medium range and close to maximum range reached 30 to 35 percent or more of the entire total errors committed when conducting destruction fires.

In order to lessen the impact of these errors, the Soviets attempted to establish a systematic meteorological survey of the region during the second half of the 1980s. Meteorological data collected daily over the course of several years was noted graphically and was used to determine calculations to conduct artillery fire to support security outposts.

The conduct of artillery fire in Afghanistan demanded thorough ballistics preparation and the use of all necessary technical support, but organizing this was difficult since about half of the guns and howitzers were deployed separately by batteries and even by platoons in positions and outposts that were physically separated by a considerable distance. Ammunition resupply to these positions, as well as to those involved in maneuver combat, was not always conducted from regimental or division ammunition points. Basically, ammunition resupply was conducted by passing convoys from army and central depots and bases. Under these circumstances, organizing the distribution of ammunition by type was very complicated. Finally, the Soviets decided to deliver artillery ammunition only when the entire battalion was deployed. The battalion would break out the ammunition by type and sometimes by lot number. Distribution of ammunition to the guns depended on the remaining barrel life and other peculiarities of each piece. This demanded a significant amount of record keeping, time, and energy to keep track of all this data.

The difficulty in conducting artillery reconnaissance, of connecting topographic sites and the shifting meteorological conditions, made it difficult to determine the firing data necessary to destroy various targets. To these problems, one must add the dominant heights, steep slopes, narrow canyons, significant "dead" space, and hidden fields that demand the use of high trajectory fire. This terrain demands more exact firing calculations than when firing at a linear target with a moderate trajectory. And, finally, fire adjustment was done differently, not from a forward CP/OP as one would do on the plains, but from the flank or even from behind a group of advancing forces while other terrain factors complicated accurate fire support.

The conduct of artillery fire demanded target registration or the advanced preparation of complete firing tables. Analysis of combat showed that target registration was the primary method used. Target registration was used when and where maximum accuracy in firing was required, even at the expense of surprise. As a rule, target registration was used to block villages during the conduct of operations, to destroy groups of Mujahideen that were close to friendly forces, to carry out artillery missions conducted by officer FOs who did not have a range finder at their observation post, and in a variety of other circumstances.

During registration in the mountains, the conduct of fire depended on the target and the distance from the target to friendly forces (200 to 400 meters separation were strictly observed for safety). In some case, Soviet gunners began registration with smoke rounds. Combat analysis showed that when the time for preparation for fire was short and fire was conducted without registration, the probability of hitting friendly forces reached 30 percent. If fire was adjusted to within 200 meters of friendly forces, the probability of hitting friendly forces fell to 7 percent. If fire was adjusted to no closer than 400 meters, the probability of hitting friendly forces fell to 1.5 percent.

Complete preparation demanded thorough calculation of all the firing data, a significant expenditure of time and manpower and fully minimizing the possibility of hitting friendly forces. At the same time, the complex meteorological conditions limited the conduct of safe, accurate artillery fire to eight kilometers for the D-30 and 2S1 howitzers, to nine kilometers for the 2S3 152mm howitzer, to 13 kilometers for the 152mm 2S5 cannon, and to ten kilometers for the BM-21 MRL.

Combat in the mountains of Afghanistan stressed the coordination of artillery, aviation, and motorized rifle units and subunits. Coordination of the forces and resources of fire destruction helped achieve the effective, timely exploitation of the results of fire support by units and subunits and was organized to the depth of the tactical mission by phase lines, time, missions, and firing systems. More detailed coordination was involved to the depth of the near [intermediate] mission. Primary attention was allotted to sequencing artillery fire and aviation strikes along with the actions of the combined arms units and subunits.

Basic coordination was usually worked out early while giving the mission to the units (as a rule on a terrain model). Special attention was devoted to tight coordination between artillery and aviation in the three measures of space: to the front, depth, and height.

In the course of combat, commanders made serious mistakes when they preferred one artillery system over another, such as howitzers over mortars. This led to circumstances in which artillery was not able to fire for a time for safety considerations since the trajectory of their rounds would pass through the helicopter gunships' fly zone. In turn, army aviation might not be able to fly their strike missions due to lack of coordination with the artillery.

Combat experience showed that positive results were possible only by applying the entire range of fire support systems. For example, during the seizure of the Mujahideen central base of Khost-o Fering in Baghlan Province in February 1985, fire support coordination specified that artillery would fire during the odd hours and aviation would strike during the even hours. While the artillery was firing, helicopter gunships were located on the flanks of the combat zone ready to strike advancing or withdrawing groups of Mujahideen and targets in the depth of the base region. However, artillery set the targets allotted to aviation on fire, making the aviation strikes pointless due to the smoke. This inevitably lessened the effectiveness of aviation strikes.

Direct artillery fire, aviation, and indirect artillery fire was coordinated. While direct fire artillery hit the Mujahideen weapons systems located on commanding heights and in the villages, the aviation hit assigned targets in the depths. As a rule, aviation strikes preceded the final artillery strike during the artillery preparation of the attack phase, hitting targets located in the enemy central base located some five to seven kilometers from the line of contact. While aviation carries out its fire missions, direct fire artillery does not quit firing. Thanks to this system, the destruction of enemy targets increased. At the same time, indirect-fire artillery, which was shut down during the air strikes, opened fire at the moment the air strikes ended and the jets and helicopter gunships left the impact area.

Combined arms and artillery commanders coordinated their actions by ensuring that both had the same understanding of the combat mission; agreeing on methods and the order of their fulfillment; deploying their CP/OPs together; tying in communications between them; and establishing common signals and reference points. In order to establish uninterrupted coordination in battle in Afghanistan's mountains, the artillery group commander's CP/OP was located with the CP/OP of the Motorized Rifle Regiment Commander, and the CP/OP of the artillery battalion or battery commander was colocated with the CP/OP of the commander of the motorized rifle battalion or company.

Every motorized rifle or reconnaissance company had an officer FO attached during combat. The FO's mission was to adjust and direct fire for the company. This arrangement not only secured uninterrupted coordination between the artillery and combined arms units and subunits, but it also created two channels for passing fire requests during the fire support of the attack phase. Fire missions could be passed simultaneously over the fire control channel and the command channel. The fire control channel passed the fire request from the company commander to the FO to the artillery battalion commander to the RAG commander. The command channel passed the fire request from the MRC company commander to his MRB commander to his MRR commander to the RAG commander.

Complex artillery missions demanded thorough preparation by commanders, staffs, and forces. The organization and conduct of these missions were much different than those conducted in peacetime training. Artillery subunits and units were used to resolve various combat missions. Thus, in one of the divisions of the 40th Army, artillery subunits and units were committed to battle eight to ten times during 1985. Each of these battles lasted from five to twenty days.

It was difficult for artillery officers to maintain a high state of combat readiness in their artillery subunits and units and to plan thorough fire support while conducting personnel training. Therefore, training in Afghanistan was conducted differently using the so-called "standard week." The principle components of the standard week were intensive crew drill, separate specialty training, and preparation of weapons, combat equipment, and gear for combat.[23]

In the standard week, the first day was used for technical preparation while the second day was for specialist training (singularly, by crew and platoon). The third day involved a battery tactical exercise. Political and medical training occupied the fourth day. On the fifth day, the sergeants and privates conducted small arms firing while the officers attended commander's training. The entire sixth day was taken up with a battalion controlled firing and fire control exercise. The seventh day was set aside for washing and personnel rest.

The next training period before planned combat lasted 10 to 12 days. The first three days were devoted to tactical training and the next three days to specialist training. The seventh and eighth days were taken up with battery tactical exercises. The ninth day was run according to the plan for unified political training. The tenth day was devoted to range firing by the sergeants and soldiers while the officers attended commander's training. On the eleventh day, the artillery battalions conducted a planned controlled exercise for artillery firing and control. The twelfth day was a day of rest for the personnel.

Time for training was not always available. Practice showed that often the subunits had to shorten the standard week because they received a combat mission. It was important to ensure that subunits had at least three days of a standard week in order to conduct essential measures to prepare for combat.

Commander's training was the principle link in training artillery specialists. In the course of training, the officers prepared vigorously for their duties and the duties of their next higher superior. They adhered to the principle that the direct supervisor taught his subordinates and accepted responsibility for their training. Officer training was conducted, as a rule, in groups based on duties and specialties. When it was necessary to form temporary groups, the exercises were conducted in assemblies. Artillery FOs, for example, trained in assemblies. The assemblies lasted for three to five days.

Commander's training for artillery officers was usually conducted in four training groups. The first group, headed by the regimental commander, included those who worked directly with the regimental commander and consisted of the artillery battalion commanders and their assistants. The second group was headed by the regimental chief of staff and consisted of all the regimental staff officers. The battery and platoon commanders were in the third group. Battalion commanders taught these officers. All the other officers were in the fourth group and were instructed by the regimental deputy commanders for armaments and rear services.

The principal focus of artillery officer training was improving special knowledge and experience. To meet this goal, the artillery training included a multifaceted exercise involving seven training sites. The idea of the exercise was that the artillery officers would move from one training station to another and increase their experience working with sights, performing the necessary firing calculations, conducting normative firing, and controlling fire missions. Simulators and sub-caliber devices were used at these training stations.

Combat experience showed that training should resemble actual combat as much as possible. This necessitated the selection of a small-arms and artillery firing range similar to the region of anticipated combat. Targets had to be placed to correspond to enemy tactics. Thus the small arms and artillery firing range for artillery subunits of the 108th MRD located near Kabul resembled the terrain of the Panjshir valley. The 201st MRD, located in Baghlan Province, set up its training area on desert terrain. Artillery fire exercises used not only actual maps of the combat zone, but also photomosaics to provide experience in using overprinted, scaled, aerial photographs. The gunners would draw the targets on the artillery plotting board and remove the rectangular coordinates in order to fulfill fire missions.

Practice showed that such a system for planning and organizing combat training served to raise the professional training of artillery personnel and commanders of units and subunits.

Training personnel in outposts and security detachments was conducted in accordance with generally accepted methodologies, but due to their location, there were several differences. Thus, the "standard month" was established for training artillery subunits in combat outposts and was conducted in four phases. During the first week, they conducted individual skills training. During the second week, they trained as crews. During the third week, they trained as a platoon. During the fourth week, they trained as a battery or platoon on outpost duty.

Security outposts, as a rule, were organized on a three shift tour of duty. Every four hours they had to change the duty shift. This made it difficult to schedule and conduct training. Therefore the level of training of personnel at combat outposts depended on individual readiness and adherence to principles, and now and then from the awareness of the outpost commander.

Commander's training for the leaders of the security posts was conducted monthly at a regimental or division assembly. This training lasted for three to five days and consisted of specialized training and management and administrative training to improve logistics and improve procedures for working with enlisted men.

In this fashion, the artillery fought alongside other Soviet Forces in the Republic of Afghanistan and confirmed their dominant role by conducting fire missions during combined arms battle. Combat disclosed the weak state of training of artillerymen and the poor design of weapons systems for fighting in the mountains. This was particularly true in the first phase of the war. Combat in Afghanistan served to highlight future developments in the fatherland's artillery for fighting in difficult circumstances in mountainous theaters.

Editors' comments: The artillery played a dominant role in Soviet Army plans and execution. Artillery has always held pride of place in the Russian and Soviet Army, and the Soviets developed a mighty artillery arm. Central to the concept of Soviet artillery planning was normative firing where hectares were physically removed by firing a number of rounds against a target or area to guarantee destruction or neutralization. This required time, lots of ammunition, and an enemy who was fixed in position. The Mujahideen refused to stay in one place and so Soviet normative artillery fires in Afghanistan seldom achieved the desired results. Soviet artillery needed to be quicker, more precise, and more responsive. It took time for the Soviets to respond and to abandon the normative firing methodology. As this section shows, Soviet gunners were reluctant to abandon concepts and even inappropriate terminology to come to grips with the demands of supporting maneuver forces in a counter-insurgency. The Soviets tested new weapons and procedures in Afghanistan and managed to develop the capability to conduct separate fire mission using split fire-direction centers in the same battalion—a capability they had neglected in the larger Soviet Army.

Afghanistan provided an opportunity for the Soviet Army to combat-test its artillery systems. New systems tested in Afghanistan included the 2S4 240mm self-propelled mortar, the Krasnapol 152mm laser-guided round, the Smelchak 240mm laser-guided mortar round, the 2S9 Nona-S 120mm mortar-howitzer, the 82mm Vasilek automatic mortar, the BM22 Uragan multiple rocket launcher, and the 152mm Giasint self-propelled cannon. The Soviets even brought SCUD mis-

siles into Afghanistan for use against remote guerrilla bases—and to threaten Pakistan and Iran. Despite the new systems, the Soviet gunners had significant problems conducting artillery planning and then adjusting firing data to compensate for the peculiarities of Afghanistan.

Soviet artillery represented a very lethal portion of Soviet combat power, but Soviet target acquisition was not able to acquire fleeting guerrilla targets rapidly enough that the overwhelming power of Soviet artillery could be fully brought to bear. One of the breakthrough innovations of Soviet artillery during the war was the use of ground sensors to acquire artillery targets.

ARMORED FORCES[24]

There were tank regiments in the motorized rifle divisions serving in the LCOSF. However, the nature of combat conducted by the Mujahideen and Afghanistan's terrain significantly limited the Soviet command's opportunity to use tanks in operations. Principally, tanks participated in combat as subunits. They were attached to motorized rifle and airborne battalions and fought as tank platoons and sometimes as tank companies.

The basic tactical subunit was the tank battalion. Its TO&E structure did not differ at all from tank battalions located in the Soviet Union. The tank battalion consisted of the command section, the combat subunits, and the support subunit. The command section included the commander, chief of staff, and deputy for political work and a deputy for armaments. Three tank companies comprised the combat subunits. Every tank company had a company commander and three tank platoons. Each tank platoon had three tanks. Thus, every tank company had ten tanks and the battalion had 31 tanks, including the battalion commander's tank. The tank battalion support subunit had a signal platoon, a medical point, and a support platoon.

Tank subunits were armed with the T-55 and T-62 medium tanks.[25] The T-55 tank was introduced into Soviet service in the second half of the 1950s and the T-62 at the start of the 1960s. Both systems have a high combat potential. The T-55 tank has a 100mm rifled gun and the T-62 has a 115mm smooth-bore gun with excellent ballistics and a high rate of fire. Besides the main gun, these tanks had additional armaments—a coaxial machine gun and an air defense machine gun.

Fire from the tank guns destroyed or suppressed targets located behind adobe walls, in caves, and in other shelters. The coaxial machine gun was used on targets in the open. Coaxial machine gun fire was more effective at distances under one kilometer. Afghanistan veterans note that when a tank was blown up, the coaxial machine gun could be dismounted to protect the crew and the damaged machine from the enemy until the arrival of reinforcements or the repair subunits.

At the same time, the tanks were not without some shortcomings. Due to the limited angle of elevation of the main tank gun and coaxial machine gun, they were not able to fire on an enemy located over 30° above the chassis. The Mujahideen knew this and established their firing positions in the heights above the firing capability of the tank armament.

The tank's air defense machine gun was used to fight with the enemy in the heights. However, the loader had to fire this machine gun from an exposed open hatch where he was vulnerable to enemy sniper fire. However, this was the only limitation on this weapon in combat. In many instances, the fire from this machine gun had a psychological impact on the enemy.

At first, the main gun tank ammunition unit of fire consisted of fin-stabilized discarding-sabot (FSDS) and high-explosive fragmentary rounds. However, since the enemy did not have armored vehicles, the next unit of fire consisted solely of high-explosive fragmentary rounds. When the fuse was set for maximum fragmentation, these rounds were capable of destroying enemy and weapons located in less-robust bunkers. When it was necessary to destroy a target located in a heavy adobe bunker with walls no thicker than 30 centimeters, the fuse settings on the rounds were set for high-explosive delayed action. After the rounds penetrated the bunker wall, they exploded inside, killing the occupants.

The presence of stabilized weapons and improved gunsights on the tanks assisted the crew in fire control, battlefield observation, accurate aiming, and highly effective fire, whether stationary or moving.

The tank crew consisted of the commander, gunner, loader, and driver. They were armed with Makarov pistols, Kalashnikov assault rifles, fragmentation hand grenades, and signal rockets. The small arms were for individual protection in close combat. The Kalashnikov rifle proved the more effective small arm in Afghanistan, so crew members armed with the pistol rearmed themselves with assault rifles.

In Afghanistan, tankers' uniforms were simple and comfortable for working in tanks. Strict uniform rules and regulations were not observed. Everything was determined by the outside temperature. As Afghanistan combat veteran Lieutenant Colonel S. A. Amelichkin observed, tankers' gear was designed not to hinder their movement inside the tank or interfere with their exit in the event that the tank was hit.

T-55 and T-62 tanks had high combat effectiveness and exploitation potential when tank subunits successfully worked together with motorized riflemen conducting cordon and search actions, convoy escort, and the securing of regimental base camps, airfield bridges, passes, tunnels, and other important installations.

When conducting a block of the enemy, tanks would usually move to the designated region as part of a motorized rifle subunit. In order to assure secrecy and achieve surprise, movement was conducted during periods of limited visibility—during the night or at dawn. There were also occasions when tank platoons moved to blocking positions by themselves, following the motorized rifle subunits. Most often this occurred in the summer, when the tank movement would kick up great clouds of dust, warning the enemy of the movement of

Soviet forces into the combat zone. Therefore, the separate movement of motorized rifle and tank subunits was determined, to a great extent, by the requirement for surprise at the initiation of combat.

As tanks moved into a region, they took up firing positions to prevent the enemy withdrawal from the cordoned area. The gap between tanks was from 200 to 300 meters and the gap between tank platoons was 600 to 800 meters or more. In all cases, the gaps were covered with fire from small arms, mortars, and artillery.

The tank subunit leader commanded his subunit from the motorized rifle battalion CP/OP or that of one of the motorized rifle companies. This provided tight coordination between the tankers and motorized rifle men and allowed them to react to any changing situation.

A second, no-less-important, mission that tankers carried out with motorized riflemen was sweeping an area to destroy the enemy. There were various methods of conducting sweeps, depending on the region, the terrain, and the support of the local populace. During sweeps, attached tanks used their armor to shelter the motorized riflemen, and the fire from their main guns and machine guns destroyed various targets.

Thus, in May 1984, a tank company was attached to a parachute battalion, commanded by Lieutenant Colonel V. Romanov, during the sweep of an area in Helmand Province.[26] By order of the battalion commander, two tank platoons headed the battalion column, which moved on two parallel march routes. A sapper squad moved in front of the tanks. The sappers' movement was covered by paratroopers who were riding on top of the tanks. The sappers checked the march routes in order to discover any mines. Should any enemy be discovered, the tanks would suppress the enemy with fire, and when necessary, with the fire from the paratroopers.

Thanks to his effective use of his personnel and equipment, the battalion commander successfully accomplished his mission. In the course of three days, the enemy was mopped up in the region and a large quantity of weapons and ammunition were captured. There were no Soviet casualties among the TO&E and attached personnel and equipment, despite the fact that the enemy shot at each company over ten times and the tanks were shot at up to 40 times by RPGs.

During the cordon and search of a large populated area, tanks could serve in positions in the initial encirclement (which was established at a distance of two to three kilometers from the outskirts of the area) or in the second encirclement (located contiguous to the populated area). In all circumstances, the tank firing positions were sited where they had uninterrupted observation throughout their sector of responsibility, their fires prevented the enemy movement in different directions, and their fires were linked to the fires of other tanks and motorized rifle subunits. As experience showed, such sites were normally at cross roads, squares, gardens, and valleys.

Tank platoons were included in assault groups to destroy enemy sheltering in fortresses and other sturdy positions. Assault groups were based on motorized rifle platoons also reinforced with flame-thrower crews, artillery FOs, and sappers.

During the movement to the assault objective, tank main gun and machine gun fire suppressed enemy firing positions from a distance and sheltered the infantry that followed the advancing armor on foot. During the course of battle, tanks could, when necessary, destroy buildings and evacuate the wounded and damaged equipment.

Much of the success of a search and destroy mission depended on achieving surprise. In this case, the enemy lost the initiative and the seeds of panic started to spread throughout the enemy ranks. Experience showed that commanders needed to apply different methods of military cunning to achieve surprise. Thus, during the sweep of a section of terrain, a motorized rifle battalion encountered a fortress that was an architectural treasure under the protection of UNESCO. The enemy rightly believed that the Soviets would not fire tank rounds into the fortress and the ten-meter thick walls would absorb bullets. Further, one side of the fortress was secured by a cliff while the other side was secured by a moat filled with water. The only entrance into the fortress was across two bridges, which were raised.

The Soviets used cunning to cause the enemy to lower the bridge in this difficult situation. The Soviets simulated damage to a tank located near the fortress. The Mujahideen decided to capture this tank as a trophy and lowered one of the bridges in order to leave the fortress and capture the tank. Once the bridge was lowered, Warrant Officer Yu. Aikin, who was hiding inside the "knocked out" tank opened fire with the tank main gun. He destroyed the bridge lifting mechanism. A rapid attack by motorized riflemen then crossed the bridge into the fortress and captured it.[27]

In the course of combat in Afghanistan, armored subunits also secured LOCs and escorted convoys. Combat outposts, sited by the motorized rifle divisions to secure important sections of highway, were reinforced with tank platoons. Tank firing positions were sited based on the probable direction of enemy advance and the terrain. Firing positions were selected outside the zone of possible landslides, falling rocks, and flooding. The tank platoon also had alternate firing positions and the crews had bunkers or slit trenches to shelter in. They erected tank firing positions in the mountains, as a rule, either by digging the tank halfway in or by building up the protective walls with stone or sandbags from the ground up. They put trip flares on the approach to the firing positions, as well as minefields, and various wire obstacles (MZP,[28] concertina, wire entanglements, and wire knife rests). All engineer obstacles were covered with tank and small arms fire.

The tank subunit's fire plan was included in the security outpost's fire plan and was oriented on the main approaches and combined with the planned artillery fire and small arms fire. The tanks were also used as a mobile firing position during war gaming and battle planning. During this process, the commander determined the principle and supplementary approaches and the limits and sectors of fire for each approach.

The use of tanks at security outposts proved very effective when organized wisely. Thus, in the spring of 1982, Mujahideen convoy ambushes sharply increased near security outpost number 3, located on the northeast outskirts of Kandahar. The Soviets decided to reinforce the security outpost with Senior Lieutenant Sorokin's tank platoon in order to limit Mujahideen attacks.

Upon arriving at the security outpost, the tanks took up positions in a garden while the crews prepared five firing positions along the northeast outskirts of the city. When they received the signal that a convoy was moving, BTRs moved into the firing positions and increased observation in the area of the more threatened sector. When the enemy appeared, they opened fire on them with small arms. When the enemy force was good-sized or had crew-served weapons, the security outpost commander summoned the tanks. During the course of battle, they might move from one position to another, bringing aimed fire on the enemy. The presence of tanks at the security outpost had positive results. Earlier, practically every convoy suffered personnel and vehicle losses in this dangerous sector, but after the tanks were assigned, the enemy attacks dropped way off and their infrequent attempts were unsuccessful.

Tanks were often included in convoy escort forces as part of the movement support detachment or as covering forces in the main body. Usually, a reconnaissance group and mine neutralization team were part of the movement support detachment, as was a tank with a KMT-5 mine plow or KMT-7 mine flail. The tank moved some 50 to 100 meters in front of the detachment covered by the fire of a motorized rifle squad. In order to prevent injury from fragments from exploding mines, the tank crew moved fully "buttoned-up" with closed hatches. If the roadway to be cleared was wide, then several tanks with mine-clearing devices moved in echelon. In order to increase the thoroughness of the mine clearing, the tanks with mine-clearing devices made several passes over suspicious sites.

Tanks located in the main body served as a covering force and were equally distributed throughout the whole convoy. The leading tank in the forward patrol had several motorized riflemen seated on the turret. The tank at the tail of the convoy moved with the technical maintenance echelon. A group of motorized riflemen were also detailed for its protection.

There were several variants when using tanks to escort convoys. In all instances, they would move to the side of the road where the enemy was attacking and open fire with all tank armaments, allowing the trucks to drive out of the kill zone. If a truck was hit, the tank could tow it out of the battle, and, where necessary, they could clear the road by pushing off the destroyed vehicles.

Tank subunits could also be detailed to secure and defend airfields, base camps, depots, and other important installations. In these cases, the tanks served as firing points. They occupied firing positions at sites where they could fire to the maximum range of all the tank's armaments. The tank main gun fire and machine gun fire was integrated into the motorized rifle subunit's fire plan.

Often, because of the terrain, tank firing positions were selected away from the motorized rifle subunit's strong point. This was the case, for example, of the security and defensive positions at a regimental base camp in the Kabul suburbs. A tank platoon was deployed on one of the heights in order to cover the valley with interlocking fields of fire. The gap between the tank platoon and motorized rifle subunit strong points stretched some 400 meters and was covered by a mine field and an electrified wire fence. The tank platoon CP/OP was located on a height providing long-range observation of the terrain. There was a telephone line between the tank platoon CP/OP and the motorized rifle battalion CP/OP to support coordination and command and control. The tank crew of the alert tank was always ready.

This arrangement of tanks supported the effective destruction of the enemy on the more threatened axis. Convinced of this, the Mujahideen henceforth did not venture to attempt an attack on the security posts and on the western suburbs of Kabul.

The commander and staff thoroughly prepared tanks and tank crews for combat in Afghanistan. Thus, at the end of December 1982, tank company commander Captain V. P. Stuliy was ordered to advance to the Panjshir valley, to secure the crossing across the Panjshir river, to secure the approach into the canyon by motorized rifle subunits of Soviet and Afghan forces and to cover their further advance into the combat zone.

Having analyzed the mission, the company commander did an estimate of the situation with the aid of a map. His evaluation of the enemy situation paid special attention to possible ambush sites, mine fields, demolition sites, and available routes of maneuver and withdrawal. Evaluating the condition and potential of his own subunits, the company commander decided to train his tank crews repeatedly for the specific aspects of this mission and conducted practice in clearing mines from roads. He devoted special attention to the fact that his personnel were not trained to find plastic Italian mines.

Further, since the subunit had to move to the crossing at night, the company checked its night-vision devices and conducted supplemental limited visibility drivers' training. This training led to the successful completion of the company's mission.

During this time, commanders of tank subunits often underestimated the enemy and his tactics and did not intimately know the terrain along the march route to the combat zone. This resulted in significantly increased expenditures of time to carry out missions, and sometimes in personnel and equipment losses. For example, this happened to a tank platoon attached to a motorized rifle battalion that was sent to relieve Soviet subunits trapped in the villages of Maravara, Sangam, and Daridam in April 1985.

The commander of the separate motorized rifle battalion did not provide engineer reconnaissance on the march route. The tank platoon was located at the head of the march column. As the column entered the narrowest portion of the road, the enemy detonated a radio-controlled explosive charge and destroyed the lead tank. Movement of motorized rifle subunits, hurrying to the rescue of their comrades, also stopped. It took some four hours to secure and repair the road and begin moving on it again. During this time, the trapped Soviet subunits, which were five to seven kilometers apart, each fought off attacks. During the delay, while the trapped subunits repulsed Mujahideen onslaughts in Daridam and Sangam, their personnel and equipment losses doubled and they lost over 50 percent of their TO&E strength.

Combat in Afghanistan showed that mission success for tank subunits depended on thorough preparation of the commanders, crews, equipment, and weapons. Tank commander training emphasized the mastery of command of subunits and fire control in battle. Sometimes lack of necessary experience caused setbacks to tank subunits. Therefore, groups of tank officers gained this experience during exercises and communications exercises by working with motorized riflemen, FOs, FACs, and sappers and practicing quickly overcoming breakdowns in coordination and control.

Tank subunit pre-combat preparation and training lasted for 10 to 12 days and concluded one to two days before the scheduled start of combat. The main training events were crew drill, platoon, and company teamwork and coordinating actions with the motorized riflemen and supporting artillery. Serious attention was devoted to maintaining weapons and equipment. This preparation was followed by a thorough inspection of all systems, sights, mechanisms, assemblies, and communications gear that support command and control. The subunits were issued additional ammunition, water, POL, and spare parts that tank crews could use to repair broken-down tanks. The training concluded with a full-field layout inspection,[29] which demonstrated the readiness of the personnel to carry out the combat mission.

Thus, the experience of combat in Afghanistan confirmed that there was a place for the tank in this type of war. However, it also highlighted the need to reevaluate the role and place of tanks in combat, particularly considering the terrain and climate of a country, different enemy tactics, and the capability of Soviet forces to carry out their combat missions under these circumstances.

Editors' comments: Armor had limited application in Afghanistan, but the Soviet Army had a lot of tanks, and tanks figured prominently in their war plans. Armor, which is viewed as a decisive maneuver force, was primarily relegated to a follow and support role or a quick reaction role. Often, tanks were relegated to security outpost duties where their shock action and maneuver was lost and they became stationary pillboxes. The motorized rifle divisions that deployed to Afghanistan brought along their full tank regiments. They were underemployed and withdrawn, along with the divisions' air defense regiments, in 1986. This over-publicized troop withdrawal eventually ended up bringing more troops into the country than actually left, but the extraneous tanks were gone.

This did not mean that the 40th Army was left without tanks. Each motorized rifle regiment still had an organic battalion of tanks that were sufficient to handle the armor missions. The Soviets did not combat-test their newest tanks in Afghanistan. In fact, the Soviets sent their older model tanks to the war. Since the Mujahideen lacked tanks, there was no need for the latest tanks and the older tanks were equal to any task, were a bit roomier than the new tanks, were rugged and fully tested, and lacked many of the newer systems that could easily break or go out of adjustment in Afghanistan's harsh climate and terrain. 40th Army tanks had a four man crew—commander, gunner, driver, and loader. The newer tanks had an automatic loader and three-man crews. It was much easier to provide security for a stationary tank and to provide an around-the-clock responsiveness with a four-man crew than a three-man crew.

Instead of leading the assault, tanks were deployed by platoons and companies to support the mission. Often, because of the highly visible "rooster tails" that moving tanks raise in the desert, tanks would move later or over a different route to get to the fight. Since tankers are, by nature, aggressive soldiers who expect to be at the key juncture of the battle, the habitual follow-and-support role did not do tanker morale any good.

AIRBORNE AND AIR ASSAULT FORCES[30]

Afghanistan's rugged terrain and the enemy guerrilla tactics foreordained an especially important role for airborne and air assault forces in the conduct of various combat missions. At the very start of the entry of the LCOSF into the country, the airborne forces had to seize the major airfields, government centers, and vital installations in Kabul and to secure and blockade the nearby garrisons that were held by the opposition. From 28 to 30 December 1979, as part of the operations plan, paratroopers landed at the Kabul and Bagram airfields while air assault forces landed at the Kunduz airfield.

Veterans of these events recalled the planning for first landings. At each of the targeted airfields, a reinforced airborne battalion would parachute onto the field to seize the control tower and the take-off and landing strips, to neutralize the security forces, and to support the landing of the main airborne force. However, it turned out that the Afghan forces guarding the airfields were neutralized well in advance, their resistance did not hold up the operation, and the airborne forces merely disembarked from the aircraft as they landed at the airfields.

The first to disembark at the airfields were groups that seized the fields and scouted the area. They occupied the key points of the airfields, conducted reconnaissance, and supported the air landing of the main forces. Over the course of several hours, dozens of IL-76, AN-12, and AN-22 military transport aircraft landed the main body of an airborne division at Kabul and Bagram airfields. At Kunduz airfield, Mi-6 and Mi-8 helicopters landed subunits of an air assault brigade. At intervals of every one-and-a half to three minutes, aircraft landed with their rear fuselage loading hatches open and, without shutting down their engines, taxied to the end of the landing strip, where the paratroopers disembarked from the aircraft and quickly moved to their planned objectives. The empty aircraft taxied to the take-off strip and flew off, leaving the landing strip and taxi area free for the next aircraft. After the main force of the division was on the ground, subsequent flights brought in the division's vehicles, necessary supplies, and support units and personnel.

This phase involved a very complex air traffic control process. Only a minimum number of aircraft and helicopters could be at the airfields at any one time. However, not all the air crews worked together precisely. Several aircraft had to make more than a single landing approach or had to circle the airfield while other aircraft that had already landed were unloaded. Nevertheless, landings at the three airfields proceeded swiftly and successfully, mainly due to multiple training exercises conducted at their home airfields.

After the parachute units [regiments and separate battalions] were on the ground, they left part of their force to secure the airfield and their stockpiled material and set out on their assigned missions. Two parachute regiments that landed at Kabul airfield secured the Ministry of Defense, the Ministry of Communications, the television center, the Soviet embassy, and the *microrayon*—the modernized area of the city where Soviet specialists and advisers lived. They seized the army staff building, nearby depots, and President Amin's palace, where there was some slight resistance.[31] Besides this, the paratroopers established posts on dominant terrain overlooking the city and on bridges across the Kabul river. They established road blocks on the main roads leading into Kabul. The third parachute regiment, which landed at Bagram airfield, conducted a swift march to Kabul and on the morning of 31 December concentrated in the city center and deployed in the army corps headquarters building. After a week, this regiment moved to the Bala-Khisar fortress, located on the southern outskirts of Kabul. They were stationed there, together with the DRA "Commando" brigade. This fortress, rising over the southern portion of the city, blocked the approaches from the south and, further, controlled the center of the capital. This fortress played a decisive role in suppressing the February 1980 revolt in the city.

The airborne and air assault forces in the LCOSF in Afghanistan were assigned to an airborne division,[32] an air assault brigade,[33] a separate parachute regiment,[34] and two separate air assault battalions assigned to separate motorized brigades.[35]

The airborne division had three parachute regiments, an artillery regiment, and other specialized units. Each parachute regiment had three battalions and a special troops subunit. The parachute battalion had three parachute companies and artillery, air defense, and reconnaissance subunits. Depending on the assigned mission, the parachute regiments and subunits could be reinforced with artillery, engineer, and reconnaissance subunits. Also, aviation control groups might be detailed to support coordination with supporting aviation.

The weapons and combat vehicles assigned to airborne and air assault forces were less powerful and capable than those assigned to the motorized rifle units and subunits. At the same time, the weapons and combat vehicles were specially designed to meet the needs of these sky-assault forces. They were shorter and lighter so that they could be carried by aircraft and airdropped by parachute.

Thus, the BMD-1[36] is 2.2 times lighter and 1.2 times shorter than the BMP-1. It still packs a lot of fire power. It has the 73mm cannon that can fire fragmentation and shaped-charge rounds. It has a co-axial machine gun and two bow-mount machine guns. The machine guns were particularly useful during an assault against lightly armed enemy subunits that were often encountered in the depth of the enemy rear.

The low clearance of the BMD-1 was an important design feature. It allowed the crew to use any cover, even an insignificant terrain fold, to hide the vehicle during combat. The designers incorporated a mechanism in the BMD-1 that allowed it to raise some 30 centimeters from its covered position, fire at the target, and then lower itself again to the ground. Further, it might move forward, after firing, at minimum clearance to new cover. This gave the BMD-1 a high rate of survivability and allowed it to achieve surprise fire. The BMD-1 exerted a reduced ground pressure, a feature that was very important in an area where the enemy widely employed land mines. There were many occasions when a BMD-1 would run over a mine that did not explode, although it would have exploded with the passing of any other combat vehicle. The BMD is air-transportable on military airlift transport aircraft and helicopters. When necessary, the BMD may be dropped by parachute. The BMD has special brackets for attaching the parachutes and the rocket-braking system. Besides all this, the BMD-1 has a powerful water jet propelling system that allows it to cross unaided any water obstacle with a speed of 10 to 12 kilometers per hour.

Airborne and air assault small arms were distinct from those of the motorized rifle forces. They had folding stocks that shortened their length almost by half. These shortened weapons were more suitable for air landing and also when riding in a combat vehicle or when dismounting the vehicle.

Paratroopers and air assault troopers were generously and suitably equipped. This included a Panama field hat, cloth cap, or helmet; airborne coveralls or the winter airborne field uniform; jack books, jump boots, or sneakers; the PD-54 airborne rucksack; a flak jacket; an assault rifle, machine gun, or grenade launcher; a bayonet; two or three F-1 or RG-42 hand grenades; eight to ten magazines loaded with ammunition plus additional ammunition; two to four signal or illumination flares; two to four orange smoke canisters; a UHF radio; compass and flash light; matches; first aid kit; and dry rations. Belts of machine gun ammunition were carried draped on the personnel or in metal ammunition cans.

There were special features involved in preparing subunits and individuals for an airborne assault in Afghanistan. It was absolutely necessary to thoroughly conceal the planning for an air assault as well as the time and LZ. In the USSR, preparing subunits for an air assault was conducted in an assembly area, whereas in Afghanistan, this preparation was conducted in the base camp. Measures taken depended entirely on the nature of the upcoming mission and concluded with the preparation of personnel, armaments, and equipment and stockpiling necessary supply and equipment reserves.

Personnel training included training of the commanders, staffs, and force. During commander and staff training, particular attention was paid to the enemy and his tactics, the terrain in the combat zone, and earlier battles fought under similar circumstances. This training would usually include a command post map exercise as well as a communications exercise.

Personnel training in the subunits included weapons firing, vehicle driving, battle-drill, reconnaissance, land navigation, and individual skills. Special training was devoted to the selection and fortification of firing and observation positions; combat in built-up areas; movement in the mountains; first aid and evacuation of the wounded; and hand-to-hand combat.

Mission planning was conducted on maps or aerial photographs. This complicated planning since it was impossible to plan on the actual piece of ground. Missions were given to the subunits and coordination was conducted at the base camp using a map or a terrain model.

Significant effort was put into misleading the enemy as to the timing and mission plan. Misleading the enemy included deception, disinformation, surprise, and conducting the mission with comparatively small forces.

Planning for the mission was based on the commander's concept. In order to preserve the secrecy of the plan, it was worked out by a limited circle of men, usually the commander, the chief of staff, the chief of the operations section or his deputy, and one other officer of the operations section. They worked out the combat order and combat instructions. The staff worked out the plan for moving men, vehicles, armaments, and material by helicopter and worked out an air assault schedule and a coordination planning table. The coordination planning table depicted the primary missions; which subunits would carry them out; the order in which they would be carried out; the order in which forces and resources would be committed to the mission; the objectives; the timing; the phase lines; the communications plan; and the signals for recognition, warning, target identification, and guidance.

Reconnaissance was very important when preparing for an air assault and combat. Reconnaissance was conducted not only with the organic forces and resources of the airborne division, air assault brigade, and parachute regiments, but also with 40th Army assets. Further, they used reports and information from agents, the DRA KHAD, the DRA Sarandoy, Afghan Army units, and local inhabitants. On the basis of this data, they would modify the commander's concept of the battle and missions to the subunits and insert corrections in the battle plan and the utilization of forces and resources.

Sometimes the commander would send a reconnaissance group into the enemy rear area beforehand in order to get more reliable information about enemy activities. They would be inserted by helicopter or would walk in.

Final preparation of the formation was completed at the base camps or while the assault subunits were assembled at the airfield or helipad. After final preparations, the forces would board the helicopters. An air assault in the mountains often required almost twice the number of helicopters of normal circumstances. The air temperature and the height above sea level of the helipad and LZ affected the lifting power of the helicopter engines and reduced their load-carrying capacity. For example, an Mi-8 helicopter can carry 24 fully equipped troopers at sea level, but in the mountains, no more than 12, and in some cases even fewer.

It was necessary to emphasize these special features when determining the time and movement of the air assault. In conventional warfare, air assaults would land in the enemy rear after a breakthrough of enemy defenses and when the success of the offensive was assured. In Afghanistan, in order to achieve surprise, the assault flight went in before the start of the movement of the main ground forces or as these forces began to move from their base camps to the combat zone. Further, in order to deceive the enemy that an air assault was going into another LZ, the helicopters had to first fly to another likely LZ and then make a subsequent sharp shift in the flight route and approach to the actual LZ.

Depending on the mission, the air assault force might be a parachute platoon up to a parachute battalion. Usually the force was reinforced with mortar crews, AGS-17 crews, flame-thrower operators, and sappers. Air assault forces went in on transport helicopters and armed lift ships. Helicopter gunships provided fire support along with fighter-bomber aircraft.

The combat formation for an air assault usually consisted of several groups. The first group was composed of Mi-24 HIND helicopter gunships, MIG-21 jet fighter-bombers, and SU-25 FROGFOOT close air support jet aircraft. This group suppressed enemy air defenses and conducted preparatory fires on the LZ. Mi-8mt armed helicopter lift ships followed this group and landed a group that seized the LZ. Part of this group were FACs who adjusted helicopter gun ship strikes.

The main body of the air assault followed this group in a flying column. Mi-6 helicopter transports and Mi-8mt armed helicopter lift ships flew in pairs, maintaining their intervals and distance, which made the flight safer, provided freedom of maneuver, and aided control. The number of helicopters in this group depended on their availability and the size of the assault force. In the event that there were not enough helicopters to lift the entire main body at once, the main body was carried in several lifts, although this had a negative impact on surprise, simultaneity, and massing of forces.

A covering force over-flew the main body and provided fire support to the air assault force. There were two to four Mi-24v HIND helicopter gunships in this group that overflew the area, maintaining radio contact with the assault force and the FACs. When necessary, they would suppress enemy weapons that had survived the initial aerial preparation of the LZ.

A group of helicopter gunships followed the main body to provide fire support to the assault force, and, when necessary, another group followed to continue to suppress enemy air defenses. A combat command and control group accompanied this trail group. The command and control group had one or two MI-9 VZPU[37] command and control helicopters that were linked to an airborne AN-26 command and control aircraft. The helicopters circled the LZ at low altitude. Due to the nature of the war, enemy air defenses were not always fully suppressed.

Usually tactical air assaults would land simultaneously at several LZs. If there were no suitable LZs in the area, the lift ships would hover one to two meters above the ground while the assault troopers would jump out. In this case, it was best to use helicopters that had been lightened by removing the gun mounts and doors.

After they landed, the first group of assault troopers, supported by helicopter gunships, killed the enemy on the LZ and in the area, captured the high ground, and dug in. Sappers searched the area and neutralized mines. Scouts looked for the enemy and provided more exact data on enemy actions to the assault commander, the FACs, and the FOs.

There were a limited number of LZs in the mountains that were large enough to accommodate a company or battalion landing. Therefore, the Soviets had to use a number of smaller LZs and a smaller force to accomplish the mission. The scattered subunits quickly moved from the LZs to an assembly area where the commander assembled his forces and resources into an assault group. Sometimes it happened that a subunit of the main body landed on one of these small LZs and had to immediately defend itself and start the battle under extremely inauspicious circumstances.

In November 1981, a reconnaissance company of a parachute regiment was involved in an air assault 70 kilometers north of Kabul. Senior Lieutenant A. I. Lebed[38] commanded the company. The company had six LZs, located one to three kilometers from each other. The area in which the LZs were located encompassed some 30 square kilometers. Each LZ would only handle one helicopter at a time, so the other helicopter of the pair had to circle waiting for its turn to land. The assault landing took over twice as long as usual. This in turn delayed the assembly of the assault force and their subsequent movement to the designated line. As a result, some of the targeted enemy managed to escape the assault group's strike.

In the course of combat in Afghanistan, the air assault units and subunits sometimes conducted combined arms offensive and defensive ground combat, and other times they conducted specialized missions. In the first instance, their tactics and techniques did not differ from the tactics of the motorized rifle forces. In the second instance, tactics as a whole depended on the specific requirements of the combat mission. These missions were usually establishing a blocking position, conducting ambushes, conducting raids, and escorting convoys.

Establishing a blocking position from the air was done to prevent the withdrawal of the enemy from an occupied region and the arrival of enemy reinforcements from outside the area. Air assault forces were inserted in advance or during the course of the operation.

Blocking positions were established in advance when and where it was established that the enemy had concentrated in that region and the terrain and situation allowed the secret air landing of subunits. With the goal of preserving secrecy, the air assault subunits seldom landed on the site of the designated blocking positions. They landed elsewhere and then walked to the site. Thus, in the course of one of these operations, conducted to the east of Kabul in November 1985, a parachute battalion[39] landed some eight kilometers from the designated blocking positions. Due to the rugged terrain and the necessity of moving at night, it took over four hours to move to the site. As a result, part of the Mujahideen withdrew from the region and hid in the mountains.

Air assault forces established blocking positions simultaneously with the advance of ground forces only when it was impossible to conduct the air assault landings in advance, when the sweep was conducted only over part of the region, when the enemy was held in position, or when the situation demanded that surprise be added during the course of combat. It was difficult to establish surprise blocking positions and avoid personnel, weapons, and equipment losses.

An example of such an air assault occurred in February 1982 in a green zone in Paghman some 15 kilometers to the northwest of Kabul. Ten minutes before the main attack, 12 Mi-8tv helicopters lifted a reconnaissance company and a parachute company from the same parachute regiment from the Kabul airfield.

The flight took a wide detour around the region and, after a 30-minute flight, approached the LZ from the north. The ground force had already entered the green zone and begun forcing the enemy out of his strong points. However, the Mujahideen put up a stubborn fight, counting on the arrival of reserves or eventual withdrawal into the mountains.

From 0630 to 0650 hours, the air assault force landed on the eastern slope of the mountain adjacent to the green zone. This was in plain view of the Mujahideen and cut off their withdrawal route. Panic broke out in the Mujahideen camp. The Soviet forces took advantage of this panic and quickly and completely destroyed a strong enemy detachment.

Air assault landings to block the enemy could be conducted at one location or at several locations simultaneously. An air assault into one LZ was conducted when and where the terrain would not permit establishing a perimeter around the entire region and where there was only one possible withdrawal route for the enemy.

For such a mission, the senior commander required highly centralized control of forces and resources and comprehensive support. This significantly eased coordination. However, such air assaults expended a significant amount of time. It was inevitable that the enemy group would leave the area when he saw a large number of helicopters landing at a single site or saw the ground force blocking subunits begin withdrawing to their own lines.

It was more effective to establish blocking positions with air assaults on several LZs, located along the perimeter of the area where the enemy was concentrated. However, this demanded a high degree of professionalism by the helicopter pilots who had to accurately navigate while flying nap of the earth over rugged terrain. It also demanded a high degree of professionalism by the air assault squads and platoons who had to act independently for a long period of time while separated from the main body.

In November 1981, a multiple blocking insertion took place to trap a strong enemy group in the green zone near Estalef—some 15 kilometers southwest of Bagram. A reinforced reconnaissance company from a parachute regiment landed at dawn to interdict a possible western withdrawal route from the green zone.

The air assault force boarded their helicopters at their assembly area at the southern part of Kabul airfield. Eight Mi-8 helicopters were supposed to land simultaneously on six LZs located along a seven-kilometer front. The landings were supposed to be complete 30 minutes before the ground force began to move.

Due to the rugged terrain, the helicopter crews were unable to quickly find the LZs. It took longer to land the assault force than planned. However, the uncoordinated landings of several groups at different times prevented the enemy from determining the Soviet intent and launching counter actions.

In the course of an hour, the troopers seized the LZs and started to move to their blocking positions, destroying small groups of the enemy as they went. At 0700 hours, the movement to the blocking line was complete. There were 250 Mujahideen in the trap who were quickly destroyed.

Air assault subunits conducted ambushes deep in the enemy area to interdict weapon caravans and capture prisoners and documents. These ambushes were very difficult and dangerous. Subunits selected for ambush had to function independently for a period of several days far from their base camps while under the constant threat of discovery and attack by the enemy. However, the high state of individual training of the air assault troopers and paratroopers allowed them to accomplish most difficult missions successfully.

Air assault troopers and paratroopers conducted ambushes in conjunction with practically every operation. Each ambush was different, due to differences in mission, objective, ambush composition, and available resources.

The more frequent ambushes were those conducted to interdict caravans carrying weapons and ammunition across Afghanistan's international borders with Pakistan and Iran. As a rule, a parachute company was assigned to interdict each caravan route and was reinforced with machine gunners, AGS-17 crews, and sappers. The company would conduct two or three ambushes, each of which consisted of a reinforced parachute platoon.

Preparation for the conduct of an ambush began with the analysis of reconnaissance information received from various sources. After conducting an appraisal of the terrain, the planners selected the ambush site, determined the optimum course of action, determined the forces and resources necessary to carry out the mission, and specified the combat formation, the withdrawal plan, and those measures taken to deceive the enemy.

Preparation of personnel, weapons, and equipment began simultaneously alongside planning. Training was conducted in hand-to-hand combat, movement by stealth, observation, first aid, and evacuation of the wounded. Armaments and equipment were carefully checked for good working order and combat reliability. Soldiers conducted range fire and adjusted their sights; mounted and checked night sights; and did the same for weapon silencers. The platoon leaders and squad leaders conducted personnel training.[40]

Subunits were transported to the ambush site secretly on armed Mi-8tv transport helicopters. During the flight, the helicopters conducted several false insertions in the region of the ambush to deceive the enemy. The troops exited on the last insertion, which was conducted an hour to an hour-and-a-half before sunset. The insertion was some five to eight kilometers from the ambush site. The subunit moved on foot under cover of darkness. Reconnaissance and the strict observation of security measures were important. Reconnaissance and security elements moved fairly close to the main body, communicating by special light and sound signals and short-range radios.

When the subunits reached the designated area, they occupied suitable observation and firing positions, camouflaged them, and scouted the terrain looking for the enemy. Reconnaissance often discovered possible enemy movement routes against which they could deploy forces and resources. Scouting also disclosed sites for mines and other obstacles. Scouts also marked the withdrawal routes from the ambush site to the assembly area and on to the pick-up LZ. The scouts determined the security positions and defensive positions around the LZ.

The difference between an ambush established by a motorized rifle subunit and an ambush established by a parachute subunit was that a group of armed transport-helicopters or helicopter gunships was part of the parachute subunit ambush. In order to ensure tight coordination with the helicopters, an FAC with the necessary communications gear accompanied each platoon. During the entire time that the subunit was on ambush, the helicopters were waiting in a concealed, secure hide position or at the nearest Soviet regimental base on strip alert.

The ambush could summon the helicopters with a special predetermined radio signal. Two helicopters would fly to the ambush site and conduct fire support for the ambush commander as directed by the FAC.

The ambush opened fire on the enemy at close range. In the course of battle, the Soviets would capture prisoners, weapons, and ammunition. Enemy groups, attempting to flee, would be intercepted by specially selected groups positioned on probable escape routes. These groups would also ambush the enemy. The conduct of the ambush considered enemy activity; the size and composition of the enemy; the training, strength, and combat readiness of their own troops; and the terrain.

Ambushes organized as above were quite effective. In July 1986, a parachute company was ordered to conduct an ambush. The commander selected 35 men. Armaments included four PKM machine guns, four RPKS machine guns, and ten MON-100 directional mines. Every paratrooper had two units of fire, four hand grenades, and a low-power radio. An FAC and two sappers accompanied the paratroopers. Four Mi-8 armed helicopter transports were assigned to carry and support the ambush party. Further, four Mi-24 HIND helicopter gunships were kept on alert at their base camp to support the ambush.

The ambush party flew from their base camp at 1930 hours on 21 July and flew nap-of-the-earth toward their ambush site. Every 10 to 15 minutes, the helicopters would conduct a false insertion. At 2030 hours, the helicopters landed the ambush party some six kilometers from their ambush site. After this, the helicopters flew to the pick-up LZ and set down. The pick-up LZ was 15 kilometers from the ambush site. The ambush party took reconnaissance and security measures. At 2200 hours, the ambush party secretly moved to the designated area and established two ambush sites on a probable enemy route. The company commander organized observation, determined the firing positions for his weapons, and showed the sappers where to place the mines.

At 0400 hours, the observers reported that a column of six trucks was moving down the road toward the ambush kill zone. The trucks maintained large intervals between each other so they could not all be destroyed simultaneously. Two trucks were outside the kill zone and attempted to escape. However, the commander had called for helicopter support at the start of the combat and helicopter gunships caught up to the trucks and destroyed them. At 0700 hours, the sun was up and the mission was complete. The company withdrew, covered by part of its own force, and moved to the assembly area where the helicopters were waiting. They loaded their trophies and personnel on board the aircraft and flew back to base camp.

Raids were conducted mainly to seize and destroy weapons and ammunition dumps, command posts, training centers, small strong points, and enemy groups. Most often, these raids were conducted against military depots that were located in the mountains and difficult for ground forces to reach. As a rule, the security on these depots consisted of several dozen personnel armed with small arms. On the approaches to these depots and on the tops of dominant terrain the Mujahideen established observation and defensive positions manned by mortar and DShK machine gun crews and shoulder-fired air defense missile gunners. The Mujahideen manned these positions around the clock and buried mines around the observation posts.

To take out such a target with a raid required a group of 20 to 40 raiders armed with assault rifles, knives, and plenty of hand grenades. To transport this group to the objective required from two to six helicopters. If the enemy had a strong security and air defense force, two to six helicopter gunships would reinforce the raid to provide fire suppression.

Colonel V. A. Gorshkov participated in several raids and was decorated with two Cavalier Orders. He remembers how every raid was thoroughly prepared for. The parachute battalion commander, the raiding parachute company commander, and the helicopter pilots planned the raid together. They carefully studied the terrain using maps and aerial photographs, determining the more advantageous flight paths and the combat formation after landing. They calculated the time required to fulfill the mission. The personnel trained on ground similar to that of the objective. During the course of training, they paid particular attention to quick, precise actions by the helicopter crews and raiders.

Most often, raids were conducted at noon, when the Mujahideen were eating and involved in worship and religious rituals. The helicopters flew nap-of-the-earth to approach the objective secretly. As a rule, they flew along the side of the highest mountain and conducted the air assault by landing close to the depot. If there was no LZ, the raiders quickly jumped out of the helicopters and rapidly rushed the depot to seize it from all sides. At the same time, when necessary, the helicopters fired on the objective to prepare it for the raiders.

The raiders quickly captured and destroyed the objective. After they accomplished their mission, the raiders moved to the assembly area and called for pickup by the armed transport helicopters. The helicopters returned the raiders to their base camp.

Frequently, airborne and air assault units and subunits were detailed to provide security and convoy escort for military and economic cargo. The basic method of carrying out these missions was to establish temporary guard posts along the convoy's route of march with the help of helicopters and to inflict a preventative strike on enemy groups preparing to attack. V. M. Varushinin, the former chief of staff of a parachute regiment, recalls providing security and convoy escort along the Jalalabad-Barikot highway during June and July 1981. Four air assaults landed four parachute companies in the mountains along the banks of the Kunar river. The troopers seized the dominant heights and interdicted the enemy paths leading to the road.

In a number of instances, the airborne and air assault subunits conducted preventative strikes on moving enemy groups and small detachments. These actions took the form of a raid. Subunits would board helicopters that would fly nap-of-the-earth to secretly penetrate into the enemy rear. The subunit would quickly land and rapidly attack and destroy the enemy. In the event that a significant enemy force was spotted, several parachute or air assault companies and helicopter gunships were detailed to deal with it.

The experience of employing airborne and air assault forces in Afghanistan showed the exceptional complexity of organizing and supporting the withdrawal of subunits from the combat zone after they completed their mission. Withdrawal was conducted by stages, as a rule, under the cover of helicopter gunships and a specially constituted rear guard. The rear guard occupied and fought from a series of lines along the path to the assembly area. During this rear guard battle, special efforts were made to find and destroy enemy air defense weapons, which would be particularly dangerous to the troopers during the boarding and take-off of the helicopters.

As a whole, combat experience in Afghanistan demonstrated that airborne and air assault forces could be used expediently to fulfill special combat missions, most of which could not be effectively accomplished by motorized rifle units and subunits. The more productive types of combat carried out by airborne and air assault forces were ambushes, raids, establishing blocking positions, and providing security to convoys. The success of these types of combat depended greatly on the preparation of commanders, staffs, and airborne and air assault troopers, as well as the combat mastery of the helicopter gun ship crews.

Editors' comments: The airborne, air assault, reconnaissance, and Spetsnaz troopers, along with those of the two separate motorized rifle brigades, executed the bulk of the offensive combat. They conducted the raids, ambushes, and deep battle that brought the fight to the Mujahideen. While motorized forces were involved with security of garrisons, LOCs, cities, and airfields, the airborne and air assault troopers launched the majority of combat assaults. Tactical innovation naturally appeared earlier among these forces. Perhaps 10 percent of motorized rifle officers served in Afghanistan. A much higher percentage of airborne and air assault officers served there. During the postwar period, the influence of the airborne and air assault "mafia" was apparent, as many of these officers became the ranking officers in the Soviet Armed Forces.

Although parachute assaults were not conducted in Afghanistan, air assaults from helicopters were used frequently. The Mujahideen had initial difficulty adapting to the sudden appearance of air assault forces in their territory. The Soviets had invested a great deal of attention to the development of airborne forces beginning in the 1920s. By the time the Soviet Union invaded Afghanistan, airborne and air assault forces were well-equipped and essential components of the Soviet military. Unlike the U.S. airborne and air assault forces, the Soviets had developed combat vehicles that could be air-dropped or carried by helicopter to the landing zone. These combat vehicles included armored personnel carriers, assault guns, portable artillery, engineer vehicles, command vehicles, and reconnaissance vehicles. When a U.S. airborne or air assault unit landed, it was on foot. When a Soviet airborne or air assault unit landed, it mounted its accompanying combat vehicles and rode to battle. When the U.S. force landed, it tried to land on or very close to its objective. The Soviet force would always land away from its objective in order to organize its force carefully before it mounted its vehicles to move on the objective.

The Soviets brought all their airborne and air assault combat vehicles along to Afghanistan. However, the rugged terrain in Afghanistan often dictated that the vehicles could not be used, due to the limited landing zones, the difficulty of lifting vehicles in the thin air of the mountains, and the nature of the terrain. Consequently, the combat vehicles that accompanied a 40th Army air assault often drove to the area where they could support the air assault troopers who landed from helicopters. Airborne and air assault combat vehicles were, by necessity, less roomier than the standard BTR and BMP personnel carriers of the motorized rifle forces. During the war, the airborne and air assault forces were supplemented with additional combat vehicles—such as the larger BMPs and BTRS. With these, the airborne and air assault forces could perform routine missions, such as convoy escort, while not wearing out their specialized vehicles.

Airborne and air assault forces were elite forces in the Soviet Army and enjoyed special privileges, uniforms, and a pick of the conscripts. Since the airborne and air assault forces were involved in bringing the fight to the Mujahideen, often in the Mujahideen's back yard, these forces experienced much of the combat and garnered many of the awards and accolades.

ARMY AVIATION[41]

A year prior to the introduction of Soviet forces in Afghanistan, Soviet aviation was already carrying out various missions in the border regions and throughout the country. Fixed wing and helicopter flights primarily carried out reconnaissance and data-gathering missions. Soviet Army aviation helicopters, carrying the markings of the Afghan air force, flew using minimum radio communications.

During this time, the Soviets formed a composite team of ethnic Tadjik and Uzbek air force officers at the airfield of one of the aviation regiments. They were air force pilots, on-board aviation technicians, ground aviation specialists, aviation engineer services specialists, and civil aviation personnel. They were given an accelerated course on aviation theory, followed by flight school at one of the helicopter academies. They further perfected their flight techniques in Soviet Central Asia. After all this, they began to conduct independent missions in Afghanistan. Hardly any of them suspected that their preparation was the preparation for a long and difficult war in the skies over Afghanistan. During the war, hundreds and thousands of aviators would be killed and maimed and their aircraft would be struck and shot down.

From its first combat, aviation proved to be of special significance. Helicopters were given a variety of fire support, air assault, and special missions. The Soviets used a variety of gunship, armed-transport, and transport helicopters for these missions in the skies above Afghanistan.

The Mi-24 was the Soviet production rotary-wing helicopter gunship. This helicopter was assigned to provide close aviation support to ground forces and to destroy ground targets (primarily moving) from the forward enemy fighting positions to the depths of their position. Mi-24 helicopters were also used to lay land mines, conduct reconnaissance, and carry out a variety of special missions.

The Mi-8mt armed transport helicopter was used for the conduct of air assault landings, transporting personnel and cargo, destroying ground targets, and carrying out special missions.

The Mi-6 transport helicopter was used for the conduct of air assault landings, transporting personnel, or transporting up to 12 metric tons of cargo in the cargo bay and suspended beneath it. The Mi-6 may also be refitted as a fuel bowser. The helicopter is armed with a heavy machine gun and 250 rounds.

A small quantity of the Mi-9 VZPU helicopter airborne command posts were used in Afghanistan to control combat.

Helicopters were equipped with a variety of weapons systems and munitions to meet mission requirements. The standard armaments included rocket pods full of unguided rockets, machine guns, and grenade launchers. For special missions, helicopters were armed with antitank guided missiles and aerial bombs of various types.

Flying helicopters in Afghanistan was very difficult. The majority of the airfields and heliports were located from 1,000 to 1,800 meters above sea level and were very dusty. External wind temperature in the summer reached 45° to 52° Celsius [113° to 126° Fahrenheit] in the southern region and 40° to 45° Celsius [104° to 113° Fahrenheit] in the northern region. In the central and western parts of Afghanistan, strong winds arose, especially in the second half of the day. These winds obscured visibility and created dust storms. Combat missions took helicopters into the high mountains. All these conditions reduced the engine power and the lifting capacity of the aircraft, lowered the flight ceiling, and worsened the take off and landing characteristics and the technical reliability of the helicopter.

The territory of Afghanistan was divided into four regions that were controlled by subunits of army aviation and partly by the ground forces. The northern region included the cities of Kunduz, Khanabad, Faizabad, Puli-Kumri, Tashkurgan, and Mazar-i-Sharif. The eastern region included the cities of Khost, Asadabad, Jalalabad, Gardez, Ghazni, Kabul, and Bagram. The southern region included the city of Munarai to the southern border zone of Pakistan, Kandahar, and Lashkargah. The western region included the cities of Farah, Shindand, and Herat.

Each of these regions had its own geographic and climatic conditions with its own peculiarities that affected the helicopters. In particular, there are the mountain regions, characterized by slopes, canyons, and mountain ranges where the average mountain height is between 3,000 to 4,000 meters. Furthermore, there are zones containing great deserts. The terrain and climate had a decided effect when selecting the optimum helicopter flight path, the proper safety altitude for overflying a danger zone, the target attack approach route, the amount of hover time available to aim and fire, and the exit route to take after the attack. Further, the operational capabilities and ease of flying the helicopter were influenced by the constant rising and descending air currents over mountain passes and canyons.

Helicopter flight personnel in Afghanistan wore a simple, suitable flight uniform consisting of flight coveralls and a steel protective helmet. During flights supporting the ground forces, they also wore flak jackets. Further, every member of the flight crew was armed with TO&E weaponry—a pistol and short-barreled Kalashnikov assault rifle. The crew was also equipped with parachutes, radios, life-saving gear, and smoke and light signaling devices for emergencies.

The opportunity to use helicopters depended partially on where the helicopters were based. Regiments and subunits in Afghanistan were usually based at civilian airfields or at specially prepared heliports at the garrisons of combined arms units and subunits. Helicopter bases had a parking area for the helicopters, a command post, a rocket and ammunition preparation site, buildings for engineering-technical subunits, an ammunition storage area, a POL storage area, and a building for equipment for airfield-technical support. Communications and radio-technical support were located at each airfield and heliport.

Aviation garrisons were usually located adjacent to the airfield or heliport. An aviation garrison consisted of the headquarters, barracks, or prefab sleeping quarters, a mess hall, a movie theater, steam baths with small swimming pools, and other service buildings.

Special engineering-construction subunits built and equipped heliports and aviation garrisons. They were assisted by the personnel of the army aviation units and subunits.

Combined arms subunits protected and defended airfields, heliports, and aviation garrisons by manning defensive perimeters designed to exclude enemy mortar and small-arms fire. The aviation units and subunits provided their own internal guard on the parked helicopters and aviation garrison buildings.

The combat employment of helicopters in Afghanistan depended on the nature and tactics of enemy actions. The Mujahideen fought in small groups and frequently at night. In all circumstances, their clothing was indistinguishable from that of the general populace. It was very difficult to find and destroy such an enemy from the air.

Enemy air defense systems also hindered the employment of aviation. Mujahideen senior commanders paid special attention to combating aircraft and helicopters since these mobile, lethal systems could find, block, and destroy the Mujahideen. The Mujahideen presented their highest awards and rewards to those groups that succeeded in knocking down aircraft and helicopters, as well as those who captured pilots.

The primary Mujahideen air defense weapons were the DShK heavy machine gun, the mountain air defense machine gun mount, small arms fire, and RPG-7 grenade launchers. In the mid-1980s, the Mujahideen began to use large amounts of "Strella-2" and "Stinger" shoulder-fired air defense missiles.[42] Air defense fire was usually combined with salvo fire from small arms. Further, the Mujahideen routinely fired normal automatic weapons at aerial targets using improvised mounts that provided the angle of elevation and arc of fire. Mujahideen air defense weapons were as a rule deployed, dispersed, and echeloned in lines. Air defense fire opened up simultaneously on a given signal, when an aircraft or helicopter was on a bombing run or when they were pulling out from a bombing run. The dispersed air defense systems allowed the enemy to fire in various directions. Further, the Mujahideen kept their air defense systems in their firing positions only when necessary. At other times, they were kept in special fortified hidden positions. This made it very difficult to find the Mujahideen air defense weapons and destroy them.

In later years, the enemy used the air defense "nomadic ambush" widely to combat Soviet aviation. These ambushes were established close to airfields at the ends of the take-off and landing strips and also on the likely flight routes of aircraft and helicopters. In order not to give away their positions, the Mujahideen did not fire tracer ammunition while they were firing at aerial targets. They would fire on the aircraft and helicopters during their approach and as they flew away and, as a rule, concentrate the fires from several air defense ambushes on both the lead aircraft and its wing aircraft. When possible, fires would come from the front, rear, side, and even above.

Army aviation flew at different heights during different periods of the war in order to counter enemy air defense. Thus, at the start of combat, right up until 1981, they flew at the minimum allowable height. With the increase in the number of enemy weapons, it was no longer safe to fly at this altitude as the quantity of combat-damaged helicopters rapidly grew. As a consequence, army aviation had to fly at a working altitude of 500 to 700 meters. This somewhat reduced the number of bullets and rounds striking the helicopters. However, the incidence of damage remained high. Thus, in June 1982, while a Mi-24 helicopter was carrying out a mission in the area near the city of Kandahar, a bullet penetrated the armor beneath the fuselage and entered the cargo compartment, wounding the on-board technician in the leg and hitting the main reduction gear.

With the appearance of the "Strella-2" shoulder-fired air defense missile in the Mujahideen arsenal, army aviation had to fly at the higher altitude of 1,500 meters above the ground. Further, to protect the helicopter during this period, army aviation widely employed the exhaust deflecting skirt installed on the engine nozzle to disperse the hot stream of exhaust gases. Also, they installed flare dispensers that fired flares at intervals behind the aircraft when over those areas where enemy air defenses might be located. These flares would draw infrared homing missile guidance systems away from the aircraft.

The Mujahideen acquisition of the American-manufactured "Stinger" shoulder-fired air-defense missile gave them the ability to hit an aircraft out to a distance of 4,800 meters and up to 2,000 meters in elevation. The Soviet command had to severely limit the employment of helicopters, especially during daylight. However, it was impossible to abandon the use of rotary-wing aircraft completely. Helicopter pilots had to become even more skilled to survive.

Combat pilot training was conducted in several phases. It began in the mountain-desert terrain of Soviet Central Asia and continued after the crew's arrival in Afghanistan. In Afghanistan, the crew received general training, designed to integrate the crews into the formation, and direct training for combat. Usually the training was conducted in subunits and units.

Upon receipt of a combat mission, an aviation commander would ensure that he understood his mission and his senior commander's concept of the operation. He reviewed the terrain and the mission of the unit he was supporting and the missions of subunits of that unit. He reviewed coordination procedures with other aviation subunits and ground units and determined the time available to prepare for the coming combat. During training and preparation for combat, one of the basic tasks of the unit and subunit army aviation staffs was to provide an accurate picture of the combat situation and the condition of subordinate subunits. Particular attention was paid to the enemy situation—the composition of his groupings, his intentions, and his air defense lay-out. Further, a thorough study of the terrain was key in determining how to conduct the upcoming combat. To support this terrain study, army aviation would conduct reconnaissance flights over the region and take aerial photographs used to create photo mosaics to supplement large-scale maps. As a result of the evaluation of the terrain, planners determined the accessibility of the region, landing zones for armed helicopter transports, potential use of the terrain to support action against the enemy, possible firing positions for enemy air defense systems, and the routes that Mujahideen forces could use for maneuver and withdrawal.

As a result of the evaluation, specific missions were assigned to every aviation combat subunit and armed-transport helicopter subunit. The plan included artillery and frontal aviation suppression of enemy air defenses in the high-mountain regions and enemy air defense zones. Specific targets, flight routes to them, and helicopter gun ship armaments were specified in verbal combat orders.

Mission training for flying personnel began with an analysis of the previous combat mission, review of other relevant examples, and a discussion of past errors and their causes. A very important step in mission training was active coordination between the army aviation subunits and the subunits and units of the ground force. In the course of the operation, coordination was stressed to ensure uninterrupted contact between the commander of the ground force and supporting aviation.

A group of command and control officers and FACs controlled aviation during the conduct of operations.[43] The effectiveness of aviation strikes and the success of combat at the objective depended, to a great deal, on the preparations, coordination, and precise actions of this group. FACs, attached to ground battalions, received their missions from the battalion commander and directed army aviation strikes against specified enemy targets. All questions of coordinating army aviation and artillery were handled on the spot with the FOs who were also attached to the battalion headquarters. Having verified the location of targets, determined the location of enemy air defense systems, and checked the terrain relief, the FACs determined the sequence of target strikes by the aviation group and determined the best flight attack and exit routes to guarantee the safety of their aviation group. When enemy positions were detected and identified, the FAC marked them for the helicopter crews. The FAC would use signal rockets and tracer bullets to show the direction to the target. After the helicopters carried out their first attack, the FACs would make the necessary corrections for the next attack. During the course of the aviation support of the ground forces, it was often necessary to redirect the helicopter strikes to other, more important targets. This required well-trained pilots and FACs with a detailed knowledge of the situation on the ground.

In Afghanistan, army aviation missions were classified as fire, air assault, and special. The most important fire missions were in direct support of ground combat. The primary method of fire support was for helicopter gun ship subunits and groups to launch successive strikes on planned targets and targets of opportunity while accompanying the ground units that were engaged in combat. These strikes were conducted in accordance with a predetermined schedule or on call when the FAC alerted aircraft on strip alert or circling in the air.

Often, tactical aviation support to combat in the mountains was severely limited. Maneuverability of helicopters is drastically reduced at heights of 2,500 meters and more, and the accuracy and effectiveness of helicopter armaments falls off. Helicopters would have to attack targets while covered by other helicopter groups conducting air defense suppression missions. The attacking helicopters would try to exit over an area not covered by enemy air defenses. These attack helicopters would not hover, but would attack at maximum speed to minimize their exposure time over target.

Helicopter flights were made at 1,500 meters above the ground. These altitudes were reduced only when conducting a gun run to launch rockets and fire the on-board cannon and machine guns. In this case, the "form a circle" helicopter tactic was highly recommended. Attack helicopters would form a circle high above the target or to the side. In turn, attack helicopters would dive down, attack the target, and then use a horizontal combat turn or a steep climb to exit and rejoin the circle. The attack helicopters would then repeat their attack on the target in turn. This tactic was used only by those pilots who had mastered helicopter gunnery and the control of their aviation technical equipment. During these gun runs, the most effective armaments were ATGM, coupled with a salvo of free-flight rockets.

During the course of the war in Afghanistan, the army aviation units and subunits continually searched for new tactics, techniques, and procedures; ways to improve aviation equipment; and ways to improve the armaments and ordnance. Particular attention was devoted to testing and adapting weapons employing new physical principles or providing increased lethality and effectiveness. Night-combat capability was improved with various new sights and night-vision binoculars that aided target illumination at night. Experiments were conducted to improve the probability of kill by mounting homing warheads on helicopter rockets.

Helicopters provided essential support to ground forces conducting cordon and search actions in inhabited areas located within green zones. Green zones were difficult terrain to advance through, since they have a well-developed system of irrigation canals and are densely covered with vegetation. Further, the enemy often converted the adobe buildings and their enclosure walls *(duval)* located within the green zones into strong points. Helicopter gunships provided cover to the combined Soviet/DRA forces that cooperated in such actions.

When the ground commander required aviation support in the green zone, attack helicopters flew into the combat zone at an elevation of 1,500 to 2,000 meters. Normal aviation support was provided by a pair or section of circling helicopters that responded to a ground-based FAC who directed and corrected the helicopter strikes. This proved effective since all the helicopter crews observed the strikes of the leading helicopter, and then, in the event that the leading helicopter drew return fire, the following gunships could accurately destroy the enemy firing position. The helicopter conducted its gun run and exit at an angle of attack of 20° to 30°. It began its exit at a height of 1,200 to 1,000 meters and a distance of 1,000 to 1,500 meters past the target.

Helicopters frequently engaged targets located close to the forward edge of friendly forces. The minimum safe distances for using aerial ordnance near friendly forces are the following: free-flight rocket, 1,000 meters; helicopter cannon, 500 meters; and helicopter machine gun, 300 meters. These safety constraints also required that flight personnel were skilled in aerial gunnery using all the various armaments. Further, the FAC had to know the current ground situation precisely and comprehensively and be able to quickly react to changes in the ground commander's plan. When the enemy put up a stubborn resistance that attack helicopters could not overcome, the FACs called in close-air support aircraft or fighter bombers to bomb and strafe the enemy, smash his adobe structures, and destroy his strong points.

Should the aviation support requirement extend over a long time, relief heli-copter crews were substituted when the aircraft were refueled and rearmed. The same helicopters usually provided close air support to the ground force through-out the action.

When the fire support to ground forces mission ended, the helicopters would exit the combat zone. If, for some reason, an individual motorized rifle subunit was not able to exit the region before sunset, it would establish a perimeter defense and helicopter gunships would remain overhead. In some cases, armed helicopter transports would evacuate the subunit at night. In October 1986, helicopters evacuated part of a motorized rifle company from a green zone near Kandahar city. The troopers were surrounded and being shelled by enemy mortars. Heli-copter gunships destroyed four of six Mujahideen firing points. This kind of combat action was not rare. It demanded a high level of professional skill and moral-psychological conditioning [courage] on the part of the flying personnel.

One of the more important missions performed by army aviation in Afghani-stan was conducting air assault landings and supporting the air assault force. It was equally difficult conducting the assault landing and evacuating the force at mission's end.

When the helicopter subunit commander received the air assault mission, he would make an estimate of the situation and select the more suitable LZs. Flight personnel would then thoroughly study these LZs on a photomosaic of aerial photographs. In the process of preparing for the mission, aviation planners paid particular attention to calculating the maximum flying weight of the helicopter, the weight of the air assault cargo, the altitude of the LZ above sea level, the size of the LZ, and the locations of sites for refueling the helicopters. They selected a flight profile and flight route to the LZ based on the terrain while circumvent-ing those areas saturated with enemy air defense systems.

Frontal aviation and combat helicopters conducted fire preparation to destroy and suppress targets, enemy personnel, and enemy air defenses along the flight route and in the region of the LZ. The air assault landing took place imme-diately after the fire preparation. During the landing, helicopter gunships isolated the region while the assault group landed, provided safety to the lift birds, and engaged newly discovered and recovering enemy air defense sites. If the location of enemy air defense sites was not fully known, helicopter flights would conduct a feint to draw fire and thus pinpoint their firing systems.

As the air assault groups flew to the area, the helicopters of these groups might fly at different altitudes in order to forestall enemy fire from the mountain slopes and canyons. Su-25 close air support aircraft often reinforced covering groups of helicopter gunships. The SU-25s overflew the area of the assault land-ing and exerted strong psychological pressure on the Mujahideen by destroying their known air defense systems with powerful bombing and strafing attacks.

The number of LZs depended on the size of the operation, the availability of forces, and the missions to be accomplished. Frequently the LZs were barely adequate, being too small, very dusty, and very high above sea level. Therefore the helicopters might set down on one or two wheels or hover to unload air assault forces. This risked brushing the tail rotor against the steep mountain slope. The exact location of the LZ could not exceed the planned location by more than 500 to 1,000 meters. The most difficult part of flying the helicopter at that point was determining the descent to landing, since a repeat approach was often impossible. If the landing was in the mountains located over 2,500 meters in altitude, the helicopters of a landing group lightened their weight by removing some armaments and armor, limiting the number of air assault troops that they carried, and limiting their fuel load. There was a shortage of helicopters, so when large air assaults were conducted, the transport helicopters had to make several flights. Toward the end of August 1987, 14 Mi-8 helicopters landed 1,700 troopers near the Salang tunnel. Each helicopter made 12 trips during the four-hour landing.

Often air assaults landed right on top of a defending enemy. In this case, the transport helicopters independently engaged the surprised enemy with machine gun fire, and the air assault troopers went immediately into combat after landing. Each helicopter left the LZ independently, observing safety measures and avoiding helicopter collisions in the mountains.

Helicopter gunships, flying in the area of the LZs, provided cover to the assault troops and directed the lift ships to avoid collisions.

During the air assault, army aviation maintained fire support and aerial cover by phasing in aviation groups into the air space over the combat. These included helicopter gunships, close air support aircraft, and fighter-bombers. Transport helicopters provided maneuver to the forces and equipment, brought in armaments and ammunition, and evacuated the dead and wounded.

After carrying out the mission, the assault subunits moved independently to the assembly area for helicopter evacuation. Combat experience showed that evacuating air assault forces from the combat zone was frequently more difficult than the insertion. The difficulty rose from the intensity of enemy combat and the arrival of fresh enemy reserves that would seize the dominant heights and attempt to disrupt the aircrafts' activity. Therefore it was very important to divert the enemy forces from the assembly and extraction area. Pairs of helicopter gunships carried out this mission by flying a standing air patrol over an area that was one-and-a-half to two times larger than normal.

The mission to insert reconnaissance and sabotage groups and to support their actions deep in enemy territory was equally difficult but required fewer aircraft. A mixed helicopter group carried out such missions. The group had one or two pair of helicopter gunships and a flight of armed helicopter transports. The LZ should be no closer than five to eight kilometers from presumed enemy movement routes and villages. The helicopter flight carried out one or more false insertions just before sunset. The actual insertion and deployment of the Spetsnaz groups had to be conducted away from villages, shepherds, and cattle drovers.

After landing the Spetsnaz groups, the helicopters would return to their airfield or to a nearby Soviet garrison where they stayed in constant readiness to react to a call. The commander of the Spetsnaz subunit had the authority to call for these helicopters at any hour. If such a need arose, the group of helicopters quickly took off and flew to the designated region and then acted as directed from the ground. Night flights were carried out under complete black-out conditions. The crews were rapidly oriented relative to each other by sporadically turning on aerial navigation lights or periodically displaying aircraft lights for a short time. For maximum safety, the helicopters flew echeloned with 100 to 200 meters of altitude between each helicopter.

Army aviation systematically destroyed individual enemy strong points, weapons dumps, training centers, and other important targets. Every aviation unit and subunit was tasked to conduct three or four flights daily in cooperation with close air support aircraft or fighter-bombers to accomplish such missions. However, helicopter gunships could carry out such missions independently, and did so, especially in southern Afghanistan.

Lift ships assigned to attack missions performed target designation, search and rescue, and post-strike photo reconnaissance. To prepare for these missions, the helicopter crews studied the combat orders, which described the region, enemy groupings, the target coordinates, and also the enemy air defense systems, the composition of the aviation group, and the time of the fighter-bomber strike. After this, the helicopter crews studied the region and the mission objectives on large-scale maps and photo mosaics and confirmed the make-up of the strike group, its call signs, and ordnance.

The armed helicopter transport group, equipped with aerial illumination flares, arrived at the designated region one or two minutes before the arrival of the fighter-bomber strike group with whom they were in radio contact. They would drop the illumination flares (which, in this case, were not rigged with parachutes) on the target area from a height of 1,500 to 2,000 meters. Airborne FACs would then fly into the area to direct the air strikes and adjust their bomb runs.

The strike group of jet aircraft would fly out of a circular holding area to make two or more bombing runs from different directions and then return to their airfield. Helicopters would photograph the strike and forward the results to the higher headquarters. These were surprise attacks and, as a rule, were very productive.

In the course of Afghanistan combat, the Soviet forces often used army aviation helicopters to inspect caravans. In order to conduct these missions, the helicopter crews had to know the area and the times that caravans would usually move across it, enemy tactics, and how visually to distinguish a peaceful caravan from a hostile caravan, as well as how to precisely coordinate with ground forces search groups.

A group of lift ships with an on-board search group flew to the region where they suspected that caravans were crossing. The lift ships were covered by helicopter gunships. They set out, as a rule, early in the morning or toward dusk, when the hostile caravans would be arriving in the suspect area, shifting hiding places, or loading cargo.

When they found a caravan, the helicopter crews visually determined the size and nature of the caravan from what they could see. The inspection of the caravan was conducted while flying around at a height of 1,500 to 2,000 meters. In the event that the personnel escorting the caravan displayed any aggressive behavior or started to employ their weapons, the caravan was destroyed. If the caravan conducted itself peacefully, the armed transport helicopters with its on-board search groups would land in front and behind the caravan to conduct a detailed search. During this time, the helicopter gunships circled in the air ready to cover the search group and, when necessary, to support its evacuation from the field of battle.

Supply convoys moving all over Afghanistan daily resupplied Soviet forces with cargo, fuel, and ammunition. This created the problem of assuring safe passage for convoys on the country's roads. Helicopter gunships were used to secure the safe passage of convoys and provide convoy escort. They provided a standing air patrol over the convoy, conducted route reconnaissance, and provided close fire support to ground forces when they met the enemy. When an enemy ambush was detected, the helicopter guns ships would destroy it independently or as directed by the FAC riding in the convoy. During combat with a strong Mujahideen force, additional reinforcing helicopters might be called in from a nearby airfield. When the reinforcing helicopters arrived at the combat site, the escort helicopters provided target designation for them. At the completion of combat, the helicopters were used to evacuate the dead and wounded as well as the more valuable cargo.

A unique army aviation helicopter mission was the "free search and destroy." This was conducted to offset the sharp increase of guerrilla activity at night. Mujahideen moved their forces and equipment, transported cargo, and prepared for combat at night. In order to limit this activity, the Afghan government banned all nighttime movement outside of the government-controlled roads without special permission of the military authorities. In the nighttime, army aviation helicopters controlled the airspace over Afghanistan and conducted a free search and destroy mission against moving targets.

The more experienced crews of helicopter gunships and armed transport helicopters conducted the search and destroy missions. They operated in pairs or sections. Night hunters flew at arbitrary altitudes. They detected unauthorized vehicle movement by headlights and by other indicators. The helicopters would then determine the coordinates of the vehicles and report these to the nearest combat outpost. The commander of the outpost had the convoy movement plan for his region. Once the outpost commander had cleared the strike, the helicopters would destroy the ground target.

Combat experience showed that the actions of these night hunters were very effective. The local inhabitants readily adjusted to the wartime regulations, and Mujahideen nighttime activity dropped markedly in the government-controlled regions.

Airborne reconnaissance of the enemy was a continual mission of army aviation. Specially designated crews conducted reconnaissance as an independent mission, or more often, in conjunction with another mission. Aerial reconnaissance was conducted by region or axis. They often would photograph the area during the reconnaissance.

One of the more difficult missions undertaken by army aviation helicopters in Afghanistan was the evacuation of the dead and wounded, as well as battle-damaged equipment. Medevac helicopters and other helicopters carried out this mission, often under enemy fire. Search and rescue helicopters and technical assistance helicopters looked for downed aircraft and helicopters. When they found a downed aircraft or helicopter or the site of a downed pilot, the search and rescue helicopter would land under the cover of a second helicopter that would circle at 600 to 1,000 meters altitude. If the downed aircraft or pilot was located in a contested area, the search and rescue helicopters would call in reinforcing helicopters from a nearby airfield or a *bronnegruppa* from the nearest friendly base camp. When necessary, damaged aircraft were repaired on site with spare assemblies and parts or evacuated as a sling load under a transport helicopter.

The Mi-8 helicopter crews played a key role in evacuation and search and rescue work. The army aviation flight crews displayed courage and professional mastery while performing this difficult work under fire. Every aviation unit and subunit maintained an around-the-clock alert crew for this work. The alert crew included a rescue team and necessary rescue gear.

In addition to the missions already mentioned, army aviation helicopters laid mines, adjusted artillery fire, provided transport, provided illumination support to ground forces, provided command and control, and performed resupply.

Mi-8 helicopters laid mines from the air in pairs or in a section. They laid mines on movement routes of large enemy formations over rugged terrain. The mines were set to self-destruct in two to twenty-four hours.

Artillery fire was adjusted, as a rule, by a single helicopter crew on a designated route hovering at a height that provided good observation of the impact area and the strike of artillery rounds. The helicopter crew transmitted the firing corrections directly to the command post of the firing artillery battery.

The Mi-6 lift ship and the Mi-8 armed helicopter transport were widely used to transport forces. The Mi-6 can carry 40 fully equipped men, while the Mi-8 can carry 10 fully equipped men. Moreover, up to 1985, the Mi-6 was often used for this mission. In the following years, in conjunction with the increased effectiveness of enemy air defenses, the Mi-6 was primarily used to transport cargo. Personnel were transported on Mi-8 helicopters, and, for increased safety, they were equipped with parachutes.

The mission to provide illumination support to ground forces was conducted at night when it was necessary to light up a designated area or village. The selected duty helicopters were briefed on the illumination mission requirements and the time of illumination. Mi-8 helicopters, arriving in the area to be illuminated, dropped illumination flares on parachutes in the necessary number and at the necessary time intervals to provide uninterrupted illumination over the designated area. Thus, in 1983, during the course of a DRA operation in the city of Kandahar, a squadron of Mi-8 helicopters provided all-night uninterrupted illumination of the entire city.

Aviation provided command and control of ground forces by serving as a communications center and providing radio-technical support for deployed command posts and operational groups. The aircraft played a major role in increasing reliability and providing uninterrupted command and control of ground forces. Retransmission units mounted on aircraft and helicopters supported radio communications between ground command posts and also between ground command posts and the aircraft or helicopters.

The Mi-6 helicopters were used to deliver supplies to difficult-to-reach regions in Afghanistan. They were used to move vehicles, ammunition, food, POL, and other cargo necessary for sustaining the force.

Thus, the missions that were given to army aviation during combat in Afghanistan were successfully carried out. At the same time, commanders, staffs, and individual crews made serious errors that led to unnecessary casualties. During the time that the LCOSF was in Afghanistan, it lost 329 helicopters, which included 127 helicopter gunships, 174 armed helicopter transports, and 28 lift ships. These significant losses were due to poor reconnaissance of the enemy and his air defense systems, poor command and staff work at all levels in organizing and conducting combat, insufficient preparation of replacement flight personnel arriving from the Soviet Union, and the exorbitantly excessive overuse of army aviation.

The demand for army aviation helicopter support grew significantly from year to year. This resulted in the growth of the sortie rate for flight personnel. Thus, the average sortie rate for pilots reached six to eight flights in a 24-hour period and 600 to 800 flights in a year, with over 1,000 hours of combat flying time. In this period, the flying crews displayed various signs of fatigue, disorientation, and the breakdown of the cardiovascular and motor systems, and frequently displayed pronounced psychiatric breakdowns. When a helicopter crashed or was shot down, the chances of trauma and death of the flying crew were often higher due to the ineffective use of rescue equipment; the poor survivability prospects if the crew cabin, central section of the fuselage, hydraulic system, or fuel system were damaged; and the poorly designed crew seats and seat belts, which, during emergency landing, would break. Contemporary Soviet helicopters proved unsuitable for combat in high mountains or in areas of high air temperature. They were too heavy and too lightly armed. All these faults became obvious as the helicopters were used in combat.

Editors' comments: The helicopter was essential to the 40th Army effort. Its role in transport and fire support was crucial and often kept the Soviets in the fight. The helicopter gunship and the SU-25 provided much better close air support than the higher-flying, faster-moving jet aircraft of frontal aviation. Much has been written in the Western press about how the introduction of the U.S. "Stinger" shoulder-fired air defense missile "won the war" for the Mujahideen. The Stinger is an effective system, but an examination of Soviet aircraft losses shows no appreciable rise in the number of aircraft shot down after the introduction of the Stinger. Stinger did not shoot down that many aircraft. What Stinger did was cause a complete revision of Soviet aerial tactics. Once Stinger was in theater, helicopters stayed over friendly forces and limited daytime flights, jet aircraft flew much higher, and all aircraft took electronic and other countermeasures to survive. Stinger was effective—not by the number of aircraft that it downed, but by the change in tactics it engendered. Stinger made the pilots cautious and less of a threat to the Mujahideen.

There were no major parachute drops during the Soviet-Afghan War, but there were many air assaults conducted by paratroopers and air assault troopers alike. The Mujahideen initially had difficulty dealing with the heliborne threat and slowly developed countermeasures. The tactics of the airborne and air assault forces developed during the war were incorporated, to a degree, in the airborne and air assault forces of the whole Soviet Army. Perhaps the most tactical innovation was developed in the airborne, air assault, and army aviation branches.

Army aviation developed considerably during the war. The helicopter was essential to the Soviet effort. It served as transportation, mobile artillery, reconnaissance, communications relay, supply, artillery spotter, and command vehicle. The helicopter served as a force multiplier by allowing the Soviets to move forces rapidly to mass at critical points and keep the Mujahideen off balance. The Soviets had studied U.S. use of helicopters in Vietnam, but the real impetus for Soviet helicopter improvement and increased use was the Soviet-Afghan War.

The SU-25 ground attack aircraft proved a major fire support system during the war. Although jet-propelled, it could fly lower and slower than the frontal aviation fighter-bombers. Consequently, it was more accurate. The SU-25 was well-armored, carried a lot of ordnance, and could stay on target for an extended period of time. The SU-25 often flew in support of helicopters

Army aviation was essential to the 40th Army's effort, but the 40th Army did not always show the necessary restraint in using it. Army aviation pilots were constantly in the cockpit, and the strain on the aviators resulted in accidents, physical problems, and mental breakdowns. The 40th Army needed more army aviation, not more missions per army aviator.

7

Combat Support

The participation of the LCOSF in Afghanistan demanded that the senior commander and commanders and staffs at all levels pay particular attention to combat support, the most important of which were reconnaissance, security, engineers, and chemical support.

RECONNAISSANCE[1]

Guerrilla tactics and the difficult terrain allowed the Mujahideen to use small detachments and groups effectively. The nature of the war significantly elevated the role of reconnaissance in supporting the various operational and tactical missions of the Soviet forces. In Afghanistan, reconnaissance was not merely a form of combat support but also the primary factor in determining the combat potential and readiness of the force and the ability to more effectively use all the available arsenal in armed combat.

In Afghanistan, difficult missions were decided on the basis of reconnaissance information. Reconnaissance had the following tasks: keep up with the changing military-political situation in its zone of responsibility; ascertain the nature of enemy actions; determine the force structure and numerical composition of Mujahideen detachments and groups; discover the sites where the Mujahideen were deployed; calculate the Mujahideen degree of combat readiness; and reveal Mujahideen sources of weapons, ammunition, food, and other supplies.

When the LCOSF entered Afghanistan, reconnaissance units and subunits constituted no more than 5 percent of the total force. In the following years, the force quadrupled to 20 percent of the total force. However, as combat experience showed, this ratio was frequently insufficient.

The basic method of zone reconnaissance was visual observation coupled with electronic reconnaissance devices.

Observation posts were organized at picket posts to observe the Mujahideen. These were equipped with day and night observation devices (the B-6, B-12, BN-1, and BN-2 binoculars) and radar sets (PSNR-1, PSNR-5, SBR-3). These apparatus allowed scouts to find the Mujahideen at night at a distance of one-and-a-half to four kilometers and then destroy them with 82mm and 120mm mortars, AGS-17 automatic grenade launchers, and heavy machine guns. Experience showed that where observation was wisely organized and the results were exploited by artillery, the outcome was very positive.

Thus, at one of the picket posts located along the Kabul-Termez highway, the duty subunit commanded by Captain A. A. Serpov detected the passage of 23 Mujahideen groups along a two to four kilometer stretch over a two-month period. Fire missions, based on the data collected against these groups, netted 17 dead Mujahideen. In addition, the Soviets captured two Mujahideen, 14 pack animals, 12 assault rifles, a DShK machine gun, 180 rockets, and 450 kilograms of medical supplies.

In order to find the enemy located at a greater distance, the scouts positioned sensors[2] on the threatened axes. The sensors provided seismic/acoustic data. The sensors were positioned five to twenty kilometers from the picket posts and artillery fire. When the system operators received information about the movement of a group of Mujahideen, they would pass this information to the outpost commander. Within three to seven minutes, artillery would open fire on the Mujahideen group. These actions proved effective.[3]

The Mujahideen often used a particular caravan route (see Map 26). Soviet scouts established two series of sensors in conjunction with an antipersonnel minefield of 40 command-detonated mines spread over a 300 meter front. One sensor would detect a caravan of people and pack animals. Another sensor, located on the path some 400 meters from the other, would give the signal that the head of the caravan had reached the mine field.

One night, the first sensor detected a moving caravan of 20 men with pack animals. After seven minutes, the second sensor began to transmit. Simultaneously, the commander gave the order to fire the directional mines in the minefield. As a result, 12 Mujahideen were killed and 1 Mujahideen was captured, along with 20 rockets, four assault rifles, eight antitank mines, and 30 boxes of DShK ammunition.

Ambushes, raids, and planned combat were a more active means of reconnaissance. In the first year after the Soviet forces entered Afghanistan, reconnaissance ambushes were frequently not effective. There were several reasons for this. The main reason was that the commanders and staffs lacked the necessary focus and did not do a daily, exhaustive analysis of the actions of the reconnaissance forces. As a result, they did not fully understand the reconnaissance sub-

Map 26. Ambush—Spetsnaz Company and Recon Company of the 345th Parachute Regiment

units' mistakes, they did not quickly discover the reasons for the mistakes, and the lessons learned were not always passed on to the separate units and subunits. The result was that the tactics of the reconnaissance organs were primarily stereotypes. The Mujahideen quickly discovered the pattern and took appropriate countermeasures. Further, missions that were given to the reconnaissance subunits were often very general when they needed to be specific in terms of target, time, and place. This resulted in indecisiveness and lack of initiative by the commanders, which led to a lack of responsibility for carrying out assigned reconnaissance missions.

Finally, after considering earlier mistakes, the scouts began to organize their ambushes more wisely. The frequency and results of these ambushes grew sharply.

As a rule, reconnaissance groups conducted ambushes with a reconnaissance platoon or company reinforced with engineer and flamethrower subunits. The ambush force was also equipped with night sights, silencers, and CBR-3 ground radar units.

The movement of the reconnaissance groups to the ambush sites was conducted in stages, with strong precautions taken to hide their movement. The ambush had two primary groups—a [general] support group and a destruction group. [The general support group provided cover, particularly during the withdrawal.] The destruction group was subdivided into destruction, snatch, and [immediate] support subgroups. [The immediate support group covered the snatch and destruction subgroups during the actual ambush.]

As a rule, reconnaissance ambushes were decisive and swift. Thus, in the fall of 1984, a group of 14 scouts established an ambush to the northeast of Kabul. In a quick battle with 40 Mujahideen, they killed 23 and captured nine. In another such ambush, conducted in May 1986 near Jalalabad, a group of 22 scouts scattered a detachment of over 50 Mujahideen in a 20-minute battle. They killed 18 Mujahideen, captured 15, and destroyed two trucks loaded with arms and ammunition. Remarkably, the Soviet forces did not have a single man killed in either incident.

Raids were conducted to get information about the enemy and to use this reconnaissance data quickly to destroy small groups, command posts, Islamic committees, supply caches, and other Mujahideen targets, including the capture of opposition ringleaders and leaders of the counter-revolutionary underground.

Successful raids required current, timely reconnaissance data about the objective; a quick, concealed movement route for the subunit; surprise; decisive action; and precise coordination of forces and resources.

Raids were conducted at night or dawn and, as an exception, during the day. The duty reconnaissance subunit conducted the raid in its zone of responsibility (Map 27). The raid had a security destruction group, an assault group, and a fire support group. If the raiding force was flown to the combat zone on helicopters,

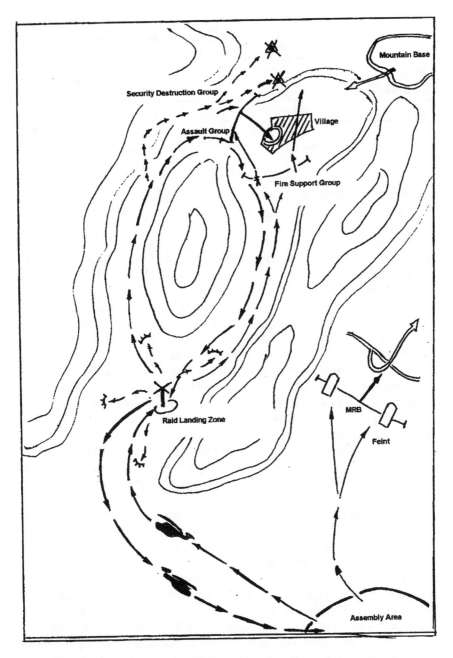

Map 27. Reconnaissance raid

Type of reconnaissance	Preparation for combat	During the conduct of combat
Agent	65%	30%
Aerial	20%	15%
Radio intercept	15%	10%
Ground forces	0%	45%

Figure 9. Sources of intelligence before and during combat

then they also constituted an air assault support group. This group would seize the LZ and support the air landing—and, after the mission, the reboarding and evacuation of the subunit.

Scouts conducted both passive and active reconnaissance in the zones of responsibility of the divisions and regiments of the LCOSF. They provided information to the commanders and staffs about the situation in their region and allowed them to quickly react to enemy actions. Often, reconnaissance data gathered in the field provided the basis for the conduct of large-scale combat.

All types of reconnaissance were fully activated during the preparation for and during the conduct of combat. However, the quantity of data received from all types of reconnaissance sources was not the same at all stages.

As Figure 9 shows, agent reconnaissance played the dominant role during the preparation for combat. The agent net of the DRA security and police forces provided the bulk of the sources. However, the efficiency and reliability of their information was not high. Considering that the agents lacked communications and that it took three to six days to conduct additional reconnaissance, part of their information became outdated during this time lapse and lost its importance.

The Soviets conducted aerial visual and photo reconnaissance of the combat region using the SU-17M3r aircraft, which had a telephoto lens on the AFA-42/100 aerial camera. At first, they used the AN-30 aircraft for aerial reconnaissance and produced aerial photographs at the scale of 40 to 80 meters per centimeter. The photographs from the SU-17M3r had a scale of 9 to 17 meters per centimeter, which permitted the photo interpreters to determine the type and nature of each targeted object better.

The great distance between the base camp and the combat zone frequently prevented radio intercept of enemy communications using stationary and mobile ground intercept stations. Therefore, it became necessary to conduct radio intercept from aircraft. The aerial radio intercept was conducted in several steps. For the first two or three days, two Mi-8 helicopters, equipped with radio reconnaissance and intercept gear, flew two missions with a duration of two to four hours each. Consequently, the Mujahideen radio stations observed radio silence and communicated only at prearranged times or only through the use of communications deception. Simultaneously, with the entry of the helicopters into the intercept area, a pair of SU-25 close air support aircraft flew on a parallel course and conducted a bombing and strafing attack on a nearby objective. The attack generated a great deal of Mujahideen radio traffic. As the radio transmitters broadcast, they were detected and their bearings determined by the airborne radio intercept stations. In the future, all airborne radio transmitters and communications links on the AN-26rr aircraft were tuned to monitor these discovered Mujahideen frequencies. Radio intercept data supplemented information from agent reconnaissance and provided intelligence to conduct successful combat in that region.

At the start of combat, the ground forces linked up with the reconnaissance forces in order to scout the enemy actively. The ground forces established observation posts, listening posts, ambushes, and raids. The reconnaissance elements supported this with observation posts and reconnaissance patrols formed from the reconnaissance detachments.

Observation was widespread and was the most common form of combat reconnaissance. It was conducted in all types of combat by all subunits beginning at the squad, crew, and team level. A dense web of observers and observation posts watched the enemy and terrain out to the limits of their optical instruments. However, the effectiveness of this observation was significantly diminished at night in the mountains.

Experience disclosed that the number of observation posts should be increased by two or three times in the mountains. Therefore, subunits constituted these posts from their own ranks: a platoon had three or four observers, a company added one or two observers to each of its one or two observation posts, while a battalion added one or two observers to each of its two or three observation posts. Every observation post was equipped with optical instruments and the SBR-3 ground radar station. When setting up observation, it was important to exclude any "dead space." This was achieved by echeloning observation posts on the high ground and establishing a system of observation in several layers. At night, part of the observation posts moved down from high ground where they were able to get better results.

With the advance of darkness, observation was supplemented with listening, which all observers were ordered to do. Special listening posts of two to three men each were established at battalion and company level. The listeners were selected for listening acuity and the ability to ascertain what sounds meant and to determine the nature of enemy actions by sound. If the location of the listening post allowed them to listen to the conversations of Mujahideen, then a soldier who knew the local language was included in the listening post [the 40th Army did not always have enough soldier-linguists available, although many Central Asian draftees could communicate with the local populace].

During the movement of forces, reconnaissance patrols and reconnaissance detachments conducted reconnaissance. A combat reconnaissance patrol[4] (CRP) moved 600 to 1,000 meters in front of the battalion. The CRP was constituted from the TO&E reconnaissance platoon. A reinforced-platoon-sized reconnaissance patrol from regiment moved two to five kilometers in front of the regiment.

Reconnaissance detachments, made up of one to three companies, advanced on the more important axes at a distance of five, ten, or more kilometers in front of the main body. The advancing force often constituted several reconnaissance detachments. Every company serving in a reconnaissance detachment was reinforced with sappers, flame-thrower crews, snipers, and heavy weapons crews for the 82mm mortar, AGS-17, and Utes machine gun. A group of artillery scouts and FOs, and a "Romashka" [daisy] radio set (for communicating with aircraft and helicopters) were attached to the company commander. An FAC was attached to the detachment commander. Such a combination of reconnaissance forces and combat resources significantly reduced the time spent in the "detect-destruct" cycle.

During combat, a large quantity of intelligence data came from branch reconnaissance. Artillery reconnaissance was provided by the artillery reconnaissance group and FOs. These groups followed the combat formation with the combined arms or reconnaissance subunit commander. The artillery reconnaissance group, as a rule, included an officer FO, one or two artillery scouts, and an RTO. The group had optical aids, such as binoculars, an aiming circle, and an LPR-1 laser reconnaissance instrument, plus an R-107 or R-159 radio. These allowed them quickly to determine the coordinates of targets and prepare firing data and direct a firing mission.

Artillery reconnaissance systems such as the VPZK and the SNAR-10 counter-battery radar were located in the artillery regiment. These systems were not effective in detecting mortar and rocket firing positions in mountain-desert terrain. The ARK-1 also had difficulty intercepting mortar and artillery fire due to the reflection and absorption of its signals by the mountain slopes.[5] Further, the Mujahideen took suitable measures to limit the sounds and flashes of their artillery when they deployed it out of hiding. Motorized rifle and artillery reconnaissance combined their efforts to accomplish the same plan with the same goals to overcome these shortcomings.

After receiving intelligence reports on the enemy, engineer reconnaissance assumed an important role. One of their more important and difficult missions was to find enemy obstacles, particularly minefields. Finding minefields was complicated by the Mujahideen's inventiveness in setting up ambushes and diversionary actions. It was further complicated by the Mujahideen's use of plastic-bodied mines that were difficult to find with minesweepers and which forced the engineers to use more primitive methods. As a result, the tempo of engineer reconnaissance on a march route seldom exceeded three to four kilometers an hour, which made it very difficult to carry out various combat missions.

During combat, radio intercept played an active role. Experience showed that this type of reconnaissance was most effective during the artillery preparation and the first four to six hours after the beginning of combat. After this time, the Mujahideen had usually stopped broadcasting, hid their radio transmitters, and left the area. Since all helicopters support tactical air assaults, the Soviets used a pair of Mi-8 search and rescue helicopters for radio reconnaissance. They circled the combat zone and simultaneously performed aerial radio interception. The accuracy of the radio bearing acquired depended on the distance from the source but was within 150 to 500 meters.

Ground sensors were also used successfully to find the enemy. Signals from the sensors fed into the ground force command post, the artillery firing positions, and the rapid reaction force. During the Panjshir operation, scouts set up 11 sensor intercept lines. They launched six aviation strikes and 34 artillery fire missions based on the sensor signals. As a result, they hit 12 groups and four caravans, killing 36 Mujahideen and 41 pack animals and destroying four trucks loaded with arms and ammunition.

The bulk of intelligence data came from prisoners and documents that were captured during the inspection of caravans and conduct of ambushes and raids.

Specially designated reconnaissance units and large units conducted caravan inspections.[6] The inspection was carried out by finding caravans, blocking their progress with an unexpected force, and inspecting the personnel and cargo to find and seize weapons, ammunition, combat gear, documents, and prisoners. The scouts used aerial reconnaissance and ground observers backed by sensors to find caravans. After discovering a caravan, the helicopters would circle it and fire the door guns to signal the caravan to stop. Then the helicopter with a support subgroup would land 200 to 300 meters in front of the caravan or to the side.

Under the cover of the second helicopter (which continued to circle—prepared to fire), the support subgroup completed landing and took up an overwatch position and prepared for combat. The first helicopter then took off and covered the second helicopter while it landed the inspection subgroup.

The inspection subgroup, covered by the support subgroup and the helicopters, began their inspection. They moved the people away from the caravan and searched them and their belongings for personal weapons. At the same time, the inspection subgroup searched the cargo, using mine detectors, probes, and mine-sniffing dogs. In the event that they found weapons, ammunition, or subversive literature among the personnel or pack animals, the personnel were moved to a base camp for initial questioning. After this, the prisoners were transferred to the Interior Ministry. The confiscated weapons and ammunition were loaded onto the helicopters and moved to the base camp. When it was impossible to move the contraband, the scouts destroyed it on the spot.

The time spent inspecting the caravan depended on how long the helicopters could stay on station circling the site. As a rule, they could not exceed 30 to 35 minutes, and, if they were a significant distance from the airfield, the time might be much less. Such time constraints demanded precise, coordinated actions by the commander and scouts.

Interrogation of prisoners and detainees provided a large quantity of intelligence data about the enemy. However, it demanded careful organization and an in-depth understanding of the situation, the country, and its inhabitants. The main goal of questioning prisoners was to obtain reliable data about the local supply transfer bases and points where ammunition dumps, caravans, and Islamic committees were located.

Missions were resolved by such questioning—obtaining information about the enemy that was of interest to the commander, while establishing the veracity of the prisoner and the truthfulness of his testimony. Following the questioning, the interrogators decided on further exploitation of the prisoner—whether to use him as a guide or as an informer or to forward him to the intelligence organs of the higher headquarters.

The regimental commander (or separate battalion commander) and his staff were entrusted with organizing interrogation. The chief of reconnaissance was responsible for the conduct of the interrogation.

There are two basic types of interrogation—initial and comprehensive. Initial interrogation is conducted in the combat zone, while comprehensive interrogation is conducted at the unit or large unit headquarters.

Thus, Soviet combat experience in Afghanistan shows that reconnaissance is one of the most important forms of combat support. The success of combined arms battle and air assault combat, as well as the number of Soviet casualties, depended on the results of the reconnaissance forces. At the same time, quality intelligence demanded sufficient forces and resources with a high state of personnel, subunit, and unit special training.

Editors' comments: The Soviet conduct of reconnaissance in Afghanistan had some severe difficulties. The reconnaissance forces assigned to the 40th Army initially constituted 5 percent of the force. In time, 20 percent of the 40th Army were reconnaissance forces. Still, the Soviets had difficulty knowing what the Mujahideen were doing. The Soviets relied heavily on radio intercept, overhead photography, and the Mujahideen-penetrated DRA agent reconnaissance nets. The Soviets had a significant number of trained scouts, but the scouts were often used for combat instead of reconnaissance. The scouts were often the best trained soldiers available and spent more field time in combat rather than searching for the enemy. Soviet reconnaissance missions included ambush and raids—which are missions for regular ground forces in most Western armies. Commander's reconnaissance, which was part of the regular Soviet troop leading procedures, is not discussed in this chapter. Commander's reconnaissance should be routine, but was difficult to accomplish due to the extended nature of the terrain in Afghanistan.

Reconnaissance forces enjoyed an elite status in the Soviet forces, and their scouts in the field were usually good. However, the overall intelligence product was often lacking. The Soviets were looking for structure among the unstructured Mujahideen and saw the seven principal factions in Pakistan as commands that planned, coordinated, and conducted operations. Actually the factions were political and religious bodies who served as logistics conduits and tried to provide military direction to their Mujahideen field commanders—which might or might not be followed. The Mujahideen were hard to control, as CIA and other foreign intelligence services discovered. The Soviet search for structure and predictability, coupled with their Marxist-Leninist blinders, frustrated their intelligence effort in an already difficult theater.

Spetsnaz forces were elite reconnaissance forces that belonged to the General Staff's Intelligence Directorate. The Spetsnaz were trained and developed for long-range reconnaissance behind enemy lines. The Soviet Union deployed two Spetsnaz brigades to Afghanistan, where they focused on interdicting Mujahideen logistics by ambushing caravans and raiding logistics bases in the areas bordering Pakistan. There was little Spetsnaz long-range, long-term reconnaissance in Mujahideen-held areas. Instead, the Spetsnaz spent much of their effort on combat instead of reconnaissance. Like other reconnaissance forces, the Spetsnaz were mechanized and well equipped with heavy machine guns and other crew-served weapons. In some instances, the Spetsnaz even had artillery assigned for long-term support.

SECURITY[7]

Combat in the Republic of Afghanistan was characterized by the lack of a continuous front line. The enemy conducted guerrilla warfare. As the LCOSF discovered during their first months in the country, the enemy preferred to attack important government and manufacturing installations, military garrisons, and the lines of communication. Under these circumstances, a significant portion of the Soviet subunits were assigned security duties, which, in the majority of cases, were organized in guard picket posts and guard posts.

One of the most important duties of the Soviet forces in Afghanistan was to safeguard the so-called security zones and LOCs. Security zones were established around airfields, electric power stations, Soviet and Afghan military garrisons, and important government installations, with the aim of providing security and public order and preventing and curbing enemy actions.

Within these classified zones, the population's life and activities was organized and closely controlled by a special regimen. The DRA Ministry of Internal Affairs, the DRA Ministry of State Security, and Afghan army regiments were responsible for enforcing this public order. However, Soviet forces played the major role in guarding security zones and particularly the LOCs. They did this by establishing permanent picket posts. The 40th Army established 862 picket posts in which 20,200 personnel served. This guard force constituted about one-fifth of the entire Soviet force in Afghanistan.

The picket posts were equipped for long-term residency and performance of duty. The Soviets usually constructed these posts from the ruins of various fallen buildings and the posts were prepared for perimeter defense. Many picket posts were located in barren areas and were constructed of local materials. Commanders and personnel at all levels displayed a high degree of initiative and inventiveness at these posts.

The security of joint Soviet-Afghan installations was provided by some 20 combined Soviet-Afghan picket posts that were organized in accordance with the instructions of the Council of Ministers of the USSR. Their mission was the security and defense of some 20 Soviet-Afghan cooperative projects. They guarded these projects with a general security zone and further established special guard posts and patrols. The majority of these projects had dual security—internal and external, provided by Soviet and Afghan subunits.

The chiefs of the Soviet garrisons were charged with the organization and defense of the airfields. Airfield security was organized in three lines. Guard picket posts were sited on the distant approaches and along the security perimeter. Interior patrols secured airfield sites. 149 picket posts were built and manned, which included the security of ten airfields within their security regimen. Further, 224 picket posts provided double duty. They were built along the roads that passed through the security zones of the airfields and at the entrances to the road system within the security zone (Map 28).

The second motorized rifle battalion, reinforced with a battery of D-30 howitzers and two tank platoons, secured one of the many security zones in Afghanistan. Lieutenant Colonel A. P. Yunakov recalls how this zone contained the headquarters for an air assault brigade, an air-assault battalion, a signal battalion, an electronic warfare company, a helicopter squadron, and an artillery battery.[8] In addition to securing this garrison, his battalion had two other missions—to escort a convoy some 80 kilometers two or three times a week and to combat Mujahideen groups in the adjoining region.

To carry out these missions, the forces and resources of the battalion were distributed as follows. The 12-kilometer garrison perimeter had seven picket posts, each with one or two reinforced motorized rifle platoons. One or two motorized rifle platoons, reinforced with one or two 82mm mortar crews, were detailed for convoy escort. A motorized rifle company, a reconnaissance platoon, an artillery battery, and two mortar platoons were usually detailed to join a Sarandoy battalion in combating the Mujahideen scattered in the region.

The Mujahideen began firing rockets at the base camp shortly after this security zone was established near the city of Lashkar Gah in 1985. The rockets were fired from the green zone along the Helmand river. Therefore, at the beginning of 1987, the Soviets and units of the Afghan Army conducted an operation to drive the enemy away from the city and establish picket posts in the green zone. A battalion of Sarandoy occupied the picket posts. After completing the operation, the Soviets established another picket post in the Qala-Bust fortress. This site allowed them to control the green zone adjacent to the Sarandoy picket

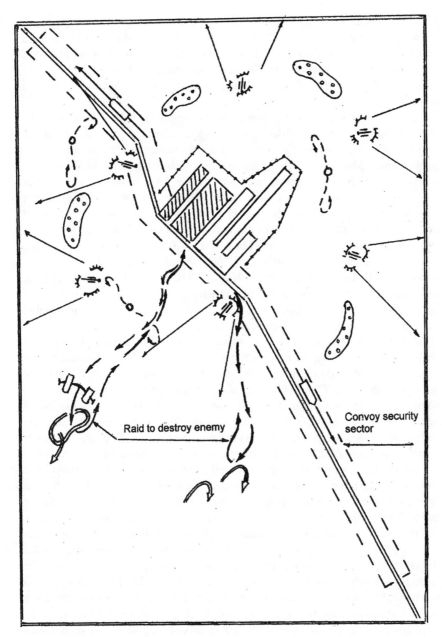

Map 28. Security zone for a garrison and airfield

posts. There was a close coordination between the picket post and the Afghan subunits. A Sarandoy liaison officer, with his own communications, played a major role in this coordination. A tank platoon located in the fortress provided fire support to the picket posts, as did the artillery battery. These fire support systems were able to ward off several Mujahideen attempts to destroy the Afghan subunit's picket posts.

Over time, the Soviets developed close cooperation with the staffs of the Sarandoy battalion and the border guard brigade and the local party organizations. This allowed the Soviets and DRA to control the situation near the security zones and to identify Mujahideen deployment bases, detachments, posts, and movement routes. As a result of their coordinated actions, they were frequently able to succeed over time in foiling the enemy schemes. By the end of 1987, the Mujahideen leadership had abandoned combat in this region, and peace ensued, which lasted until the withdrawal of Soviet forces from the territory of Afghanistan.

In order to protect the personnel in picket posts from light machine gun and mortar fire, a great deal of effort was devoted to constructing field fortifications. Every squad had a fortified position. The squad positions, in every picket post, were connected with a platoon trench. Further, picket posts fortified the sleeping quarters, the ammunition dump, the headquarters, the Lenin room, the dining hall, the water point, the washroom, and the latrine.

Carrying out the duties of a guard picket post demanded a high degree of organization. First of all, the most difficult mission was night observation. Guard posts were established to increase observation. Guard posts, as a rule, consisted of three personnel: a BTR machine gunner, a driver, and a motorized rifleman. Sometimes guard posts had only two soldiers, but never less. The personnel assumed their duties at 1800 hours after receiving their orders and the challenge and password. After four hours, the platoon leader or his deputy changed the personnel at the guard post. Their performance of duty was checked every two hours.

At night, from 1800 hours to 0500 hours, the sentries were permitted to fire preventive small arms shots at the terrain. These were only single shots. Should the guards fire a burst of automatic weapons fire, then the entire post was alerted and took up battle positions. Artillery could also conduct harassing and interdiction fire on designated targets. Artillery FACs earlier worked out the coordinates and firing data of all targets located in the picket zone of responsibility, so the fire could be conducted at night without warning. During the inspection of the guard post sentries, they were provided the time of arrival and the challenge and password. At dawn, the guard posts were withdrawn. In order to ensure the safety of the withdrawing sentries, the picket post fired on all moving personnel, convoys, and caravans passing within four kilometers of the post. No personnel were allowed to withdraw from the guard picket posts.

Every six months the personnel of the picket post were rotated during daylight. Such an approach to organizing guard post security provided well-being to the garrison.

The first priority of Mujahideen commanders was to disrupt the movement of convoys traveling on the main roads of Afghanistan. Motorized rifle subunits were responsible for route security. Normally, a motorized rifle battalion would be responsible for a 40 to 150 kilometer stretch of road, whereas a company would cover from 2 to 10 kilometers. For example, the 3rd Motorized Rifle Battalion, reinforced with a tank company and two artillery batteries, was responsible for the security of a 102 kilometer stretch of road along the Puli-Charkhi to Jalalabad highway.[9] The battalion could field 11 tanks, 42 BMPs, 12 self-propelled howitzers, 27 82mm mortars, 9 ZSU 23-2 twin-barreled antiaircraft guns, and 23 AGS-17 automatic grenade launchers. Lieutenant Colonel M. A. Tubeev, the battalion commander, divided his zone of responsibility into three parts. The 7th MRC had a 32-kilometer stretch, the 8th MRC had a 30 kilometer stretch, and the 9th MRC had a 40 kilometer stretch (Map 29).

Another motorized rifle battalion, commanded by Guards Major V. I. Trashchak, was assigned to guard a 40-kilometer stretch of the Kandahar-Shindand highway in 1988. His 7th MRC guarded a ten-kilometer stretch, his 8th MRC guarded a nine-kilometer stretch, and his 9th MRC had a 2.5 kilometer stretch.[10] Further, the battalion commander distributed his reinforcements to the more vital sectors. Thus, the 7th MRC received two tanks and a mortar platoon, and the 9th MRC received four tanks, a ZSU-23-4M, three mortar platoons, and a squad of sappers. The length of the zone and sector of responsibility of the battalions and companies was determined by the importance of what was being guarded, the terrain, the availability of forces and resources, and the nature of the enemy.

The motorized rifle subunits providing security were also responsible for finding and destroying Mujahideen in their zone of responsibility; supporting the unimpeded passage of convoys on the main routes; and preventing the mining of the roads, bridges, and tunnels; as well as other special missions.

The basic security element was the guard security picket based on a platoon reinforced with one or two AGS-17 automatic grenade launchers, one or two RPK machine guns, one or two "Utes" or DShK heavy machine guns, one or two mortars, and a tank.

Security detachments (reinforced companies or battalions) could occupy security pickets. Security detachments were reinforced with artillery subunits, tanks, and engineer subunits (to construct and maintain minefields, provide overhead cover for the detachment's positions, and clear mines from the road and area).

Subunits that guarded roads and government installations rotated after three months' security duty, while subunits guarding military garrisons rotated after a month. Rotation of security subunits was conducted in the presence of the subunit's immediate superior commander and was made official by a document signed by the company and battalion commanders and approved by the regimental commander. The transfer of minefields was also accomplished with a document in the presence of a representative of the regiment's chief engineer.

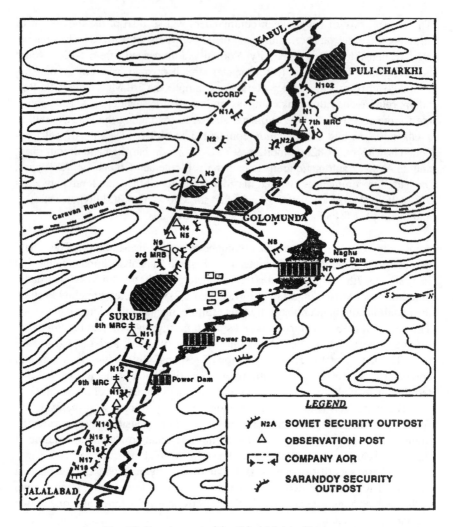

Map 29. Securing part of the Kabul-Jalalabad highway

However, the planned regular rotation of security units often did not occur as scheduled. This was particularly true for the units located in Kandahar, Jalalabad, Kunduz, and Faizabad. The failure to rotate these motorized rifle subunits reduced their combat readiness. The main reason for delaying these rotations was that the other subunits at the unit base camp were performing other combat missions assigned by a higher commander.

The security picket posts functioned around the clock. During the day, one man per squad or tank was on watch while a two-man patrol worked the area. The Soviets established secret or forward guard posts to discover the enemy quickly as he secretly approached and to alert the force. Every picket normally organized one or two mobile guard posts of four to six men each. These mobile guard posts were located some 500 to 800 meters from the picket post. This distance was close enough for visual and wire communications in case it was necessary to support the mobile guard post with fire from the picket post. The routes to the picket posts were guarded by positions that provided for the safe ascent and descent of the personnel and were well situated for firing.

Picket posts were prepared for a full perimeter defense and to repel an enemy attack from above and below. In support of this, platoons had primary and alternate sectors of fire, with interlocking fields of fire and targeted areas for concentrated fire. All the crew-served weapons had primary and reserve firing positions and firing sectors.

A great deal of attention was devoted to planning artillery fire. Artillery subunits at picket posts were located within supporting distance of each other. Artillery fires were planned on all likely enemy approaches to every picket post in the region. Concentrations were registered and numbered and their coordinates and firing data were maintained by every firing crew and by the picket commanders in order to open fire rapidly.

Fire missions were conducted from planned targets or were adjusted on the orders of the picket post commander. In the event that the picket post lost direct communications with the artillery subunits, they could communicate with the artillery through their battalion command net. Normally, it took not more than two to four minutes for a mobile guard post or picket post to bring artillery fire onto a group of detected Mujahideen.

Picket posts were built and fortified to take advantage of the terrain and were designed for long-term service. Dug or built of piled-up rock, the picket posts had a complete trench system, dugouts, and shelters for ammunition, food, and water. Two necklaces of barbed wire entanglements surrounded the positions. Antipersonnel mines armed by trip wire were laid between the rows of barbed wire. Trip flares and sensors were laid on the far and concealed approaches to the outpost. At night, the picket post entrance and exit were blocked and mined. Rules of conduct were posted at the perimeter of the security zone and outside the picket posts. The sign posts were written in Afghan, Russian, and English.[11]

Each picket post had five combat loads[12] of ammunition and ten days' worth of food, water, and fuel. Night-vision devices, "Blik" binoculars, night scopes, parachute flares, and tracer ammunition were available for nighttime employment.

Each picket post maintained the following documents and maps:

- combat mission of the outpost and the sequence of mission fulfillment;
- commander's map marked with positions, fire plans, and the known enemy position;
- diagram of the firing positions, mine fields, and barriers;

- diagram of the strong point;
- orders from the battalion commander;
- combat orders of the picket post commander;
- observation schedule;
- patrol schedule;
- duty weapon schedule[13] and sectors of fire;
- signal tables;
- observer's journals, combat journals, and journals of enemy activities.

The battalion produced the security plan, which showed the number and composition of each picket post; their locations; the quantity of vehicles, weapons, and ammunition at each post; the security belt at each post; the defensive plan for key sites; the coordination measures between Soviet posts and DRA posts; the defensive fire plan; and the signal plan for communications between picket posts, garrisons, convoys, dispatch posts, and the fire support elements. In addition, the battalion had a shift schedule for its subunits and also the battalion commander's order for organization of the security zone. Subunits had their TO&E equipment, plus additional radios, telephones, and cable communications gear for command and control.

Radio was the primary means of communication among the picket posts. A picket post had two or three telephones and one or two ultra-short-wave radios set on the same frequency. All armored vehicles, TO&E, and attached subunits and passing convoys were required to monitor this common frequency at all times. Passing convoys also monitored this frequency. At other times, the frequency was monitored in the battalion commander's command vehicle and the man-pack radios of the company commanders and artillery subunits. Then, the separate picket posts entered the command-observation net according to the signal tables, usually hourly or when necessary. This supported solid coordination and a high level of combat readiness.

The picket post duty schedule was designed to ensure the safety and uninterrupted passage of military convoys on the roads during daylight hours. It was written after considering the local situation and the experience level of the commanders and personnel. Experience showed that the performance of night duty required two-thirds of the personnel. The other third performed security duties during the daylight hours. As a rule, picket post commanders inspected their sector from dawn until 1000 hours, assuring themselves that there was no threat to the passage of convoys. They then reported their readiness to the senior commander responsible for the entire sector. Once the commander received all the reports, he gave the command to start the movement and passage of the convoys.

The picket post commander's responsibilities included inspecting the sentries, listening posts, and duty firing crews. He or his deputy would personally inspect their performance of duty hourly at night and every two hours during the day. Further, the company commander would inspect every one of his picket posts daily, whereas the battalion commander would inspect two or three of his picket posts daily. During the course of one or two weeks, the battalion commander would inspect all his picket posts. Senior commanders would inspect picket posts according to their own plan. These inspections served to maintain picket post combat readiness and the proper organization of duties for the security of assigned sectors.

The battalion reconnaissance platoon was located close to the battalion CP/OP. Its goal was to cut off and destroy any small groups of Mujahideen in the battalion AOR. They usually did this by setting up ambushes on sites where the Mujahideen could approach the highway. Their ambush site was coordinated with the regiment's ambush plan. If it was necessary to move the ambush site, a report with the new coordinates was sent by the battalion staff to the regimental CP.

As a rule, the ambush stayed in position for one night. However, there were instances when the situation dictated that the subunit stay in ambush for three full days without moving. In the course of a month, the battalion reconnaissance platoon conducted 20 to 25 ambushes. However, their success was normally based on complete and reliable information on Mujahideen activity or by employing more daring and deceptive actions.

Picket posts, located along the roads and on caravan routes, significantly limited Mujahideen resupply of weapons and ammunition. Naturally, the Mujahideen would not tolerate this. In order to secure the passage of caravans, the Mujahideen would block those picket posts that were close to the caravan route. Repeatedly, the Mujahideen attempted to blockade the picket post in the region of the village of Gagamunda, which was located close to the Kabul-Jalalabad highway. The Mujahideen used a short stretch of this road for the passage of caravans from Pakistan to Kabul—a two-week trip. To take a different bypass route would lengthen the time necessary to deliver arms, ammunition, and other material by three or four times. The Mujahideen secretly moved from their fortified caves and village bases at night and moved with impunity past the road security picket posts into the mountains. The fact that the picket posts were maintained at permanent sites facilitated Mujahideen activity. The enemy could determine the composition of the force in the picket posts, study the terrain, and organize a first-rate attack on the post. Picket post duty required thorough organization, since the results of the security mission were practically the same as the results of combat in terms of effectiveness and high tension.

Combat demonstrated that security pickets were needed to support the economic life and garrisons in Afghanistan. The correct organization of the pickets was determined through combat with the Mujahideen and the conduct of convoys, the interruption of sabotage, and other enemy actions near garrisons, airfields, electric stations, mountain passes, tunnels, and other important sites.

Editors' comments: Installation, LOC, and rear area security were usually missions for the Soviet KGB divisions, MVD divisions (internal forces), and person-

nel of the Commandant's service. KGB and MVD forces served in Afghanistan, but not in the numbers necessary to secure the cities, garrisons, LOCs, installations, and airfields from the Mujahideen. Therefore, this mission fell on the already overburdened ground forces. This security mission significantly degraded the 40th Army's ability to mount combat against the Mujahideen. Further, the extended periods of time served by subunits in picket posts produced a "bunker mentality" that was hard to overcome when the subunit was taken off the defensive and readied for offensive combat.

Security and guard duty is a boring, unglamorous part of soldiering. It is also a very necessary part, and particularly so in Afghanistan. Although the text states that 20 percent of the Soviet soldiers were tied up in security duties, the orders of battle in Appendix 1 show that, depending on the year, almost 50 percent or more were so employed. A significant portion of the DRA forces were similarly employed. The Mujahideen were able to hold a major portion of their enemy by maintaining a threat to installations, airfields, factories, government facilities, and the like.

ENGINEER SUPPORT[14]

During the course of combat in Afghanistan, the Soviets encountered an enemy whose tactics heavily relied on mine warfare. The enemy also mined the LOC and destroyed sections of road and transportation infrastructure. Further, the hot climate and general scarcity of water made it difficult to supply water to the Soviet soldiers. At the same time, the almost complete lack of forests, the dominant mountain terrain, and the poorly developed road network seriously complicated carrying out engineer support missions.

Under these conditions, the principle missions of engineer support were the following: conducting engineer reconnaissance of the enemy and terrain; fortifying and maintaining the water crossings; preparing and maintaining the roads for the movement and maneuver of subunits; surmounting mine fields, land slides, and rubble; supporting the passage of forces through fortified regions and positions occupied by friendly forces; constructing engineer obstacles; and extracting, purifying, and supplying water to the forces.

All of the branches carried out these missions. However, the specially trained and equipped engineer units and subunits carried out the more important missions and those involving difficult engineer missions. Special engineer units included engineer reconnaissance, sappers, highway engineers, static assault crossing engineers, pontoon and bridging subunits, field fortification subunits, mine-clearing subunits, water support units, and others.

One of the main missions of engineer forces in Afghanistan was engineer terrain reconnaissance, particularly march route reconnaissance conducted to determine route trafficability for force movement and to find enemy land mines.

In the first weeks and months after the entry of the 40th Army into Afghanistan, the primary form of Mujahideen resistance was the destruction of bridges, the construction of obstacles and craters on the difficult sections of mountain roads, the construction of antitank ditches and gullies, the deliberate collapsing of road ledges and supporting walls, and also the laying of individual mines and mine fields on troop movement routes. From the very beginning, the enemy chiefly concentrated on destroying bridges and building various non-exploding obstacles.

Combatants noted that practically all the bridges on the routes used by the Soviet forces were destroyed. Concrete and steel, metal, and stone bridges were most often blown up with high explosives, explosive powders, artillery rounds, and mines. The explosives were placed on one bridge section that partially destroyed that section. Wooden bridge spans were burned or sawed up into unusable sections.

The enemy would collapse sections of road and retaining walls around road crowns and on sloping sections of road. The destruction was done with explosives and then completed by hand by the mobilized populace. This was especially difficult damage to repair. The sections of destruction stretched from 10 to 100 meters and to a depth of three to ten meters. The Mujahideen might also prepare a surprise by undermining a section of road, which would cause vehicles to plunge off the road. The Mujahideen also built "wolf pits"—holes full of stakes that cut the road. The Mujahideen also dug antitank ditches using explosives or hand tools. The antitank ditch cut across the entire road and had a width of five to six meters and a depth of three to five meters.

In the south, the enemy often used irrigation canals and culverts to destroy roads. The Mujahideen would divert a stream or channel water across the road to cut it. This did not require too much effort. After one and a half to two hours, the running water would cut a gully with a width of five to ten meters and a depth of three to five meters [this may be an exaggerated erosion rate].

As the Mujahideen transitioned to guerrilla warfare, mine warfare became very important to them. The Mujahideen used the Soviet PMN, the American M-18, the British No. 5 Mark 1, the Italian TC-50, and Pakistani and Chinese antipersonnel mines. To destroy armored and other vehicles, the Mujahideen used the U.S. M19; the British Mark 5 and Mark 7; the Italian TC-2.5 and TC-6.1; the Soviet TM-46; and the Belgian H55 and M3 antitank mines. Further, the Mujahideen used a wide variety of homemade mines and explosive charges made from unexploded aerial bombs, mortar rounds, artillery rounds, and other explosives.

The Mujahideen laid mines to protect defensive positions, important military installations and supply bases, and also to impede road travel by supply and troop convoys. They used antitank, antipersonnel, and mixed mine fields, as well as single mines and groups of mines.

The enemy put booby traps in villages, gardens, houses, schools, mosques, and on footpaths. They put booby traps in ballpoint pens, pocket flashlights, books, earthenware crocks, other household articles, and children's toys.[15]

The Mujahideen would lay mines and explosives on the route before the force arrived or as the convoy was approaching. Usually, they dug the holes for the mines ahead of time and would lay the mines in the road and surrounding region a half hour to an hour before the convoy arrived. They would mine the road after the reconnaissance and mine-clearing subunits had passed by. As a counter, Soviet engineers recommended that when conditions allowed the distance be shortened between the reconnaissance and mine-clearing groups and the main convoy body so that they had constant visual contact between them.

The more probable sites for Mujahideen mines and explosive charges were the following: entrances into populated areas; ascending or descending road sections; narrow road sections on which vehicles cannot pass or turn around; bridges, water drains, culverts, and water sources; river fords and exits from canyons onto roads; potential helicopter LZs; rest and bivouac sites; and positions and trenches periodically occupied by Soviet and DRA forces.

The Mujahideen laid antitank mines on the roads in the vehicle tracks, in the space between vehicle tracks, and on the sides of the road. They would lay them in a linear or chessboard pattern or without a pattern, with a single mine here and a group of mines there. They would place their blast mines singly or in groups. Sometimes they would join their fragmentation mines and blast mines together with detonation cord or electric wire and electric fuses. To increase the destructive potential, they would sometimes put one mine on top of another in the same hole. Fragmentation mines and blast mines were buried from a depth of two to three centimeters, up to 60 centimeters or greater. In order to add to the difficulty in finding the mines, the Mujahideen would cover the mine pressure plates with rocks or pieces of wood. Sometimes the Mujahideen would put mines and explosive charges in breaks in the road bed and pavement. Less often, they would dig under the road bed to lay their mines. In the majority of cases, blast mines were laid in the area between the vehicle tracks and in the tracks.

Practically all the Mujahideen mines were laid with one of several types of antilift devices. Further, they had several ways of setting off the mines. Fragmentation and blast mines could be set for selective detonation depending on the type of contact switch—only for tracked or wheeled vehicles, against tanks equipped with mine plows, igniting after several passes by vehicles, or exploding after the covering layer of soil was worn away by passing traffic.

All the mines were skillfully camouflaged to blend with the surrounding background. For example, after planting an explosive charge in the road, the Mujahideen would roll a truck tire over the area several times to give the appearance of vehicle traffic. As a rule, the Mujahideen covered all obstacles with machine gun and rifle fire.

To complicate the search for mines with mine detectors, the Mujahideen laid false obstacles and impediments. For example, they would strew metal pieces or bits of explosive in the ground. To foil the senses of mine-detecting dogs, the Mujahideen would tightly wrap the mines in cellophane bags and pour kerosene, diesel fuel, or motor oil on them. Further, to complicate Soviet efforts to disarm antitank mines and explosives, the Mujahideen would lay antipersonnel charges and fragmentation mines nearby and around the antitank mines. They would sometimes also use antipersonnel mines to strengthen various types of nonexplosive obstacles. [This section gives more credit to the Mujahideen mining skills than may be due.]

The Mujahideen marked their mines so that they could drive their own vehicles through the mined area and retrieve their mines later for reuse.[16] They would mark the fragmentation mines, blast mines, passage lines, and contact points with barely detectable reference points. These reference points might be a broken branch or a notch on a tree trunk, some spilled grain, a small group of stones on the side of the road or close to it, a plow abandoned in a field, and so on. Indicators of mining might also be previously blown-up vehicles left on the road, since the Mujahideen might lay single mines several times at the same site.

Soviet engineers conducted reconnaissance using aerial photographs, ground searches for mine fields, and close inspection. Further, the engineers obtained information from prisoner and deserter interrogations and from questioning the local inhabitants.

Airborne engineer reconnaissance patrols were conducted using specially equipped helicopters. Airborne cameras, integrated into the reconnaissance systems, provided vertical and diagonal photographs of the terrain in various scales. Aerial photographs revealed the condition of roads and bridges, the degree of their destruction, the presence of obstacles and possible bypasses, and also the location of mine fields.

Sapper subunits, which were part of combined arms divisions and regiments, were used to find and disarm fragmentation and blast mines on the roads and to repair destroyed roadway on the march route. Movement support detachments (MSD) helped divisions and regiments move. Movement support detachments had reconnaissance and mine neutralization groups, obstacle removal groups, and road and bridge groups. The composition and equipment of these groups were determined by the mission and terrain and enemy situation.

Engineer reconnaissance, sapper, and engineer road construction and repair subunits all constituted reconnaissance and mine neutralization groups. These were augmented by dogs and dog handlers of the mine-search service.[17] Motorized rifle, tank, and sapper groups were often included in obstacle removal groups. The obstacle removal groups were equipped with shaped-charges, blasting charges, motorized boring machines, the engineer obstacle clearing vehicle (IMR),[18] and tanks equipped with bulldozer blades. The Movement Support Detachment usually had one to two sapper platoons with mine detection and destruction gear, two or three mine detection dog teams, two or three tanks with mine plows, and an IMR. The MSD was reinforced with a motorized rifle platoon to cover the group.

Reconnaissance and mine neutralization groups moved on BMPs. They carried specialized gear, including portable mine detectors, probes, explosives, and fuses. The vehicle commanders were sapper officers who had fought in the region and knew the Mujahideen mining techniques and potential well.

Mine reconnaissance and detection groups usually worked in two steps: mounted reconnaissance and mine detection and dismounted reconnaissance. The group stopped when they found evidence of mining on the road or on the approaches to a section of road, or when mines exploded under the mine flails. The sappers would then dismount and proceed to check the road, road shoulders, ditches, and pull-offs for the presence of mines and then disarm any they found. A security subunit would occupy the nearby slopes of dominant terrain to provide cover for the reconnaissance and mine neutralization group.

Specially equipped sappers conducted road reconnaissance and mine neutralization to find and manually disarm fragmentation mines and blast mines. Armored mine neutralization vehicles followed some 40 to 50 meters behind the sappers. Tanks with mine plows, BTRs, or BMPs followed behind these vehicles. As a rule, there were two reconnaissance and mine neutralization groups. These would switch off at the intervals designated by the MSD commander. This provided uninterrupted movement for the MSD. The sappers would destroy the mines that they discovered in place by setting off an explosive charge on top of them, or they would use grapnels to drag the mines away from the road for destruction. Sappers disarmed directional mines one at a time after cutting their command-detonation wires.

The effectiveness of the engineer forces in mine neutralization improved sharply, as did their volume of work. In 1980, engineers neutralized 1,032 mines and blast mines. In ten months of 1986, the sapper subunits reported that they neutralized 35,000 mines and 650 blast mines.[19]

Another important engineer combat support mission in Afghanistan was to support and maintain river crossings on the movement route. The engineers had their first such mission during the 1979 entry of the 40th Army into Afghanistan. The engineers had to conduct a river crossing of the Amu-Darya river, which had a 700 meter width, a depth of .3 to four meters, and a current of two meters per second or greater. The river flood plain extended some 40 to 90 meters along both banks.

After studying the site conditions, the engineers decided to construct a bridge site using five PMP[20] bridge sets.

The engineers laid the bridge by assembling the pontoons into sections and then towing them into place with cutter vessels. Tracked amphibious transports (PTS)[21] hauled the pontoons and cutters through the shallow flood plain to the clear water. Prior to the invasion, the engineers, disguised as civilians, built bridge abutments and off-load sites for the cutters and the sections of PMP bridging. They laid reinforced concrete slabs on the departure shore and on the islands over which the axis of the bridge would pass. When they made the first crossing, the engineers ferried engineer equipment on barges to the far shore to reinforce the opposite bank and bridge exit. Further, in order to prevent bank erosion at the bridge sites, they paved the banks where the PMP bridge entry and exit were. The engineers used layered sections of pierced steel plate from the PMD bridging sets for the paving. To hold the bridge's position in the river, the engineers anchored sections of the bridge into the ground using screw tie rods, truck winches, and tractor cables, augmented with a simple windlass, which they installed on the decks of the pontoon-carrying vehicle.

One of the more difficult tasks was to keep the bridge intact and serviceable in the drifting current. The special anchors in the PMP bridging sets, which supposedly had "improved holding capabilities," did not work well on the silty river bottom. The current shifted the river bottom silt and unburied the anchors, the anchor cables periodically slackened, and the anchors slipped and tangled under the bridge.

River debris, such as wood, vegetation, and other trash, fouled the anchor cables. This also made it difficult to keep the bridge intact and serviceable.

In order to anchor the bridge sections in the river, the engineers substituted 10 to 20 meters of sea anchor chain for the PMP anchors. The local steamships often used these sea anchor chains to anchor barges in the Amu-Darya river. Once the heavy chain was dropped on the river bottom, the river quickly buried the anchor chain with silt that did not wash away. As a further precaution, the engineers positioned barges up river from the bridge. They sank these barges, which decreased the speed of the current and, consequently, helped maintain the bridge's position.

As a result of thorough planning and preparation, the engineers were able to construct a 160 meter and a 350 meter section of bridge in seven hours and fifteen minutes and to bridge the Amu Darya river in 12 hours. This successful bridging was crucial to the successful invasion operation as it enabled the Soviet forces to cross rapidly into Afghanistan.

After the invasion, it was necessary to protect the Amu Darya bridges against sabotage groups, floating mines, explosive charges, and floating objects. The Soviets posted a commandant's service detachment on the far shore to defend the bridge. They also created detachments to man up-river and down-river posts, in conjunction with a bridge guard force and duty subunit.

The force detailed to secure and defend a river crossing varied from a motorized rifle company up to a motorized rifle battalion. Their defensive fires included flanking fires and interlocking fields of fire, incorporating artillery and BMP fire, tied in with engineer barriers and natural obstacles. Subunit positions were thoroughly prepared and fortified. Barbed wire entanglements, combined with signal mines, were built in front of the positions and in the gaps between positions.

The up-river and down-river posts consisted of one or two pontoon platoons, a BMP-mounted motorized rifle platoon, and an ATGM crew. The up-river post was two to two-and-a-half kilometers from the bridge, while the down-river post was a kilometer from the bridge. The river pickets maintained 24-hour watch on the river crossing with observation posts and reconnaissance patrols. During the night, the posts deployed a boom barrier on the water's surface and lit the approaches with search lights.

During the years that the 40th Army was stationed in Afghanistan, the engineer forces continually worked to improve the roads and bridges that were vulnerable to devastation by the enemy and nature. Therefore, the engineers stockpiled construction materials on all march routes and posted stand-by mobile road-bridge groups in those areas where natural or manmade damage was likely. These groups consisted of an engineer road company with five bridge-laying MTU-20s[22] or a TMM bridge.[23] These were used to bypass a destroyed bridge, construct a river crossing, or clear obstructions away from sections of the road.

The Soviets constituted road groups to help move forces through mountain passes. Road groups had an IMR and road clearing machines to maintain the passes. The main tasks of these groups were to clear snow drifts and avalanches from the mountain passes. As a result of frequent Mujahideen gunfire directed at the BAT[24] engineer road-clearing vehicles, the Soviets curtailed the use of these very vulnerable machines. The bulk of the snow clearing tasks fell to the IMR and the S-100 armored bulldozer.[25]

Since there were a limited number of routes available for military traffic, a large number of vehicles had to use those routes. This led to overuse of the roads and promoted the rapid deterioration of parts of the highway. Further, the enemy constantly used rocks and overturned vehicles to build road blocks, which limited the traffic-carrying capability of the road significantly. Therefore, every motorized rifle regiment had a movement support detachment (MSD) in its area of responsibility. The MSD had an IMR, BAT, MTU-20, and a TMM bridge set, which allowed the engineers to restore the road quickly to a serviceable condition.

Often, repairing mountain roads was complicated by insufficient working space. In that case, the engineer road subunits had to move from point to point, working only on one section at a time. This significantly slowed down the tempo of road repair. In some cases, transport helicopters helped the engineer forces by moving engineer subunits, vehicles, road and bridging material, and the TMM and MTU motorized bridge sets over long distances. Engineer subunits, moved on helicopters, were equipped with D42 bulldozers, GAZ-SAZ-53B and GAZ-66 trucks, drilling equipment, and small mechanical tools. These subunits possessed the necessary autonomy and could independently undertake various engineer missions simultaneously on several sections of destroyed road.

Destroyed bridges presented a major challenge. Sometimes a partially destroyed bridge could be repaired by filling in the destroyed section with earth. However, most often the damage was so severe that restoration of the bridge on the old foundations was practically impossible in a short period of time. In that case, a new bridge could be laid using the motorized MTU-20, TMM, and "crossing" elements.

If the destroyed bridge span exceeded 20 meters, it was restored with the PMM-4 bridge.[26]

It was particularly difficult to restore collapsed sections of roads that were built on ledges. The primary method to repair these sections was to build up a supporting wall and broaden the section of road by deepening the rock face. Restoring roads was conducted sequentially by sections. When building up supporting walls, the engineers used a lot of local material such as earth and rocks, as well as sand bags and industrial cloth. In order to build a supporting wall from rocks, the engineers reinforced it with brushwood and metal netting. For filling hollows, the engineers laid stones in layers to which they added earth. In the course of restoring supporting walls, the engineers also successfully used the empty artillery ammunition packing boxes filled with earth or crushed stone, which were nailed together and reinforced with earth and tie rods.

Other designs were also used to restore supporting walls. Practice showed that the most effective way to repair supporting walls was with gabions made of metal netting and other highly durable, flexible material such as industrial cloth.

The Soviets usually deployed platoons in strong points to secure points on the lines of communication, bridges, dams, tunnels, and supporting walls located in canyons. Engineers constructed these strong points, digging out and fortifying primary and reserve fighting positions for motorized rifle squads, BMPs or BTRs, attached tanks, artillery pieces, and mortars. They also constructed small ammunition magazines. The engineers constructed CP/OPs for the platoon commanders for observation and directing combat. They also built dugouts and shelters for the personnel. All fortified works and structures were linked by communications trenches. Observation posts were sited in the unoccupied region, located some 500 to 1,000 meters in front of the main defensive positions. The observation posts had prepared fighting positions with covered slit trenches and field-expedient devices to help conduct fire.

The engineers used large pieces of crushed rock, adobe, prefabricated reinforced concrete pillboxes, and written-off BMPs, BTRs, and tanks to fortify the fighting positions. The engineers fully utilized the defensive and camouflage potential of the mountainous terrain. When building fortifications, they had to make allowances for large boulders, rocky crags, ledges, and hollows. The engineers built many structures by half-digging out the positions and then building them up using rock, sand bags, and earth.

While deploying platoons in strong points and fortresses or other dispersed sites, they supplied them with everything necessary for life and lodging. They provided stores of ammunition, equipment, and food and a CP for the platoon commander. They built firing embrasures in the adobe walls and enclosed courtyards and they built adobe firing pits as well as firing steps next to the walls, which let them conduct fire along the wall and in the territory inside the court-yard. They built covered enclosures on flat-roofed buildings to conduct fire and observation. They used sand bags, adobe, and ammunition boxes filled with dirt to build these structures. They closed windows with brick clay. In front of the entrance, they built a protective wall of stone or brick. Around the fortress or building, they scraped out emplacements for tanks, BMPs, BTRs, artillery pieces, mortars, and motorized rifle squads and built shelters for vehicles. The fortress or building itself was linked to external fortifications along the LOC.

Motorized rifle subunits provided the basis for the security and defense of air-fields, base camps, hydroelectric facilities, and other important installations. The motorized rifle squads and platoons were reinforced with tanks, artillery, and mor-tars. The squads were distributed 700 to 800 meters apart around the installation perimeter and also positioned on the near and far approaches to the installation. The squad positions were in dugout sections of trenches, while BMPs and BTRS were placed in emplacements and dugouts, with communications trenches run-ning between them. Ammunition storage bunkers and crew dugouts were built into the tank emplacements. Communication trenches were built so that the crews could quickly and easily get into the tank through the floor escape hatch, without exposing themselves to enemy fire. The platoon leader's CP was set up in one of the squad's positions and linked to the other squads by communications trenches.

Earth work was done by hand or, if the terrain permitted, with engineering equipment. Equipment included the regimental GZM-2 earth moving machine, the BTM-3 trenching machine, the TMK-2, and MDK-3 rotary evacuator. The tactical-technical characteristics of the earthmoving machines are shown in Fig-ure 10.

In all instances, fortified installations were built on the best available terrain and located outside the area of possible avalanche, rockslide, landslide, mountain torrents, flooding from cloudbursts and snow melt, and snow slide. To protect the installations from surface flooding, the engineers built diverting canals, and to protect them from drifting sand the engineers built barriers and vertical screens.

Most of the space in the installation was built up to protect personnel, ammunition, and POL from Mujahideen bullets and shrapnel, as well as direct hits by their mortars and launch bombs. The available local building material was usually limited to adobe and stone which was used to thicken structure walls. The engineers built parapets with sandbags filled with clay or stone and then plas-tered over them with wet clay, or they plastered the clay to the structure by mix-ing it with mortar. To prevent bullets and fragments from ricocheting off stone parapets, the engineers coated them with soft dirt or stacked up turf.

The forces used unrepairable armored vehicles, trucks, and vehicle frames and bodies in constructing fortified positions. They also used ammunition pack-ing boxes and metal cases as well as airfield pierced steel plate. The engineers

	GZM-2	BTM-3	TMK-2	MDK-3
Weight (metric tons)	12.8	27.6	27.2	39
Propulsion	Wheel	Track	Wheel	Track
Crew	2	2	2	2
Earth moving capacity(cubic meters per hour)	100-110	350-400	350-400	500-600
Depth of trench in meters	1.2	1.5	1.5	3.5
Trench width at top (meters)	0.9	0.9-1.1	0.9-1.1	
Trench width bottom (meters)	0.65	0.5	O.6	3.7
Road speed (km/hour)	to 45	to 35	to 45	to 35

Figure 10. Tactical-technical characteristics of earthmoving machines

built regulation individual emplacements, trenches, and communication trenches. The engineers reinforced walls and built protective positions for tanks, BMPs, BTRs and artillery pieces using sandbags, adobe blocks, bricks, ammunition boxes, stones, and so on.

The engineers built covered slit trenches to protect personnel. They used strips of corrugated steel, planks, ammunition boxes, vehicle frames, and dump truck bodies for the overhead cover. The engineers used closed vehicle bodies and the bodies of BTRs and other vehicles that were nonrepairable for personnel shelters. They made similar shelters for ammunition and POL. They piled dirt on top of these as protection from bullets and shrapnel.

During the course of combat, personnel in assembly areas were usually protected by trenches built under their vehicles, as well as by rock walls. They built walls of stone and adobe to increase the protection of personnel at security posts. Besides protecting personnel from bullets and shrapnel, these walls allowed the secret deployment of forces during combat. In order to conceal the forces' activities, they used a wide variety of various masking covers and vertical screens. As a rule, the engineers used the KVS-A and KVS-U prefabricated fortified shelters to build command posts and to store ammunition and explosives at regimental and subunits base camps.

Laying mine fields was one of the most important engineer support missions to the LCOSF in Afghanistan. This was complicated by the lack of a clear front line and a guerrilla enemy. Further, the predominantly hard ground made it difficult to lay mines.

The division and regimental commanders made the decision to use obstacles to protect the installations in their areas of responsibility. Based on the commander's decision, the division or regimental chief of the engineering service developed a plan to build engineering obstacles. These plans were approved by the higher commander.

TO&E and attached engineer units and subunits constructed mine fields. Non-TO&E sappers also laid mine fields for combat support and service support subunits and special forces. The engineers sometimes used the PMZ-4 mechanical mine layer to lay mine fields.

Those mine fields that protected subunit security positions and installations were surrounded by two barbed wire fences and covered with small arms fire. In order to prevent the Mujahideen from dragging out the mines with a grapnel, the defenders linked signal mines or bounding fragmentation mines to the fence. In order to warn soldiers and the local population about the danger of mines, the defenders hung warning signs on the barbed wire fence or put them close to it. "Stop, mines" was written on the signs in Russian and the Afghan language.

Installations were protected by antipersonnel blast mines, bounding mines, and directional mines. All the area within installations was fenced off with a continuous barbed wire fence. The more important sites within the installation, such as aircraft parking areas and depots, were fenced off with additional fencing. Antipersonnel fragmentation mines were placed on the interior side of installation fencing at those areas where the enemy could secretly approach. Signal mines were sited 150 to 200 meters outside the installation fence. The engineers laid tangle foot[27] in those sections outside the installation fence where they could not lay mine fields. They covered all the approaches to the installation and all mine fields with machine gun fire from fortified machine gun nests.

All the mine fields were recorded in mine field registration books that were forwarded to regiment and division. Further, the subunit commanders maintained drawings depicting the mine field locations, the number of rows, the distance between the rows and mines, and reference points.[28]

The Soviets widely used the OZM-72 bounding fragmentation mine, the MON-50 directional mine, the PMN antipersonnel blast mine, and various types of booby trap mines for combat in the mountains. They used them to lay antipersonnel barriers in canyons on reconnoitered or probable Mujahideen movement or caravan routes. They mined roads, slopes, dry river beds, mountain passes, and other sites that the Mujahideen moved on by foot, truck, or cart.

In the desert, where the enemy had more maneuver room, the Soviet mine fields stretched further and contained few groups of mines [and were often scatterable mines].

The Soviets used antivehicular and antitank mines on roads and bridges. They used command-detonated directional mines for ambushes. Spetsnaz subunits also used mine fields for combat. The Soviets would lay mine fields in those areas that the Mujahideen would likely move through: at the cross roads of several trails; where natural barriers do not permit a withdrawal; at the entries and exits to canyons; at the ascent and descent from mountain passes; and at other sites. They would use blast mines as well as bounding fragmentation and command-detonated directional fragmentation mines. For ambushes, they would lay mines at the entry and exit to the ambush as well as in the kill zone itself. In addition, they would mine possible withdrawal routes that the Mujahideen might take to escape the ambush. They would lay the mines at a safe distance from the covering force positions and the command detonation point, but within visual and optics range and covered by the fire of assault rifles and machine guns.

In the majority of cases, the Soviets laid mine fields by hand. They laid remotely delivered mine fields with aircraft and artillery. Most often they laid these remote minefields during combat on well-established enemy movement routes and also on difficult-to-reach passes.

The Soviets installed booby traps and anti-lift devices on their mines that they laid to protect strong points, installations, and base camps. When the Soviets laid mines during combat in an area that might later be used by peaceful inhabitants, they equipped these mines with self-destruct devices.

A very important engineer mission in Afghanistan was providing clean water and establishing water supply points. In order to provide water to the forces, Soviet engineers established water points at springs of subsurface water, water bore holes, and wells and also in *karez* (underground irrigation tunnels) and open water sources.

The type and quality of water supply points supporting the divisions, regiments, and subunits were determined by the deployment of forces and the availability of water in the region.

Water supply points were established using TO&E equipment. Thus, for example, when the 40th Army entered Afghanistan, they used the truck-mounted MAFS water filter system and the TUF-200 woven-charcoal filter exclusively. In some very few garrisons, they used the existing drilled water wells located at installations. They chlorinated this water without fail. The engineers drilled for water in those remote regions where Soviet forces deployed. The engineers prepared a total of some 180 drilled wells throughout Afghanistan. These produced a total of 60,000 cubic meters of water a day.

The sanitary-epidemiologic service selected the sites for the water points based on the water sources and their water quality and the lack of disease-causing microbes, and also the security, defendability, and ability to camouflage the site. The maintenance of the water supply point was performed by the TO&E crew, while motorized rifle subunits provided security and defense.

Water supply was centralized in the base camps, which would then supply water to the subunits' water points. At division and regimental water supply points, the Soviets developed an autonomous security plan for those exposed water supply points that their security detachments and posts used.

The senior commander was responsible for delivering water to his small platoon and company posts and garrisons that guarded the LOC or important installations. Water was stored in various reservoirs and containers that were dispersed in sheltered sites, to safeguard the water from evaporation by the sun's rays, from being fouled by dust and dirt, and from being lost to punctures from bullets and shrapnel. In the event that there was a breakdown in the supply of water, these garrisons used the woven charcoal filter TUF-200 and the MTK-2M small, tubular well-borer, along with trained operating crews who could collect and purify water on site.

Convoys that transported supplies to the combat zone had a TO&E water purification system—either the MAFS or the TUF-200.

The quality of the water at water supply points was checked by laboratories, mobile laboratories at filtration stations, or quality control kits. A doctor or physician's assistant gave the final release for potable water. Water storage and transport containers (canteens, barrels, reservoirs, and cisterns) were routinely disinfected.

The successful accomplishment of the various difficult engineer support missions contributed to successful combat by Soviet forces in Afghanistan.

Editors' comments: As with most armies, the 40th Army had more engineer requirements than available engineers. Modern warfare requires a developed theater infrastructure to support a modern army, but Afghanistan was hardly well developed. The roads were few and inadequate, the railroad was nonexistent, the industrial production facilities were few and generally inefficient. Engineers had to provide some rudimentary infrastructure. The standard engineer missions of mine and obstacle clearance, mine and obstacle construction, and water supply were supplemented with the requirement to maintain a long LOC over very rugged territory and the need to fortify a series of security posts along that LOC and around cities, airfields, and garrisons. The engineer equipment, designed to function on the Northern European Plain, had difficulty digging in the hard Afghanistan soil. Clean water provision was particularly difficult, due to the many outposts that the 40th Army had strung out along the roads of Afghanistan.

There were many engineer troops in Afghanistan, but they still were not enough. The 40th Army had an Engineer Road Construction Brigade and the 45th Engineer Regiment assigned to army headquarters. Each division had its own engineer battalion and each regiment had its own engineer company. Local contract labor provided muscle and skill for engineer projects. Motorized rifle and artillerymen did much of the engineering work in the construction of outposts, firing positions, base camps, and the like. Engineers supervised much of this work. DRA engineer units worked on projects that also benefited the Soviets. Despite all these assets, the Soviet engineers were stressed to meet all the demands imposed by the Afghanistan countryside and the 40th Army. That they were able to do as much as they did is a credit to their professionalism.

	RPO	RPO-A
Caliber in millimeters	110	93
Length in millimeters	1440	920
Maximum range (meters)	400	1000
Maximum effective range(meters)	250	600
Direct fire range at a 3-meter high target (meters)	150	200
Weight of warhead (kilograms)	4	2.1-2.4
Weight of launcher (kilograms)	12.6	11
Temperature range for use (Celsius)	-40° to +50°	-50° to +50°
Time to ready the weapon for firing (seconds)	60	30

Figure 11. Characteristics of rocket-assisted, man-portable flame throwers

CHEMICAL SUPPORT[29]

Soviet use of chemical weapons during combat in Afghanistan was limited. Only the enemy employed chemical weapons in strength.[30] The enemy used an unstable poisonous substance that acted as an irritant. The Soviets widely used flame throwers and smoke.

The Soviets used two models of rocket-assisted, man-portable flame throwers—the RPO and the RPO-A. These had a maximum range of 400 and 1,000 meters, respectively. Moreover, up until 1964, the Soviet forces only had the RPO, which has a limited maximum effective range of 250 meters and required a great deal of time to ready it for firing. This increased the threat to the flame thrower gunner while moving up to the firing position and limited the effectiveness of this type of weapon in combat.

With the receipt of the RPO-A in the Soviet armory, gunners could now conduct aimed fire out to a maximum effective range of 600 meters. Further, it took half the time to get ready to fire that its predecessor had taken. These factors significantly increased the effectiveness of this chemical weapon.[31] More of the complete characteristics of these rocket-assisted, man-portable flame throwers are included in Figure 11.

At the same time, there remained the unresolved problem of how to protect the flame thrower gunners, who were a primary target for enemy snipers. The Soviets undertook a series of calculated steps to resolve this issue.

The Soviets constructed a special fitting in the revolving turret of the BTR from which the flame thrower gunner could fire his RPO-A. The construction still allowed the turret to rotate and to elevate and lower the weapon. Four to eight flame thrower rounds were stored inside the BTR. The flamethrower was linked to the turret machine gun and was aimed by aiming the turret machine gun. Firing could be done from a short halt or while moving at a speed of up to ten kilometers per hour. The gunner could conduct single or volley fire. The armored vehicle protected the flame thrower gunner from enemy small arms fire.

Flame throwers were effective in destroying single enemy firing positions located in adobe structures, caves, and other enclosed structures.

In May 1985, during combat near Khost, the Soviets encountered a Mujahideen fortified strong point inside a village surrounded by an adobe wall. The most dangerous firing position was located on the southern outskirts. The flame thrower crew commanded by Junior Sergeant S. V. Mgar' was ordered to suppress this firing position. The flame thrower round fell accurately on the target and destroyed a mortar and four Mujahideen. This opened up the advance for the assault troops.

In October 1987, a Soviet subunit fighting in Logar Province was halted by the fire from several caves located on the mountain slope. All attempts to suppress the firing points with small arms and mortar fire were unsuccessful. Therefore, the company commander ordered a flame thrower crew, commanded by Sergeant A. V. Sergunov, to engage one of the firing points. The flame thrower round flew some 300 meters directly into the cave, destroying a machine gun and killing five Mujahideen.

Seeing how effective the flame thrower was, the company commander then ordered the flame thrower crews to engage a recoilless rifle that was firing from another cave. This was located 500 meters away. Two flame throwers engaged the target. The first round fell short of the target but raised a dust cloud in front of the Mujahideen. Taking advantage of this dust, Junior Sergeant S. V. Komarov got closer to the target and destroyed it with the next shot.

Afghanistan provided the opportunity to combat test flame throwers against Mujahideen who were sheltering in the underground *karez*. The flame throwers proved effective under these conditions, although the gunners were in danger of enemy fire if they tried to aim a shot down the *karez* shaft. Therefore, the flame throwers were used only when necessary and only after repeatedly demanding that the enemy surrender. The RPO was readied for firing and cocked. Ropes were tied to the flamethrower and trigger and then the flame thrower was lowered into the *karez* shaft where it was fired. The flamethrower could be fired down a side passage where it would destroy the enemy or force him to surrender or withdraw to the surface.

In February 1985, the Soviets fought groups of Mujahideen in Kabul Province who had their bases in several *karez*. One of these groups, numbering up to 20 men, was discovered not too far away from the village of Ben Zadi. A flame thrower shot killed five men on the surface. Another flame thrower shot killed the rest of the group in their shelter.

Two days after this, another group of Mujahideen was neutralized in the area of the village of Karez-e Mir. In all, over a six day period, flame thrower actions destroyed or captured 70 Mujahideen in various *karez*.

Flame thrower gunners were included in every battle and were chosen after considering the scope and the difficulty of the mission. As a rule, every company was reinforced with a group of two to six flame thrower gunners. Further, the regiment or battalion commander had a small flame thrower reserve at his disposal. Flame thrower gunners moved on foot or in their TO&E vehicle while in combat. As they moved up to their firing position, they were supported by a special security group drawn from the subunit to which they were attached. The gunners selected their own firing positions and shelter. They would fire on the target until it was suppressed or destroyed.

The Soviets used various types of smoke during combat in Afghanistan. The smoke lessened the effectiveness of enemy reconnaissance and fire while facilitating the maneuver of Soviet forces. The Soviets established blinding and masking smoke screens using special systems, smoke generators, and the smoke induction systems on tanks, BMPs, and BTRs.

Special smoke systems include smoke grenades, incendiary-smoke cartridges, and artillery and mortar smoke rounds.

The RDG-2 smoke grenade was convenient and lightweight (about 600 grams), allowing a soldier to conceal himself for one and a half minutes with an impenetrable smoke screen that was 15 to 25 meters long. This was sufficient smoke concealment to enable the soldier to either close with the enemy or withdraw from enemy fire during combat.

The DM-11, UDSh, and BDSh-15 smoke pots weigh 2.4, 13.5, and 43.5 kilograms, respectively. The Soviets used them to provide smoke concealment for subunits. They are set up by designated personnel. Each smoke pot burns for 5 to 17 minutes and establishes an impenetrable smoke screen with a length of 50 to 150 meters.

The ZDP incendiary-smoke cartridge propels a smoke round out to 500 meters. Due to its limited smoke capacity, these as a rule are fired en masse using a launcher. They serve to not only lay smoke on the site, but also to set fire to things.

The smoke induction systems of tanks, BMPs, and BTRs served to cover the area with smoke in order to conceal the vehicles as well as subunits of other branches of service.

The TDA-2m smoke machine is assigned to military smoke subunits. It can lay an impenetrable smoke screen with a length of 1,000 meters and a duration of three to eight hours.

More complete characteristics of smoke systems are contained in Figure 12.

The military situation often demanded the use of a combination of incendiary and smoke systems. This was done by a customized BTR-70 equipped with a flame thrower mount, a ZDP incendiary-smoke cartridge launcher, and smoke pots. This vehicle was used to support various military missions and protect its crew.

	Weight (kg)	Burning time (sec)	Time smoke screen maintained (min)	Length of smoke screen (meters)	Projection distance (meters)
RDG-2 smoke grenade	0.5-0.6	to 15	1-1.5	15-25	-
ZDP incendiary smoke cartridge	0.75	to 7.5	1-2	10-15	to 500
DM-11 smoke pot	2.2-2.4	to 30	5-7	to 50	-
BDSh-15	13.5	to 30	15-17	100-120	-
UDSh	13.5	10-15	10	100-150	-
81mm vehicle-mounted smoke grenade	2.4	7-16	to 2.5	30-45	300
TDA-2m smoke generator			3-8 hours	1000	-

Figure 12. Characteristics of smoke systems

The combat employment of flame throwers and smoke to support motorized rifle, airborne, and air assault subunits gradually improved tactics.

During an advance into a well-fortified Mujahideen base region, flame thrower gunners usually traveled on combat vehicles as part of the combat formation. The movement was hidden by smoke (Map 30). At a line some 800 to 1,000 meters from the enemy fortified positions, RPO-A flame thrower gunners would first engage the enemy and troops would launch incendiary-smoke cartridges and ZDP smoke grenades. Under the cover of the smoke, the flame thrower gunners would move closer to the enemy. The smoke screen was maintained some 300 meters in front of the advancing force.

The flame throwers and smoke systems were used to help subunits break contact and withdraw. They would lay a smoke screen some 300 to 400 meters in front of the limit of advance using the RPO-A smoke round, smoke grenades, and UDSh smoke pots. They would lay successive smoke screens as they fell back (Map 31). These measures were combined with the fire and maneuver of the motorized rifle or air assault troopers and guaranteed the success of their action. Combat in Afghanistan showed that when the forces and resources were skillfully applied, the number of successful missions quickly grew and friendly casualties substantially lessened.

When advancing in a green zone, the flame thrower gunners attempted to move closer to the enemy in secret. They moved to their firing positions under the cover of smoke, fired at the enemy, and then returned. A specially chosen group covered their secret advance with smoke and small arms fire. The flame throwers were employed at fairly closely range. The gunners took special care to ensure that there were no trees or large branches in the firing sector that could deflect the flight of the projectile.

When flame thrower gunners traveled in a convoy, they were either part of

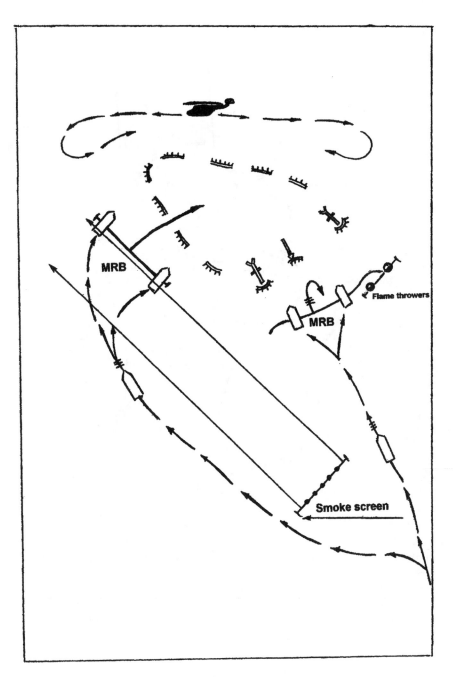

Map 30. Chemical support of an advance

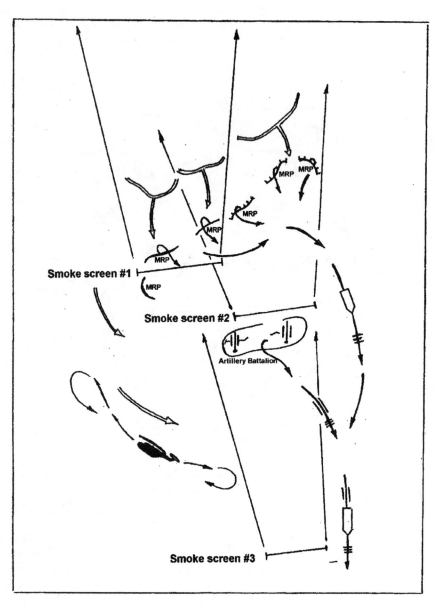

Map 31. Chemical support of a force when breaking contact and withdrawing

the march security element or the main body. If they were in the main body, they were located at the head of the column or at the tail or dispersed throughout the column. When the enemy would open fire on the convoy, the drivers would toss out RDG smoke grenades to quickly lay a smoke screen. Covered by the smoke screen, the convoy would increase speed and drive out of the kill zone, while the flame thrower gunners would take up firing positions. The flame throwers fired from their combat vehicles or from ground positions in concert with small arms fire, combat vehicle fire, and antitank weapons fire. The combination of flame throwers and smoke was highly effective in these given circumstances.

Thus, in April 1988, a convoy driving from Kandahar was ambushed by the enemy in the mountains. The convoy commander quickly gave the signal to toss the smoke grenades. One of the RPO crews dismounted and moved under the cover of the smoke to a position closer to the enemy. It hit a Mujahideen firing position. Then the enemy opened fire from the other side of the road where there was no smoke screen. Instantly one vehicle was stopped and another was damaged. Senior Lieutenant S. V. Derevyakin, the commander of the chemical defense platoon, was in a BTR equipped with a flamethrower. He ordered his driver to drive alongside the convoy between it and the enemy. The flame thrower fired a salvo while the BTR continued to move. The enemy firing point was neutralized.

Smoke systems were also used independently to cover the evacuation of the dead and wounded, the evacuation of damaged vehicles, the removal of landslides, mine-clearing activities, and also to conceal helipads. Combat experience showed that the skillful use of smoke lessened personnel, equipment, and armament casualties by two times.

A no less important chemical support mission was monitoring the chemical and radiological situation to determine the radiological and chemical situation in the area where the forces were located and in the combat zone.

Due to the lack of a threat of the use of nuclear weapons, the radiological situation was simply the natural background radiation. The results of this monitoring did not have any impact on the conduct of combat; however, it was taken into account in the selection of base camps and locations for guard posts and security posts.

Monitoring the chemical threat was an active mission. This was because the Mujahideen sparingly used an unstable poisonous substance that was an irritant. Their primary delivery means were poisonous smoke and chemical hand grenades, chemical cartridges, 81 and 82mm mortar rounds, and also strychnine and phosphorus tablets manufactured in the United States and West Germany.

Monitoring the chemical threat included determining the facts about the Mujahideen use of chemical weapons, the frequency of their employment, and the consequences of their use. The TO&E radiation and chemical reconnaissance squad was used to perform these missions. They performed this while on the march from the BRDM-2RX reconnaissance vehicle as part of the movement support detachment. When the column arrived at the combat zone, they established a chemical monitoring post from which they could alert the force about a chemical threat.

The equipment of the chemical monitoring post included the authorized instruments (the DP-56 or DP-58, which measure the power of the doses and the VPKHR chemical reconnaissance instrument), the MK-3 meteorological set, signal rockets, communications sets (telephones and portable radios), the KZO-1 warning sign set, the authorized signal codes, and other survey documents.

The distinctive and difficult chemical support mission in Afghanistan demanded thorough personnel training, not only of the chemical personnel but also of the combined arms units and subunits.

Chemical branch personnel were assigned in training units prior to their service in Afghanistan. When they arrived in the combat zone, they continued their preparation at a month-long course and then continued their special training while serving with the forces.

Chemical training of motorized rifle and air assault subunits and the subunits of other branches of services and special forces was conducted at regular training sessions and during the course of combat.

The experience of the LCOSF in Afghanistan provided a rebirth in the importance of chemical support for the resolution of various military missions. During the course of combat, the chemical troops received a significant amount of experience in using flame throwers and proved that flame throwers are a powerful and advanced weapon for close combat.

The use of smoke showed that it had wide application for concealing Soviet forces and installations as well as for blinding enemy observation. Smoke significantly lessened Soviet casualties and aided mission accomplishment. Further, the availability of chemical forces and resources that monitored the chemical situation kept Soviet losses to a minimum from the chemical weapons of the enemy.

Editors' comments: The Soviet use of chemical weapons in Afghanistan remains a matter of debate. The United States made a convincing case that the Soviets had tested a wide variety of chemical agents in Afghanistan during the first half of the war. This section's claim that the Mujahideen used chemical weapons against the Soviets is hard to accept. There is some evidence that the Mujahideen had a limited number of tear gas grenades, but nothing else. Few photographs from the war show the Soviets carrying protective masks as protection from the Mujahideen chemical threat.

The Soviets have long classified smoke rounds and flame weapons as chemical systems. During the cold war, this led to misunderstandings. For example, Western analysts announced that one-fifth of Soviet artillery rounds were chemical rounds. Smoke rounds are a large portion of any country's artillery war stocks but are hardly chemical rounds in the accepted Western sense. In Afghanistan, the Soviets used a lot of smoke and flame weapons.

Although the Soviets withdrew the tank regiments and air defense regiments from the divisions of the 40th Army in 1986, they did not withdraw the equally redundant chemical reconnaissance troops. This was because the number of chemical reconnaissance troops was small, and they usually helped out with headquarters duties in addition to their chemical reconnaissance duties.

8

Combat Service Support

The LCOSF's sojourn and combat in Afghanistan required increased technical and rear area support. Afghanistan lacked the material-technical base necessary to satisfy the needs of the 40th Army forces. The technical and rear area support services of the divisions and regiments were unable to adequately support the 40th Army since the facilities they needed were located in the Soviet Union. Therefore, a major portion of the logistics support of the divisions and regiments was conducted directly from the Soviet Union, and this physical separation created additional difficulties.

TECHNICAL SUPPORT[1]

Technical support of Soviet forces in Afghanistan included all the normal requirements: bringing the amount of armaments and equipment up to required strength; training the technical and tactical specialist personnel; providing ammunition support; operating, repairing, and evacuating arms and equipment; providing military-technical stores; and directing technical support. However, the reality of technical support measures was determined by the distribution of forces, the peculiarities of the theater of military action, and armed combat. The widespread dispersal of forces over a large area in numerous garrisons, ranging from platoon-sized to that of several regiments, had a serious impact on technical support. This dispersal of the entire contingent of Soviet forces is typified by the deployment of one of the motorized rifle divisions, which occupied an area of 380 by 120 kilometers. The division was distributed throughout almost 70 garrisons, of which some 60 were strong points on the LOC. The strong points were dispersed within mutually supporting distance (two to seven kilometers) along the road and included, as a rule, a motorized rifle platoon and, in some cases, a

264

tank platoon, sometimes reinforced with a mortar platoon or other fire support systems. Typically, 40 to 60 percent of the combat equipment of a regiment or division was dispersed in strong points guarding LOCs, pipelines, and base camps.

This dispersal of a significant portion of combat power into small garrisons was further aggravated by the difficulty of maintaining contacts between those garrisons—due to the constant threat of enemy attack. The remaining military equipment not devoted to garrison support was periodically committed to combat or used to escort supply convoys and so on.

Due to the extreme physical terrain and the constant commitment of the equipment to various tasks, the Soviets could only mass a large number of vehicles in motor pools when preparing for a planned battle. The Soviets constituted composite combat groups with varying structures from the forces of different formations. A combat group usually had two or three partial motorized rifle regiments, plus attached combat arms and combat support units and subunits, plus specialized division and army forces. A limited number of tank subunits were attached for direct combat. Weapons and combat vehicles were not assigned by TO&E, but by various combinations of branch and specialized forces equipment.

As a rule, the length of time that a combat group could remain committed on enemy territory was a function of available technical support.

Separate division and unit combat was conducted from 10 to 16 kilometers up to 100 kilometers or more from garrison, usually on difficult terrain. Army operations were significantly larger in both scale and the distance to the combat zone. When the threat of enemy action gradually increased against the LOCs, it was necessary to deploy combat groups from garrison for extended combat. This also required constituting a corresponding independent technical support group, capable of functioning for an extended period of time while separated from fixed supply and repair facilities.

These separate actions sharply increased the problems of securing and defending the technical support components. In the majority of cases, their security was the determining factor in selecting the type of technical support personnel and resources for the mission. Security considerations partially disrupted technological support of the mission.

The 40th Army system of technological support was completely dependent on its own personnel and resources since there were no local resources or industrial base to draw on.

AMMUNITION SUPPORT

The basic principle of ammunition support during combat is to establish adequate self-sufficient support that meets the requirements of the group of forces, to the maximum extent possible, for the entire planned period of combat.

Planners determined the ammunition reserve necessary to support an independent group of forces by considering the planned duration of the combat or operation and the anticipated expenditure of ammunition.

Separate regiment and division combats lasted an average of five to ten days, while an army-scale operation lasted ten to twenty days. There was a wide fluctuation within ammunition expenditure parameters. The quantity of ammunition carried in similar operations was not always the same. In any event, the average combat expenditure of ammunition for BMPs, BTRs, artillery, and small arms was between 2.2 and 2.4 combat loads.

The demands for self-sufficiency led the group of forces to carry additional ammunition at all levels starting with the soldier and crew. Every rifleman, as a rule, had two combat loads of ammunition for his assault rifle. Further, every BMP or BTR carried an additional two to three boxes of assault rifle ammunition and one or two boxes of hand grenades. Further, the BMP or BTR carried an additional 0.5 to 1.0 combat loads of main gun ammunition (30mm cannon or 14.5mm machine gun). Boxes of ammunition were stored on board the vehicles.

Battalion and regimental transport and the artillery battalion transport carried additional reserves of all types of ammunition. If an action or separate operation was planned at a significant distance from fixed depots, part of the division ammunition reserve could be transported on the trucks of the material support battalion.

The ammunition reserve that accompanied the group of forces was not always sufficient to last for the entire operation, particularly if it lasted over 10 days. Therefore, in order to support combat, the force established supplemental ammunition reserves at the permanent depots of regiments and divisions from which the group of forces was drawn or at any nearby depot. The requirement to establish supplementary ammunition reserves was eased somewhat by the fact that the units and subunits involved in combat usually were not fully manned. This resulted in an increased amount of reserve weapons that the units and subunits had to carry along with them. Sometimes, the units were able to keep the ammunition uploaded on trucks ready to move to the combat zone when necessary.

In some cases, the logisticians established a separate army artillery depot to support combat. This depot was usually established at the nearest existing regiment or division depot, which, as a rule, was near an airfield and had TO&E ground transport.

During large-scale operations, logisticians increased material reserves, including ammunition, in the base region to support the entire group of forces. In one such operation, the combat service support forces established four regional bases located at an existing army depot and three regiment or division depots. The logisticians stocked about five combat loads of various types of ammunition in these depots. They determined the composition of these ammunition reserves based on the situation and the type of planned operation or combat.

Thus, ammunition support planning combined the prescribed ammunition loads habitually carried with supplementary reserves carried by the group of forces to achieve autonomy. This was backed by other reserves in nearby stationary ammunition stores. Further, if the ammunition support system was functioning correctly, any commander involved in a combat mission could draw ammunition from a nearby unit without having to arrange this in advance through his higher headquarters.[2]

During combat, direct ammunition support was first provided to the fire support systems. Artillery firing positions were laid, as a rule, near the command post of a transportation unit that carried ammunition and other material reserves. The resupply of ammunition was conducted over short distances in secure regions that lacked major obstacles.

Ammunition support of motorized rifle subunits depended on their combat mission. The battalion trucks, loaded with the ammunition reserve, might be held in a section of the regiment rear area or they might be located with the battalion *bronegruppa*.

It was far more difficult to resupply ammunition to dismounted motorized rifle subunits that were separated from their *bronegruppa*. This was especially true when the subunit had been on foot in the mountains for several days. Where possible, ammunition was resupplied from higher to lower using the transport of the senior commander to support his subordinates. Two or three BMPs or BTRs loaded with ammunition would move into the area where the dismounted motorized riflemen were located. The subunit *bronegruppa* could also be used to resupply ammunition to the dismounted subunit. If vehicles could not get into the area, helicopters would resupply ammunition. Only in the event that the higher commander was unable to deliver the ammunition to the subunit would the subunit resupply itself. In this case, the dismounted personnel would descend from the mountains and move back on combat vehicles to pick up material from the subunit and unit.

There were two ways to transport ammunition to groups in combat. In the first case, representatives of the rocket-artillery armaments and rear services—the heads of these services for the group of forces—organized ammunition convoys using truck transport that had been attached to units and subunits. A motorized rifle company or platoon, reinforced with a sapper subunit, would protect each convoy. The convoy would load up the ammunition necessary for the conduct of operation at a base camp or any nearby depot.

In the second case, helicopters would provide a continuous resupply of ammunition to the group of forces. In this case, the command formed convoys to move ammunition stores to the transport helicopters. The convoys were formed from truck support groups that might be formed from transport available at the base camp, or, if necessary, the higher headquarters could form a new convoy using other available transport.

The usage rate of armaments and equipment was entirely different than that of the peacetime Soviet army or the historic experience of the Red Army during the Great Patriotic War. The irregular tempo of combat and the rugged terrain in

Afghanistan affected usage of arms and equipment. Combat vehicles and other vehicles were used in operations on an average of once a month. Between operations, subunits participated in various battalion and company actions, many of which were unexpected. Further, these subunits used their equipment when they were periodically assigned to escort supply convoys.

The combat tempo disrupted the monthly and annual resource expenditure plan. Therefore, the logisticians threw out the peacetime norms and canceled the annual and monthly vehicle maintenance plan for the regiments and divisions. Instead, the regiments worked out a flexible general ledger and estimates of when their vehicles would require scheduled maintenance.

The actual expenditure of resources for armaments and equipment fluctuated within set limits and also within various units and divisions according to the time of year and the size of the operation. Thus, during six separate operations that lasted 9 to 25 days each, the average daily mileage was the following: BMPs, 30 to 50 kilometers; BTRs, 25 to 40 kilometers; and trucks, 25 to 60 kilometers.

In major, longer-lasting operations, the total mileage was significantly higher. This increased mileage indicated the increased strain on the armaments and equipment. Reconnaissance vehicles, the bulk of motorized rifle unit and subunit vehicles, and engineer vehicles showed especially extensive mileage. However, subunit mileage was insignificant when they secured the LOC, pipelines, and garrisons or patrolled their sectors of responsibility.

The army and division rear area support vehicles and their security escort combat vehicles also accumulated excessive mileage. These vehicles conducted continual long marches of 100 to 700 kilometers across the mountain passes and serpentine road stretches from the support base in the USSR to the separate depots and base camps of the 40th Army. These vehicles consumed a large amount of resources when they arrived at transfer bases at the Soviet border. Due to the lack of railroads, there was a serious demand placed on the vehicles belonging to the forces.

The harsh climate and physical geography further strained the vehicles. The air temperature is high, it is very dusty, and the mountain soil is rocky. All of these increased the wear and tear on practically all assemblies and joints in armaments and vehicles.

Maintenance personnel paid particular attention to vehicle moving parts, the engine and its lubrication system, the cooling system, the fuel system, and the electric system. Common problems included the premature disintegration of the rubber on tracked vehicle road wheels, the destruction of idler wheels, the breakdown of track (particularly when proper track tension was not maintained), an increase in wear and tear on the engine pistons and cylinders (from the extreme dustiness and hot air temperatures), and overheating (caused by personnel carelessness). The diesel fuel system had to work under difficult conditions that were aggravated by the difficulty in keeping the fuel clean. Dirty fuel led to the breakdown of the most complex and expensive element of the diesel fuel system—the fuel pump. The dust and high temperatures also required that the electronic apparatus, electric instruments, vehicle battery, and radio be serviced differently than under normal conditions.

The operating conditions had a substantial influence on the maintenance schedule for armaments and equipment. Maintenance was conducted an average of 1.2 to 1.3 times more often due to the high temperatures and extreme dustiness. Further, subunits took 15 to 26 percent more time servicing items of equipment than the regulations specified. The increased consumption of fuel and oil between services (up to 50 percent over the norm) led to increased maintenance time during scheduled services.

This led to a change in the system of technological servicing of armaments and vehicles. The Soviet army had a system of planned preventive maintenance. Its essence was the required conduct of scheduled maintenance after a vehicle was driven a certain number of miles or a weapon fired a certain number of rounds. Every necessary service was included in a numbered step-by-step preventive maintenance work schedule. For example, the planned preventive maintenance for the BMP included technical maintenance service #1 after 2,500 kilometers. The listed services took five to six hours of work by the crew. Technical maintenance service #2 was performed after 5,000 kilometers and took eight to ten hours of work by the crew.

In Afghanistan, the technical support personnel retained the formal planned preventive maintenance schedule, but they added new components. To begin with, due to the harsh operating conditions, they increased the frequency of services by some 25 to 30 percent. However, this increase proved insufficient. The preventive maintenance system was complicated by conditions that could not be prevented. It was clear that maintenance needed to be performed after fewer miles were driven or rounds fired than the manual dictated. It was necessary to perform maintenance when the vehicles were not being used or the weapons were not being fired regardless of mileage or the number of rounds fired. The peacetime preventive maintenance system was developed away from the battlefield where no one could predict the expenditure of resources.

The change in the frequency and scheduling of maintenance led to changes in the content and sequence of maintenance work. In fact, the technicians frequently combined some of the services from technical maintenance service #1 and #2. They determined which elements of the services to combine, based on equipment use and the circumstances under which it was used.

Naturally, this new maintenance system was planned and controlled. In many instances, the center of gravity in the organization and direction of maintenance shifted to the subunits. This significantly increased the flexibility of the system and accommodated abrupt changes in the situation as well as changes in specific local conditions.

The crux of the system was to perform the work on the weapons and equipment during preparation for combat and after returning from the operation.

Forces selected for combat underwent a seven-day preparation program. Three days of this were devoted to the preparation of weapons and equipment. The program recommended a series of maintenance tasks, chief of which were cleaning all filters, topping off lubricants, performing tune ups, cleaning radiators, and servicing batteries.

Every vehicle carried extra POL and distilled water. When the combat vehicles were originally designed, the designers did not foresee the need to equip the vehicles to carry extra POL and distilled water. Therefore, extra racks and fittings were added to provide additional carrying capacity on the sides and rear deck of armored fighting vehicles. Vehicles that were not originally equipped to carry extra oil were rigged with additional carrying capacity. Occasionally, oil was stored in one of the rear door fuel tanks of the BMP and blocked off from the fuel feed. Additional reserves were maintained in the company and battalion.

Commanders planned for the maintenance of vehicles and weapons based on the preparation program for combat. Considering the specified work required, commanders blocked off time to carry it out and planned its sequencing. All preparation of equipment for combat was carried out in the motor pools. There, personnel carried out the necessary tasks in the order required: fueling the vehicles, washing them, performing necessary maintenance and repair, performing technical diagnostics, and so on. When preparing vehicles, the maintenance units would set up points to clean filters, test and regulate the pressure and vacuum relief valves on the radiators, check and charge the fire extinguishers, check and adjust the fuel system, perform welding, and check the electric components. The points were laid out to mesh with the tasks being performed around them.

The preparations for combat were completed with a ceremonial inspection [*stroevoy smotr*] at which the regimental commission would check the readiness of armaments and vehicles as specified in the manual. Maintenance of armaments and equipment during combat was the most difficult. Combat experience showed that it was necessary to designate special times for regularly maintaining vehicles during the course of lengthy operations. On the average, this was one day in every 8 to 12 days combat, even when the vehicles were only used to carry spare parts and fluids. The main goal of such maintenance was to prevent the breakdown of armaments and vehicles during long uninterrupted use.

It was difficult to establish a typical work list for comparable maintenance. As a rule, this included fueling the vehicles, carefully checking and adjusting moving assemblies, checking fastenings, checking batteries, and several other adjustments.

As a rule, the volume of work performed during systematic maintenance was comparatively small. This led to the mistaken idea that such maintenance measures were unnecessary. However, this idea only destroyed the systematic accomplishment of work to prevent breakdowns and increased the number of armaments and vehicles out of commission.

For limited operations lasting up to ten days, the problem of conducting necessary maintenance work on armaments and vehicles was less critical and was alleviated by the systematic conduct of separate maintenance work. When soldiers were dismounted to man blocking positions, conduct ambushes, or act independently on foot, this time could be used to maintain the *bronegruppa* at their area of responsibility. Artillery, trucks, and other vehicles were also maintained while they were in firing positions, at command posts, and so on.

A difficult problem was maintaining armaments and vehicles dispersed at multiple strong points along the LOC, pipelines, and other installations. The vehicles at the strong points required systematic recharging of their batteries and other maintenance by assigned specialists and maintenance support systems.

Technical support groups, commanded by technical service officers, were established in units to provide assistance in maintaining weapons and vehicles at the strong points. These groups included specialists from the repair and maintenance subunits. They were supported by the repair and recharging PRZS-70 station and other mobile systems (technical support vehicles, tank-repair workshops, and the like). Periodically, usually once a month, the group would set out on the route and work in turn on the equipment at the units' strong points. The technical support group would usually move between strong points as part of a guarded transport convoy.

Maintaining convoy vehicles hauling material over long distances required a great deal of attention. Usually the major mandatory maintenance tasks were carried out at the transfer bases, depots, route rest stops, and dispatchers' points. TO&E technical support points, consisting of 30 to 36 repair specialists and the mobile PARM-1 repair workshop, were located on the major routes (for example, on the 500-kilometer Khariton-Kabul highway). Every required maintenance check was performed during on-loading and off-loading cargo and further, during the convoys' planned stop at the technical support point.

Following combat, complete maintenance of arms and vehicles was performed in regimental motor pools in accordance with a specially developed layout. There was a list of enumerated services that were entitled "Measures for Returning Armaments and Equipment to Combat Readiness Upon Return to Base Camp." It usually took two to three days to accomplish these measures, which, as a rule, were during designated motor pool days. In the course of events, the full plan to put the armaments and vehicles back into combat readiness was published as a regimental order.

After combat, the initial vehicle servicing included topping off the vehicle with fuel, oil, and engine coolant and unloading, inspecting, and turning in unexpended ammunition. However, in the maintenance period following combat, the Soviets often conducted the full maintenance schedule envisioned in the three-day program for preparing armaments and vehicles before an operation. Thus, the after-operations maintenance had precisely those fundamental elements of the entire system supporting the combat readiness of armaments and vehicles. The Soviets did this since the bulk of combat vehicles, as a rule, were not used again until it was time to prepare for the next operation. But, after the vehicles were maintained, a significant part of the subunits still had to carry out frequent intermittent missions. These vehicles had to be topped off with POL and fluids after their hard use before they could be used again. It was logical to perform the pre-combat maintenance program, especially for these vehicles.

The recovery of weapons and vehicles during combat in Afghanistan was very difficult and was one of the primary ways to replace material combat losses and support force readiness. There are three primary reasons to send armaments and vehicles in for major repairs. These are combat damage, scheduled overhaul after sustained usage, and accidents and breakdowns during use caused by personnel neglect.

During operations in World War II and the subsequent local wars, combat damage was the main reason for overhauling vehicles. For example, during the Great Patriotic War, only an average of 3 to 5 percent of the tanks overhauled were due to technical reasons. This was several times less than the percentage of tanks being repaired due to combat damage. During combat in Afghanistan, the relationship was reversed—the main reason for overhaul was for technical repair (scheduled repair, accidents, and breakdowns). Even during the more active period of Soviet combat (1980–1985), the correlation of technical repair to combat damage repair for various armaments and vehicles was 10–20:1.

This was explained primarily by the very difficult conditions in which the armaments and vehicles were used and also by inadequate personnel training. As a whole, Soviet equipment demonstrated a high reliability, especially as the equipment provided the force was serial production and not specially designed for use under these special conditions. The average daily rate for unserviceable armaments and vehicles was 1 to 2 percent of the overall quantity of material allocated for operations.

The material which was dead-lined for technical reasons required routine repairs involving replacing individual assemblies and several components.

The repair of armaments and vehicles that were dead-lined for combat damage characteristically were less routine. In limited operations that lasted eight to ten days, the group of forces, as a rule, suffered limited casualties. On an average, these losses were four to six armored vehicles, one or two artillery pieces, and two or three trucks. This represented a daily rate of 0.3 to 0.5 percent of the overall armaments and vehicles committed to combat. In one of the large-scale operations that lasted more than three months, the loss to combat damage was 12 to 17 percent, which is a 0.2 percent daily loss rate.

The nature of combat damage was determined by the enemy weapons. The principal armored vehicle combat loss was to mines and blast mines. These created a great deal of damage to the vehicle. More than 50 percent of combat-damaged armored vehicles required capital repair (depot or factory rebuilding) or were not repairable. Losses of trucks and jeeps hit by antitank grenade launchers and small arms fire were somewhat better.

Armaments and equipment dead-lined for scheduled repairs after firing so many rounds or running so many hours or kilometers also had their peculiarities. In order to extend the life of armaments and equipment and to curtail the delivery of new material for several types of vehicles (for example, BMPs and BTRs), the maintenance personnel performed additional unit (intermediate) repairs. Material was sent off for capital repairs only when it was impossible to perform the necessary repairs with in-country personnel and resources. Trucks and jeeps were also not sent off for capital repair if they could be repaired by additional unit repair. Of course, these repairs increased the overall quantity of scheduled intermediate unit repairs.

In the overall scheme of things, routine repairs constituted over 95 percent of repair work. In order to support the combat readiness of units and divisions, commanders organized a large-scale routine repair effort for armaments and equipment at all levels in garrison and the field.

Routine repair at base camps was carried out according to generally accepted rules without any particular exceptions. The primary exceptions to scheduled unit maintenance, particularly intermediate maintenance, were performed at permanent bases, where they did not strictly adhere to the technical norms. Simplified techniques were used to speed up the repair process. This was justified, since it was not necessary to rebuild for long-term reliability and there was a large inventory of parts on hand that allowed technicians to quickly fix the equipment and turn to the next job.

A more essential requirement was the repair and use of armaments and vehicles during combat. Subunits and units participated in operations without their full complement of men and material since part of their force had other responsibilities and some of the equipment was down for routine repair. Therefore, relatively small losses of weapons and armaments could be serious. The main agencies of restoration during combat were temporary formations called repair and evacuation groups (REG) that functioned at all levels and were created during preparation for the operation using the personnel and resources of the maintenance subunits and units.

The lowest level at which an REG was formed was at the motorized rifle company and tank company. Since subunits do not have any technical support or maintenance vehicles, they generated an REG by designating two to three combat vehicles that were included in the combat formation and fulfilled combat missions until it became necessary to perform the mission of technical support. There were tow-bars, spare parts, and oil and water drums on these vehicles. The main mission of the REGs at company level was to tow away unserviceable vehicles or extricate bogged-down vehicles. Besides, these were the first machines assigned to security and defense of the damaged vehicles of the company during restoration or evacuation. Accordingly, the crews of the REG combat vehicles were sufficiently experienced to perform the missions. These combat vehicles were directed by the company technical warrant officer (the deputy company commander for armaments and technical support).

In the REG of the motorized rifle or tank battalion, there was a TO&E technical service squad mounted on a technical support vehicle (MTO). When possible, the battalion REG would include a BTS-4 tank recovery vehicle or—in the REG of a motorized rifle battalion—a tow truck that was capable of towing a BMP or BTR. Sometimes the battalion REG was reinforced with specialists from the regimental repair company. When the REG worked separately from the combat subunit, a BMP or BTR-mounted motorized rifle platoon would provide security and protection. The REG was headed by the deputy battalion commander for technical affairs (or for armaments), to whom all the TO&E and attached elements were subordinated, including the motorized rifle security element. The missions of the battalion REG were to give assistance to crews while conducting technical services, evacuating out-of-commission and mired vehicles, performing routine repairs of armaments and vehicles, and replacing assemblies and components.

The regiments would constitute REGs with the necessary personnel and assets to restore all types of armaments and vehicles participating in the operation. For restoring armored vehicles, the REG included one to two repair squads on TRM-75 tank repair workshop vans. Another squad would handle wheeled vehicles with the MRS repair and fitting workshop van. The MRS-AR artillery repair and fitting workshop van, with its squad, was assigned to the REG to repair artillery. The regimental REG also had two to three tank recovery vehicles and tow-trucks and one or two trucks full of spare parts and POL. The Regimental Deputy Commander for Armaments or the chief of one of the technical services (armored vehicles, wheeled vehicles, artillery systems), or a commander, including an officer of the repair company, might command the regimental REG. When the regimental REG had to work separately from the regiment, it was assigned a motorized rifle platoon mounted on two or three BMPs or BTRs and an ambulance. The REG commander had a command post vehicle with the necessary communications.

The regimental REG was a collection of evacuation and repair vehicles that could work with the combat subunits and also when separated from the force. The regimental REG was assigned missions to provide assistance to crews conducting technical services, evacuating out-of-commission and mired armaments and vehicles, and performing routine repairs.

The divisions would constitute one or two REGs depending on the scale and the size of the combat zone. The division REGs were usually headed by an officer of the repair and restoration battalion. The composition of the division REG was determined by the quantity of vehicles in the operation, the length of the operation, and the distance of the combat zone from the base camp. In any case, the division REG had a pool of personnel and resources for restoring all basic models of armaments and vehicles, destined for combat. Most often the division REG included one or two armored vehicle repair squads for tanks, BMPs and

BTRs, a wheeled vehicle repair squad, an artillery repair squad, electrical equipment repair facilities, oxyacetylene welding equipment, one to two tank recovery vehicles, one to two tow trucks, two to three trucks carrying parts, and POL. Further, the chief of the REG might also command motorized rifle subunits mounted on their TO&E vehicles to provide security as well as an ambulance and, when possible, a command vehicle with necessary communications gear.

Division REGs did not usually travel to the disabled armaments and vehicles. Instead, they brought dead-lined vehicles to their field repair site and, under the cover of the combat subunits, performed routine repair.

During the conduct of major, lengthy operations, Army REGs were constituted that included repair platoons for BMPs, BTRs, wheeled vehicles, and artillery; usually a tank-repair squad; two to three tank recovery vehicles; two or three tow trucks; and one to two trailers and trucks with spare material. Further, the Army repair and restoration units constituted mobile repair brigades, usually for a single type of armament or vehicle, that were located at base camps and, when necessary, would drive to the combat zone or be flown on helicopters.

In this way, the Soviets constituted a system of self-sufficient repair and evacuation elements to support any scale combat at all force levels.

The Soviets devoted maximum attention to supporting the group of forces with military-technical material. While preparing vehicles for combat, all the REGs provided material reserves to support maintenance throughout all the planned phases of the operation.

Crews fastened up to 210 spare track links to every tracked vehicle and carried a spare tire on the wheeled BTR. The designers had not foreseen this need. Further, the majority of tanks and BMPs carried various spare parts, such as road wheels, suspension arms, and torsion bars. The REG parts trucks carried material for the entire force, and the average holding included 4 to 6 percent engines, 2 percent generators, 8 to 10 percent radiators, 3 to 5 percent separate assemblies and components.

During the preparation for large-scale operations, the Soviets established separate depots or supply bases for technical material. These bases were usually sited in those regimental or division permanent depots located closest to the planned combat zone. As a rule, the separate depots or supply bases had wheeled-vehicle transport on which they preloaded material in readiness to supply material to the group of forces. Further, these depots were also equipped to supply technical material by helicopter.

With the start of the movement of forces from their base camps to the combat zone, REGs took their positions in the convoys. Combat vehicles, designated to functions as a company REG, took their place at the tail of the company column. The battalion REG was located next to the combat subunit. The regimental REG was located with the regimental rear services in the convoy. The division

REGs moved in group of forces convoys. Sometimes the regimental REG also had a place in the division convoy along with the division REG. These were used to establish local security and defense and to organize evacuation and repair support over a wide area.

During movement along difficult mountain roads and difficult detours, the REG groups were split up, and REG vehicles, especially towing vehicles, were distributed along the regimental or division convoy in order to quickly clear the road and shorten the time needed to restart convoy movement.

The formation for movement of the REGs varied. Most often, the bulk of the tank recovery vehicles and tow trucks moved at the head of the REG. Then the workshop vans moved, followed by the parts trucks, the ambulance, and then one of the towing vehicles. Combat subunits, which were assigned to the REG for security and defense, brought up the rear of the REG, simultaneously fulfilling the role of the convoy rear guard.

When moving to the combat zone, the various REGs provided technical support. The main mission of technical maintenance was to prevent leaving damaged or broken-down vehicles on the march route. The REGs attempted to repair them in order to prevent their lagging behind the combat subunits when the danger of enemy action was imminent. This was preferred, although the technical support subunits, reinforced with motorized rifle subunits, had the capability of fighting; it was more important to preserve the forces and resources earmarked for future combat.

Soviet maintenance personnel sought to find a compromise between restoring out-of-order vehicles immediately within the march column and exposing them to excessive danger by leaving them behind the march column while they repaired them. In official documents—plans of technical support, orders, notices on technical instructions—the maintenance planners prescribed various technical support work. The planners prescribed the maximum allowable time for remaining in one place to conduct repairs—for example, at regiment it was 15 to 20 minutes and at division it was one hour—but the length of time varied according to the circumstances. Several documents stated the opposite and ordered that there would be no repairs conducted on the route of march. Frequently, the senior commander did not regulate the technical support, supposing that the decision was already made by a group of responsible leaders.

In practice, the technical support provided to moving groups of forces on the march route varied with the situation. Technical support could take more time when there was little direct danger on the march route, when the terrain and situation precluded a surprise attack, and when the section of the march route was not under fire. Often, the column moved slowly and made frequent halts to check the route and remove enemy mines. This also allowed more work time for the repair crews.

In any case, the full complement of technical service vehicles halted for out-of-order vehicles, regardless of the type, while the combat security element deployed in readiness to repulse an attack or prevent shelling.

The first thing the technical support personnel did was talk to the vehicle crew to help determine the reason for the stoppage. The technical support personnel then determined if they could repair the vehicle on site in the time available. When it was impossible to repair an out-of-order vehicle in time, the technical support people would tow it to a nearby site, where it could be guarded and repaired.

Thus, the technical support vehicles, along with the out-of-commission vehicles, entered the combat zone practically with the combat subunits or directly behind them.

In the combat zone, the company REG was co-located with the company. The battalion and regimental REGs were dispersed and deployed, as a rule, in the same region as the command post, rear services, and other regimental subunits that were next to but not participating in the fighting. The Soviets would organize a unified system of security and defense. The length of time that the REG would remain in one location varied, but on the average it was one to three days, during which time the REG could work on restoring vehicles.

In the course of events, the battalion REG was co-located with the *bronegruppa* of its subunits.

The division REGs were also dispersed and deployed in the same region as the command post, rear services, and the division's artillery. On average, the REG would remain at the same site for two to three days working on restoring vehicles.

The REGs established collection points for battle-damaged vehicles (SPPM).[3] When several REGs from various-sized forces co-located in the same region, they established a combined SPPM. Naturally, the SPPM (particularly the regimental SPPM) had a simplified layout, and frequently the collection point was also the repair site for armaments and equipment.

At the SPPM, they restored those vehicles that were towed there by technical maintenance after breaking down during the road march and those vehicle evacuated from the adjacent combat zone. Out-of-commission weapons and equipment were evacuated to the repair site disregarding some principles. For example, the normal principle in evacuating armored vehicles was that the repair and maintenance organization that would repair the vehicle would go forward and evacuate the vehicle to its site to repair it. However, during combat in Afghanistan, the company-level mechanics, led by the company technical warrant officer (deputy to the company commander for armaments), would evacuate their TO&E combat vehicles back to the REG at battalion or regiment when necessary and possible.

Further, sometimes there was out-of-commission equipment in the subunits that was not evacuated back to the SPPM. Rather, when it was expedient and possible, the REG would dispatch a vehicle to tow the disabled vehicle all the way back to the repair brigade while elements of the *bronegruppa* would provide security. They used this option when the vehicle required major repairs that could only be done at the brigade and when time lost towing the disabled vehicle was much shorter than the great deal of time required to evacuate the disabled vehicle to the repair brigade using normal procedures.

In any case, the first priority was to secure the repair and evacuation equipment during all the shifts within the combat zone.

If the command post was displacing and the SPPM had not completely fixed a vehicle, they would take necessary measures to ensure that the entire REG and all the damaged vehicles accompanied the command post and other subunits during the displacement. Only when there was an accumulation of damaged vehicles and it was impossible to evacuate the majority of these assembled vehicles would the REG remain behind to complete repair work. Then it was necessary to assign a security element consisting of a motorized rifle platoon up to a motorized rifle company to the REG. In this case, the security element would establish a separate system of observation, warning, security, and defense.

Technical support at the conclusion of combat and return to base camp was accomplished in the same fashion as the advance to the combat zone. In this case, the main mission of technical support was to clean up the combat zone and the return route. It was essential to evacuate everything, including all the damaged vehicles to their base camp or, at least, to the nearest garrison or strong point.

There were specific characteristics involved in repairing wheeled vehicles in a supply convoy. [Supply convoys, composed mostly of trucks and wheeled vehicles and traveling on cleared routes, moved much faster than combat convoys with a high number of tracked vehicles.] Experience showed that it was practically impossible to repair supply convoy vehicles on the route of march. Depending on mountain routes, the speed of the column, and the transport interval, the repair element would quickly lag behind while repairing the disabled vehicle. In a short time their separation from the main body would become unacceptably great. When a large convoy was transporting a great deal of material, it was impossible to protect all the repair groups stopped on the march route.

Therefore, the primary task of the technical support element in a supply convoy was to evacuate the wheeled vehicles to the closest garrison, point of technical assistance, or strong point. Every convoy included a wheeled vehicle repair and evacuation group consisting of one tow truck for every 20 to 30 trucks and two to three trucks carrying vehicle parts, POL, water, and brake fluid. Shop vans with specialist mechanics were not usually included in the REG. All of the out-of-order vehicles were evacuated by the REG, and if there was a shortage of tow vehicles, other trucks in the convoy would also tow broken-down vehicles. Repairs were done at the technical assistance points and at the regimental base camps where the convoys formed.

As a rule, the Soviets used a system of multi-functional technical support groups to repair vehicles at strong points located on the LOCs. The strong points (garrisoned with small subunits) were distributed systematically along the march route. The support groups included repair facilities, repair personnel, and spare parts. Sometimes, they formed special repair and evacuation groups that worked sequentially in the strong points along the march route.

Command of technical support was a component part of the overall command of the forces. The principal commander was the combat commander, who determined the substance of technical support measures and the order in which they would be accomplished.

Periodically the 40th Army commander and the commanders at other levels would issue orders concerning the organization of technical support for a planned period of time—usually a month. The orders would specify the main missions of technical support; establish the amount of required support for weapons and material; specify the amount of personnel technical training and the sequence of its conduct; stipulate the ammunition reserves; outline the general order of supply during preparation for combat; direct missions for repairing armaments and material; establish guidelines providing security and defense of technical support elements; and organize the technical support command. These orders established the basis for organizing technical support for the planned period of time.

Periodically, when necessary, the senior commanders would also issue refined plans of technical support for all force levels down to regiment for a given period of time (usually a month), as well as plans for technical support of specific operations.

As regulating documents were issued, either orders or instructions for technical support for the planned period of time and for specific combat actions were also issued.

Technical support combat documents were written in the generally accepted format but were often simplified. Indeed, in Afghanistan's difficult environs, it was not always possible or necessary to predetermine the exact site and time of deployment for combat, nor was it possible to predetermine the movement and deployment of the technical support elements or the amount of work required. Tight, timely plans and orders regulated the actions of the repair and evacuation elements and, during unforeseen circumstances, the likely circumstances that will initiate combat. In many operations, particularly limited operations, the Soviets used unconventional ways to move and protect their vehicles, such as incorporating them into a *bronnegruppa* or transferring vehicles to a safer area. Within the combat zone, the Soviets created specific methods and solutions to the technical support mission. These demanded creative application under varying circumstances and were not a part of formal regulations.

An operations group directed combat of a group of forces participating in an operation. The operations group included a deputy director of combat for armaments. Among the assistants were the chief of technical services and other technical support officers from assigned TO&E headquarters or, simply, the deputy commander for armaments.

During combat, technical support decisions were made in the operations group main command post. The operations group rear area command post was practically never set up.[4] The Soviets combined the deployed command post with the support subunits command posts and the non-TO&E subunit command posts.

Further, the Soviets did not establish the usual separate technical support radio network. Technical support traffic was broadcast entirely over the command net.

The Soviets also did not establish their usual points of technical observation (PTN) at battalion and company level. The PTN main mission was to gather basic information about the technical status of vehicles involved in combat. In conventional warfare, as a rule, PTN were located directly within the combat formations of their subunits at a distance, from where they could constantly support the effort with their communications. In combat in Afghanistan, the primary maintenance supervisors—the deputy battalion commander for technical services, the deputy battalion commander for armaments, and the technical company commander—actually performed the work of the PTN while carrying out their own duties from the area where the *bronnegruppa* was usually located. They were able to assemble the necessary information about the condition of their vehicles at this spot. The deputy battalion commander for technical services (and for armaments) was located in the regimental command post and received his information about the condition of vehicles over the commander's radio. In any event, the Soviets never set up a conventional PTN in Afghanistan. It was practically impossible for a regular PTN to carry out its independent tasks because of the threat of destruction.

Combat in Afghanistan upheld the fundamental Soviet principles for organizing technical support. However, there were important unique features involved in implementing these principles. Particularly valuable was the Soviet experience gained while supporting independent actions by the group of forces. The Soviet system of echeloned reserves of ammunition, beginning with the individual soldier and every combat vehicle, deserves special attention. Also instructional was the on-site construction of mountings and racks on combat vehicles to accommodate additional reserves of ammunition, water, and oil. In the course of combat, the significance of independent actions grew. These actions resulted in the conversion of TO&E repair and evacuation elements into temporary repair and evacuation groups that could act simultaneously over great distances. During the war, system flexibility grew in the area of maintaining and preserving armaments and material at an acceptable standard. When the enemy began targeting technical support elements, it became apparent that their survivability had to be enhanced. Therefore, the security and defense of technical support became one of the major concerns of the combined arms commander.

Editors' comments: There is an old U.S. army saying: "Amateurs talk tactics and professionals talk logistics." Put another way: "Tactics is the art of the probable, while logistics is the art of the possible." That said, most military histories deal with the exciting life and death struggle typified by tactical combat, but ignore the broader, essential topic of how the struggle was sustained. This chapter addresses the not-so-glorious, yet essential, topics of maintaining the equipment of the Soviet 40th Army while supplying it, housing it, paying it, providing exchange services for it, and saving the lives of its soldiers.

The Soviet 40th Army lacked sufficient maintenance personnel and facilities during the entire war. Not all damaged vehicles could be repaired in Afghanistan. Vehicles returned to the Soviet Union for depot overhaul and rebuild were frequently not returned—and, if they were, they were usually stripped of usable parts en route. As a result, Soviet technical support procedures were discarded, while local commanders ordered their technical support people to perform officially unauthorized repairs, to cannibalize vehicles for parts, and to take extraordinary, and frequently unsafe, measures to keep the vehicles running and weapons firing. Commanders attempted to conserve the use of vehicles until they were needed and to maintain more "spare" vehicles than authorized. The 40th Army had a Material Support Brigade and separate tank, motor vehicle, and artillery repair battalions to help with the technical support mission. Still, the technical services were hard pressed to keep the 40th Army moving and that they did as well as they did is a credit to their technical support personnel.

The 40th Army's constitution of repair and evacuation groups throughout its force is an example of how the Soviets adapted to their battleground. The Soviet Army in Europe was poised for offensive operations, and the assumption was that damaged vehicles would be located behind the advancing Soviet force. Security of the vehicle was not a problem and eventually an evacuation vehicle would tow the damaged vehicle to a repair facility or railhead where it would be shipped for repairs. In Afghanistan, a damaged vehicle was a liability that had to be protected until it could be evacuated. This put a lot of pressure on commanders to get the vehicle fixed rapidly or to tow the damaged vehicle along with the rest of the march column until it could be fixed. These temporary maintenance groups were the field solution.

This section begins its discussion of equipment maintenance with a discussion of ammunition support. This strikes a Western military man as unusual since this is a supply issue in Western armies. In the Soviet Army, the chiefs of tank, artillery, and motor vehicle maintenance were responsible for ordering unit ammunition by type and amount. Once the ammunition arrived, the supply personnel became responsible for the storage and delivery of the ammunition. Inclusion of ammunition support in this section is perfectly logical—from a Soviet perspective.

LOGISTICS SUPPORT

The LCOSF arrived in Afghanistan accompanied by a great deal of physical and morale-support baggage. To a great extent, the combat readiness and combat capability of divisions, units, and subunits depended on the quality of their logistics support, which included supply, contracting for local services, billeting, and financial support of the force.

The primary mission of supply was to furnish the force with sufficient POL, food, military clothing, and sundries to meet its demands. The TO&E divisions, units, and subunits had their own logistics organizations to carry out these tasks. In the division, there was a logistics battalion, in the regiment was a logistics company, and in battalions and batteries there was a separate material support platoon. There were various types of specialized logistics vehicles in these logistics elements.

Carrying out the supply mission required the transport of a large quantity of various material that was hauled out from the regimental and battalion base camps directly to the combat zone. The average daily amount of material that they hauled was some 2,000 to 3,000 tons, of which 60 to 65 percent was POL, 7 percent was ammunition, 20 percent was food, and 8 to 13 percent was other cargo.

The transport of consumable cargo was accomplished in stages. The cargo was moved from throughout the USSR on railroad and barges to the transfer bases at Termez and Kushka. From there, the cargo was moved on trucks to the army bases at Shindand and Kabul and then on to division and regimental depots. An insignificant part of perishable goods (5 to 8 percent) was flown on military transport aircraft directly to the forces. Thus truck transport played a major role in supplying the forces by transporting 75 to 80 percent of the cargo, excepting aviation and diesel fuel. The latter were transported by two dual main pipelines that paralleled the road Khairaton–Puli-Khumri–Bagram and the road Turagondi-Shindand. On each route, one pipeline was continually transporting aviation fuel and the other, diesel.

Truck transport experience shows that the best results were achieved by transporting goods with a truck transport company for some 200 to 250 kilometers. The weakest link in the transportation process was loading and unloading cargo, especially ammunition. Loading and unloading took up to 80 percent of the time involved in the trip. Loading and unloading was primarily done by hand.

The logisticians established a centralized directorate to coordinate the receipt and dispatch of freight and to schedule truck convoys. The centralized logistics system included a centralized dispatcher point, combat command and control centers, operations groups, and dispatcher points at division and regiment. Every day up to 600 soldiers, 90 BTRs, 20 helicopters, and 140 air-defense guns conducted convoy escort and security duty. One armored vehicle was assigned for every 10 to 15 trucks. This material support organization was unusual for the Soviet army and demanded special forethought when formulating specific missions.

The battalion commander prepared his material support platoon for combat using the regimental support plan. When possible, this plan was delivered to the subunits in plenty of time. The deputy battalion commander for logistics was responsible for logistics support of the battalion. The material support platoon was subordinate to him. This platoon, as a rule, was housed together in buildings or tents. Their logistics vehicles (special trucks, tanker trucks, and mobile kitchens) were kept in the motor pool under the open sky. The battalion's material reserves were kept uploaded on the trucks and combat vehicles and seldom were downloaded into tents or caves. In order to avoid Mujahideen small arms fire, motor pools were located carefully. Gently sloping heights or mountain plateaus with the slope on the downwind side located some one-and-a-half to two kilometers from the nearest mountain were preferred.

The logistics element prepared for a planned mission at the base camp simultaneously with the combat subunits. As a rule, this preparation period lasted for 10 to 12 days and concluded with a full-field layout inspection some one or two days before the action. During this period, they brought the logistics subunits up to strength in personnel, transport, equipment, clothing, POL, and other material. They stowed cargo on trucks; conducted combat, specialist, and political training; conducted equipment maintenance; and repaired wheeled vehicles and other equipment and specialized kit. The amount of time and the order in which the work was carried out always depended on the battalion's combat mission, the condition of the logistics subunits, the time available for preparation, the peculiarities of the terrain, and the season of the year.

The battalion commander specified measures to prepare the rear services, and these were supervised by his deputy commander for logistics and conducted by the commanders of the subunits.

The logistics support mission was announced to the logistics personnel in the detail and to the extent that they needed to know. The logistics personnel took part in special mountain training along with the rest of the personnel.

The material support battalion provided timely and complete support of everything necessary for combat and survival to the subunits and individual soldier. The battalion's primary mission was to support the successful conduct of combat and mission accomplishment under any circumstances.

In order to provide uninterrupted combat support, the battalion established increased stocks of material by constantly replenishing them with deliveries from the depot of the senior commander. The supplies were cross-leveled so that three to five days of dry rations or two to two-and-a-half combat loads of ammunition were carried on the combat vehicles. The transport battalion carried seven days of rations, one combat load of ammunition, two refuelings of POL, and also a reserve of three to five days of dried biscuit or fresh bread.

The combat rifleman carried eight loaded assault rifle magazines and up to

1,000 rounds of ammunition, four hand grenades (two F-1, two RG-5), four signal rockets, two days of dry rations, two canteens full of water (2.5 liters), an individual first aid kit, 20 tablets of pantacide for treating water, a great coat or short jacket, and a small spade. The overall weight of this kit approached 32 to 33 kilograms [70.5 to 72.75 pounds].

The senior commander reinforced the battalion logistics effort with truck transport, refueling equipment, and delivery vehicles in order to haul and deploy all these supplies.

Because of the vulnerability of trucks loaded with ammunition, the first step was to load the extra ammunition on the weapons' systems themselves (store it on tanks, BMPs, and BTRs). Practice showed that a BMP could carry up to 2.5 combat units of boxed cartridges and one combat load of hand grenades or one 82mm mortar with crew and two combat loads of mortar rounds in crates. Further, a significant amount of ammunition and gear was carried on the outside of the combat vehicles in order not to limit the use of the vehicle's weapons or those of the passengers.

Special attention was paid to securing the subunit's water. All the canteens and vehicle water containers were filled with water, including one 20-liter cannister and a ten-liter drink barrel on every squad vehicle and a 12-liter platoon insulated food container per platoon. The company carried 1,500 liters in its kitchen cauldrons, food barrels, and RDV reservoirs.[5] The battalion has a 3,000 liter water trailer. This was one-and-a-half to two days' normal supply, according to the regulations.

Additional reserves increased the reliability of logistics resupply and supported independent combat for five to ten days in the event that the regular delivery of supplies to the battalion from the senior commander's depot was disrupted.

The battalion's material support platoon had a squad that received, stored, and distributed POL at the battalion refueling point using its tanker truck. Fuel and lubricants were delivered to the battalion from the depot of the senior commander on the ARAL 375 truck with its 4.5 ton fuel tank. POL was pumped into metal drum containers and sent to the companies for refueling the vehicles. Fuel transported to the battalion was stored in tank trucks and used when necessary.

Supplying the subunits with food had its own peculiarities. The wide fluctuation in temperature and the hot climate made it difficult to transport and store food. This meant that it was necessary to supply the subunits with canned goods and food concentrates. On the other hand, the difficult climate and the psychological pressure of combat meant that the personnel required fresh food.

The battalion logistics personnel sought to establish a reserve of food that was high in calories and easy to digest. The flour was enriched with vitamins that would improve general health. Due to the lack of iodine in the water, the troops were occasionally fed ocean fish, and their potatoes and groats were prepared with iodized salt. The first, second, and third courses of a meal were usually canned, as was the groat-based food concentrate. This use of canned food saved time and limited the amount of fuel needed to heat the meal—especially since the soldiers did not have to boil the groats on site for a long time.

Personnel who were on detached duty from their subunit were issued a prepared daily mountain summer or mountain winter food ration. These rations were high in calories and easy to digest (a can of meat or mixed meat and vegetables, canned fruit with groats, and another can of meat with vegetables), fruit and berry juice, sweetened condensed milk, vitamin-enriched caramel, and a sour lemonade drink.

Further, groups and crews detached from the battalion main body were supplied with the KN-10 portable squad stove to fix hot food. The KN-10 consisted of a trivet, two cooking pans, a pressurized heating unit, and cooking utensils. This was all stored in its own pouch with straps. It could easily be carried in a rucksack and could be used to fix a meal for ten men in 30 to 40 minutes.

Back in base camp, the battalion personnel were fed hot food prepared with the KP-130 mobile field kitchen. The battalion in garrison seldom cooked on its garrison stoves, preferring to use the mobile field kitchen. The cooks used the KI-50 insulated containers to preserve perishable food.

The continually changing uniform and individual field equipment requirements for officers, sergeants, and soldiers complicated supply actions. At the start of the war, officer casualties were higher because they wore a distinctive uniform. Therefore, all the personnel were supplied with an identical uniform and rank insignia was subdued. The exchange of clothing, the issue of additional clothing, and the higher rate of wear on clothing in the mountains complicated clothing supply. Until the end of the war, there was an issue point for special cold-weather clothing (rain capes, sweaters, felt boots, quilted jackets) for high-altitude conditions. Mountain boots needed to be lightweight and durable and to provide protection to the ankles, but the Soviets were never able to design and issue an acceptable mountain boot. The great fluctuation in temperature between night and day, particularly in the mountains, required a supply of warm clothing, even in the summer (sleeping bags, warm-up jackets and trousers, sweaters, and caps that fit under helmets). Further, each soldier was issued 50 percent more clothing than was authorized back in the Soviet Union.

In order to quickly exchange unserviceable clothing at battalion level, supply personnel established a supplementary battalion reserve of clothing, boots, and equipment, as well as a reserve of bed linen. This reserve was equal to 10 to 12 percent of the subunit strength. However, this often proved insufficient, since in the mountains the wear and tear on clothing and boots was much higher than under ordinary circumstances.

In the course of combat, the battalion support platoon was situated and moved in order to supply the motorized rifle companies, mortar battery, and separate platoons in accordance with the battalion commander's concept. The battalion chief of staff and the deputy battalion commander for logistics directly coordinated the deployment of the support platoon in the convoy.

Combat experience showed that the movement of the battalion to the combat zone should usually take place at night in order to occupy the assembly area by dawn. During the movement out of base camp to the combat zone, the battalion support platoon followed at the trail end of the battalion march column. As a rule, a motorized rifle platoon provided security at the column trail end and were mounted on combat vehicles distributed through the entire convoy rear.

When the battalion halted, they topped off the vehicles using attached and TO&E equipment and fuel drums and cans. They fed personnel hot food or dry rations (dry rations consisted of 200 grams of rusks, 250 grams of canned meat, 250 grams of canned fish, 30 grams of sugar, and four grams of fruit extract per person).

After the final halt, the battalion logistics element joined the main body of the battalion and moved to the designated region, protected by the rear security detachment. Depending on the terrain, battalion logistics were usually located close to the battalion command post and helicopter landing pad. They were located further away from the CP during the battalion advance, the reconstruction of a road or bridge, or the cleaning up of a rock slide. During ambush missions, the bulk of the material support personnel were located with the subunits. They established a small reserve of ammunition, food, and water for the subunit participating in the ambush.

The timely supply of material was particularly important and was one of the main logistics missions during combat. During combat in mountain-desert terrain, the normal supply procedure from regiment to battalion to the company to the soldier was seldom used. As a rule, the senior commander moved material reserves close to the subunits. Considering the threat of Mujahideen attack on individual vehicles and small convoys, the primary resupply of material was to the companies, using truck convoys, which were protected by motorized rifle subunits mounted on BMPs and BTRs. Helicopters, which were in radio communication with the convoy commander, conducted reconnaissance and supported the combat of the security subunit.

Experience showed that logistics officers had to plan and conduct tactically sound actions to defeat the attacks of diversionary groups on the march route and had to fight using the personnel attached to protect the transport.

The company commander or separate platoon leader verbally requested replenishment of expended material. The battalion commander or chief of staff approved resupply and dispatched the supplies on battalion transport to the subunits. Often, supplies were carried on subunit armored vehicles that were dispatched to the battalion rear to pick up the supplies. Most often, BMPs and BTRs transported supplies, since they were better protected from enemy fire than trucks. Resupply was usually conducted during daylight.

In difficult terrain, material was delivered to the battalion and company using the Mi-6 and Mi-8 helicopters. These would land on site or drop cargo from a height of 5 to 30 meters at a speed of 20 to 70 kilometers per hour (12 to 43 miles per hour). The cargo that was dropped was well-packed in boxes in which rags or sand took up one-fourth of the space. They also used a heavy-duty supply container that was designed for airborne drops and equipped with shock absorbers. Small-arms ammunition and dry rations were dropped in their original containers that were reinforced with metal banding. Due to the peculiarities of high mountains, helicopters delivered material in the morning hours between 0500 and 1000 hours. The overall weight of the cargo dropped in the rarified air did not exceed 400 kilograms (882 pounds).

As a rule, it was impossible to resupply subunits conducting ambushes. Therefore, particular attention was paid to outfitting the personnel of the ambush party. For example, a motorized rifle platoon with three squads could be reinforced with a Kalashnikov medium machine gun crew, an AGS-17 automatic grenade launcher crew, and am 82mm "Tray" mortar. In addition to their TO&E weapons and ammunition, they had five to eight radios plus spare batteries, up to 30 mines of various types, several dozen water containers, and other material. As a result, every combatant, as well as the commander, had to carry 25 to 40 kilograms (55 to 88 pounds) of assorted kit.

Thus, in December 1984, when an airborne platoon conducted an ambush in Helmand Province, they carried three units of fire and ten days' worth of food and water. The average weight that each soldier carried approached 40 kilograms (88 pounds). The unit flew to the ambush area on helicopters. They landed six kilometers from their ambush site. The paratroopers were fed in the morning after they pulled back from the ambush site and in the evening before they returned to the ambush site. Each man received one liter of water every 24 hours. They continued this routine for four days until the enemy convoy arrived and they destroyed it.[6]

In several instances, when the ambush was planned for a single night's duration, they would not take extra rations along. Thus, when a reconnaissance group conducted an ambush in Kandahar Province in July 1982, they carried two units of fire for every weapon and three days' worth of food and water. As a result, the load carried by each man was reduced to 20 to 25 kilograms (44 to 55 pounds).

Considering the difficulty involved in resupplying tactical air assaults, each air assault carried enough supplies for five to six days of combat.

Air assault combat experience showed that the quantity of ammunition and food carried by the personnel depended on the length of the anticipated mission. The more-experienced soldiers always preferred to carry only high-calorie foods (evaporated milk, dried fruit, sugar, and canned meat), exchanging the canned meat mixed with oatmeal for extra ammunition. And this, as a rule, saved them in those instances when carefully planned actions did not go according to the plan.

Thus in October 1985, the Soviets discovered a Mujahideen base southwest of Kandahar and developed an operation to destroy it. In the course of this operation, an air assault company landed behind Mujahideen lines on the morning of 13 October and was locked in a fierce fire fight all day long. The advancing Soviet main force was not able to link up with the company by nightfall. The situation was further complicated by the fact that the air assault force ran out of ammunition. All attempts to resupply them with ammunition by helicopter failed. The situation became critical that night. The air assault force conducted a night maneuver and attack that enabled them to seize the Mujahideen base. They were then able to use captured enemy weapons and ammunition to stabilize the situation. If this had not happened, the entire air assault force might have been killed because of the lack of ammunition.[7]

Block and sweep missions of areas of terrain or villages required logistics support for a shorter period of time. The logisticians would provide additional supplies for vehicles and weapons. Thus in March 1982, an airborne battalion was prepared to search the village of Sher Khan Kheyl' in Parwan Province. The combatants were carrying three units of fire and had two more stored on their armored vehicles. They had three days' rations. This additional material was carried despite the fact that the operation was planned to last one day. Military experience showed that such a logistics reserve was more than adequate.[8]

Hot meals in the combat zone were provided by the ration supply point located near the battalion command post. When it was not possible to provide hot meals, the subunit commander ordered his troops to open their dry rations. This switching back and forth between regular meals and dry rations was acceptable for normal subunit activity over a period of three to five days.

It was far more difficult providing material support to forces operating apart from the main body for an extended period of time. For example, in August 1987, an airborne reconnaissance company flew in on helicopters to establish a blocking position as part of a large-scale operation. The blocking position prevented the withdrawal of a large Mujahideen force through a mountain pass. They maintained the blocking position for 18 days. Helicopters supplied the subunit with ammunition and food once every three days. The helicopters dropped supplies from four to six meters elevation. Dry rations and ammunition were dropped in their original containers. Water was dropped in hermetically sealed containers and chemical boots that were filled to two-thirds capacity and thoroughly braced. Cooking and warming fires were not permitted, in order not to disclose the subunit's position. Therefore, the soldiers ate cold rations for the entire course of the operation. According to participants, after five to seven days, they all developed stomach cramps from the dry rations, and after eight to ten days, they developed bleeding gums due to vitamin deficiency.

A more common problem was supplying security detachments and outposts. They were periodically supplied with necessary material by truck convoy or, when necessary, helicopter.

The outposts received ammunition, food, and water sufficient for three to seven days' combat. This amounted to four or five units of fire and three to seven days rations. The outpost cooked their hot meals on the MK-13 or MK-30 portable stoves. Hot food was served regularly and had sufficient calories. This significantly lessened the incidents of sickness.

Supplying subunits conducting long-distance truck convoys or escorting them was a significant supply problem. The convoys carried two-and-a-half to three units of fire and sufficient rations for an uninterrupted round trip. However, when the convoy drove to pick up supplies from the stores of its senior commander, then they only carried rations for a one-way trip since they would receive enough for the return trip at the stores. The truck drivers and security personnel usually had a hot meal during the evening break. During the day, the personnel consumed dry rations.

In this fashion, the LCOSF fighting in Afghanistan solved many of the most serious supply problems. However, a significant portion of them remain unresolved.

The necessity of reinforcing subunits with various weapons (mortars, AGS-17 automatic grenade launchers, PK machine guns, and grenade launchers) to increase their fire power when advancing along isolated axes required that the logistics elements provide the subunits with a large assortment and quantity of additional ammunition. Intensified combat raised ammunition expenditure and led to additional logistics cargo. This in turn led to an increase in the amount of assigned transport of the material support platoon and demonstrated the need for armored transport to deliver ammunition and evacuate the wounded. This issue has not been resolved. Combat showed that it was wise to prepare company "ready to go" kits in advance. These kits contained required supplies for a company (by type and assortment), had their paperwork done in advance, and were kept in the battalion rear.

A more serious shortcoming was supplying personnel with issue kit and equipment. In order to minimize officer casualties, all military personnel were issued the same field uniform. However, the "Afghan" uniform was not up to the demands of mountainous terrain. It offered little protection against the wind, absorbed moisture readily, and was easily torn.

Footwear was a special problem. Field boots with synthetic tops would wear out in a month of walking around the rocks. The soles were very slippery and the boot laces would not keep out sand and small stones. Further, these boots are very heavy and do not protect the ankles from injury or sprain.

Therefore, the soldiers preferred Czechoslovakian mountain boots (sent to supply the Afghan Army) or track shoes, sneakers, or gym shoes. The preferred combat uniform was combat overalls and overjacket. This was the normal field dress for the reconnaissance subunits and airborne and air assault forces. The "Afghan" uniform head gear was not completely satisfactory due to its short visor. Sunglasses were only issued to officers and only one pair every two years. This was clearly insufficient. The quilted sleeping bag was very cumbersome, was far from waterproof, and was hard to zip up. The Soviet soldiers preferred a Pakistani down-filled sleeping bag with "velcro" fasteners and viewed these as a very rare and desirable war trophy.

The issue ammunition pouches for rifle magazines and grenades were not comfortable when firing from the prone position and did not offer any protection to the vital organs when standing. Combat experience led commanders to have their companies make canvas ammunition vests. These vests would carry eight AKM magazines and four grenades. These vests covered the thorax and part of the abdominal cavity and protected the combatant from fragments and spent bullets. Full magazines could readily be extracted and empty magazines easily stored in these vests. However, the authorities never produced such vests.

There were major problems with individual pieces of military gear. Flak jackets were very heavy and uncomfortable and provided poor protection against fragments and bullets. Kit bags were uncomfortable to carry and had very little carrying capacity. The handle of the entrenching tool limited soldiers' mobility inside armored vehicles.

Food services also needed improvement. First of all, it was difficult to deliver perishable food and vegetables to the garrisons. Then there was the problem of regularly supplying hot meals to subunits fulfilling independent missions separate from the main force.

The soldiers did not have a way to heat up their dry rations. There was a limited assortment of dry rations (two cans of mixed meat and vegetables and one can of pâté), which did not have sufficient calories and were not vitamin-enriched. Finally, Soviet industry developed the "mountain summer" and "mountain winter" dry rations that came closer to meeting the requirements of the combat force. However, the soldiers still did not receive their required daily dosage of vitamins. Besides, as practice shows, soldiers find that a limited selection of canned foods are difficult to eat constantly in a hot climate. The soldiers quickly become accustomed to the selection and then they become sick of them. The limited selection included stewed pork in a 400 gram (.88 pound) can and a two kilogram (4.41 pounds) borscht concentrate. The soldiers often added local fruit, vegetables, and fresh meat (mutton or chicken) to the borscht concentrate.

The optimum canned ration for combat weighs 50 or 100 grams (1.75 to 3.5 ounces). Further, there should be a wide-enough assortment of canned foods so that the soldier will not get the same meal more than once every three days.

A pantocide water-purification tablet would purify a liter of water in thirty minutes, but thirsty soldiers did not observe this time constraint. It was necessary to have a faster-acting agent that the soldiers could use. Combat showed that resupply was often possible only by throwing material out of a helicopter. However, specialized shock-absorbing packaging for ammunition, food, and water was in very short supply. Therefore, a critical continuing problem was the optimum design for a container for transporting and dropping material from a hovering or passing aircraft.

Combat in Afghanistan put personnel under a great deal of moral and psychological pressure that often led to stress. The logistics system did not foresee this. There was not a drop of alcohol issued to the forces—neither vodka nor even beer (which is not forbidden in the other armies of the world). Vodka could be bought in Afghan stores. Also, alcohol was illegally brought in by helicopter pilots and then by logistics convoy personnel who sold it to personnel in combat subunits for 50 *checks* a bottle.[9] Some of the vodka was genuine while other vodka was moonshine. This alcohol smuggling attacked discipline and dissipated personnel. Further, soldiers began brewing and distilling alcohol in base camp, which led to a further deterioration of discipline and disturbed the life of the garrison.

Editors' comments: The Soviet system of support was a "push" system. It was the responsibility of the higher commander to keep his subordinates supplied. This is in contrast to the U.S. system in which the commander who is running low on material requests it from his commander. Since the Soviets had a "push" system, they maintained the bulk of transportation at the higher command levels. Ammunition and POL were priority supply items. The supply planning norms for war in Europe forecast that 40 percent of the weight carried daily would be ammunition and 40 percent would be POL. Instead, 40th Army figures showed that 60 to 65 percent of the daily weight carried was POL and only 7 percent was ammunition. This demonstrated that there was a lot less actual shooting in Afghanistan than was planned for in a general war in Europe.

The Soviet 40th Army lacked sufficient logistics personnel and transport throughout the entire war. Theft complicated the supply activities. Soldiers traded uniforms, parts, ammunition, and even weapons with the Afghans in order to get money to buy food, goods, alcohol, and narcotics. Often, the rear echelon soldiers were well supplied, but the combat soldiers in the far-flung outposts were poorly supported. Soviet soldiers lived poorly in contrast to their Western counterparts. In the Soviet Union, soldiers frequently had only one field uniform, which they wore constantly. When they washed it, they wore it damp the next day. The Soviets increased the clothing issue for Afghanistan, but it was still sparse by Western standards.

Every army gripes about its chow, but the Soviet army had good cause. The combat ration did not provide sufficient calories and vitamins, there was little variety in the combat ration or regular meal, and soldiers seldom received enough food. To the Soviet army's credit, its commanders made every effort to feed at least one daily hot meal to its forces in combat.

The 40th Army's equipment was designed for a war in northern Europe or northern China. Therefore, much of it failed to perform optimally in Afghanistan. Uniforms, footwear, load-bearing equipment, rucksacks, sleeping bags, and other personal equipment was not up to the demands of Afghanistan's rugged climate and terrain. This chapter is unusually candid about the equipment shortcomings.

Vodka and narcotics were a problem. Although both were readily available, their price was beyond the reach of most soldiers and widespread theft of government property increased so that soldiers could obtain these stress-relieving substances. During World War II, Red Army soldiers were issued a 100 grams [3.5 ounces] of vodka per day, with an increased issue before battle. This was a significant amount of spirits that created many alcoholics among the veteran survivors, but it provided a degree of stress relief to the Soviet soldiers. The total prohibition on vodka in Afghanistan merely drove it underground and encouraged experimentation with narcotics. The alcohol and narcotics trade created serious morale and discipline problems within the 40th Army and followed many Afghanistan veterans home.

POST EXCHANGE (PX), HOUSING, AND PAY

A network of post exchange [*voyentorg*] shops was established in division and regimental garrisons to satisfy the personnel demands for several types of articles and food. There were no PX facilities at the small detachments and remote sites. However, the soldiers who served there could order and receive a minimum amount of goods when the frequent supply columns brought them food and ammunition. The division and regimental headquarters personnel, as well as the women who had volunteered for Afghanistan service, were better served by the PX. The privates and soldiers, due to their constrained circumstances, could only buy candy and lemonade. There were several people who sold illegal spirits, primarily vodka, in every base camp. As a rule these were women, who were non-combatant warrant officers and officers. Officers (platoon leaders and company commanders) and soldiers who served in far-flung security detachments and outposts were given the opportunity to buy a Japanese-manufactured tape recorder or radio and a West German track suit when they were preparing to return to the Soviet Union.

Despite the attempts of the command and "the people's control" to regulate the sale of goods from the PX, a significant portion of goods ended up in the Afghan shops where they were sold to the people and Soviet soldiers at a significantly higher price.[10] The leadership was unable to establish a "relatively equitable" distribution of goods in the PX shops in the command.

The PX system was not prepared to carry out its mission in Afghanistan and failed to adequately support the soldiers' needs. The PX situation created unhealthy relations within the military collective and this had a significant impact on the quality of combat missions.

The housing service was created to provide the minimum necessary billets for permanent party and temporary duty personnel in divisions and regiments. Housing was part of the mission of the deputy commander for rear services, but most of the housing was built by the soldiers themselves.

In base camps, unit and battalion officers were billeted in prefabricated modular housing and the soldiers in tents of various sizes. Officers lived in four to eight man rooms. Practically all the quarters lacked air conditioning. Soldiers, warrant officers, and company-grade officers lived in tents. In winter, the tents were heated with oil or coal-burning stoves. Occasionally the soldiers built regular barracks and billets with material from the Soviet Union.

At the security detachments and outposts, the first shelters constructed were trenches and bunkers. Minefields were placed on the approaches to the positions. Then they started to construct some kind of shelter using cement, boards, beams, nails, and wire. Almost all of this construction material was scrounged, bartered for, or purchased by the security post personnel. Only a very small portion was furnished by the rear services commander. Wherever possible, the living area, dining area, and store rooms for ammunition, food, and POL were underground. In those security posts located on rocky soil, the personnel built these shelters out of rock held together with cement. When the detachment or post was moved, they would salvage and move all the construction material that they could to reuse at the new security site. These sites were very uncomfortable and limited the combat actions of Soviet forces in Afghanistan.

Financial support of the soldiers was inadequate. Soldiers received allowances and pay. All soldiers received an allowance that was based on their rank and position.

Pay was divided into two parts. The portion received in Afghanistan was paid in government scrip or *checks*. The portion of their pay that was in rubles was deposited and held for the officers and soldiers in accounts in the Soviet Union. The amount of this pay was very insignificant. Senior officers received 300 to 350 *checks* a month, junior officers received 230 to 275 *checks* a month, warrant officers received 230 to 260 *checks* a month, while sergeants and privates received 8 to 18 *checks* a month depending on their duties. In the last years of the war, personnel leaving the service after Afghanistan were each paid an additional 100 rubles mustering out allowance.

Thus, in two years of continuous service in Afghanistan, a junior officer (platoon leader or company commander) might be able to horde 5,000 *checks,* while a senior officer might be able to horde 7,000 *checks*. This was not enough to buy an inexpensive automobile like the Zhiguli. When a soldier or sergeant mustered out, he might be lucky enough to buy a pair of blue jeans.

It is true that there were other "sources of income." Soldiers received a one-time payment for being wounded. These payments were ludicrously small. A soldier would receive a month's pay for a light wound, two months' pay for a more serious wound, and three months' pay for a serious wound. Thus, if our junior officer wanted to buy a car when he returned home from Afghanistan, he also had to be wounded seriously five times. Our senior officer, who also wanted to buy a car, would also have to be seriously wounded three times or lightly wounded nine times. Of course, any wound treated improperly could result in death.

Regardless of where soldiers served, they all received the same pay. The rear area supply clerk received the same pay as the front-line combatant. The women who worked in the PX in downtown Kabul received the same pay as junior officers who risked life and limb in close combat.[11] Thus, there was no financial incentive or prestige attached to serving in the combat units or carrying out the combat missions.

Editors' comments: There were no Afghan bordellos available to Soviet soldiers, so sexual tension was high and centered around the few available Soviet women. The Soviet World War II tradition of the "field wife" was revived in Afghanistan. Soviet women working in the headquarters, communications sites, hospitals, PXs, and support areas were avidly courted by Soviet officers. Duels were fought in some garrisons for their favors. Some mercenary women sold their sexual favors, while others formed short or long-term relationships with officers— regardless of their marital status in the Soviet Union. Some of the relationships endured beyond the war.

The goods available through the PX system were supposed to aid troop morale, but the inequitable distribution of its scarce goods had the opposite effect. Senior officers and rear echelon personnel had access, while the warriors did without. Allegations of graft and corruption in the PX system abound—and appear justified. Further, soldiers complained that Soviet customs officials frequently seized their radios, stereos, or other coveted acquisitions when they returned home.

Although not covered, postal service should have been included in this section. As with any army, mail was very important to the soldiers' morale. Mail was delivered regularly, but postal censorship in both directions slowed that delivery. A constant complaint of the soldiers was that packages were rifled en route or never delivered at all.

Garrison housing was not fancy, and privates, sergeants, and company-grade officers endured the summer heat and winter cold in tents. Officer modular housing for field grade officers was better. General officers had apartments. The garrisons lacked many of the amenities expected by Western armies, but almost all posts had a Russian steam bath [banya].

Most of a soldier's pay was deposited in a bank or postal account in the Soviet Union. Although the official exchange rate was one ruble = $1.59, this

was an inflated rate since the ruble was not a convertible currency. When the
ruble became a convertible currency, it initially traded at 5 to 6 rubles per dol-
lar, so the ruble was actually worth some 17 to 20 cents at this time. The Soviet
soldier was paid very little for hazarding his life. The idea that a combat soldier
should receive more pay than a rear echelon soldier is not new or original to the
Soviet army. The U.S. army also pays its warriors and its support personnel the
same amount—regardless of the risk to life and limb.

MEDICAL SUPPORT[12]

The health and lives of the servicemen of the LCOSF were placed in great risk
as they entered Afghanistan. This was not only due to their exposure to combat,
but also to the very rugged terrain, the extreme climate, and the sanitary and
epidemiological conditions of the country. Long exposure of soldiers to altitudes of 1,500 to 1,800 meters [4,922 to 5,906 feet] and higher exposed them
to altitude sickness. During the summer, the daytime temperature reached 45°
to 50° Centigrade [113° to 122° Fahrenheit] in the shade and fell during the
night. During the winter, people went from overheating and dehydration to
chills and freezing.

Added to this was the considerable problem of moving men and material in
this terrain. The road network is under developed and has a limited carrying and
through-put capacity. Valleys and canyons are separated and do not join each
other and there is a lack of bridges across rivers. This severely limited the ability of medical support personnel and equipment to move. Narrow roads wound
through mountain canyons and up and down extensive slopes. These did not
allow the wheeled medical transport to drive over 10 to 15 kilometers per hour
[six to nine miles per hour]. The rugged terrain, the monotonous sameness of the
color of sun-scorched earth, the extreme dust, the limited visibility due to the
constant wind that blows during the daylight hours (nicknamed "the Afghan"),
and the sand storms complicated the performance of medical support and often,
searches for casualties. These geographic and climatic factors had an impact on
first aid and medical evacuation and affected the eyes and lungs of the soldiers.

The presence of a large amount of poisonous snakes meant a need for constant vigilance and maintaining a supply of anti-venom serum down to the battalion medical point.

The sanitary and epidemiological situation in the country was severe and
characterized by a universal presence of serious medical problems throughout
the population. These included acute intestinal disorders, typhus and paratyphus,
viral hepatitis, tuberculosis, leprosy, malaria, and chicken-pox. These had an
influence on the health of the Soviet personnel, particularly when they were living in the field and their bodily resistance was weakened.[13]

The outbreak of disease was spread, to a large extent, by the concentration
of forces in a single area. Thus, in the period when the first six regiments of

Soviet forces were preparing to withdraw from Afghanistan in the fall of 1986, the personnel were temporarily concentrated in one area after being withdrawn from throughout the country.[14] Viral hepatitis broke out and rapidly spread throughout these six regiments. The number of sick shot up, and, as a result, the medical facilities were working as infectious disease wards with three to four times their normal load. Even the various specialized field medical subunits (therapeutic; neurological; and eye, ear, nose, and throat) were temporarily converted to infectious disease duties. Only the surgical teams, anaesthesiology teams, and intensive care wards were not converted.

Normally, qualified medical care was provided by the medical subunits of the separate medical battalion. They provided medical support to the division and brigade and studied and determined the sanitary-epidemiological situation in the combat zone and in the base camp area. They would identify and liquidate centers of infection and conduct preventive measures to reduce the possibility of disease among the personnel.[15]

Medical support was seriously impeded by the poorly developed system of health care in Afghanistan. It was undermined by a severe lack of medical personnel, a low level of professional training, and insufficient medical supplies and facilities. Thus, for example, an Afghan who spent three or four months training at the central Afghan hospital in Kabul, receiving the equivalent training for a Soviet medical corpsman, could be commissioned as an officer and practice medicine. The national cadre of healing practitioners included those who trained as veterinarians. Thus, the head of the Shindand hospital in Farah Province was a trained veterinarian with the military rank of senior captain. Therefore, the Soviet medical services, particularly the specialists in the separate medical battalions and military field hospitals, constantly provided consultative assistance to the local population and provided laboratory services, technical testing, electrocardiograms, and X-ray examination, as well as providing local medical facilities with medications, Soviet-made materials, and medical implements.

By petition of the Afghan High Command, individual Afghan service personnel and members of their family were examined and treated in the military field hospitals and separate medical battalions of the 40th Army. This imposed additional responsibilities on the medical service of the LCOSF, while expanding the scope and increasing the amount of their work. It follows that it also reduced the quality of care.

During the conduct of combat, the principal missions of the medical service were the following: search for and find casualties; provide initial emergency medical treatment; and gather and arrange for evacuation (or do the evacuation) of the wounded from the battlefield. They also evacuated sick patients from disease outbreak centers and evacuated sick and wounded from the subunits and units to the regimental medical point (MPP[16]) and the separate medical battalion (OMedB[17]). Further, they would establish temporary hospitals in the medical battalion for those sick and wounded who could not be moved. The separate medical battalion would also treat and hold lightly wounded and mildly sick patients for five to ten days. They also reinforced the medical support to the line regiments of the divisions and the medical subunits of the line regiments with medical personnel. They provided ambulances and medical stores. They secured and defended medical subunits, conducted medical reconnaissance of the division combat zone and base camp, and supported the regiments of the division with medical stores.

The Medical Service supported all the units and divisions, but the scope and scale of this support varied by medical subunit and unit.

Thus, regimental medical personnel provided first aid, screening, and the first medical treatment by a doctor of sick and wounded, as well as the assembly and evacuation of the patients to the regimental medical point. The division medical battalion would often cooperate in carrying out this mission. Evacuation of the sick and wounded from the regimental medical point and further medical treatment was the responsibility of the division medical battalion and the military field hospital.

Medical service in the line regiment included corpsmen-riflemen in motorized rifle platoons, senior medical corpsmen in the motorized rifle companies, battalion medical points in the tank and motorized rifle battalions, and also senior medical corpsmen and physician's assistants in those subunits of the regiment other than the line battalions.[18]

During combat, the medical personnel of the motorized rifle regiment carried out a larger amount of the medical support tasks and were assigned more forces and resources than other units of the division. They played a leading role in searching for and assembling the wounded, evacuating them from the battlefield, providing first aid and medical screening, and evacuating them to qualified surgical care at the division medical battalion or the multi-functional military field hospital.

Division medical battalions and multi-functional military field hospitals were deployed to provide qualified military treatment to the sick and wounded. They were located at the primary troop concentration sites, while specialized medical care was provided centrally in Kabul. In all, there were seven major treatment centers in Afghanistan. First of all, there was Kabul with a 400-bed military hospital and a 500-bed infectious disease military hospital. These were both called central hospitals and were designated to provide specialized care. Their facilities included a blood-dialysis unit attached to an artificial kidney. The more critically ill patients were evacuated to these central hospitals from throughout Afghanistan using the fixed-wing, propellor-driven, light AN-26M "Savior" aircraft or the Mi-8MB "Bisector" medical evacuation helicopter.

A military clinic and a military stomatologic clinic were also located in Kabul, as was the blood transfusion center (which also had a branch in the Shindand military multi-functional field hospital), a pathological/anatomical laboratory, and a medical-forensics laboratory. Kabul was also the place from which the

AN-12 aircraft (nicknamed the "Black Tulips") flew, carrying the dead Soviet soldiers home to the Fatherland for burial. There was also a sanitary-epidemiologic detachment in Kabul that implemented sanitary and epidemiologic controls and conducted medical reconnaissance. Further, there was a medical supply depot for medicines and medical supplies, as well as a central pharmacy to support medical service and treatment facilities. The second largest concentration of medical facilities was in Shindand, located in Farah Province. It was connected to the well-constructed airfield with its cement runways. These allowed the uninterrupted resupply of the forces and allowed the evacuation of sick and wounded to the hospitals in Kabul or directly to hospitals in the Soviet Union. There was a 350-bed military multi-functional hospital in Shindand.

The TO&E structure and main deployment of the general military field hospital (VPMG)[19] is shown on the sketch map (Map 32). Further, a separate medical battalion, a sanitary-epidemiologic detachment (SEO),[20] medical stores, and a mobile stomatological surgery were stationed in Shindand.[21]

In Kandahar, a medical company ran a 175-bed military general hospital to support the Soviet brigade.[22]

Medical service in Kunduz Province was based on a 180-bed infectious disease military field hospital. A separate medical battalion provided treatment for the sick of the garrison.[23] Kunduz also had a mobile stomatological surgery, a portable X-ray unit, and a sanitary-epidemiologic detachment.

There was a 200-bed military general field hospital and medical depot in Puli-Khumri.[24]

In Bagram, there was a 400-bed military infectious-disease field hospital and a separate medical battalion. There was also a recovery center that could accommodate 1,000 beds during an epidemic. This was the second largest medical facility after Kabul.[25]

There was a 200-bed military infectious-disease field hospital in Jalalabad. It was staffed by the medical company of the separate motorized rifle brigade.[26] They were set up to provide good treatment, using excellent medical machines and instruments for conducting complex surgery.

The major medical sites held enough medications to provide the full range of medical support. The medical service of the 40th Army further had enough medical supplies and equipment to support the timely examination and treatment by preventive medicine and to provide medical assistance and treatment to the sick and wounded.

The daily strength of a motorized rifle division included some 0.2 to 1 percent of the personnel who were wounded. The percentage of sick personnel was relatively constant and fluctuated within the limits of 0.3 to 0.6 percent of division strength, regardless of the type of combat being conducted.

The reasons for illness and wounds varied widely. Repeated analysis of mil-

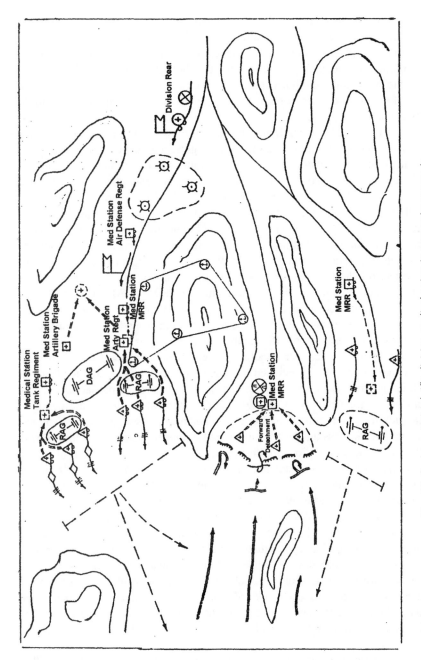

Map 32. Soviet motorized rifle division medical points in mountainous terrain

itary pathology discloses that 10 to 15 percent, and sometimes more, trauma was the result of careless weapons handling, truck accidents, and terrorist acts. About 0.8 percent of the wounded suffered severe depression, while about 2 to 3 percent of the wounded displayed various psychological abnormalities. Knowledgeable and literate personnel could use the figures of the division or regimental chief of medical services to predict the probable medical casualties prior to the start of combat.

As a rule, a battalion acting independently would have a doctor, an ambulance, and necessary kit attached from the regimental medical point at the start of combat and throughout its course. A grouping of two or more battalions was reinforced with a surgeon, a field dressing station, and enough supplies (from the separate medical battalion) to provide emergency qualified care.

The movement of the sick and wounded depended mostly on the time it took to evacuate the casualties from the battlefield to qualified surgical care. In comparison with the Great Patriotic War, the time spent evacuating personnel was shortened. In particular, during World War II, 61.7 percent of wounded were evacuated to a division medical point (DMP)[27] or the mobile field surgical hospital (KhPPG)[28] within six hours after being wounded. In Afghanistan, 90 percent of the wounded were evacuated within that time. Only 2 percent of the wounded were evacuated over 24 hours after being wounded, but that usually depended on the difficulty of the combat situation.

In the field, medical personnel had special kits that contained various medicines and supplies. They included bandaging material, splints, and medications for treating wounds and frostbite. Treatment was given in dispensaries, dressing stations, and medical operating theaters. The medical services were equipped with truck-mounted fumigation and shower and bath units, a sterilization and distillation unit for dressing stations, and a truck-mounted laboratory equipped with an electric generator, radio, and other gear.

The medics used the standard medical stretchers to move and group the wounded. Sick and wounded were evacuated from the battlefield on a BTR, BMP, or LUAZ-967 wheeled field ambulance.

The UAZ-452A or AS-66 ambulances were used for longer-range transport of the sick and wounded. Further, the seriously wounded in a remote area could be moved by an emergency evacuation flight using one of the medical services' eight specially equipped Mi-8 "Bi-sector" medical evacuation helicopters.[29]

There were two AN-26M "Savior" fixed-wing medical evacuation aircraft that could transport sick and wounded while providing on-board surgical capability and intensive therapy during the flight. The crew of the "Savior" included doctors, anesthesiologists, medical nurses, and nurse anesthesiologists.

Combat experience showed that it was necessary to train soldiers in first aid. The regimental medical service personnel conducted this training during preparation for combat. Troop training covered self-administered first aid and first aid to others, prevention of gastro-intestinal diseases, personal hygiene, and water discipline. Non-TO&E stretcher bearers from the rifle platoons were taught bandaging, the use of a tourniquet, splinting broken limbs, administration of pain-killers, and the priority of evacuation. Medical support preparation for combat included meetings with the doctors at the supporting hospitals, specifically with the infectious-disease doctors, epidemiologists, and surgeons.

During the same preparation period, the division and regimental chiefs of medical service were briefed on the commander's battle plan and the rear services support plan for the upcoming mission. The medical service chiefs evaluated the situation and made decisions concerning medical support to the forthcoming fight. The medical service chiefs' concept was developed in the medical support plan, which consisted of the basic document and the coordination measures between TO&E and attached medical service personnel and resources during preparation for and conduct of combat. Combat in mountains and desert required advanced preparation for both combat forces and medical support personnel to determine treatment and evacuation measures. The substance and volume of treatment and evacuation measures was determined by the number and type of casualties and how they were incurred.

In Afghanistan, the daily average casualty population was 69.7 percent combat casualties and 30.3 percent noncombat casualties. All military field hospitals, particularly the designated infectious disease military field hospitals, could field up to six infectious disease wards, in addition to the surgical, therapeutic, and neurologic wards.

During preparation for combat, all soldiers were provided two field dressings. Every third or fourth soldier carried a rubber tourniquet. The company senior medic and platoon stretcher bearers carried field dressings, promedol injectors,[30] antidote injectors, various medications, a tourniquet, and an emergency tracheotomy tube.

The company senior medic or battalion physician's assistant handled the evacuation of the lightly wounded from the battlefield. They gave medical aid to the severely wounded, when necessary, splinted limbs using the available issue material, bandaged wounded, and repeatedly injected painkillers.

Special attention was devoted to organizing the casualty search and evacuating the wounded from the battlefield. Every maneuver company designated a BTR or BMP for this purpose, and every maneuver platoon trained two or three stretcher bearers. Battalions deployed their medical aid stations at entry points onto roads, and during the influx of a large number of casualties, they relocated to the regimental medical point.

A universally accepted idea is that aviation was the more effective means of evacuating the sick and wounded in Afghanistan. Besides the specially equipped Mi-8 "Bi-sector" helicopters, fire support and search and rescue helicopters conducted medical evacuation. As a rule, a regimental doctor flew on board a helicopter during every sortie in order to provide first aid. Combat experience showed that helicopter medevac was often conducted under the most difficult combat and terrain conditions. When the helicopter was unable to land to take on wounded, they would load on the wounded while the helicopter hovered. These wounded were evacuated to a nearby airfield in an area where a separate medical battalion was deployed and, in the best of circumstances, next to a military hospital. In the rest of the cases, the first complete treatment by a doctor was provided at the regimental medical point. All these wounded received their first medical chart there, which accompanied them as they were transported to the next medical facility.

Sick and lightly wounded who were expected to recover within five to seven days after seeing the doctor and receiving the necessary medical treatment might be held at the regimental medical point until they fully recovered. The remaining wounded were sent on to a separate medical battalion or a military field hospital.

During hot weather, medical personnel would treat the sick and wounded for dehydration along with their medical problems. For this purpose, they kept a large assortment of fluids on hand, and, starting with the regimental medical point, these were reinforced with special chemicals. The average daily demand for fluids by a wounded soldier was seven to ten liters.

During cold weather, medical personnel organized warming points in every company to prevent frostbite. These warming points could accommodate one-third of the force at a time. The warming points had stoves, exhaust pipes, and stacks of coal and firewood. Fuel supplies were replenished by a detail from the *bronegruppa* that transported boxes of sawed and chopped firewood and sacks of coal during the entire period of combat.

Medical support played an important role in the life of the LCOSF in Afghanistan and in the fulfillment of operational and tactical missions. The goal of their efforts was to satisfy the needs of the force. At the same time, several problems were never satisfactorily resolved throughout the conflict. These were primarily concerned with preventing various diseases and providing quick, quality first aid to the soldiers.

In this way, the maintenance and rear area support of Soviet forces in Afghanistan passed a rigorous and comprehensive examination. In a variety of areas, they performed at the highest levels. However, there were shortcomings along with the successes. These shortcomings had a negative impact on the daily life of the force and had an impact on their combat actions. The majority of the shortcomings were a result of the weak material-technical base of the maintenance and rear area support services and the insufficient quality of personnel training. These demand serious evaluation and resolutions for the future.

Editors' comments: Serious disease was a much bigger problem than this section would indicate. Serious disease hospitalized 67.09 percent of all Soviet soldiers in Afghanistan. Viral hepatitis, cholera, shigellosis, amebiosis, typhus, paraty-

phus, and other water-borne diseases decimated the ranks of the 40th Army. At least 2.33 percent of those who served in Afghanistan were killed, and at least 8.67 percent were wounded. Disease was clearly a far-bigger problem for the 40th Army than was combat.

During the early years of the war, the bulk of wounds were from bullets. Over time, the Mujahideen received mortar and mines, and the Soviet wounded by shrapnel grew. Gradually, the number of severely wounded Soviets who survived grew as Soviet medical procedures improved. Helicopter-evacuation and the formation of special surgical teams that were set up prior to the start of a major operation and moved as far forward as possible were particularly effective in reducing the deaths from severe wounds.

Soviet medical support was well distributed throughout Afghanistan, and Soviet soldiers were reasonably close to a physician's care when it was needed. Soviet wounded were supposed to be routinely evacuated by ambulance to the regimental aid station. The few specially outfitted medical evacuation helicopters were supposed to be reserved for the critically wounded. In fact, the nature of the guerrilla war meant that a ride in an ambulance might end in ambush. More and more wounded were evacuated by helicopter—either the special evacuation helicopters or more commonly on the returning transport and supply helicopters. Physicians often rode in these general purpose helicopters so that they could work on the wounded while the helicopters flew to the nearest hospital.

Conclusion[1]

For Soviet forces, the war in Afghanistan concluded with the withdrawal from the country on 15 February 1989. The Soviets should have withdrawn earlier, but it was first necessary for the Afghan leadership to begin the slowly developing politics of "national reconciliation" in the country in 1986. The first practical step in this direction was the withdrawal of six Soviet regiments from Afghanistan in 1986. These were a tank regiment, two motorized rifle regiments, and three air defense regiments.[2]

In January 1987, the Revolutionary Council of the DRA issued the declaration "On National Reconciliation," which envisaged curtailing combat by Soviet and government forces and restoring the situation in the country through negotiations. From this moment, the General Staff of the Armed Forces of the Soviet Union began to plan the withdrawal of the LCOF of the 40th Army to the territory of the Soviet Union.

The final international démarche on Afghanistan was signed in Geneva on 14 April 1988. It was an agreement by the Afghan Ministry of Foreign Affairs with four interested countries: Afghanistan, Pakistan, the Soviet Union, and the United States.[3] This bound the Soviet Union to fulfill its obligations completely, and Soviet forces ceased combat in Afghanistan.

During its entire sojourn, the Soviet forces in Afghanistan compellingly demonstrated the results of the lack of political support for its actions by the government of the USSR. When the highest political leaders of the USSR sent its forces into this war, they did not consider the historic, religious, and national particularities of Afghanistan. After the entry, these particularities proved the most important factors as they foreordained the long and very difficult nature of the armed conflict. Now it is completely clear that it was an impetuous decision to send Soviet forces into this land. It is now clear that the Afghans, whose history includes many centuries of warfare with various warring groups, could not see these armed strangers as anything but armed invaders. And since these strangers were not Muslim, a religious factor was added to the national enmity. Both of these factors were sufficient to trigger a large mass resistance among the people, which various warriors throughout history had been unable to overcome and which the Soviet forces met when they arrived in Afghanistan.

The Soviet High Command compounded this serious mistake when they initially included a large percentage of Central Asians (Uzbeks, Tadjiks, and Turkmen) in the divisions and regiments of the 40th Army. These Central Asian peoples were also national minorities in Afghanistan. The High Command's hopes, that Soviet soldiers of these nationalities would have a greater understanding of their kinsmen in Afghanistan, were not realized. The Pushtun tribes, which had composed the most active part of the antigovernment movement, had historically always fought with the national minorities in the north, and the appearance of Uzbeks and Turkmen from a foreign land only strengthened the nationalities' discords[4] and fanned the flames of a war into which thousands of Soviet citizens were being drawn along with the Afghans.

From the viewpoint of the size of the country and the quantity of forces and resources involved, Afghanistan could be classified as a local war, but when considering how these forces and resources were used in combat, Afghanistan should be classified as a special category local war. It soon became apparent that the regular forces of the Soviets and Afghans were equipped with all types of weapons (except nuclear) and combat vehicles, while the opposing irregular forces had some new weapons, some ancient examples of rifles and light artillery, practically no combat vehicles, and no aircraft. Further, combat was conducted throughout the country, since there were no clearly defined front lines. The Soviet and Afghan government side fought a counter-guerrilla war, and the resistance conducted a guerrilla war. This turned out to be the key factor, since it determined the nature of the war and influenced the force structure and development of the Soviet military art in Afghanistan.

The war in Afghanistan gave the Soviet forces their first significant experience in the preparation and conduct of operations and combat against irregular guerrilla formations on mountain-desert terrain.[5] The operational art was formed in the chorus of soldier-intensive, large-scale offensive operations by the forces of the 40th Army. Divisions and regiments of various branches and special forces, as well as Afghan government forces, participated. During these operations, their combined force would advance along a 60-kilometer front to a depth of 220 kilometers with an average rate of advance of five to six kilometers per hour.

A new feature of the operational art in Afghanistan was the operations conducted with limited forces to resolve special operational missions. They were prepared and conducted by the commander and staff of the 40th Army with designated separate units and subunits of various branches and special forces and had a smaller scale and shorter duration than the large-scale operations. Despite being smaller and quicker, the results of these limited operations were often significantly better.

Despite the series of large-scale operations, the real war in Afghanistan for the LCOSF was conducted at the TACTICAL-COMBAT level. The basic formations that resolved specific combat missions were the regiment and battalion. They were reinforced with tanks, artillery, engineers, chemical troops, and army aviation subunits. Practically every battle was a combined-arms battle that demanded thorough and comprehensive preparation by the commanders and staffs at all levels.

The peculiarities of counter-guerrilla war and the rugged terrain determined the Soviet tactics in Afghanistan, where it was impossible to conduct classic offensive and defensive warfare. In Afghanistan, the principal forms of combat were the raid, block and sweep, ambush, and those actions connected with convoy escort and convoy security.

Raids were a "cleaner" variety of offensive combat. They were conducted by a raiding detachment consisting of one or two reinforced battalions moving along a previously designated march route or axis for a great distance with the goal of finding or destroying the enemy located there. Combat showed that this type of combat was frequently not very effective. In the majority of cases, raids were conducted not to destroy the enemy, but to displace him and occupy his region.

The block and sweep [cordon and search] was a completely new and widely employed tactic for the Soviet military in Afghanistan. It combined offensive and defensive combat in a single plan to destroy the enemy in a previously designated region. Considerable force was required for a block and sweep mission—usually some five to eight motorized rifle or infantry battalions and reinforcing subunits of tanks, artillery, engineers, chemical troops, airborne or air assault troops, helicopter gunships, and transportation helicopters. Success, to a significant degree, depended on the actions of the blocking forces, which, when possible, surprised the enemy by closing off the more-likely enemy escape routes. This forced the enemy to fight under disadvantageous conditions. In the event that the blocking portion of the tactic was successful, the sweep was conducted very much like a classic attack on a hastily prepared defense. This normally achieved good results and sometimes resulted in the encirclement and complete destruction of the enemy.

In some instances, the block or the sweep were conducted as individual actions. The block might be used to guard an important section of the international border or to hold some tactically significant terrain. This appeared to be very similar to defensive combat. These blocks were conducted for a lengthy period of time (from several weeks to several months), used a large number of forces and resources, but did not always give the hoped-for results. The enemy knew the terrain quite well and, as a rule, was able to bypass the blocking force. In turn, the blocking force was subject to significant casualties from an enemy surprise attack on their defensive positions or lines of communication. Independent sweeps were rarely conducted by Soviet forces and then only against small enemy forces. Their effectiveness was very limited.

Ambushes, as an independent combat tactic, attempted to carry out reconnaissance and prevent the resupply of personnel, weapons, ammunition, food, and other material to the opposition groups from contiguous countries. Motorized rifle, airborne, or air assault regiments conducted ambushes, using forces ranging from a platoon to a battalion. Higher demands were made on the soldiers, commanders, and subunits while preparing for this mission. The results of a well-prepared ambush were productive. They served to get necessary reconnaissance data, brought about control of the enemy lines of communication, and inflicted significant personnel casualties and material losses.

Soviet forces had to battle the enemy during the escort and security of the convoys that moved cargo for the forces and the civilian population from the USSR and also within the borders of Afghanistan. These convoys were primary targets for Mujahideen attack. Convoy escort was usually performed by a motorized rifle company reinforced with subunits of sappers, flame thrower gunners, ZSU 23-4 air defense machine guns, and recovery vehicles. During movement, these forces maintained close contact with the subunits of the commandant's road service and helicopter gunships. The escort force entered combat from the march, frequently under tactically disadvantageous conditions and, most often, piecemeal. This resulted in significant casualties among the Soviet forces on the road, casualties that made mastering this particular kind of action very important.

Combat in Afghanistan was not only conducted by motorized rifle forces, but also by various branches: artillery, armor, airborne, air assault, and army aviation. Artillery proved to be the primary means of fire destruction of the enemy and was widely used for all types of combat. The artillery used a large variety of different systems that were able to conduct all types of fire in order to support the effective destruction of the enemy on mountain-desert terrain. Further, artillery was often used to lay down smoke on an area or to illuminate an area at night. Combat showed that motorized rifle subunit commanders were poorly trained to call for and adjust artillery fire.

Independent actions by tank regiments and subunits hardly ever took place in Afghanistan. At the same time, tank platoons and companies were attached to motorized rifle subunits and units to accomplish various combat missions.

Airborne and air assault subunits were successfully used to conduct independent, surprise actions in far-off and hard-to-reach regions to destroy enemy combatants and bases. They were also used for combined actions with motorized rifle subunits and units advancing to link up. Combat demonstrated that these forces were very effective when well prepared and wisely led. At the same time, there were some serious shortcomings in the training and outfitting of these troopers that limited their ability to influence the outcome of their combat missions.

The rugged terrain and guerrilla warfare determined that army aviation would play a very significant role in supporting the LCOSF in combat in Afghanistan. Further, army aviation facilitated the Soviet maintenance and rear area support missions. From the first day of the war, helicopters proved to be an integral asset, a true friend of the ground forces, and often their sole support and salvation. At the same time, analysis of combat disclosed serious shortcomings in pilot training and the capability of the aircraft to perform adequately in Afghanistan. Further analysis disclosed very weak preparation of combined arms commanders and staffs in organizing and maintaining coordination with army aviation on the battlefield.

Combat support forces were absolutely critical to success in operations and combat in Afghanistan. Reconnaissance played a leading role in this. In counter-guerrilla warfare, reconnaissance was the only combat support branch that could determine enemy combat potential and ability to employ all of their arsenal effectively in combat. Combat experience showed that, during preparation for operations and combat, reconnaissance received 65 percent of their data from agent reconnaissance and, during the course of the battle, up to 40 percent from their own forces. The most effective source of ground force intelligence was the ambush, which provided 80 to 90 percent of the reliable data about the enemy. Further, the new ground sensors were effective and were widely used in the mountain-desert terrain of Afghanistan. Still, the intelligence provided to the commanders, staffs, and forces was often insufficient, which significantly harmed the results of combat by Soviet forces.

A no less significant combat support branch in Afghanistan was the engineers. Their main efforts were conducting engineer reconnaissance, determining the location of enemy mines and explosive obstacles, inflicting casualties on the enemy with engineer munitions, and fortifying and preparing positions and regions occupied by Soviet forces. Further engineer missions included preparing and maintaining thousands of kilometers of mountain road and hundreds of bridges and crossings and also providing water to the forces. Combat showed that the engineers rapidly carried out all these missions. However, engineer forces experienced difficulty with their equipment, which severely limited their potential and their support to the Soviet forces in Afghanistan, whether in combat or in daily life.

Chemical troops' support of combat in Afghanistan was primarily reduced to providing flame weapons and smoke. Combat demonstrated that flame weapons were effective in the mountains. Smoke was used in significant quantities to hide the forces and reduce personnel and vehicle casualties.

The lengthy sojourn of Soviet forces in Afghanistan was considerably improved by the maintenance and rear area support, not only in achieving operational and tactical success, but also in the daily life of the 40th Army. The rugged terrain served to increase the wear and tear on weapons and combat vehicles, and there were not always enough maintenance personnel and resources to repair them quickly. During combat, the maintenance personnel would evacuate damaged vehicles from the battlefield and then repair them out in the field. However, the problem of evacuating damaged vehicles has still not been resolved satisfactorily.

Serious deficiencies were uncovered in the supply of Soviet forces, particularly in the areas of food service and personal equipment, the types and quantity of which frequently did not correspond to the realities of combat in Afghanistan. Far away from Afghanistan, an unfortunate decree was made that everyone would be paid the same, with no extra pay for performing the most hazardous combat duties nor compensation for increased moral and psychic trauma. This further demoralized the soldiers.

Significant difficulties arose with medical support to the force. The amount of medical support assigned was figured solely on the intensity and nature of combat. It disregarded the difficult sanitary and epidemiological conditions in the country. The result was that, even after intensive battles, the regiments found that the sum total of sick greatly outnumbered the sum total of wounded.

The war in Afghanistan did not pass without leaving a trace on the Soviet people and their armed forces. The personnel of the LCOSF in the 40th Army and the Soviet advisers all passed through the fiery crucible of war. There were over 525,500 officers, sergeants, soldiers, workers, and support staff of the Soviet armed forces who served there. Casualties were high. As of February 1989, there were 13,833 killed or died of wounds reported, with 49,985 wounded and 311 missing in action. Thus, one in every eight who served there was killed or wounded, or is missing.[6]

There is definite interest in conducting a qualitative and quantitative analysis of those killed in action, reflecting the types of combat in the different years of the war in Afghanistan.

The figures of data attest that the Soviet forces suffered their greatest casualties from 1980 to 1985. The average was 8,240 a year. These fell off by a factor of two or three times during the following years. However, the casualties of the first days of the war are more significant. During the bloodiest days of 1984, the 40th Army was daily losing 26 men killed or wounded.[7] During the period 26 December to 31 December 1979, the Soviets suffered an average of 69 casualties a day.

The specific conditions of the war in Afghanistan foreordained a significantly high percentage of noncombat deaths among the total killed. The percentage of officer deaths was also noteworthy. From the available statistics, it can be shown that noncombat deaths averaged 17.7 percent. This meant that every fifth or sixth soldier who died was not killed by the enemy but as a result of disease, accident, or other occurrences not associated with the battlefield. However, during the course of the war, the percentage of noncombat deaths decreased somewhat. During the period 1979 to 1983, the average noncombat deaths fell to an average of 16 percent per year.

Officer deaths averaged 14.3 percent of total dead. In this war, the officer casualties had a pronounced tendency to grow. Thus their specific proportion in the overall dead from 1979 to 1985 averaged 13.4 percent, but in the following years it reached 17 percent.

And, in sum, considering the political misfortunes and heavy casualties, the war in Afghanistan clearly demonstrated the high morale and combat quality of the Soviet forces, thousands of whom were decorated for courage and valor.[8]

Witness these military decorations. During the period 1979 to 1989, 76 servicemen were designated Heroes of the Soviet Union, 103 received the Order of Lenin, 1,972 received the Order of the Red Banner, 52,520 received the Order of the Red Star, and several tens of thousands received other Soviet awards. Overall, over 196,000 soldiers, sergeants, warrant officers, officers, and generals received Soviet orders and medals for this time. Many of these continued to serve in the ranks of the armed forces of the USSR.

Editors' comments: The Soviet Union had plenty of experience subjugating and controlling discontented people and breakaway communist governments. During the Russian Civil War and afterward, the Bolsheviks used subterfuge, pressure, and military force to reintegrate the regions and nationalities that had broken away from the Russian Empire. As the Red Army advanced through German-occupied territory in 1944 and 1945, it again faced resistance from nationalist forces, which it finally subjugated in the early 1950s. During World War II, the Red Army successfully ran one of the largest guerrilla forces in history.[9] Therefore, the initial inept approach of the 40th Army to fighting guerrillas was not due to a lack of historic experience to draw on. Further, British experience on their Indian Northwest Frontier is replete with tactical solutions to fighting the ancestors of the Mujahideen. Mujahideen tactics were basically unchanged over the decades, and the British lessons were still valid.

The Soviets designed their armed forces to fight large-scale, high-tempo offensive operations exploiting nuclear strikes on the northern European plain and China. In this type of war, massed Soviet air and artillery fire would blast gaps through enemy positional defenses. Soviet armored columns would dash through these gaps and move deep within enemy territory. In this type of war, tactical predictability was preferred to tactical agility. The war would be won on the operational level. Soviet force structure, weaponry, tactics, and support infrastructure were all designed to support this operational vision. These were all inappropriate for a long counterinsurgency effort in Afghanistan.

Despite the passage of time and the authors' unprecedented access to materials about the war, there is ample evidence that the Soviets never really understood their enemy or the neighboring country in which they were fighting. Clearly, some aspects of the war are still deep secrets—even to trusted members of the General Staff. The authors clearly believe that Soviet casualties were at least double those reported, yet they end the book repeating the official figures. The authors have done an excellent job at analyzing the conduct of the war from the viewpoint of using an army, with all its branches and services, in conducting a counter-guerrilla war. The authors of this study have made a good start toward determining where the Soviet effort went wrong and what they did right. Unfortunately, their efforts are not having an immediate impact. The Russian army is unwilling or unable to apply the lessons of this conflict to their present situation. Large-scale, theater-level conventional war is highly unlikely today, yet Russian officers continue to devote their studies to such a conflict in their academies. Conflicts like Afghanistan plagued the Russians in Chechnya, Ossetia, Dagestan, Georgia, and Tadjikistan, yet the lessons of Afghanistan are not being fully applied. The lessons of this book should be read by the Russian military professional. Incredibly, they are available first to English-speaking professionals. These lessons are not uniquely Russian. They apply to any high-technology force trying to contend with a guerrilla force, fighting on its own territory and enjoying popular support. Some additional key lessons that the Russians should be drawing from their experience follow:

TACTICS

In many respects, the tactics of the Anglo-Afghan Wars still applied. Technology has added range and accuracy; but the terrain still dictates tactics, and the Mujahideen were quite comfortable applying their time-honored tactics against a modern foe. Much more innovation was required from the Soviet forces. Two modern systems, the helicopter and the antipersonnel mine, created serious tactical problems that were outside the Mujahideen historical experience. Tactical innovation occurs only where tactical innovation is required, and the Mujahideen eventually found ways to work around the problem technology. Where innovation was not required, the Mujahideen stayed with the tried and true. Thus, the basic Mujahideen ambush and pursuit were little changed from the last century whereas their actions against an air assault or a fortified security post were quickly developed out of necessity.

The Soviet ground forces developed the bronegruppa *concept to use the firepower of the personnel carriers in an independent reserve once the motorized rifle soldiers had dismounted. It was a bold step, for commanders of mechanized forces dislike separating their dismounted infantry from their carriers. However, terrain often dictated that the carriers could not follow or support their squads. The* bronegruppa *concept gave the commander a potent, maneuverable reserve that could attack independently on the flanks, block expected enemy routes of withdrawal, serve as a mobile fire platform to reinforce elements in contact, serve as a battle taxi to pick up forces (which had infiltrated or air-landed earlier and had finished their mission), perform patrols, serve in an economy-of-force role in both the offense and defense, and provide convoy escort and security functions.*

The Soviet ground forces adopted bounding overwatch for their mounted and dismounted ground forces. Combat vehicles or a dismounted element would occupy dominant terrain to cover other vehicles or elements as they would advance. The advancing group would then stop on subsequent dominant terrain to cover the forward deployment of their covering group.

Air assault tactics and helicopter gunship tactics changed and improved steadily throughout the war. However, the Soviet never brought in enough helicopters and air assault forces to perform all the necessary missions. Helicopter support should have been part of every convoy escort, but this was not always the case. Dominant terrain along convoy routes should have been routinely seized and held by air assault forces, yet this seldom occurred. Soviet airborne and air assault forces were often the most successful Soviet forces in closing with the resistance, yet airborne and air assault forces were usually understrength. Air assault forces were often quite effective when used in support of a mechanized ground attack. Heliborne detachments would land deep in the rear and flanks of Mujahideen strongholds to isolate them, destroy bases, cut LOCs, and block routes of withdrawal. The ground force would advance to link up with the heliborne forces. Usually, the heliborne force would not go deeper than supporting artillery range or would take its own artillery with it.

Enveloping detachments [obkhodiashchii otriad] were used frequently in Afghanistan. Battalion or company-sized forces were split off from the main body and sent on a separate route to the flank or rear of the Mujahideen to support the advance of the main body, perform a separate mission, prevent the withdrawal of Mujahideen forces, or to conduct a simultaneous attack from one or more unexpected directions. If the enveloping detachment was dismounted, it was usually composed of airborne, air assault, or reconnaissance forces. If the enveloping detachment was mounted, it was frequently just the unit's bronegruppa.

TECHNOLOGY

Technology can provide advantages but is not decisive in this type of war. Soviet smart bombs had a decided impact when an appropriate target set could be identified. U.S.-supplied, shoulder-fired Stinger air defense missiles, in the hands of the Mujahideen, created a great deal of consternation and led to a dramatic change in Soviet air tactics. Neither system, however, was a war winner. The Soviet equipment was designed for a different war on different terrain. It failed to function optimally in the mountains and deserts of Afghanistan. The Kalashnikov assault rifle was not always better than the World War I–designed British bolt-action Enfield rifle. The Enfield shot further accurately and would penetrate flak jackets designed to stop Kalashnikov bullets.

The Soviet RPG-7 antitank grenade launcher was the Mujahideen weapon of choice. It is a lightweight technology killer that destroys tanks, armored personnel carriers, trucks, and helicopters. The Soviets and DRA tried to stay at least 300 meters away from the Mujahideen—out of Kalashnikov and RPG-7 range. This tactical timidity led to Mujahideen acquisition of crew-served weapons. Over time, heavy machine guns, recoilless rifles, mortars, and portable multiple rocket launcher systems became an essential part of the Mujahideen arsenal, which the Mujahideen used to pin their enemy in place in order to get close enough to use their Kalashnikovs and RPGS. These crew-served weapons also limited guerrilla mobility.

Soviet high performance jet fighters and bombers played a significant strategic role, but not a tactically significant one. The Soviets used their air forces to devastate the countryside and force the populace to leave in order to deny food to the Mujahideen. The Soviet air force destroyed farms, crops, animal herds, orchards, and irrigation systems and forced millions of people to flee. The Mujahideen were then forced to carry their rations along with the other impedimenta of war. However, the Mujahideen seldom presented a target set that the Soviet air force or artillery could fully exploit to influence the tactical fight. Helicopters and the SU-25 close air support aircraft were the most effective aircraft of the war.

Technology did serve the Soviets as a force multiplier. Besieged garrisons could be maintained indefinitely by aerial resupply. Carpet bombing could stave off immediate disaster. Helicopter medical evacuation could save personnel who could later be returned to duty. Sensors could provide reconnaissance data in isolated areas.

MORALE

During the war, draft-age Soviet youth increasingly tried to avoid the draft and Afghanistan duty. Large bribes were paid to exempt or safeguard the children of the privileged. A disproportionate number of youth from factories and collective farms served in Afghanistan. The conscript's morale was not great when he was drafted. At the training centers, conscripts were told that they were going to fight Chinese and American mercenaries. When they got to Afghanistan, they soon discovered that they were unwelcome occupiers in a hostile land. Morale further plummeted at this realization. As in other armies, the field soldiers were too busy to get into much trouble, but those soldiers in the rear with routine supply, maintenance, and security duties had too much time on their hands. Many conscripts developed a narcotics habit in Afghanistan. They financed their habit by selling equipment, ammunition, and weapons. Some turned to violent crime. Soviet soldiers robbed merchants and passersby. At Soviet checkpoints, the soldiers would search Afghan civilians' luggage for weapons. Routinely, those Afghans carrying large amounts of money were "sent to Kabul." Being sent to Kabul meant isolating the civilian and his luggage behind a wall and out of sight of the checkpoint. There, the soldiers would kill the civilian and take his money. In the field, villages were razed and the occupants murdered in retaliation for ambushes or suspected aid to the guerrillas. Some of these incidents seem to have been officially sanctioned, while others appear to have resulted from a breakdown in discipline.

The Soviet policy terrorized the population and did little to win them over to the government's side. Despite all the press photos showing Soviet soldiers with Afghan adults and children, genuine fraternization between Soviets and Afghans was discouraged. During combat, the Soviets called in artillery and air strikes on villages without warning the inhabitants. Press gangs followed many sweeps and Afghan youth were conscripted into the Afghanistan army on the spot. The most infamous Soviet crimes against Afghans were prosecuted, but many more were ignored. Often, Soviet actions seemed deliberately designed to harden the resolve of the resistance.

It is easy to dismiss the Soviet failure in Afghanistan, but it is not wise. Armies seldom get to chose the wars in which they fight and this type of difficult war is as likely a future conflict as a war involving high-technology systems in which the sides seldom get close enough to see each other. Russia continues to fight guerrilla wars. Other nations may also have to.

Appendix 1: 40th Army Order of Battle

Lester W. Grau has compiled the following orders of battle from various unclassified Russian sources.[1] They showed the 40th Army shortly after it arrived in 1980-1981, at the peak of its strength in early 1988, and then half-way through the withdrawal on 15 October 1988.

Garrison Locations of Soviet 40th Army Units in Afghanistan, 1980-1981

Major Ground Units of the 40th Army–5th, 108th & 201st Motorized Rifle Divisions; 103rd Airborne Division; 66th & 70th Separate Motorized Rifle Brigades; 56th Air Assault Brigade; 191st & 860th Separate Motorized Rifle Regiments; 345th Parachute Regiment; 28th Separate Multiple Rocket Launcher Regiment; 45th Engineer (Sapper) Regiment

Major Air Units of the 40th Army–115th Fighter Regiment; 136th Fighter-bomber Regiment; 50th Composite Air Regiment; 181st , 280th & 292nd Separate Helicopter Regiments; 146th Separate Helicopter Detachment; 4th Aviation Squadron of the 335th Separate Helicopter Regiment; 263rd Separate Tactical Reconnaissance Squadron; 262nd & 302nd Separate Helicopter Squadrons

Organization	Location	Remarks
40th Army Troops		
40th Army HQ	Kabul	
1074 Artillery Regiment	Kabul	
28th Separate MRL Regiment	Shindand	5th MRD AO
1839 Separate Air Defense Regiment	Kabul	
45th Engineer (Sapper) Regiment	Charikar	
Engineer Road Construction Brigade	Kabul	
103rd Separate Signal Regiment	Kabul	
247th Separate Repair & Maint Bn	Kabul	Artillery
258th Separate Repair & Main Bn	Kabul	Armored Vehicles
40th Army Ground Forces		
5th Motorized Rifle Division	Shindand	
101st Motorized Rifle Regiment	Herat	AT platoon-outpost Taragun
1st MRB (- 1 MRC)	Kushk-e-Kohna	Six MRP OPs north of Herat
2nd MRB (-1 MRC)	Qala-e-Naw	
3rd MRB	Herat	
371st Motorized Rifle Regiment	Shindand	
24th Tank Regiment	Shindand	
1st TB	Shindand	
2nd TB	Girishk	
4th TC	Talkhak	
5th TC	Girishk	
6th TC	Kushk-e-Nakhod	
3rd TB	Shindand	
1060th Artillery Regiment	Shindand	
1122 Air Defense Regiment	Shindand airfield	
5th MRD HQ Troops		
650th Separate Recon Bn	Shindand	
Anti-tank Bn	Delaram	Two sep plt OPs from 2d Coy

315

388th Separate Signal Bn	Shindand	
68th Separate Sapper Bn	Shindand	
46th Separate Medical Bn	Shindand airfield	
108th Motorized Rifle Division	Bagram	
177th Motorized Rifle Regiment	Jabul-Seraj	
1st MRB	Jabul-Seraj	
2nd MRB	Highway 76	
3rd MRB	Highway 76	
180th Motorized Rifle Regiment	Kabul	
181st Motorized Rifle Regiment (-)	Kabul	
1st MRB	Highway 1 between Surobi and Darunta	
3rd MRB	Darunta	
285th Tank Regiment (-)	Bagram airfield	
TB (-)	Kishm	Attached 860th Sep MRR
1st Tank Company	Faizabad	
2nd Tank Company	Faizabad	
479th Artillery Regiment	Kabul	
1049th Air Defense Regiment	Kabul Airfield	
108th MRD HQ Troops		
781st Separate Recon Bn	Bagram	
738th Separate Anti-Tank Bn	Bagram	
303rd Separate Repair & Maint Bn	Bagram	
1003rd Separate Bn	Bagram	Spetsnaz?
271st Separate Sapper Bn	Bagram	
201st Motorized Rifle Division	Kunduz	
122nd Motorized Rifle Regiment (-)	Mazar-e Sharif	
1st MRB (-)	Afghan-Tepa	
1st MRC		OP north of Afghan-Tepa w/AD plt
2nd MRB	Aibak	Highway 76 from Baghlan to Termez
Tank Bn (-)	Sheberghan	
1st Tank Coy	Afghan-Tepa	
2nd Tank Coy	Sheberghan	
3rd Tank Coy	Mazar-e Sharif	
149th Motorized Rifle Regiment (-)	Kunduz	
MRB	Talgan	
395th Motorized Rifle Regiment (-)	Pul-e Khomri	
3rd MRB	Doshi	Highway 76 from Doshi to Baghlan
? Tank Regiment	?	
998th Artillery Regiment	Asqalan	
990th Air Defense Regiment	Kunduz	
201st MRD HQ Troops		
783rd Separate Recon Bn	Kunduz	
252nd Separate Signal Bn	Kunduz	
541st Separate Sapper Bn	Asqalan	
349th Separate Repair & Maint Bn	Asqalan	
103rd Airborne Division	Kabul	
317th Parachute Regiment (-)	Kabul	
3rd Para Bn (-)	Lashkargah	Two companies at Darveshah
350th Parachute Regiment (-)	Kabul	
1st Para Bn	Jalalabad airfield	66th MRR AO
3rd Para Bn	Shindand airfield	5th MRD AO

357th Parachute Regiment (-)	Kabul	
1st Para Bn	Miterlam	
66th Separate Motorized Rifle Brigade (-)	Jalalabad	
2nd MRB	Asadabad	
70th Separate Motorized Rifle Brigade	Kandahar	Formed from 5th MRD MRR
56th Air Assault Brigade (-)	Kunduz	
3rd Air Assault Bn	Imam Sahib	
191st Separate Motorized Rifle Regiment (-)	Ghazni	
1st MRB	Baraki Barak	
860th Separate Motorized Rifle Regiment	Faizabad	
345th Parachute Regiment (-)	Bagram airfield	From 105th Airborne Division
2nd Parachute Battalion	Bamian	

40th Army Air Forces

115th Fighter Regiment	Bagram airfield	
136th Fighter-bomber Regiment	Shindand & Kandahar airfield	5th MRD & 70th MRR AO
50th Composite Air Regiment	Kabul airfield	
181st Separate Helicopter Regiment (-)	Kunduz airfield	
1st Helicopter Battalion	Faizabad airfield	
280th Separate Helicopter Regiment	Kandahar airfield	70th MRR AO
292nd Separate Helicopter Regiment	Jalalabad airfield	66th MRR AO
146th Separate Helicopter Detachment	Kunduz airfield	
4th Sqdrn of 335th Sep Helicopter Regiment	Kunduz airfield	
254th Separate Helicopter Squadron	Kunduz airfield	
263rd Sep Tactical Recon Squadron	Kabul airfield	
262nd Separate Helicopter Squadron	Bagram airfield	
302nd Separate Helicopter Squadron	Shindand airfield	5th MRD AO

Ministry of Defense Forces in Afghanistan

59th Brigade	Pul-e-Khomri	Spetsnaz?
1003rd Separate Bn	Bagram	Spetsnaz?

Total Maneuver Battalions in Divisions	73
Battalions in LOC security	20
Battalions in airfield defense	14
Battalions in security of vital sites	4
Battalions providing security to DRA government sites	11
Garrison security and post, camp and station details	16
Battalions available for combat	8

Garrison Locations of Soviet 40 Army Units in Afghanistan 1988

Major Ground Units of the 40th Army–5th, 108th & 201st Motorized Rifle Divisions; 103rd Airborne Division; 66th & 70th Separate Motorized Rifle Brigades; 56th Air Assault Brigade; 191st & 860th Separate Motorized Rifle Regiments; 345th Parachute Regiment; 15th and 22nd Spetsnaz Brigades; 28th Separate Multiple Rocket Launcher Regiment; 45th Engineer (Sapper) Regiment

Major Air Units of the 40th Army–120th Fighter Regiment; 134th Fighter-bomber Regiment; 378th Ground Attack Regiment; 50th Composite Air Regiment; 181st, 280th & 292nd Separate Helicopter Regiments; 146th Separate Helicopter Detachment; 4th Aviation Squadron of the 335th Separate Helicopter Regiment; 263rd Separate Tactical Reconnaissance Squadron; 254th, 262nd & 302nd Separate Helicopter Squadrons plus two more squadrons

Organization	Location	Remarks
40th Army Troops		
40th Army HQ	Kabul	
15th Spetsnaz Brigade	Jalalabad	Code name 150th Spetsnaz Bde
334th Spetsnaz Bn	Asadabad	Code name 500th Spetsnaz Bn
154th Spetsnaz Bn	Jalalabad	Code name 100th Spetsnaz Bn
Spetsnaz Bn	Ghazni	
Spetsnaz Bn	Puli-Alam	
22nd Spetsnaz Brigade	Lashkargah	
Spetsnaz Bn	Daulatabad	
Spetznaz Bn	Lashkargah	
Spetsnaz Bn	Kandahar	
Spetsnaz Bn	Alaqadari Shahjoy	
1074 Artillery Regiment	Kabul	
28th Separate MRL Regiment	Shindand	
1839 Separate Air Defense Regiment	Kabul	
Separate MRB	Kabul	Security Battalion
45th Engineer (Sapper) Regiment	Charikar	
Engineer Road Construction Brigade	Kabul	
103rd Separate Signal Regiment	Kabul	
247th Separate Repair & Maint Bn	Kabul	Artillery
258th Separate Repair & Main Bn	Kabul	Armored Vehicles
650th Central Military Hospital	Kabul	500 bed
Infectious Disease Hospital	Kabul	500-bed
Infectious Disease Hospital	Bagram	500-bed
Infectious Disease Hospital	Kunduz	150-bed
Infectious Disease Hospital	Jalalabad	200-bed
Field Hospital	Puli-Khumri	200-bed
Field Hospital	Kandahar	175-bed
Field Hospital	Shindand	300-bed
40th Army Ground Forces		
5th Motorized Rifle Division	Shindand	
12th Motorized Rifle Regiment	Highway 1	Replaced 24th Tank Regiment
101st Motorized Rifle Regiment	Herat	
371st Motorized Rifle Regiment	Shindand	
1st MRB	Daulatabad	
2nd MRB		
1060th Artillery Regiment	Shindand	

5th MRD HQ Troops		
650th Separate Recon Bn	Shindand	
Separate MRB	Daulatabad	Security Battalion
Separate Anti-tank Bn	Delaram	
388th Separate Signal Bn	Shindand	
68th Separate Sapper Bn	Shindand	
46th Separate Medical Bn	Shindand airfield	
108th Motorized Rifle Division	Bagram	
177th Motorized Rifle Regiment	Highway 76	
180th Motorized Rifle Regiment	Kabul	
181st Motorized Rifle Regiment	Kabul	
682nd Motorized Rifle Regiment	Pandshir valley	Replaced 285th Tank Regiment
Tank Bn	Bagram airfield	
479th Artillery Regiment	Kabul	
108th MRD HQ Troops		
781st Separate Recon Bn	Bagram	
738th Separate Anti-Tank Bn	Bagram	
303rd Separate Repair & Maint Bn	Bagram	
271st Separate Sapper Bn	Bagram	
201st Motorized Rifle Division	Kunduz	
122nd Motorized Rifle Regiment	Mazar-e Sharif	
MRC	Sheberghan	
149th Motorized Rifle Regiment	Kunduz	
395th Motorized Rifle Regiment	Pul-e-Khomri	
998th Artillery Regiment	Asqalan	
Separate MRB	Kunduz	Security Battalion
201st MRD HQ Troops		
783rd Separate Recon Bn	Kunduz	
252nd Separate Signal Bn	Kunduz	
541st Separate Sapper Bn	Asqalan	
349th Separate Repair & Maint Bn	Asqalan	
103rd Airborne Division	Kabul	
317th Parachute Regiment (-)	Kabul	
3rd Para Bn (-)	Alaqadari Shahjoy	
Para Coy	Kalat	
Separate MRB	Alaqadari Shahjoy	Security Battalion
350th Parachute Regiment (-)	Kabul	
357th Parachute Regiment (-)	Kabul	
66th Separate Motorized Rifle Brigade (-)	Jalalabad	
2nd MRB	Asadabad	
Separate Motorized Rifle Bn	Jalalabad	Security Battalion
Separate Motorized Rifle Bn	Asadabad	Security Battalion
70th Separate Motorized Rifle Brigade	Kandahar	
Separate Motorized Rifle Bn	Kandahar	Security Battalion
56th Air Assault Brigade (-)	Gardez	
3rd Air Assault Bn	Puli-Alam	
Separate Motorized Rifle Bn	Puli-Alam	Security Battalion (Regt?)

| 191st Separate Motorized Rifle Regiment | Ghazni | |
| Separate Motorized Rifle Bn | Ghazni | Security Battalion |

860th Separate Motorized Rifle Regiment (-)	Faizabad	
1st MRB	Khairabad	
3rd MRB	Kishm	
Separate Medical Battalin	Faisabad	

| 345th Parachute Regiment | Bagram airfield | |
| Separate MRB | Bagram airfield | Security Battalion |

40th Army Air Forces

120th Fighter Regiment	Bagram airfield	Replaced 115th
134th Fighter-bomber Regiment	Shindand & Kandahar airfield	Replaced 136th
378th Ground Attack Regiment	Bagram and Kandahar	
50th Composite Air Regiment	Kabul airfield	
339th Separate Composite Air Squadron	Meimene	
181st Separate Helicopter Regiment	Kunduz airfield	
Squadron of 181st	Faizabad airfield	
280th Separate Helicopter Regiment	Kandahar airfield	
292nd Separate Helicopter Regiment	Jalalabad airfield	
146th Separate Helicopter Detachment	Kunduz or Gardez airfield	
335th Attack Helicopter Regiment	Jalalabad	
263rd Sep Tactical Recon Squadron	Kabul airfield	
205th Separate Helicopter Squadron	Lashkargakh	Dets at Farah, Shakhdzhoy and Kandahar
239th Separate Helicopter Squadron	Ghazni and Gardez	
262nd Separate Helicopter Squadron	Bagram airfield	
302nd Separate Helicopter Squadron	Shindand airfield	
320th Separate Helicopter Squadron	Kunduz airfield	

40th Army Statistics

Description	Total	Western Corridor	Eastern Corridor
Total Personnel (Thousands)	100.3	42.8	57.5
Personnel in headquarters	3.6	0.8	2.8
Personnel in combat units	70.7	36.4	34.3
Personnel in logistics & maintenance	14.3	2.4	11.9
Total Battalions	93	21	72
Securing government vital areas	40	7	33
Securing LOCs	15	4	11
Reinforcing vital areas & LOCs	9	2	7
Convoy Escort	3	1	2
Securing Industrial areas	5	0	5
Available for combat	30	8	22

Garrison Locations of Soviet 40th Army Units in Afghanistan on 15 October 1988

Major Ground Units of the 40th Army–5th, 108th & 201st Motorized Rifle Divisions; 103rd Airborne Division; 345th Parachute Regiment; 45th Engineer (Sapper) Regiment

Major Air Units of the 40th Army–120th Fighter Regiment; 134th Fighter-bomber Regiment; 378th Ground Attack Regiment; 263rd Separate Tactical Reconnaissance Squadron; 262nd & 302nd Separate Helicopter Squadrons

Organization	Location	Remarks
40th Army Troops		
40th Army HQ	Kabul	
1074 Artillery Regiment	Kabul	
45th Engineer (Sapper) Regiment	Charikar	
Engineer Road Construction Brigade	Kabul	
103rd Separate Signal Regiment	Kabul	
247th Separate Repair & Maint Bn	Kabul	Artillery
258th Separate Repair & Main Bn	Kabul	Armored Vehicles
40th Army Ground Forces		
5th Motorized Rifle Division	Shindand	
101st Motorized Rifle Regiment	South of Herat	
371st Motorized Rifle Regiment	Shindand	
1060th Artillery Regiment	Shindand	
5th MRD HQ Troops		
650th Separate Recon Bn	Shindand	
Separate Anti-tank Bn	Delaram	
388th Separate Signal Bn	Shindand	
68th Separate Sapper Bn	Shindand	
46th Separate Medical Bn	Shindand airfield	
108th Motorized Rifle Division	Bagram	
177th Motorized Rifle Regiment	Highway 76	
180th Motorized Rifle Regiment	Kabul	
181st Motorized Rifle Regiment	Kabul	
682nd Motorized Rifle Regiment	Jabul-Seraj	
479th Artillery Regiment	Kabul	
108th MRD HQ Troops		
781st Separate Recon Bn	Bagram	
738th Separate Anti-Tank Bn	Bagram	
303rd Separate Repair & Maint Bn	Bagram	
271st Separate Sapper Bn	Bagram	
201st Motorized Rifle Division	Aibak?	
122nd Motorized Rifle Regiment	Mazar-e Sharif	
395th Motorized Rifle Regiment	Pul-e Khomri	
998th Artillery Regiment	?	
201st MRD HQ Troops		
783rd Separate Recon Bn	?	
252nd Separate Signal Bn	?	
541st Separate Sapper Bn	?	
349th Separate Repair & Maint Bn	?	

103rd Airborne Division	Kabul
317th Parachute Regiment (-)	Kabul
350th Parachute Regiment (-)	Kabul
357th Parachute Regiment (-)	Kabul

| 345th Parachute Regiment | Bagram airfield |

40th Army Air Forces

120th Fighter Regiment	Bagram airfield	Replaced 115th
134th Fighter-bomber Regiment	Shindand airfield	Replaced 136th
378th Ground Attack Regiment	?	
263rd Sep Tactical Recon Squadron	Kabul airfield	
262nd Separate Helicopter Squadron	Bagram airfield	
302nd Separate Helicopter Squadron	Shindand airfield	
254th Helicopter Squadron	?	

40th Army Statistics

Description	Total	Western Corridor	Eastern Corridor
Total Personnel (Thousands)	50.1	10.1	40.0
Personnel in headquarters	2.4	0.4	2.0
Personnel in combat units	29.2	6.7	22.5
Personnel in logistics & maintenance	18.5	3.0	15.5
Total Battalions	56	10	46
Securing government vital areas	29	6	23
Securing LOCs	15	3	12
Convoy Escort	2	0	2
Securing Industrial areas	5	0	5
Available for combat	5	1	4

Appendix 2: Soviet Artillery Planning

For those unfamiliar with Soviet artillery planning, a clarification is necessary so that the General Staff explanation of the different approach to artillery planning in Afghanistan is clear. Artillery was central to Soviet battle planning. They employed normative artillery fires in which a given number of rounds fired within a certain time would produce desired results. For example, to destroy 30% of an enemy infantry platoon dug in on a hectare of ground, the Soviets would fire 200 rounds of 120mm mortar, 100 rounds of 240mm mortar, 200 rounds of 122mm howitzer, 150 rounds of 152mm howitzer or 240 rounds of 122mm multiple rocket launcher within 20 minutes.

Soviet artillery planning initially identified targets, which were planned as artillery concentrations. The artillery concentrations would identify the firing batteries and number of rounds required for each concentration. Then, the targets would be connected by lines. These lines would be fired consecutively to insure that no identified targets were missed or that they were fired out of turn, giving the survivors time to recover and fight the advancing Soviet maneuver force.

Soviet classifications of artillery fire were fire against an individual target, fire concentration, standing barrage fire, rolling barrage fire, successive fire concentration, offensive rolling barrage and massed fire.[1]

Fire concentration [*sosredotochennyy ogon'*] (SO) is artillery fire conducted by several batteries or battalions simultaneously against one target. Fire concentrations are planned to provide even distribution of impacting rounds on the target area. On the map, fire concentrations are depicted a black numbered rectangle for cannon artillery and by a black numbered square for multiple rocket launchers. The fire concentration symbol on the planning map delineates the physical area of impact to scale. The following depicts a cannon artillery battalion firing a concentration in support of an attacking maneuver battalion. As is normal, the artillery battalion command post is colocated with the maneuver battalion command post.[2]

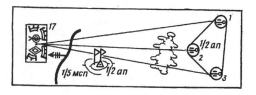

The successive fire concentration [*posledovatel'noye sosredotocheniye ognya*] (PSO) is used to support the attack of motorized rifle subunits and units. It can be fired on one, two or three lines simultaneously and is designed to neutralize enemy personnel and weapons to the front and on the flanks of the attacking elements. The lines of fire are shifted successively against targets in the enemy depth.

Graphically, the successive fire concentration is depicted in black as follows:

Planned targets are associated by lines with those targets located approximately the same distance from the friendly positions being grouped on the same line. Lines are named after predatory animals and were 300 to 1000 meters apart. Targets on the lines are given three-digit numbers with the first number representing the line number and the other two digits the number of the target on that line. An artillery battalion would normally service two or three targets on a line.

The following illustration depicts an artillery battalion supporting the southern attacking maneuver battalion:

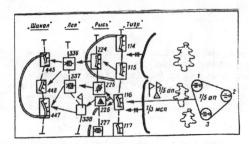

The artillery battalion services target 116 and then shifts to battery engagement of target 225 and 226 (on line "Lynx"). When the fire is shifted to line "Lion", the battalion's batteries fire on targets 337 and 338. When the fire is shifted to line "Jackal", the entire battalion engages target 447.[3]   Mujahideen defenses were usually shallow and lacked the depth of conventional armies--against which Soviet artillery methodology was developed. Not wanting to redo artillery procedures for the war in Afghanistan, Soviet gunners modified their procedures. Against the shallow Mujahideen defense, they developed the oxymoronic single-line successive fire concentration (OdPSO) where only one line was developed and fired.

Standing barrage fire [*nepodvizhnyy zagraditel'nyy ogon*'](NZO) is a solid curtain of fire set up along one line. This is usually a defensive fire characteristic designed to stop an attacking enemy, but it was used to prevent enemy withdrawal in Afghanistan. A deep standing barrage consists of more than one line. It can be fired by a single battalion on a narrow approach (300 meters with an 18-gun battalion, 400 meters with a 24-gun battalion) or by several battalions on a wider approach. Usually, all lines of the deep-standing barrage are fired simultaneously and continuously throughout the duration of the fire mission.[4]

The offensive rolling barrage is used when the enemy defense has a dense network of trenches and connecting passages that hinders precisely determining the location of strong points when fighting through a fortified area. The offensive rolling barrage is a solid curtain of fire shifted ahead of attacking maneuver subunits to neutralize enemy personnel and weapons. One or two lines can be fired simultaneously. The first line is planned along the first trench of the enemy defense. Intermediate lines are planned to neutralize the enemy located between the primary lines and to prevent his maneuver along communications trenches. The distance between intermediate lines is 100 to 300 meters. Graphically, the offensive rolling barrage is depicted in black as follows:

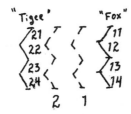

The rolling barrage line is divided into battery sectors with not more than 15 meters of frontage per mortar and not more than 25 meters of frontage per howitzer. Primary lines are named for predatory animals. Fire is shifted from the primary line by the maneuver commander as the attacking troops reach the troop safety line. Fire is shifted from the intermediate line by the artillery commanders at the end of the prescribed time of fire, which is normally two to three minutes.[5] The following shows a rolling barrage against a dense enemy trench network:

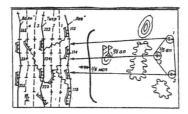

Soviet artillery planning was a very effective way of engaging a conventional enemy who defended in positions laid out in depth. It was not effective against an illusive guerilla force. The Soviets struggled hard to adapt their system to guerrilla war, rather than seeking innovative approaches to use their artillery.

Notes

EDITORS' PREFACE

1. James J. Schneider, *The Structure of Strategic Revolution: Total War and the Roots of the Soviet Warfare State* (Novato, CA: Presidio Press, 1994), 166–167.

2. Harold S. Orenstein is currently involved in the imposing task of translating and publishing these war experience volumes. Interested readers are directed to *Soviet Documents on the Use of War Experience* (London: Frank Cass Publishers) for the first three volumes.

3. Lester W. Grau, *The Bear Went Over the Mountain: Soviet Combat Tactics in Afghanistan* (London: Frank Cass Publishers, 1998).

4. Peter Vigor, *The Soviet View of War, Peace, and Neutrality* (London: Routledge and K. Paul, 1975), 56–58.

5. The *bronegruppa* is a temporary grouping of four to five tanks, BMPs or BTRs, or any combination of such vehicles. The BMPs (tracked combat vehicles) or BTRs (wheeled combat vehicles) are deployed without their normally assigned infantry squad on board and fight away from their dismounted troops. The grouping has a significant direct-fire capability and serves as a maneuver reserve.

6. Three paragraphs are from Lester W. Grau and Yahya Nawroz, "The Soviet Experience in Afghanistan," *Military Review* (September–October 1995), 20.

7. Ali A. Jalali, "Clash of Ideas and Interests in Afghanistan," paper given at the Institute of World Politics (Washington, DC, July 1995), 4. Much of this section is based on Ali A. Jalali and Lester W. Grau, *The Other Side of the Mountain: Mujahideen Tactics in the Soviet-Afghan War* (Quantico, Va.: U.S. Marine Corps Study), xiii–xx.

8. This section is derived from Richard F. Nyrop and Donald M. Seekins, eds., *Afghanistan: A Country Study,* 5th ed. (Washington, DC: Government Printing Office, 1986), 22–73; and Peter Hopkirk, *The Great Game* (New York: Kodansha International, 1994).

GENERAL STAFF INTRODUCTION

1. The introduction was written by Colonel V. A. Runov.

2. The Limited Contingent of Soviet Forces was the official term for Soviet Armed Forces in Afghanistan. It is abbreviated as the LCOSF throughout the book.

3. But these lessons were not available to Soviet soldiers until after the war and much later.

4. Oxus River.

5. Actually, these facilities were built several years before the war.

6. This is true for the southern deserts, but the central and northeast mountains are populated.

7. This is very high. Most authorities put the Turkmen population at some 125,000.

8. It took two years to conquer and organize the Central Asian provinces of the Persian empire–of which present-day Afghanistan was a part. Percy Sykes, *A History of Afghanistan,* vol. 1 (London: Macmillan, 1940), 62–66.

9. The main points of the Treaty of Gandamak were that Britain would control Afghanistan's foreign affairs; that English-born representatives would reside in Kabul and other areas under Afghan protection; that the Emir ceded Kurram, Pishin, and Sibi to the British; and that the British would control the Khyber and Michni Passes. In return for these concessions, the British agreed to pay the Emir £60,000 per year and might provide assistance in case of foreign aggression. Louis Dupree, *Afghanistan* (New Delhi: Rama Publishers, 1980), 409.

10. The siege preceded the Battle of Maiwand.

11. The "Durand line" marked the boundary between Afghanistan and British India. Named after the Indian Foreign Secretary, Sir Mortimer Durand, the line cuts across tribal and cultural areas. It remains an area of contention between Afghanistan and Pakistan today.

12. This is an oversimplified account. Interested readers are directed to Percy Sykes, *A History of Afghanistan,* vol. 2 (London: Macmillan, 1940).

13. The Marxist-Leninist view of history takes over at this point, and facts are bent. There was no coup. Rather, Nadir Shah returned from Europe and fought from Paktia to Kabul in the "War of Salvation" to take the throne. This period of history is well covered in Louis Dupree, *Afghanistan* (Princeton: Princeton University Press), in several editions starting in 1973 and ending in 1980.

14. Scholars are hard-pressed to find a civil war during this time.

15. This paragraph is very Marxist and very debatable.

16. The reforms, which included marked changes in the status of women and the nature of marriage, the abolition of usury, and land reform, were radical policies that opposed traditional Afghan values and the well entrenched rural power structure. They imposed an alien communist ideology and brutally repressed the intellectuals, tribal leaders, and Islam.

17. Islam needed no rebirth in Afghanistan. The fundamentalist movement had strong nationalist underpinnings.

18. The resident Afghan population began the resistance–which spread to the refugee camps outside the country.

19. Actually, Kabul was comparatively quiet during this time.

20. The gold rubles are a matter of debate.

21. Soviet technical specialists began serving in Afghanistan during the late 1950s and continued for the next three decades.

22. The narrative leaves out a significant piece of Afghan politics. In September 1979, communist president Taraki was deposed and executed by Hafizullah Amin, the head of a rival communist faction. Amin began to move out of Moscow's orbit and look for other allies. The Soviets were faced with losing control of a new nominally communist state and decided to intervene.

23. At that time, General Tukharinov was the First Deputy of the Turkestan Military District. It is interesting that the authors do not mention the lengthy reconnaissance of Afghanistan made by the CINC Ground Force, General of the Army Pavlovski, and sixty of his officers from July to December 1979. General Pavlovski made a similar reconnaissance of Czechoslovakia before the Soviet invasion. See Boris Gromov, *Ogranichennyy kontingent* [Limited contingent] (Moscow: Progress Publishers, 1994), 115–121.

24. At that time, the Chief of the General Staff was Marshal of the Soviet Union Nikolai Vasilevich Ogarkov.

25. World War II.

26. 108th Motorized Rifle Division. According to General Gromov, the 108th spent a year getting ready for the invasion, although they did not know what they were preparing for. The Turkestan Military District mobilized the 108th several times during 1979. Gromov, *Ogranichennyy kontingent,* 115.

27. The 108th MRD's original mission was to seize and hold the northern area of Afghanistan including Mazar-e Sharif, Baghlan, and Kunduz. This new order required the division to take a long and difficult road march through the Hindu Kush mountains. Evidently, the high command had a sudden fear that the 103rd Airborne Division would be unable to handle Kabul on its own.

28. 5th Motorized Rifle Division.

29. The combat units of the 40th Army consisted of the 5th, 108th, and 201st motorized rifle divisions; the 103rd Guards Airborne Division; the 66th and 70th Separate Motorized Rifle Brigades (upgraded from two of the separate motorized rifle regiments); the 191st and 860th Separate Motorized Rifle Regiments; the 345th Separate Parachute Regiment; the 56th Air Assault Brigade; the 15th and 22nd Spetsnaz Brigades; one fighter regiment; one fighter-bomber regiment; one separate ground attack air regiment; one separate composite air regiment; three helicopter regiments; and seven helicopter squadrons.

30. Spetsnaz were Troops of Special Designation. They were Soviet forces trained for long-range reconnaissance, commando, and special forces type combat.

31. Regiments withdrawn were a tank regiment and an air defense regiment from each of the motorized rifle divisions. There was no real role for either type of regiment due to the geography of Afghanistan and the lack of a guerrilla air force. Another Spetsnaz brigade and several motorized rifle regiments were brought in during this same time.

1. PHASES AND COURSE OF THE CONFLICT

1. This chapter was written by Colonel P. F. Vashchenko.

2. At that time, the Chief of the General Staff was Marshal of the Soviet Union Nikolai Vasilevich Ogarkov.

3. World War II.

4. According to General Gromov, the 108th spent a year getting ready for the invasion,

although they did not know what they were preparing for. The Turkestan Military District mobilized the108th several times during 1979. Gromov, *Ogranichennyy kontingent,* 115.

5. As in Czechoslovakia, the main Soviet objective appeared to be to seize the capital and establish and protect the new regime.

6. 5th Motorized Rifle Division.

7. These were the 5th and the 108th Motorized Rifle Divisions, the 103rd Airborne Division, the 56th Separate Air Assault Brigade, and probably the 191st and 860th Separate Motorized Rifle Regiments. The 345th Separate Airborne Regiment was also there.

8. Actually, Amin was killed by a group of Soviet Spetsnaz and paratroopers who were initially helping guard Amin and his palace.

9. The Basmachi were resistance fighters in Central Asia who resisted the imposition of Red rule from 1918 to 1933. The Bolsheviks' attempt to extend their revolutionary order into Muslim Asia was resisted by hit-and-run raids and ambushes. A good English-language account of the Basmachi resistance is in Dr. Robert F. Bauman, *Russian-Soviet Unconventional Wars in the Caucasus, Central Asia, and Afghanistan* (Leavenworth Paper Number 20, Combat Studies Institute, Fort Leavenworth, KS, 1993).

10. During conversations in 1995 with a serving officer who is an Afghanistan veteran, Les Grau asked if Soviet officers had studied the Vietnam War, since Soviet officers made the same mistakes in Afghanistan that American officers had made in South Vietnam. The officer replied that they had indeed studied the war in great detail—but all from the North Vietnamese perspective.

11. At times, up to 85 percent of the LCOSF was committed to security and defense.

12. Subsequent actions in Chechnya show that the Afghanistan experience was not incorporated and passed on.

13. The approximate size of the support forces was only 20 to 25 percent of the total force. This is clearly inadequate for an extended war.

14. Usually, the 103rd Guards Airborne Division.

15. Before Afghanistan, the Soviets considered the operational level of war as actions conducted by armies, fronts, and groups of fronts. A front is a war time formation consisting of several armies.

16. This same incident is recounted, with some different details, in Lester W. Grau, *The Bear Went Over the Mountain: Soviet Combat Tactics in Afghanistan* (Washington, DC: London: Frank Cass Publishers, 1998), 2–4.

17. *Karez* is an Afghanistan system of underground tunnels used for the collection of ground water and for carrying water for surface irrigation. The Mujahideen used them for shelter and ambush. There are actually no *karez* in this area. Irrigation water comes directly from two local rivers.

18. BMP is a Soviet tracked infantry fighting vehicle *[boevaya mashina pekhoty]* that carries a three-man crew and a squad of eight soldiers. The BMP-1 mounts a 73mm cannon, a 7.62mm machine gun, and an antitank missile. The BMP-2 carries a 30mm automatic gun and a different antitank missile and launcher.

19. This was not the case but is one of the myths surviving the war. The real irritant was the invasion of their land by the Soviets.

20. The peak Soviet strength was about 130,000. DRA strength is greatly over represented throughout this book, since the Soviets counted the tribal militias, whose strength was always over reported in order to receive additional Soviet funding.

21. The Soviets spent a lot of time and energy trying to discover a recognizable structure among the Mujahideen forces. There was little structure and consistency. However, the "fronts" were much smaller than these.

22. With 40 percent of the force involved in securing installations and population centers, another 35 percent involved in LOC security, and other forces involved in supply and maintenance, there were few forces left for combat.

23. These were the 5th, 108th, and 201st Motorized Rifle Divisions; the 103rd Airborne Division; the 66th and 70th Separate Motorized Rifle Brigades; the 56th Air Assault Brigade; the 15th and 22 Spetsnaz Brigades; the 345th Separate Parachute Regiment; and the 191st and the 860th Separate Motorized Rifle Regiments. The author may be mistaken as to the presence of another separate regiment.

24. Zhawar 2.

25. Most accounts, including Soviet, cite the withdrawal of three tank regiments and three air defense regiments—all clearly unneeded fighting guerrillas in a mountainous country. The tank and air defense regiments were from the 5th, 108th, and 201st Motorized Rifle Divisions. The withdrawal made military sense and allowed General Secretary Gorbachev the chance to proclaim that the Soviet Union was unilaterally cutting back combat power while actually easing his resupply problems and not affecting his effective combat power. In fact, at this same time, Gorbachev secretly replaced the tank regiments with motorized rifle regiments and sent another Spetsnaz brigade into Afghanistan.

26. Operation Magistral succeeded in opening the road to Khost and keeping it open for a few weeks. Then the Mujahideen cut the road again. The Soviets also conducted several major operations along the Arghandab river during the fourth phase.

27. Chronology of operations derived from David C. Isby, *War in a Distant Country: Invasion and Resistance* (London: Arms and Armour Press, 1989); and Mark Urban, *War in Afghanistan* (New York: St. Martin's Press, 1988). Originally published in Lester W. Grau, *The Bear Went Over the Mountain: Soviet Combat Tactics in Afghanistan* (London: Frank Cass Publishers, 1998).

2. ORGANIZATION, ARMAMENT, AND TRAINING OF THE LCOSF AND DRA

1. This chapter was written by Colonel V. A. Runov.

2. Not all Soviet soldiers would agree. The BTR-70 has a bad reputation among those who know it intimately—as combat soldiers do.

3. The 5.45mm Kalashnikov was only issued to Soviet troops.

4. The Forward Security Element *[golovnaya pokhnaya zastava]* was a reinforced company-sized element that normally moved in front of the battalion during a road march.

5. Soviet commanders were reluctant to issue flak jackets to their troops since the commanders were responsible in case the soldier lost the flak jacket. The earlier flak jackets cost 250 rubles. The new flak jackets cost 10,000 rubles.

6. There is time to learn one's job in two years, if one concentrates on the job. Officers were kept busy with other tasks.

7. War dead include killed in action, died of wounds and disease, and killed in accidents.

332   THE SOVIET-AFGHAN WAR

8. Official 40th Army war dead number 13,833. Others include 572 KGB, 28 MVD, and 20 miscellaneous, for a total of 14,453. Official 40th Army officer war dead are 2,595 (4 generals, 1,975 officers, and 616 warrant officers). Total officer war dead amount to 2,765. G. F. Krivosheev, *Grif sekretnosti snyat* [The secret seal is lifted] (Moscow: Voyenizdat, 1993), 402–403. The authors of this study claim casualty figures that are almost double the official figures!

9. These are very optimistic figures. The prewar 1978 authorized army strength was 110,000, and actual strength was probably 80,000. Desertions and casualties kept the DRA ground forces at some 40,000 throughout the war. The Air Force and Air Defense Forces had a combined actual total of some 7,000, while the Sarandoy internal security forces may have had a wartime strength of 15,000. The border guards may have reached 4,000 men. The tribal militias, on paper, may have had 40,000 members—but many of these were part-time. Extracted from *Afghanistan: A Country Study*.

10. The Suvorov military schools were two-year-long secondary schools that accepted qualified 15- and 16-year-olds. Completion of a Suvorov school was particularly helpful in acceptance into a military academy. There was one lycee in Afghanistan.

11. This describes the Soviet Army as well, where family connections, friendship, and political connections determined promotions and assignments. The Mayorov, Sokolov, and Varennikov military family dynasties are prime examples.

3. ORGANIZATION, ARMAMENT, AND TACTICS OF THE MUJAHIDEEN

1. This chapter was written by Colonel V. A. Runov.

2. No ultra-leftists come to mind. Perhaps the author is confusing recipients of Chinese aid with true believers.

3. The April Revolution is the military coup d'etat on 27 April 1978 that brought the communist regime into power in Afghanistan.

4. Actually, the split was in August 1981.

5. *Islamskaya partiya Afganistana* (IPA) in Russian.

6. He did not graduate but left prior to the end of the four-year course. His followers also included Turkmen and Uzbeks.

7. *Islamskoe Obshchestvo Afganistana* (IOA) in Russian.

8. *Islamskaya partaya-krylo Khalesa* in Russian.

9. The split was in 1979.

10. Mullahs are paid religious teachers who instruct their communities in the fundamentals of Islam. Ulamas are Islamic scholars.

11. *Islamskiy soyuz osvobozhdeniya Afganistana* (ISOA) in Russian. This was actually the name of a previous alliance headed by Sayf that lasted until March 1981. He turned this alliance into a single faction and renamed it Islamic Unity *(Etehad-e Islami)*.

12. Actually, Sayaf was imprisoned in Afghanistan and was released after the Soviet invasion as part of a mass release of political prisoners.

13. *Natsional'nyy front spaseniya Afganistana* (HFSA) in Russian.

14. *Natsional'nyy islamskiy front Afganistana* (NIFA) in Russian.

15. Actually the title is *Pir,* not *Moreed. Pir* means the spiritual leader or source of guidance. *Moreed* means "the follower."

16. *Hazrat* is a title for respected religious leaders. It roughly means "Excellency." The author has mistaken Gailani for Mojadeddi.

17. *Dvizhenie islamskoyu revolyutsii Afganistana* (DIRA) in Russian. Again, this is the title of an earlier alliance of four parties that dissolved in 1980.

18. These are very optimistic figures.

19. The Russians are looking for structure where there was none. This is the case here.

20. The sections were usually leadership, military, judiciary, and cultural.

21. In most districts, more than one party was represented and they worked together. The example given was a isolated instance.

22. This paragraph and the chart are an attempt to create order and structure for planning. They show imagination, but little relation to reality.

23. The British Lee-Enfield rifle. This magazine-fed, smokeless powder rifle was a great favorite among Afghans.

24. This paragraph is mostly fantasy and reflects either wishful thinking or disinformation funneled to the Soviets by hired informants.

25. The Mujahideen were unpaid volunteers who supported their families with the spoils of war.

26. Again, the Russians are searching for the organization and structure that withstood the Soviet onslaught. That organization and structure are lacking. The Mujahideen were very amorphous and non-standard.

27. *Podgruppa preduprezhdeniya,* literally anticipatory subgroups.

28. *Otvlekayushchaya podgruppa.*

29. The Russian is *fugas,* similar to the western *fougasse.* The Russian term means a large explosive charge buried in the ground and covered with rocks and debris. The western term describes a flame weapon that is a buried 55-gallon drum of thickened gasoline with a propelling explosive charge at the base.

30. *Inzhenernaya mashina razgrazhdeniya* (IMR) is a tracked engineer vehicle that removes obstacles. At this time, the bazaar rate was approximately 200 Afghans to the U.S. dollar. These alleged rewards are a lot of money for a country where the per capita income was 6,852 Afghans per year ($34.26), and it is extremely doubtful that any of these rewards were ever actually paid by the cash-poor resistance groups. However, rumors of such payments were effective psychologically against the Soviets. The concept is hardly new. Editor Les Grau allegedly had a price on his head when he was an adviser to the South Vietnamese Army. No one knows of any Viet Cong actually collecting, but it gave the adviser one more reason to be cautious.

4. OPERATIONAL ART

1. This chapter was written by Colonel A. M. Fufaev.

2. DRA security was none too good and the Soviets felt that any plan was compromised as soon as the DRA was included.

3. The *stroevoy smotr,* or full-field layout, is a formal inspection where all the unit's

equipment is laid out on tarps in front of the combat vehicles. It is a stringent inspection, more appropriate for peacetime, that has little to do with combat readiness but does account for equipment availability. It was also a major indicator that the Soviets were preparing to conduct an operation.

4. There is no Province of Astana, but there is the large village of Astana.

5. The Taleqan sector is in northeast Afghanistan between Kunduz and Faizabad. The mined section appears to be some 40 kilometers in length. A *fougasse* is a blast mine that is often command-detonated and usually homemade.

5. COMBINED ARMS TACTICS

1. This section was written by Colonel P. D. Alekseev.

2. This definition is very close to the American definition of a "search and destroy" mission.

3. The same vignette is recounted, with some differences in details, in Lester W. Grau, *The Bear Went Over the Mountain: Soviet Combat Tactics in Afghanistan* (Frank Cass Publishers: London, 1998), 11–14. Many of the vignettes in this chapter are also found in *The Bear Went Over the Mountain* since both are taken from the Frunze Academy Combined Arms Staff Academy data base. The vignettes in *The Bear* are more detailed. For this vignette, both use the same map. This map has been corrected from the Soviet copy. The distance from Ghorband to Bamian is about 80 kilometers.

4. Major S. V. Nikitin served in Afghanistan from December 1979 to October 1981. He was awarded the Order of the Red Star. He was evidently assigned to the reconnaissance battalion of the 5th Motorized Rifle Division.

5. The SU-25 is a very effective close air support aircraft. Its Soviet nickname was *Grach* [rook] and its NATO designation is FROGFOOT. It has a two-man crew, a radius of action of 410 to 560 kilometers (depending on its load), is armed with a 30mm cannon, and can carry a variety of air-to-air and air-to-ground missiles, smart bombs, conventional bombs, fragmentation bombs, napalm, unguided rockets, and even nuclear weapons. It entered the Soviet inventory in 1980, making this one of the system's first combat flights. See Yuri Zuenko and Sergey Korostelev, *Boevye samolety Rossii* [Russia's Combat Aircraft] (Moscow: Arsenal Press, 1994), 88–92.

6. General-Lieutenant Yuri Vladimirovich Tukharinov.

7. This was probably the battle for Tangira canyon. Battles for the Lor Koh mountain canyons are described, from a Mujahideen perspective, in Ali Ahmad Jalali and Lester W. Grau, *The Other Side of the Mountain: Mujahideen Tactics in the Soviet-Afghan War* (Quantico, Va.: U.S. Marine Corps Study, 1998), 284–295.

8. Lieutenant Colonel A. L. Makkoveev served in Afghanistan from December 1979 until November 1981 as the commander of the 7th Motorized Rifle Company in a regiment of the 108th Motorized Rifle Division. He was awarded the Cavalier Order for Service to the Fatherland, 3rd Class. This vignette is also found in Grau, *The Bear Went Over the Mountain,* 5–8.

9. The machine gun/grenade launcher platoon was the fourth platoon of a motorized rifle company and provided suppressive fire from PKS or *Utes* machine guns and AGS-

17 automatic grenade launchers. This platoon disappeared during force reorganization in the mid-1980s.

10. Major S. V. Poleshchuk served in Afghanistan from December 1979 to November 1981. He commanded a motorized rifle platoon and a motorized rifle company in the 5th Motorized Rifle Division. He was awarded the medal "For Bravery."

11. Soviet personnel did not ride inside their armored personnel carriers due to the threat of land mines. Personnel riding on top of carriers had a better chance of surviving a mine blast on top of the carrier where the blast might throw them clear of the blast area.

12. This was probably Tangira canyon and may be a continuation of the action described by Major Nikitin previously in this chapter. Actually, Shaykh Baba canyon, Kale-e Amani canyon, Kale-e Kaneske canyon, Jare-e Ab canyon, Khwaja Morad canyon, and Tangira canyon in Lor Koh mountain all had water. Tangira canyon had the most water, but the Mujahideen eventually left it since the Soviets could get their tracked vehicles inside the canyon.

13. Alert forces (*dezhurnaya sily*—literally duty forces) were forces earmarked for rapid deployment that were immediately available to the commander. A division normally had up to a battalion as an alert force and the 40th Army had a regiment as an alert force. Alert force duty was rotated through the combat units. Alert forces were usually deployed on missions close to the sending headquarters for a limited period of time.

14. This section was written by Colonel P. D. Alekseyev.

15. The NKVD were the predecessors to the KGB. Following World War II, NKVD forces were used to fight secessionist guerrillas in the Ukraine, Baltic states, and Caucasus.

16. The *Watanparast* [patriots] were paramilitary forces recruited from communist party volunteers, local communist sympathizers, and paid mercenaries.

17. Dry rations are similar to the old U.S. Army C-ration. There were three types of dry rations. The first contained a can of meat, some crackers or toast, some jam, and a tea bag. The second contained two cans of meat mixed with oatmeal. The third contained a can of meat and a can of vegetables or fruit. Normally, Soviet units carried a minimum of three days' dry rations to preclude the very problem this unit experienced.

18. Major B. L. Polovinkin served in Afghanistan from January 1980 to December 1981, first as a reconnaissance platoon leader and then as a reconnaissance company commander.

19. The commandant's service provided traffic control, local security, and garrison police functions. Neither the Soviet or DRA Armed Forces had a military police branch, and the commandant's service handled many of these functions. Due to the limited number of commandant's service personnel, combat forces had to provide personnel to carry out many of their functions, decreasing the number of personnel available for combat.

20. This vignette is described in more detail in Grau, *The Bear Went Over the Mountain,* 9–10.

21. Soviet-cited villages are often hard to find. In this case, the villages may have been identified by the names of the Mujahideen commanders based there. Kayum and Najmuddin are common names in Afghanistan.

22. Major A. M. Kovyrshin served in Afghanistan during the period September 1982 to November 1984 as a platoon leader and company commander. He was awarded the Order of the Red Star.

23. This vignette is described in more detail in Grau, *The Bear Went Over the Mountain,* 19–23.

24. Lieutenant Colonel S. V. Zelenskiy served in Afghanistan from 1981 to 1983 as the commander of the 1st Air Assault Company and as the senior assistant to the Chief of the brigade operations section of the 70th Separate Motorized Rifle Brigade. He was decorated with the Order of the Red Star. This vignette is described in more detail in ibid., 15–18.

25. Major A. V. Odinochnikov served in Afghanistan as a motorized rifle platoon leader in the 5th Motorized Rifle Division. He was awarded the Order of the Red Star.

26. Major A. S. Burov served in Afghanistan from July 1985 to September 1987 as the commander of a motorized rifle company. He was awarded the medal "For Bravery."

27. This section was written by Colonel V. F. Yashin.

28. In Soviet conventional warfare, the dismounted ambush was primarily used to capture prisoners and documents in order to gather intelligence. Tank ambushes were used to provide early warning on armor approaches. The mission of the ambush in Afghanistan was much different.

29. The senior commander who made the decision to conduct the ambush was normally two to three levels higher than the ambushing unit. Thus a regimental commander gave an ambush order to a platoon and a division commander to a company.

30. Unit of fire is a Soviet logistics term specifying a certain number and type of round for every type of weapon in the Soviet inventory. The unit of fire is considered the amount necessary for one day of combat—although battery artillery preparation fires would often expend a unit of fire in less than an hour.

31. Soviet officers V. Alekseyenko, A. Borisov, I. Ivonnik, L. Tret'yakov, and others who fought in Afghanistan all agreed on the need for foreseeing, preparing, and rehearsing for changes to the basic ambush plan [General Staff note].

32. Hiding a full battalion in an ambush is close to impossible. Planning on trapping and killing a 200-man enemy force in a battalion ambush is fantasy at best. If the intelligence actually pinpointed the movement of such a large force, a blocking position, coupled with artillery and aviation support, and a pursuit force would have a much better chance of success.

33. This vignette is described in more detail in Grau, *The Bear Went Over the Mountain,* 159–162.

34. This vignette is described in more detail in ibid., 190–192.

35. Soviet troops frequently rode on top of their personnel carriers. In hot weather, riding inside a personnel carrier becomes rapidly unbearable. Further, if an armored personnel carrier hit a mine, the chances of survival were much higher for those personnel riding on top of the carrier.

36. Blinding or dazzling the enemy with illumination rounds or flares fired just at the horizon was a standard Soviet action.

37. Major V. P. Podvorniy served as the senior assistant to the chief of the operations section of the 66th Separate Motorized Rifle Brigade. This vignette is described in more detail in Grau, *The Bear Went Over the Mountain,* 180–184.

38. This vignette is described in more detail in ibid., 193–196.

39. 1.5 metric tons of water is 1,500 liters. For a 25 man ambush staying on site for ten days, this would work out to six liters (1.58 gallons) per day per man. What is astound-

ing is that Soviet forces would cook meals on or near their ambush site! The Soviets had adequate dry rations, so why would they cook on site? The odors and smoke from a cooking fire are giveaways to a position. If they had to cook, there are other fuels (propane, white gas) that are far less obtrusive—although these were not available to the Soviet forces. Firewood may be a reason why more Soviet ambushes were not successful.

40. This vignette is described in more detail in Grau, *The Bear Went Over the Mountain*, 185–189.

41. This vignette is described in more detail in ibid., 152–155.

42. 70th Separate Motorized Rifle Brigade.

43. This vignette is described in more detail in ibid., 167–170.

44. Directional, antipersonnel mines are similar to the U.S. claymore mine. They can be detonated by trip wire or with a firing device.

45. This section was written by Colonel V. F. Yashin.

46. This vignette is described in more detail in Grau, *The Bear Went Over the Mountain*, 136–139.

47. This vignette is described in more detail in ibid., 143–146.

48. Highway movement was regulated by organic commandant's service elements. In the regular Soviet Army, a division had an organic commandant's service company, an army had an organic commandant's service battalion, and a front had an organic commandant's service brigade. Separate armies, such as the 40th Army in Afghanistan, had a highway commandant's service regiment composed of two traffic battalions and a security battalion. The primary mission was to regulate the movement of the headquarters and to provide security to the headquarters. Since there were not enough traffic control personnel, each motorized rifle regiment trained a motorized rifle company to also perform traffic control duties.

49. *Ratsionalizator* in Russian.

50. Motorized field kitchen *[Polevaya avtokukhnya]* mounted on a ZIL 131 truck with a 200-liter cooking kettle capacity.

51. *Broneblok* in Russian.

52. Battalions trained personnel to serve as forward air controllers since regular FACs were not always available.

53. This vignette is described in more detail in Grau, *The Bear Went Over the Mountain*, 140–142.

54. This vignette is described in more detail in ibid., 147–150.

55. *Podvishnaya gruppa* in Russian.

6. COMBAT ARMS BRANCH TACTICS

1. Colonel V. I. Litvinenko is the author of the artillery section.

2. Mortars, antitank guns, and antitank guided missiles were part of the Soviet artillery, and artillerymen manned these systems in motorized rifle, airborne, air assault, Spetsnaz, and tank units and subunits.

3. The MTLB is a multi-purpose, armored, tracked vehicle that was used as an artillery tractor and an armored cargo vehicle in Afghanistan.

4. NATO designation is the AT-5 Spandrel. It has a maximum range of 4,000 meters,

flies at 208 meters/second, and carries a three kilogram warhead. Steven Zaloga, "Russian Anti-Tank Guided Missiles—Part 1: Heavy Systems," *Jane's Intelligence Review* (February 1994), 59.

5. NATO designation is the AT-4 Spigot. It has a maximum range of 2,000 meters, flies at 185 meters/second, and carries a three kilogram warhead. David C. Isby, *Weapons and Tactics of the Soviet Army* (London: Jane's Publishing Company Limited, 1988), 211.

6. NATO designation is the AT-7 Saxhorn. It has a maximum range of 1,000 meters and flies at 200 meters/second. Isby, *Weapons and Tactics of the Soviet Army,* 214.

7. 122° Fahrenheit.

8. The basic planning element for Soviet artillery fire planning was the artillery battalion.

9. An understanding of Soviet artillery planning for conventional war is helpful in understanding this section. For those readers not familiar with Soviet artillery planning, an abbreviated description is provided in Appendix 2.

10. Nona is a female name, probably that of the designer.

11. The Soviet standard for minimum safe distance between artillery impact of rounds and friendly forces is 300 meters from entrenched, protected troops and 400 meters from unprotected, defending troops.

12. The "Realiya-U" is a seismic motion detector that allows the operator to determine the number and type of objects moving near it.

13. *Ognevoy blok* in Russian.

14. This was a constant problem for British forces fighting on the Northwest Frontier. The Soviets would have been well-served to study the British lessons-learned in those conflicts.

15. *Dal'nomer Artilleriskiy Kvanovy* in Russian. This is a laser range finder.

16. *Stereoskopicheskiy dal'nomep* in Russian. This is a stereoscopic range finder, of which there are several models.

17. *Periskopicheskaya artilleriyskaya bussol'* in Russian for the periscope artillery aiming circle.

18. There are 6,000 Soviet mils in a circle—as compared to 6,400 Western mils. The Soviets use the same rule of thumb that a shift of one mil will shift the strike of a round by one meter at 1,000 meters. 1-50 mils is 9°. The 1-50 signifies 150 mils.

19. 90° to the right and 48° to the left.

20. *Artilleriyskie ballisticheskie stantsii* in Russian.

21. *Desantnyy meteorologicheskiy komplekt* in Russian.

22. *Vetrovye ruzh'ya* in Russian.

23. Soviet training was usually by conscription call-up group, whereas the standard week integrated all call-up groups.

24. Colonel N. S. Nakonechnyy is author of the armored forces section.

25. General Gromov, former 40th Army Commander, states that T-55, T-62, and T-64 tanks were used in Afghanistan. Boris V. Gromov, *Ogranichennyy kontingent* [Limited contingent] (Moscow: Progress Publishers, 1994), 121.

26. This event is described in more detail in Lester W. Grau, *The Bear Went Over the Mountain: Soviet Combat Tactics in Afghanistan* (London: Frank Cass Publishers, 1998), 24–26. The vignette gives particular credit to Soviet artillery that kept a wall of steel in front of the advancing tanks and paratroopers.

27. The location of this fortress is a mystery as is the architecture of the bridge. These moat bridges were common in medieval Europe but are unknown in Afghanistan. Parts of this vignette may be pure imagination.

28. *Malozametnye prepyatstviya* [concealed obstacles] is a Soviet tanglefoot obstacle that is a large, compressed spring made of high-quality wire. It is similar to an uncontrolled "Slinky" toy. When unbanded during set up, it uncoils wildly in every direction. It will stop dismounted soldiers, animals, vehicles, and even tanks. It is almost impossible to extricate anything from this without heavy-duty wire cutters, pliers, and lots of time.

29. *Stroevoy smotr* [ceremonial inspection]. The unit would lay out all of its equipment on the parade ground. All equipment would be laid out on tarps in front of the vehicles. Every piece of equipment would be formally checked and accounted for, the correct spacing on uniform items would be checked with a template, and displays would be aligned with pieces of string. The process could take three days by the time commanders at all levels had inspected the unit. Although inspections are good ideas, these massive formal inspections were almost always conducted before a planned action. This would tip off the Mujahideen that an action was impending.

30. The Soviet airborne did not make any combat parachute drops in Afghanistan. They conducted all of their air assaults from helicopters. The actual difference between the airborne and air assault forces in Afghanistan was their origins and traditions. Colonel V. M. Varushinin is author of the airborne and air assault section.

31. There was more than slight resistance. The presidential palace was guarded by Afghan troops and "the Muslim Battalion"—a Soviet Spetsnaz battalion of Central Asian soldiers in DRA uniforms. When the paratroopers arrived, the Spetsnaz and airborne forces accidently became engaged in a fire fight that killed half a battalion of Soviets.

32. 103rd Airborne Division in Kabul.

33. 56th Air Assault Brigade in Gardez.

34. 345th Separate Parachute Regiment in Bagram.

35. 66th Separate Motorized Rifle Brigade in Jalalabad and 70th Separate Motorized Rifle Brigade in Kandahar.

36. *Boevaya mashina desanta*. A Soviet air-droppable, armored personnel carrier that carries up to nine men (usually a maximum of seven). It has the same turret as the BMP, so the BMD-1 has the 73mm cannon of the BMP-1 and the BMD-2 has the 30mm automatic gun of the BMP-2. They were widely used by Soviet airborne and air assault forces.

37. *Vozdushnyy punkt upravleniya* [airborne command post]. This was an unarmed Mi-8 command and control helicopter with an increased number of radios.

38. Lebed later became a General Officer and commanded the 14th Army in Moldova. He ran for president against Boris Yeltsin in 1996.

39. Related by Major S. N. Pariy, the battalion chief of staff.

40. Soviet NCOs were regular conscripts who attended a six-month NCO school following basic training. Thus, in most cases, the squad leaders were the most inexperienced soldiers in the outfit and were the wrong people to conduct training.

41. The Soviet Air Force divided aviation into strategic aviation, aviation of the front, army aviation, and transport aviation. Army aviation included helicopter gunships, transport helicopters, and SU-25 close air support aircraft. Aviation of the front included fighters, bombers, and fighter-bombers. After the Soviet-Afghan War, army aviation became part of ground forces. Colonel V. S. Kozlov is the author of the army aviation section.

42. The Strella-2 [Arrow-2] is a Soviet- or Chinese-made SA-7 air defense missile. The Stinger is a U.S. air defense missile.

43. Forward Air Controllers [FACs] were TO&E and non-TO&E. The authorized TO&E FACs were pilots assigned to ground duty to direct airstrikes and regulate aviation support. In theory, authorized FACs were supposed to be the best pilots available. In practice, they were the pilots who had experienced difficulties or run afoul of the system. There were never enough authorized FACs, so additional FACs were created for whom there were no TO&E slots. Sometimes these were non-rated air force officers and sometimes they were ground officers who learned the job.

7. COMBAT SUPPORT

1. The reconnaissance section was written by Colonel V. K. Puzel'. Reconnaissance forces included two GRU Spetsnaz brigades, a reconnaissance battalion per division, and a reconnaissance company per regiment.

2. Reconnaissance signal apparatus (RSA) or *Razvedyvatel'no signal'noy apparatury* in Russian.

3. It was also dangerous to peaceful civilians since sensors cannot readily distinguish between civilians and combatants.

4. *Boevoy razvedyvatel'nyy dozor* (BRD) in Russian.

5. The ARK-1 *(artilleriyskiy razvedivatel'nyy kompleks)* is a radar/sonar system linked with a computer and an artillery unit. It detects and pinpoints enemy fire and provides firing data to the artillery unit. Nicknamed the Lynx *(rys')*, it is a reconnaissance-fire complex designed to detect and destroy an enemy target in real time.

6. There were two Spetsnaz brigades in Afghanistan. One was headquartered in Lashkar Gah in Helmand Province and the other was headquartered in Jalalabad. Each brigade had some 3,000 personnel.

7. This section was written by Colonel Yu. P. Babich. The Soviets ignored their own vast experience with partisan warfare during World War II and treated the war in Afghanistan as a unique experience.

8. The layout of this post is illustrated in Lester W. Grau, *The Bear Went Over the Mountain: Soviet Combat Tactics in Afghanistan* (London: Frank Cass Publishers, 1998), 126–128. The air assault brigade headquarters was actually a Spetsnaz brigade headquarters.

9. This example is contained in ibid., 129–132.

10. This should add up to 40 kilometers, but does not. Either the 2.5 kilometer stretch was 22.5 kilometers or there were sections of the 40 mile stretch that were not secured.

11. There is no single Afghan language. Pushtu and Dari are the official languages, while Uzbek, Baluchi, and Turkmen are also spoken. The prewar literacy rate in Afghanistan was about 10 percent.

12. Combat load *[boekomplekt]* is a logistic planning term that differs somewhat from the U.S. "basic load." It was generally (but not consistently) considered adequate for one day's heavy combat.

13. Duty weapons were manned, crew-served weapons in temporary positions. Only these weapons would engage enemy reconnaissance or probing elements while the rest of the force moved to battle positions. The duty weapons would then move to battle posi-

tions. Enemy return fire would be on the temporary position and the enemy knowledge of the locations of defending Soviet crew-served weapons would be faulty.

14. This section was written by Colonel V. V. Zakharov.

15. The Mujahideen claim that this was a Soviet activity. It seems to be a fairly common claim by combatants in post–World War II conflicts and is perhaps more the stuff of legend than reality.

16. Most of the time, Mujahideen did not mark their mines if they had them under observation. Mine markings varied among Mujahideen groups.

17. *Minno-rosysknoy sluzhby* (MRS) in Russian.

18. *Inzhenernaia mashina razgrazhdeniya* in Russian is a combat engineer vehicle based on a tank chassis with an extendable, hydraulic manipulator, a hydraulic dozer blade, and an earth bucket. The IMR can clear obstacles, dig emplacements, and repair roads under fire.

19. This is also an indicator that the Mujahideen had stepped up their mine warfare efforts considerably during this time.

20. *Pontonno-mostovii park* in Russian. A PMP set has 32 river and four shore pontoons. A complete pontoon set can provide 236 meters of 60-ton bridging or 450 meters of 20-ton bridging.

21. *Gusenichni plavayushchii transportr* in Russian.

22. A 20-meter cantilever bridge carried on a tank chassis.

23. *Tyazhelii mekhanizirovannii most* is a truck-mounted scissors bridge with four sections that join for a total length of 40 meters.

24. The BAT is an unarmored bulldozer.

25. This was also a common task for tanks fitted with mine plows.

26. *Razbornyy metallicheskiy most* is a sectional steel bridge.

27. Soviet tangle foot is a different obstacle than that used in western armies. It is a large, compressed, banded spring made of high-quality wire. It is similar to an uncontrolled "Slinky" toy. When unbanded during set up, it uncoils wildly in every direction. It will stop dismounted soldiers, animals, vehicles, and even tanks. It is almost impossible to extricate anything from this without heavy-duty wire cutters, pliers, and lots of time. These obstacles are called MZP *(malozametnye prepyatsviya),* or concealed obstacles.

28. After their withdrawal, the Soviets did not submit minefield maps to international demining groups.

29. The author of this section is Colonel S. S. Sharov.

30. The Soviets considered smoke and flame weapons as chemical weapons. This statement is quite controversial, since there is a great deal of evidence that the Soviet Union used a variety of lethal and nonlethal chemical agents against the Mujahideen during 1979–1982. U.S. State Department, *Chemical Warfare in Southeast Asia and Afghanistan: Report to the Congress from Secretary of State Alexander M. Haig, Jr., March 22, 1982* (Washington, DC: Government Printing Office, 1982), 14–18.

31. The RPO-A is a single-tube launcher with a simple optical sight calibrated to 600 meters. There are three warheads available. The RPO-A is a thermobaric (fuel-air) round used against caves, buildings, bunkers, and other enclosures. It creates a cloud of gas that explodes and creates a tremendous crushing overpressure. The RPO-Z is an incendiary round; the RPO-D is a smoke round. The RPO-A can destroy an 80 cubic meter building or anyone in the open within a four-meter radius of the burst.

8. COMBAT SERVICE SUPPORT

1. This chapter was written by Colonel B. P. Gruzdev.

2. This was a marked departure from regular garrison procedures in which ammunition accountability regulations made such transfers slow and cumbersome.

3. *Sbornye punkty povrezhdennykh mashin* in Russian.

4. This is a major departure from regular Soviet procedures in Europe.

5. The RDV is a water bladder.

6. This ambush is described in *The Bear Went Over the Mountain: Soviet Combat Tactics in Afghanistan* (London: Frank Cass Publishers, 1998), 167–170.

7. This incident is described in ibid., 94–96.

8. This episode is described in Chapter 1 and in ibid., 2–4.

9. *Checks* were a form of government script issued as a pay supplement. A *check* was worth 10 rubles and a ruble was officially worth $1.59 at the time. Thus, vodka was being sold for $79.50 a bottle to desperate soldiers.

10. Peoples' control was a Communist Party apparatus invention that used quasi-official courts to confront people with their misdeeds, extract public confessions, and shame the perpetrators into better behavior. Peoples' control was just one more job for the overworked junior officer.

11. Many of the Soviet women in Afghanistan sold sexual favors for *checks*. These "sex-for-checks" women were known as "chekistkas"—a pun on "chekists," which was an earlier term for the KGB.

12. The medical section was written by Colonel Yu. G. Avdeev.

13. For additional information, see Lester W. Grau and William A. Jorgensen, "Medical Support in a Counter-Guerrilla War: Epidemiologic Lessons Learned in the Soviet-Afghan War," *U.S. Army Medical Department Journal* (May/June 1995), 41–49.

14. By 1986, it was apparent that the air defense regiment and the tank regiment in each of the three motorized rifle divisions were superfluous to the needs of guerrilla warfare. Gorbachev made their withdrawal a political statement while secretly replacing them with additional Spetsnaz and motorized rifle forces.

15. The division's medical battalion could run a field hospital handling up to 400 patients a day, conduct surgery, and run a 60-bed recovery ward. The battalion had three or more surgeons, a therapist, a doctor of internal medicine, epidemiologist, and toxicologist. Department of the Army, *FM100-2-2, The Soviet Army Specialized Warfare and Rear Area Support* (Washington, DC: Government Printing Office, 1984), 13-20 to 13-21.

16. *Meditsinskiy punkt polka* in Russian.

17. *Otdel'niy meditsinskiy batal'on* in Russian.

18. Soviet TO&E medical personnel were assigned at maneuver company level and higher. There was a senior medical corpsman and corpsman at company. A physician's assistant or a newly commissioned doctor commanded the maneuver battalion medical section that handled initial treatment and evacuation. The regimental medical post had a medical company consisting of two or three doctors, a dentist, two physician's assistants, a technician, a pharmacist, nurses, a cook, a radio operator, orderlies, and drivers. The regimental medical post served as a dressing station and provided immediate surgery, transfusions, treatment for lightly wounded, and evacuation to the division medical battalion. Soviet Studies Research Centre, *The Sustainability of the Soviet Army in Battle* (The Hague: Shape Technical Centre, September 1986), 286–296.

19. *Voennoy polevoy mnogoprofil'nyy gospital* in Russian.

20. *Sanitarno-epidemiologicheskiy otryad* in Russian.

21. These medical facilities supported the 5th Motorized Rifle Division and the western corridor of Afghanistan.

22. 70th Separate Motorized Rifle Brigade.

23. The 149th Motorized Rifle Regiment of the 201st Motorized Rifle Division.

24. This supported the remainder of the 201st Motorized Rifle Division.

25. The 345th Separate Parachute Regiment was stationed in Bagram, and this complex would routinely treat soldiers from the 108th Motorized Rifle Division and the entire country.

26. 66th Separate Motorized Rifle Brigade.

27. *Divizionniy meditsinskiy punkt* in Russian.

28. *Khirurgicheskyy polevoy podvizhnyy gospital'* in Russian.

29. Eight medevac helicopters were probably not enough to support the 40th Army when its elements were involved in heavy fighting. See Lester W. Grau and William A. Jorgensen, "Handling the Wounded in a Counter-Guerrilla War: The Soviet/Russian Experience in Afghanistan and Chechnya," *U.S. Army Medical Department Journal* (January/February 1998), 2–10.

30. Promedol (trimeperidine hydrochloride) is a painkiller.

9. CONCLUSION

1. This section was written by Colonel V. A. Runov.

2. There is controversy as to the type of regiments involved. Western sources indicate that these were the air defense and tank regiments of the 5th, 108th, and 201st Motorized Rifle Regiments—regiments not needed for combat in Afghanistan. The Soviets sent in another Spetsnaz brigade and more motorized rifle regiments at this time. This is reflected in Appendix 1—which is compiled solely from Russian sources.

3. Actually, this was a Bilateral Agreement between Afghanistan and Pakistan on Mutual Relations. The Soviet Union and United States were signatories as interested parties and guarantors. The Mujahideen were not involved in the negotiations for the agreement, although it was presumed that Pakistan and the United States acted on their behalf.

4. This is incorrect. Afghanistan did not experience ethnic war.

5. Actually, the Soviet Union spent 1918–1933 fighting the Basmachi guerrillas in Central Asia to impose communist rule and reimpose the Russian/Soviet empire on the break-away republics. A good source is Robert F. Bauman, *Russian-Soviet Unconventional Wars in the Caucasus, Central Asia and Afghanistan* (Leavenworth Paper Number 20, Combat Studies Institute, Fort Leavenworth, KS), 1993.

6. As Chapter 2 shows, the actual war dead are probably double the official figure. Severely wounded personnel who were evacuated to the Soviet Union and died there were not counted as war dead, nor were those who died en route to the Soviet Union. Servicemen assigned to units in the Soviet Union, but located in Afghanistan for temporary duty or participating in a combat mission originating in the Soviet Union were also not counted as war dead if killed in Afghanistan.

7. There is a math problem here. This would give a maximum total of 9,490 killed and wounded in 1984. The annual average of killed and wounded during the time frame

of March 1980 through April 1985 is 27,660, as derived from official, low-sided figures. This works out to a daily average of some 76 killed or wounded. G. F. Krivosheev, *Grif sekretnosti snyat: Poteri vooruzhennykh sil SSSR v voynakh, boevykh deystviyakh i voennykh konfliktakh* [The secret seal is removed: Casualties of the Armed Forces of the USSR in war, combat, and armed conflict] (Moscow: Voyenizdat, 1993), 405.

8. Not to detract from the performance of many soldiers, but private conversations with serving officers revealed that some soldiers were decorated for self-inflicted wounds. Self-inflicted wounds are indicative of low morale, and the Soviet command punished platoon leaders and company commanders who reported that their soldiers shot themselves to avoid combat. After the command punished those junior officers who reported self-inflicted wounds, other officers awarded decorations to their soldiers who shot themselves. It was the easiest way to get the soldier out of the unit with no questions asked.

9. The Soviet *Sputnik partizana* [Partisan's companion] was published by the Ministry of Defense during the war and provided a detailed how-to guide to guerrilla war that is still applicable today.

APPENDIX ONE: 40TH ARMY ORDER OF BATTLE

1. These orders of battle were compiled from many unclassified Russian sources. Principal sources include Aleksandr Mayorov, *Pravda ob Afganskoy voyne* [The truth about the Afghan War] (Moscow: Prava cheloveka, 1996); Aleksandr Lyakhovskiy, *Tragediya i doblest' Afgana* [The tragedy and triumph of the Afghan veteran] (Moscow: Iskona, 1995), and other works of General Lyakhovskiy; and Viktor Markovskiy, *Zharkoe nebo Afganistana* [The hot skies of Afghanistan] (Moscow: Tekhnika-molodezhi, 2000). Other sources came from articles in *Soldat udachi* [Soldier of fortune], *Armeyskiy sbornik* [Army digest], *Krasnaya zvezda* [Red Star], *Bratishchka* [The little brothers], *Spetsnaz,* and *Orientir* [Reference point].

APPENDIX TWO: SOVIET ARTILLERY PLANNING

1. A. A. Grechko, *Sovetskaya voennaya entsiklopediya* [Soviet military encyclopedia], vol. 2 (Moscow: Voyenizdat, 1976), 132.

2. G. E. Peredel'skiy and M. P. Pankov, *Artilleriyskiy divizion v boyu* [Artillery battalion in combat] (Moscow: Voyenizdat, 1989), 25; and I. D. Pombrik and N. A. Shevchenko, *Karta ofitsera* [The officer's map] (Moscow: Voyenizdat, 1985), 162.

3. Peredel'skiy and Pankov, *Artilleriyskiy divizion v boyu,* 28–30; and Pombrik and Shevchenko, *Karta ofitsera,* 163.

4. Peredel'skiy and Pankov, *Artilleriyskiy divizion v boyu,* 25; and Pombrik and Shevchenko, *Karta ofitsera,* 162.

5. Peredel'skiy and Pankov, *Artilleriyskiy divizion v boyu,* 30–31; and Pombrik and Shevchenko, *Karta ofitsera,* 164.

Glossary

This is a list of common abbreviations and terms used in the book. Since the Soviet system is very different from the U.S. system, many of the translated terms are approximations. Where necessary, the transliterated Soviet term is included for the specialist.

AAslt. Air Assault [*takticheskiy vozdushnyy desant*]. Helicopter-borne assault into an area.

AAsltB. Air Assault Battalion [*desanto-shturmoviy batal'on*].

AAsltC. Air Assault Company [*desanto-shturmovaya rota*].

AAG. Army Artillery Group [*armeyskaya artilleriyskaya gruppa*]. A temporary group of three to five artillery battalions under the control of the Army Chief of Rocket Troops and Artillery for a particular mission. During army operations, a gun AAG and an MRL AAG are usually formed.

Afghanistan National Liberation Front (ANLF). [*Jebh-e-Nejat-i-Melli Afghanistan*]. Founded by Sebqhatullah Mojadeddi. This Mujahideen party is moderate.

AGS-17. Soviet-manufactured, tripod-mounted automatic grenade launcher that fires 30mm grenades from a thirty-round drum magazine. The maximum range of the AGS-17 is 1,700 meters.

AO. Area of Operations [*naznachennyy rayon*]. The area in which a unit is authorized to conduct combat or other actions.

Airborne. Parachute trained forces [*parashutno-desantiy*]. Deployed by parachute or helicopter.

AOR. Area of Responsibility [*zona otvetstvennosti*]. The area that a unit is responsibile for securing and controlling.

APC. Armored personnel carrier. Any of the wheeled or tracked Soviet-manufactured combat vehicles used to transport soldiers.

ATGM. Antitank guided missile [Russian PTUR].

BM-1. Single barrel 107mm rocket launcher.

BM-12. An obsolete Soviet multiple rocket launcher. The Chinese improved and manufactured it as the Type 63. Most Mujahideen BM-12s were actually Chinese Type 63s. It is ground-mounted, has twelve barrels, and fires 107mm rockets to a distance of 8,500 meters. It weighs 611 kilograms.

BM-21. A truck-mounted, 40-tube multiple rocket launcher that fires 122mm rockets to a distance of 20.5 kilometers. The Mujahideen mostly called this the BM-40.

BM-22. A truck-mounted, 16-tube multiple rocket launcher that fires 220mm rockets to a distance of 40 kilometers. The type of rocket warheads include high-explosive fragmentation, chemical, incendiary, and remotely delivery mines. The Soviet nickname for this lethal system is *Uragan* (Hurricane). Western analysts initially identified this system as the BM27.

BMD. [*Boevaya mashina desanta*]. A Soviet air-droppable, armored personnel carrier that carries up to nine men (usually a maximum of seven). It has the same turret as the BMP, so the BMD-1 has the 73mm cannon of the BMP-1 and the BMD-2 has the 30mm automatic gun of the BMP-2. They were widely used by Soviet airborne and air assault force.

BMP. A Soviet tracked infantry fighting vehicle [*boevaya mashina pekhoty*]. Carries a three-man crew and a squad of eight soldiers. The BMP-1 mounts a 73mm cannon, a 7.62mm machine gun, and an antitank missile. The BMP-2 carries a 30mm automatic gun and a different antitank missile and launcher.

BrAG. Brigade Artillery Group. A temporary group of two to five artillery battalions under the control of the Brigade Chief of Rocket Troops and Artillery for a particular mission.

BRDM. A four-wheeled armored reconnaissance vehicle. It has two auxiliary wheels for extra mobility. In its various configurations, it carries either a 12.7mm machine gun, a 7.62mm machine gun, or both.

BTR. A Soviet eight-wheeled armored personnel carrier [*bronetransporter*]. Can carry up to an 11-man squad. It mounts 14.5mm and 7.62mm machine guns and can carry antitank weapons as well. The BTR and BMP were the most common infantry carriers of the Soviet Forces.

Bronegruppa. An armored group of 4-5 tanks, BMPs, or BTR, or any combination of such vehicles. The BMPs and BTRs are employed without their normally assigned motorized rifle squad on board and fight away from their dismounted troops.

CINC. Commander in Chief.

Combat load [*boekomplekt*]. A logistic planning term that differs from the U.S. "basic load." It was generally considered adequate for one days heavy combat.

CP/OP. Command Post/Observation Post [*komandno-nablyudatel'nyi punkt*].

DAG. Division Artillery Group [*divizionnaya artilleriyskaya gruppa*]. A temporary group of three to five artillery battalions under the control of the Division Chief of Rocket Troops and Artillery for a particular mission.

DRA. Democratic Republic of Afghanistan. The communist government of Afghanistan.

DShK. Soviet-manufactured 12.7mm heavy machine gun. It is a primary armament on Soviet-manufactured armored vehicles and is effective against ground and air targets. It has a wheeled carriage, tripod, and mountain mount for ground and air defense firing. It has rate of fire of 540 to 600 rounds per minute, with a maximum range of 7,000 meters and an effective range of 1,500 meters against ground targets and 1,000 meters against air targets.

Etehad-e Islami (EIA). Mujahideen faction led by Abdurab Rasul Sayaf.

FAC. Forward Air Controller [*gruppa boevogo upravlenie*]. An airman or soldier who requests, coordinates, and adjusts aviation strikes in support of the ground force. He can be on the ground or flying above the battlefield.

FDC. Fire Direction Center [*punkt upravleniya ognyem*].

Fougasse. The Russian *fugas,* similar to the western *fougasse.* The Russian term, when applied to the Mujahideen, means a large explosive charge buried in the ground and covered with rocks and debris. When applied to Russian ordnance, it means a blast mine (as opposed to a fragmentation mine). The western term describes a flame weapon that is a buried 55-gallon drum of thickened gasoline with a propelling explosive charge at the base.

FSC/FO. Fire Support Coordinator or Forward Observer [*artilleyskiy korrektirovshchik*]. A soldier who requests, coordinates, and adjusts artillery fire in support of the ground force.

FSE. Forward Security Element [*golovnaya pokhodnaya zastava*]. A reinforced company or platoon-sized element that normally moves in front of the battalion during a road march.

Full-field. An exhaustive inspection by a higher headquarters layout of forces field gear and personnel with everything laid out on tarps in front of the vehicles [*stroyevoi smotr*].

Green zone. Agricultural region of gardens, orchards, fields, and vineyards bisected by a network of irrigation ditches. These normally border rivers and some sections of highway and most are practically impassible for vehicles.

Goryunov. The heavy machine gun SGM [*Stankovy Goryunov Modernizovanniy*]. M-49 was adopted by the Soviet Army during World War II and modernized versions are in service with the Russian Army today. It is a gas-operated, air-cooled, company-level, 7.62mm weapon that has vehicle and ground mounts. It has a rate of fire of 650 rounds per minute and a maximum range of 2,500 meters and an effective range of 1,000 meters.

Hazara. A people in the mountainous central part of Afghanistan. They are said to be descendants of the hordes of Ghenghis Khan and have a different physical appearance from many of the other Afghan peoples. Most of the Hazara are Shia Moslems. Iran, a Shia neighbor, was usually concerned about their treatment.

Islamic Party (HIH). [*Hezb-e-Islami-Gulbuddin*]. Founded in 1974 to fight the Daoud government, it later split, as cofounders Rabanni and Khalis founded their own factions. Its leader, Gulbuddin Hikmatyar, is a fundamentalist internationalist. Hikmatyar's party received more outside aid from Pakistan, the United States, and Saudi Arabia than any other Mujahideen party.

Islamic Party (HIK). [*Hezb-e-Islami-Khalis*]. Founded by Mawlawi Mohammed Yunis Khalis who left Afghanistan for Pakistan in 1973 after the Daoud coup. Khalis is from Nangahar Province. His most famous commanders include Abdul Haq in Kabul and Jalladuddin Hagani of Paktia Province. This Mujahideen party is fundamentalist.

Islamic Revolutionary Movement (IRMA). [*Harakat-e-Inqilab-i-Islami*]. Founded by Mohammad Nabi Mohammadi. This Mujahideen party is moderate (traditional Islamist).

Islamic Movement (HI). [*Harakat-i Islami*]. Founded by Ayatollah Asef Muhsini in Iran as a minority Shia faction. This Mujahideen party has a traditional Islamic orientation.

Islamic Society (JIA). [*Jamiat-i-Islami*]. Founded by Burhanuddin Rabbani who fled to Pakistan in 1974. His most famous commanders are Ahmd **Shah Masood and Ismail Khan.** This Mujahideen party is primarily fundamentalist and is dominated by ethnic Tadjiks.

Islamic Unity of Afghan Mujahideen (IUAM). [*Ittehad-i-Islami Mujahideen-i-Afghanistan*]. The name of the two coalitions of Mujahideen groups that formed in May 1980 in Peshawar. One contained four major and three smaller fundamentalist groups and became known as the Group of Seven. The other included three traditionalist parties and was known as the Group of Three.

Islamic Union for the Liberation of Afghanistan (IUA). [*Ittihad-i-Islami*]. Founded by Abd Al-Rab Abdul-Rassul Sayyaf. This was called the EIA until 1981. This Mujahideen faction is fundamentalist. In the mid-1980s, they again changed the name to the Islamic Union of Afghanistan.

Jihad. Holy war conducted for preservation of the faith.

Kalashnikov. Soviet automatic assault rifle. The AK-47 and AKM Kalashnikovs fire a 7.62mm round, while the AK-74 fires a 5.45mm round.

Karez. An Afghanistan system of underground tunnels used for the collection of ground water and for carrying water for surface irrigation. The Mujahideen used them for shelter and ambush.

KHAD. The secret police of the Afghan government responsible for detecting and eradicating domestic political opposition, subverting the Mujahideen, penetrating opposition groups abroad, and providing military intelligence to the armed forces through its military wing. The KHAD was patterned after the Soviet KGB and GRU and apparently reported to the KGB.

Khalq. [(Farsi) *masses* or *people*]. One of the two communist factions of the PDPA.

Kochi. Nomadic tribesmen of Afghanistan. They live primarily by herding and trading sheep, goats, and camels.

KIA. Killed in Action.

Large unit. A division-sized force [*soedineniya*].

Limited Contingent of Soviet Forces (LCOSF) [*ogranichennyy kontingent.sovetskikh voysk v Afganistane* (OKSVA)]. The official term for Soviet Armed Forces in Afghanistan.

LOC. Lines of Communications [*put' soobshchenniya*].

LTC. Lieutenant Colonel.

LZ. Landing Zone [*ploshchadka prizemleniya*].

MEDEVAC. Medical Evacuation [*meditsinskaya evakuatsiya*].

MIA. Missing in Action.

MOD. Ministry of Defense.

MRD. Motorized Rifle Division [*motostrelkovaya diviziya*]. The Soviet equivalent to a western mechanized division.

MRR. Motorized Rifle Regiment [*motostrelkovyy polk*].

MRB. Motorized Rifle Battalion [*motostrelkovyy batal'on*].

MRC. Motorized Rifle Company [*motostrelkovaya rota*].

MRP. Motorized Rifle Platoon [*motostrelkovyy vzvod*].

MRL. Multiple Rocket Launcher [*reaktivnaya artilleriya or reaktivnyi sistem zalpovogo ognya* (RSZO)]. A truck-mounted rocket artillery system capable of firing a salvo of rockets at a target.

MRS. Motorized Rifle Squad [*motostrelkovoe otdelenie*].

MTLB. A multi-purpose, armored, tracked vehicle that was used as an artillery tractor and an armored cargo vehicle in Afghanistan.

Mujahideen. Afghan resistance [holy warrior].

National Islamic Front of Afghanistan (NIFA). [*Mahaz-e-Melli Islami*]. Founded by Pir Sayed Ahmad Gailani, this moderate Mujahideen party attracted a number of former officers from the Afghan Army and moderate technocrats.

Parcham. [(Farsi) *flag*]. Faction of the communist PDPA.

PDPA. Peoples Democratic Party of Afghanistan. The communist party of Afghanistan.

PK. Soviet 7.62mm company machine gun that replaced the Goryunov machine gun. It weighs 16.5 kilograms and has an effective range of 1,000 meters. The Mujahideen call them 100-shooters since they fire out of a 100 round box of linked ammunition.

POL. Petroleum, oil, and lubricants [*goryuche-smazochnye materialy*].

Pushtun. The dominant ethnic group (nearly 50 percent) of Afghanistan, who speak Pashtu. The British historically referred to these people as Pathans.

PX. Post Exchange [*voyentorg*]. A store for soldiers where they can buy non-issue items.

RAG. Regimental Artillery Group [*polkovaya artilleriyskaya gruppa*]. A temporary group of two to five artillery battalions under the control of the Regimental Chief of Rocket Troops and Artillery for a particular mission.

RDM. Remotely Delivered Mines [*sredstva distantsionnogo minirovaniya*]. Mines that can be emplaced by aviation, artillery, or MRL fire. Similar to the U.S. FASCAM (Family of Scatterable Mines).

Recon. Reconnaissance [*razvedka*].

RPG-7. Soviet-manufactured, shoulder-fired antitank weapon that fires a shaped-charge rocket. It has an effective range of 300 meters.

RPG-18. Soviet-manufactured, single-shot, shoulder-fired antitank weapon that fires a

66mm shaped-charge rocket. The rocket is stored in an extendable storage tube that also functions as a launcher. The launcher is thrown away after use. It has an effective range of 135 meters and is a copy of the U.S. M72A2 LAW.

RTO. Radio-telephone óperator [*svyazist*].

Sapper. Combat engineer.

Sarandoy. [Defenders of the Revolution]. DRA Ministry of the Interior armed forces. A heavily armed police force. They were organized into six brigades or regiments (numbering about 60,000 men) and were based in Kandahar, Badakhstan, Baghlan, and Paravan provinces, plus two in Kabul. The Sarandoy had an additional estimated 6,000 men in operational and mountain battalions.

Shia. The minority Islamic community in Afghanistan following the Imami Shiism (the dominant faith in neighboring Iran) or Ismaili Shiism.

SOP. Standard Operations Procedures [*poryadok deystviy*]. Those designated actions that will be executed by the force when certain events occur.

SP. Self-Propelled [*samokhodnaya*]. Self-propelled artillery.

Spetsnaz. Troops of Special Designation. For this book, Soviet forces trained for long-range reconnaissance, commando, and special forces type combat.

Subunit. [*podrazdeleniya*]. Tactical elements of a unit (brigade, regiment, or separate battalion). Subunits are battalions, companies, platoons, and squads and do not have their own colors.

Sunni. The majority Islamic community in Afghanistan. Over two-thirds of the populace are Sunni—followers of the Hanafi School.

Tadjik. Ethnic Afghans from the northeastern regions of Afghanistan who make up about 25 percent of the population.

Tanglefoot. A different Soviet obstacle than that used in western armies. It is a large, compressed, banded spring made of high-quality wire. It is similar to an uncontrolled "Slinky" toy. When unbanded during set up, it uncoils wildly in every direction. It will stop dismounted soldiers, animals, vehicles, and even tanks. It is almost impossible to extricate anything from this without heavy-duty wire cutters, pliers, and lots of time. These obstacles are called MZP [*malozametnye prepyatsviya*], or concealed obstacles.

TCP. Traffic control point.

TO&E. Table of Organization and Equipment [*shtat*]. An official document specifying the number of personnel by military specialty, the types of weapons, and the type of equipment that an organization should have assigned.

Unit. [*chast*]. A brigade, regiment, or independent battalion with its own colors.

Uzbek. Ethnic Afghans primarily in the north-central part of Afghanistan who make up 10 percent of the population and speak Turkic.

WIA. Wounded in Action.

ZGU. [*Zenitnaya gornaya ustanovka*]. Mountain air defense weapons mount. Any Soviet air defense weapon that can disassembled for transport into the mountains by pack animals or porters. Usually this means that the weapons mount or pedestal has no wheels.

ZGU-1. A ZPU-1 mounted on a ZGU mount.

ZPU-1. A Soviet 14.5mm ground-mounted antiaircraft machine gun that is towed on a light, two-wheeled carriage. The system is built around a single-barreled KPV heavy machine gun that has a cyclic rate of fire of 600 rounds per minute and a practical rate of fire of 150 rounds per minute. The belt-fed machine gun feeds from a 150 round box and has a maximum horizontal range of 7,000 meters and a maximum effective antiaircraft range of 1,400 meters. It weighs 581 kilograms.

ZPU-2. The twin-barrel version of the ZPU-1.

ZSU-23-4. A Soviet self-propelled air defense weapon that fires four 23mm machine guns simultaneously. The Soviets used this weapon for counter ambushes and in the destruction of ground targets.

Key to Map Symbols

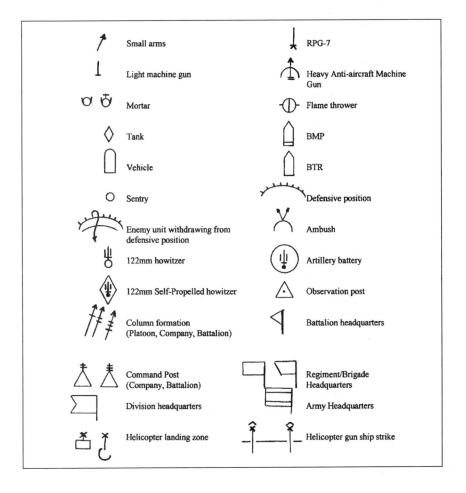

Symbol	Description	Symbol	Description
	Small arms		RPG-7
	Light machine gun		Heavy Anti-aircraft Machine Gun
	Mortar		Flame thrower
	Tank		BMP
	Vehicle		BTR
	Sentry		Defensive position
	Enemy unit withdrawing from defensive position		Ambush
	122mm howitzer		Artillery battery
	122mm Self-Propelled howitzer		Observation post
	Column formation (Platoon, Company, Battalion)		Battalion headquarters
	Command Post (Company, Battalion)		Regiment/Brigade Headquarters
	Division headquarters		Army Headquarters
	Helicopter landing zone		Helicopter gun ship strike

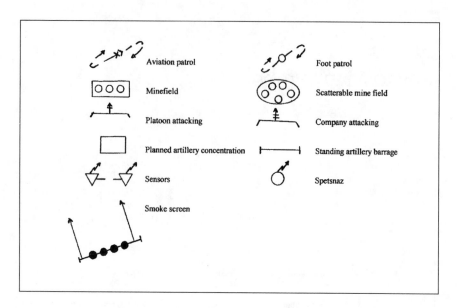

Aviation patrol

Foot patrol

Minefield

Scatterable mine field

Platoon attacking

Company attacking

Planned artillery concentration

Standing artillery barrage

Sensors

Spetsnaz

Smoke screen

About the Editors

Les Grau is a retired U.S. Army Infantry Lieutenant Colonel who fought in Vietnam and served in Germany, the Netherlands, and Korea. As a Soviet Foreign Officer, he studied Russian at the Defense Language Institute in Monterey, California, and completed a postgraduate program at the U.S. Army Russian Institute in Garmisch-Partenkirchen, Germany. He had a posting in Moscow and has written extensively on Soviet and Russian military topics. He produced two prior books on the Soviet-Afghan War—*The Bear Went Over the Mountain: Soviet Combat Tactics in Afghanistan* and *The Other Side of the Mountain: Mujahideen Tactics in the Soviet-Afghan War*, which he coauthored with Ali Ahmad Jalali.

Michael Gress is a Russian émigré who served in the Soviet army for an extended period of time. He maintains a very hectic schedule—learning a new language and culture, getting involved in the American business world, and developing the many projects he is always generating. Mike feels that the General Staff retrospective is a piece of history that has to be published and generously devoted his time and talents to preparing it for publication. His in-depth knowledge of Russian military expressions, acronyms, and culture has proven invaluable. This is his first book.

Index

Kalafghan garrison, 34
Kalashnikov, M., 38
Kama district, cordon and search in, 108
Kandahar, 3, 6, 9, 34, 139, 210, 212, 216, 221;
    British at, 7; convoys at, 149; fighting in,
    31, 32, 33, 137; hospital at, 298; Kabul
    Kingdom and, 6
Kandahar Kingdom, 6
Kandahar Province, 175, 287
Kapista Province, Islamic committee of, 83
Kapitonov, A. A., 111
Karagodin, B., 47
Karez, 22, 253, 256–257
Karmal, Babrak, 8, 14, 18, 23, 31, 33
Kayum, Mujahideen at, 117–118
KGB, 149, 241–242
KHAD, 25, 75, 93, 200
Khalis, Mawlawi Mohammed Yunis, 54
Khanabad, 210
Khejob valley, offensive in, 33
Kholod, A., 136
Khomenko, A., 131
Khost, 9, 27, 28, 33, 34, 210, 256
Kill zones, 66, 67, 131, 132, 133, 141, 144,
    194; ambush, 134, 137, 206, 253; smoke
    screens and, 261
Kirgak, raid at, 97, 98(map)
Kokabulak, 119, 120
Komarov, S. V., 256
Korchagin, A. A., 11, 15
Korobob, V. N., 116
Korotkikh, B. I., 133
Kovyrshin, A. M., 119
Kozhbergenov, T., 177
Kravchenko, A., 131
Krivosheev, G. G., 48
Krokhin, V., 119
Kulikov, V., 131
Kunar Province, 57, 62
Kunar river valley, 34, 116, 207; offensive in,
    30, 31, 33
Kunduz, 17, 26, 129, 210, 238, 298
Kunduz airfield, 119, 197, 198
Kurdish guerrillas, xi
Kushka, transfer base at, 282

Laghman Province, cordon and search in, 108
Laghman valley, offensive in, 32
Lakarosar mountain, blockade at, 124
Language groups, described, 5–6
Lashkargah, 210, 234
Lebed, A. I., 202
Levintas, Yu. P., 97
Limited Contingent of Soviet Forces (LCOSF),
    11, 12, 47; combat effectiveness of, 26,
    42; guerrilla warfare and, 62, 233; mission
    of, 1, 15, 23, 73, 138, 306; training for, 43;

withdrawal of, 29; weapons used by,
    38–40
Lines of communication (LOCs), xxiv–xxv, 19,
    25, 82, 92; attacks on, 58, 242, 265, 312;
    security for, 13, 168, 149, 193, 250, 253
Lobanov, L. N., 11, 15
Logar Province, fighting in, 9, 27, 31, 85, 256
Logistics, xxv, 29, 138, 233, 281; support,
    282–292
Lomakin, A., 10
Lor Koh mountains, 95, 103–104
Lowgar valley, 32, 33

Machine guns, 38, 39, 39(fig.), 199, 256; air
    assault force, 199; air defense, 212, 307;
    ambushes and, 206, 207; tank, 190, 191
Maidan valley, offensive in, 33
Maimana, convoy at, 141
Maintenance, 49, 268–269, 280, 302, 307;
    evacuation and, 308; operations and,
    270–271; problems with, 281; schedules,
    269, 271–272; support, 275; technical,
    269, 276, 277
Maiwand, British at, 7
Makkoveev, A. L., 97
Maksimov, Yu. P., 11, 15
Maliykhel' region, convoy in, 147
Mamykin, Nikolai Ivanovich, 18
Maravara, 195
Marzek, 119, 120
Masood, Ahmad Shah, 176
Mata, 80–81, 82
Material support, xx, 264, 279, 281, 282–283,
    289
Maksimov, Yu. P., 12, 17
Mazar-i-Sharif, 3, 210
Medical support, 295–298, 299(map), 300–303,
    309
Mgar', S. V., 256
Mikhalko, E., 143
Minefields, 20, 64, 69, 132, 193, 195, 242, 253;
    ground searches for, 245; registration
    books for, 252; transfer of, 237
Mine flails/plows, 148, 194, 246
Mines: antipersonnel, 72, 88, 91, 124, 126, 224,
    239, 243, 245, 252; antitank, 88, 124, 126,
    139, 192, 243, 244, 245, 252; blast, 244,
    245, 246, 252–253, 272; clearing, 132,
    153(photo), 194, 195, 202, 230, 231, 242,
    244–246; directional, 137, 224, 246, 252,
    253; fragmentation, 244, 245, 252–253;
    laying, 26, 70, 80, 124, 125, 126, 137,
    139, 210, 243–244, 251–252; signal, 247,
    252
Ministry of Communications, 198
Ministry of Defense, 10, 11, 15, 17, 18, 198;
    organizations and, 48; withdrawal and, 30